CHINA
AND THE
CHINESE
OVERSEAS

Wang Gungwu

TIMES ACADEMIC PRESS

©1991, 1992 Times Media Private Limited

Times Academic Press
An imprint of **Times Media Private Limited**
A member of the Times Publishing Group
Times Centre, 1 New Industrial Road, Singapore 536196
Fax: 2854871
Email: fps@tpl.com.sg
Website: http://www.timesone.com.sg/te

First published 1991
Reprinted 1992, 1993, 1994, 1995, 1997, 2000

ISBN 981 210 029 0

Printed by B & Jo Enterprise Pte Ltd, Singapore

For Margaret

Acknowledgements

Part I

Chapter 1 – Patterns of Chinese Migration in Historical Perspective: *Observing Change in Asia*, R.J. May and W.J.O'Malley (eds.), (Bathurst: Crawford House Press, 1989).

Chapter 2 – Southeast Asian Huaqiao in Chinese History-Writing: *Journal of Southeast Asian Studies*, vol. 12, no. 1, 1981.

Chapter 3 – Ming Foreign Relations: Southeast Asia: To be published in *The Cambridge History of China*, vol. 8, F.W. Mote and D. Twitchett (eds.), (Cambridge University Press).

Chapter 4 – Merchants without Empires: the Hokkien Sojourning Communities: *The Rise of Merchant Empires*, James D. Tracy (ed.), (Cambridge University Press, 1990).

Chapter 5 – Song-Yuan-Ming Relations with Southeast Asia: some comparisons: *Proceedings of 2nd International Conference on Sinology*, (Tapei: Academia Sinica, 1989).

Chapter 6 – "Public" and "Private" Overseas Trade in Chinese History: *Sociétés et Compagnies de Commerce en Orient et dans L'Ocean Indien*, Michel Mollat (ed.), Paris, 1970.

Chapter 7 – Political Chinese: their Contribution to Modern Southeast Asian History: *Southeast Asia in the Modern World*, Bernhard Grossman (ed.), (Otto Harrassowitz, Wiesbaden, 1972).

Chapter 8 – Lu Xun, Lim Boon Keng and Confucianism: *Papers on Far Eastern History*, no. 39, (Australian National University, 1989).

Chapter 9 – The Chinese as Immigrants and Settlers: Singapore: *Management of Success: The Moulding of Modern Singapore*, K.S. Sandhu and P. Wheatley (eds.), (Institute of Southeast Asian Studies, Singapore, 1989).

Part II

Chapter 10 – The Culture of Chinese Merchants: Working Paper No. 57, Joint Centre for Asia-Pacific Studies, (University of Toronto-York University, 1990).

Chapter 11 – The Study of Chinese Identities in Southeast Asia: *Changing Identities of the Southeast Asian Chinese since World War II*, Jennifer Cushman and Wang Gungwu (eds.), (Hong Kong University Press, 1988).

Chapter 12 – External China as a New Policy Area: *Pacific Affairs*, vol. 58, no. 1, 1985.

Chapter 13 – South China Perspectives on Overseas Chinese: *The Australian Journal of Chinese Affairs*, no. 13, 1985.

Chapter 14 – Little Dragons on the Confucian Periphery: (Keynote Lecture, New Zealand Association of Asian Studies Conference, Christchurch, 17 August 1989).

Chapter 15 – Education in External China: (Keynote Lecture, Conference on Contemporary Education and Cultural Tradition, Chinese University of Hong Kong, 13 October 1988).

Chapter 16 – The Chinese: What kind of Minority?: An earlier version was published in *Southeast Asian Affairs 1976*, (Institute of Southeast Asian Studies, Singapore, 1976).

Contents

The Author

WANG GUNGWU, Director of the East Asian Institute at the National University of Singapore and Distinguished Senior Fellow at the Institute of Southeast Asian Studies, was born in Surabaya, Indonesia, and brought up in Ipoh, Malaysia. His first degrees were from the University of Malaya, Singapore, and his doctorate from the School of Oriental and African Studies, University of London.

He has taught at The University of Malaya (in Singapore, 1957-1959; in Kuala Lumpur, 1959-1968), where he was Dean of Arts (1962-1963), and Professor of History (1963-1968). From 1968 to 1986, he was Professor of Far Eastern History in the Research School of Pacific Studies, Australian National University. During that period, he was also Director of the Research School for five years. In 1986, he was appointed Vice-Chancellor of the University of Hong Kong and was there until 1995.

Outside his universities, Wang Gungwu has been a Fellow of the Australian Academy of the Humanities since 1970 and the Academy's President in 1978-1980. He has twice been President of the International Association of Historians of Asia and was President of the Asian Studies Association of Australia from 1978-1980. He is a Member, Academia Sinica; Honorary Academy Member, Chinese Academy of Social Science; Foreign Honorary Member, American Academy of Arts and Science. He has also received honorary doctorates from the following universities: Sydney, Monash (Melbourne), Griffith (Brisbane), Soka (Tokyo) and ANU (Canberra). He is Honorary Fellow of the School of Oriental and African Studies, London; and Honorary Professors of Peking and Fudan (Shanghai) Universities.

Among his books are *The Nanhai Trade* (1958); *The Structure of Power in North China during the Five Dynasties* (1963); *China and the World since 1949* (1977); *Community and Nation* (1981); *Dongnanya yu Huaren* (Southeast Asia and the Chinese) (1987); *The Chineseness of China* (1991); *The Chinese Way: China's Position in International Relations* (1995). He also edited *Changing Identities of Southeast Asian Chinese since World War II* (1988) (with Jennifer Cushman); *Global History and Migrations* (1997); and *Xianggang shi xinbian* (Hong Kong History: New Perspectives) (1997).

Preface

Ten years ago, Anthony Reid, my former colleague at the Australian National University, selected some of my writings on Southeast Asia and the Chinese and had them published in a volume entitled *Community and Nation*. Since then, I have shifted my focus more towards the Chinese themselves and have paid more attention to aspects of migration, trade and culture. Thirteen of the sixteen essays in this volume were written after *Community and Nation* was published. Indeed, when it was suggested that I collect them together for this volume, five were still in press and two (Chapters 14 and 15) unpublished. As for the three published in the 1970s (Chapters 6, 7 and 16), they may need updating in parts, but have been included without revision in order to retain their place as background pieces for the more current themes.

Many Chinese have migrated from China, Taiwan and Hong Kong during the past decade and many others of Chinese descent have re-migrated, largely from Southeast Asia to North America and Australasia. In contrast to the three decades after World War II, when the major issues were the political containment of China and the assimilation of local Chinese, attention has returned to the trading and entrepreneurial skills of the Chinese. In addition, there is fresh interest in the relevance of their cultural values and in the new Chinese urge to move between countries and even continents. My aim in the essays in this volume is not to cover these developments directly but to create a historical and historiographical picture that reflects my professional interests rather than contemporary trends. I hope thereby to prove that it is not really possible to understand what seems to be new without reference to the past.

Wang Gungwu

Preface

PART I

In Historical Perspective

CHAPTER 1

Patterns of Chinese Migration in Historical Perspective[1]

MIGRATION IS A UNIVERSAL phenomenon made more conspicuous today by international attention in an era of nationalism. The paradox of better and easier transportation over longer distances and the erection of stronger barriers against the movement of people deserves to be studied as a global problem. Many studies have taken the worldwide perspective and the common features of what migration means for nations, communities and individuals are better appreciated now than ever before. Certainly the study of Chinese migration has benefited from comparisons with that of other migrating peoples.

Professor Mackie, as a distinguished scholar of Southeast Asia, has found the role of Chinese migrant communities particularly interesting. He has contributed several studies which have greatly illuminated the field for all of us. It would seem appropriate to register our debt to him with an essay that explores the historical characteristics that delineate some of the main patterns of Chinese migration during the past two centuries. Chinese migration has meant different things at different periods and to different peoples. While it may seem easy to generalize about it, it is also very easy to draw conflicting conclusions — conclusions which can be misinterpreted and which certainly do not help understanding. The complexities of the history of Chinese migration has contemporary relevance in so far as they would help our understanding of more recent manifestations of this ancient phenomenon.

I

I shall not attempt any narrow definition of "Chinese migration" but try to introduce the subject in broad terms. Broadly, Chinese migration refers to the departure from Chinese soil for the purpose of living and working abroad. I leave open the question of whether the migrants intended to settle permanently abroad or whether they meant to return to their homeland eventually. For our purposes here, the problem of intentions is not a central issue. More to the point is that in some periods, many Chinese migrants settled down and did not return while in other periods, very few did. We need to understand why this was so at different times, that is, what induced migrants to stay or to return; and also, what happened when they did settle and what happened when they actually returned. For those who settled, what changes occurred to these migrants and their families, to their migrant communities, to their relations with other local communities and, not least, to their relations with their ancestral communities in China?

Chinese migration, therefore, refers to the phenomenon of Chinese living and working abroad with the likelihood of settlement, whether or not these Chinese intended to do so from the start. By this, I would exclude diplomatic and other officials sent from China to serve China's interests; private agents who travelled on specific short-term missions; as well as students and, of course, tourists. But, as we know, that does not exclude many and for most periods during the past five to six hundred years "Chinese migrants" would have included the majority of those Chinese who left the borders of their country.

I shall not try to cover the whole history of Chinese emigration here but shall limit myself to the modern period, that is, the last two centuries since about 1800. For this period I shall use one of the historian's favourite devices and look for patterns of migration during different parts of that long period. For these two hundred years, I suggest that there have been *four* main patterns. These patterns overlapped in time as well as in many other ways but are quite easily identifiable. They are the trader pattern, the coolie pattern, the sojourner pattern and the descent or re-migrant pattern. Let me first deal with each of them individually.

The Trader Pattern

The trader pattern refers to merchants and artisans (including miners and other skilled workers) who went abroad, or sent their colleagues, agents or members of their extended families or clans (including those with little or no skills working as apprentices or lowly assistants) abroad to work for them and set up bases at ports, mines or trading cities. When this proved successful, the business abroad, or the mining business, could expand and require more agents or young family members to join it; or new businesses and mines were established into a network, also requiring more agents or family members to be sent out to help the new ventures. Over a generation or two, the migrants, mostly male, would settle down and bring up local families. But even if they themselves did not settle down, their local families did and, more often than not, remained as recognizably Chinese families to keep the businesses going. The more successful the businesses, the more likely their families kept up their Chinese characteristics, if not all their connections with China. But, where there was sufficient inducement or political pressure to do so, some of these families abandoned their Chineseness and became local notables. However, for the most part, the requirements of their businesses ensured that not all members of these families could depart too far from the Chinese connections necessary for their continuing success.

I call this the "Huashang" (Chinese trader) pattern of migration. This was the dominant pattern from early times in various parts of Southeast Asia. In all its essentials, it was a migration pattern that had been established by traders, artisans and miners *within* China since at least the Song dynasty. A later parallel involving Han Chinese settling among minority peoples may be seen in migration to provinces like Yunnan, Guizhou, Guangxi and Taiwan. The crucial difference, however, was that those provinces were under imperial Chinese administration so that the Chineseness of their families was rarely in doubt. Indeed, it was traditionally in this context that the word *qiao*, meaning temporary residence, was appropriately used. *Qiao* originally referred to temporary residence away from home, from one's own village, country or province, but still *within* China. It was appropriate in particular for people who retained the registration (*jiguan*) with their home towns and had not registered in their place of residence (*ruji*). But it was a common phenomenon for traders and artisans from the same home town or country to retain that connection in order to sustain their successful line of business for generations. Excellent examples within China were those merchants of Shanxi, Anhwei, Fujian and Guangdong, who dominated the long-distance trade within China for several centuries.

This Huashang pattern of migration was an extension abroad of this traditional practice, most notably among the Hokkien (South Fujian) merchants in Japan, the Philippines and Java, the Hakkas in West Borneo and the Teochius in Thailand. It was clearly the dominant pattern by the eighteenth century, and the only significant pattern before 1850.

The Coolie Pattern

The second pattern, the "Huagong" (Chinese coolie) pattern, derived from the migration of large numbers of coolie labour, normally men of peasant origin, landless labourers and the urban poor. This was not significant before the 1850s. It took a most dramatic form with the gold rushes in North America and Australia, but that did not provide the pattern of settlement. More important was the coolie labour phenomenon. This had many variations but its main characteristics are well known. It was associated with plantation economies of one era as well as the beginnings of industrialization in another, most notably the building of railways in North America. On the whole, this pattern of migration may be described as transitional. It was transitional in that a large proportion of the contract labourers returned to China after their contract came to an end. But it was also transitional in that it was quickly put to an end — very quickly in the Americas by the end of the nineteenth century; and not long afterwards in Southeast Asia (by the 1920s).

Nevertheless, it is an important pattern historically, especially outside Asia, in the countries of European settlement whether in the Americas or in Australasia. Although it occurred also in Southeast Asia, and was certainly significant in certain parts of Sumatra and the Malay peninsula, it was never the dominant pattern there but was largely subordinated to the Huashang pattern of migration.

The Sojourner Pattern

The third pattern was the Huaqiao (Chinese sojourner) pattern. The term "Huaqiao" is still a controversial one, but one that urgently needs definition and clarification. It is quite different in nature from the terms for traders and coolies in that it is not descriptive of the occupations of migrants but referred broadly to all Overseas Chinese. Furthermore, it had political, legal or ideological content soon after the term came into use towards the end of the nineteenth century. It came to be used to apply to all those previously known as Huashang and Huagong, but also included those teachers, journalists and other professionals who went out to promote greater awareness of Chinese culture and national needs.

At one level, that of linguistic convenience, its introduction was understandable. There had been a proliferation of terms for the Chinese abroad like Huashang, Huagong, Huaren, Huamin, Huamang (the last three are various ways of saying "Chinese" or "Chinese people") in addition to *Min Guangren, Min Yueren* and *Tangren* (people from Fujian and Guangdong, who traditionally called themselves "people of the Tang" [dynasty]) and none of them seemed accurate enough to cover all the Chinese living outside China. These Chinese were increasingly conscious of the weakness of China, of a China opening its doors and seeking to modernize through more contacts with the West. It was soon apparent that they needed China's help and protection and that China needed their experience — and in the case of Southeast Asia, also their wealth and expertise and their interest in investing in modern business and industry in China itself. To find a term that might include all Chinese and convey the idea of the official protection of China's citizens temporarily resident abroad was most useful.

But it was at another level that the pattern took its primary shape. This was the political, legal and ideological level at which the Qing imperial government and the Republican government acted and which the revolutionary movement of Sun Yat-sen and his followers later brought to a climax in the Nanking government of 1928.

The first political step was the claim that the Huaqiao owed their allegiance to China and to the Qing throne, thus negating British and Dutch claims to the loyalty of the Chinese subjects in their colonies. But this also meant the right of the Qing empire to intervene to prevent disloyalty and rebellion — to stop foreign countries from harbouring outlaws and rebels like Kang Youwei and Sun Yat-sen. The legal step provided protection for all Chinese abroad through embassies and consulates, but it also led to ambiguities about the application of legal systems to such Chinese. To what extent were these Chinese under Western law in areas over which the Chinese government had no control, or under Chinese law when inside China if some of them could show that they were foreign citizens?

But perhaps the most important feature of the Huaqiao pattern was the ideological one. This was primarily determined by nationalism, but it was also enhanced by a close association with revolution — first as espoused by Sun Yat-sen, but later in both its manifestations under the Guomindang and the Chinese Communist Party. In this way, it gave shape to a conscious migration policy that brought both the Huashang and the Huagong patterns under its umbrella. The Huaqiao pattern was to become the only pattern through which Chinese governments could protect Chinese migrants and intervene in overseas Chinese affairs.

The nationalist principles were clear. All Chinese, wherever they were, were part of the Chinese nation. They wanted protection and must be duly protected. All Chinese should give their primary loyalty to China. They must therefore have their consciousness raised and, if necessary, adequately politicized in order to ensure that the political loyalty was fully understood. To this end, the Huashang and Huagong patterns were not enough. They had to be supported by officials, teachers, journalists, party workers and a wide range of China-trained intellectuals to do the following: to re-sinicize those who had been acculturated by local or Western ways, to sustain the Chinese who wanted their local progeny to remain Chinese and not least, to serve the Overseas Chinese as direct and strong links with China. Eventually, an additional dimension was added, especially after the revolutionary movement was divided between Left and Right and the Overseas Chinese were drawn into certain aspects of the Civil War in China. An even more powerful development came with the Sino-Japanese War and the patriotism it aroused among most Overseas Chinese. The impact of that experience was to stay with them for at least a decade after the end of the war in 1945.

This Huaqiao pattern, including all migrants whether traders, coolies or educated professionals, developed only after 1900 but it reached high emotional levels very quickly after 1911. Although it was influenced by the numbers and wealth of Overseas Chinese, the chief feature that distinguished it from the two patterns of migration above was that it focused on quality, especially the quality of Chineseness among all the Chinese abroad. Thus this pattern had at its centre a deep commitment to education in the Chinese language and a willingness to help and encourage all Overseas Chinese to do battle with local authorities, whether colonial or nationalist, on behalf of that education. It was a pattern that was dominant until the 1950s and some aspects of it have survived till this day.

The Descent or Re-migrant Pattern

The fourth pattern I have called the Huayi (Chinese descent or re-migrant) pattern. This is mainly a new phenomenon, Huayi being foreign nationals of Chinese descent. While they are largely foreign-born, they also include some who were born in China, Taiwan or Hong Kong who have acquired foreign citizenship and are, strictly speaking, not Huaqiao temporarily resident abroad.

Before I continue, I must emphasize one point strongly. By this Huayi pattern, I am not referring to the earlier and basic kinds of migration that ended with many Chinese becoming foreign nationals. All three patterns of Huashang, Huagong and Huaqiao migration produced such naturalized or foreign-born Chinese. What I am referring to is the more recent development when Huayi in one foreign country migrated or re-migrated to another foreign country. Obvious examples are Southeast Asians of Chinese descent who migrated to Western Europe (Netherlands, Britain, and France), North America and Australasia during the past three or four decades, especially since the 1950s when some Southeast Asian nations made those of Chinese descent feel unwanted. Their numbers are not large, but they have produced a different pattern of migration which deserves attention.

It is not, of course, an entirely new development. Foreign nationals of Chinese descent have existed since the middle of the nineteenth century and there are some families — still recognizably Chinese families — who have been foreign nationals for generations. And among them have been those who have migrated from their adopted country to a third country and then settled down and acquired a new nationality. What is of great interest is whether this secondary or even tertiary migration, or re-migration, helped to sustain the sense of Chinese identity. In some cases, there is evidence that the second or third move was related to the migrants' search for less discriminatory conditions to bring their children up as ethnic Chinese. We are familiar with the re-sinicization of Baba or Peranakan Chinese in Malaysia and Indonesia during the period when the Huaqiao pattern was dominant. Now that the Huaqiao pattern is quiescent and at best low key, one wonders whether the new Huayi pattern of secondary or tertiary moves may keep open the possibility of re-sinicization for a longer period. An extra and probably disorienting move might loosen a foreign attachment and open such migrants to a revival of interest in their origins in China. It could, of course, produce the opposite effect. The new generations who have to endure a second change of identity might well abandon all desire to find links with the ancestral country.

One additional point worth making is that this Huayi pattern of migration is strongly represented by well-educated professionals who are a more cosmopolitan kind of migrant than any other kind of Chinese. Many are doctors, engineers, scientists, economists, lawyers, accountants, educationists, administrators and business executives. By being professionally well-trained, mobile and often open-minded, they can settle down quickly almost anywhere that is non-discriminatory, especially in modern states established by immigrants. Thus in a period when their professional skills appear to be needed in a modernizing China, there may be a stimulus for them to re-open contacts with the country of ancestral origin. It is still too early to offer answers to these questions concerning the Huayi pattern of migration, but they are ones that are worth keeping in view.

I have identified four major patterns of migration and broadly arranged them in chronological order; the Huashang pattern being the oldest and the most basic; the Huagong pattern added quantity but was transitional for the period from the 1850s to 1920s; the Huaqiao pattern was all-embracing, protective and interventionist in every aspect of overseas Chinese life but lasted mainly during the first half of this century to the 1950s; and the Huayi pattern is the newest and is yet to unfold. I must now draw attention to the fact that I gave no period to the Huashang pattern but called it *basic*. I believe that a closer examination of historical evidence points to the dominance of this pattern where migration has been long and continuous, especially in Southeast Asia. The Huagong pattern in countries of European settlement was exceptional and lasted only for a limited period. That pattern has received a great deal of attention largely because of the importance of Sino-American relations. Its actual place in the history of Chinese migration is minor compared with that of the Huashang pattern in Asia. Indeed, the Huagong pattern died out in the Anglo-American world before the end of the nineteenth century and survived only in Southeast Asia for another two decades. And the lack of a strong Huashang presence in the Americas and Australasia was a major factor in keeping the Chinese communities there weak and hard to sustain for a long time.

What blurred the basic underlying Huashang pattern of migration was the high-profile, politically supported Huaqiao pattern after 1900. The blurring by the Huaqiao/sojourner pattern occurred in at least two ways. The latter pattern gave the highest priority to patriotism and the transmission of nationalist ideals to all Chinese abroad. Although this nationalism was modern, it also revived some traditional attitudes about the inferior status of the Huashang merchants. It brought back the significance of political commitment and morality as superior to commercial success and wealth. Huashang were not themselves seen as agents of change and modernization but were merely invaluable financiers of reform and revolution, of modern schools and other political organs which were in the vanguard of all social and political change. Understandably, revolutionaries favoured the just cause of the urban poor among Chinese migrants and lectured the Huashang on their social and patriotic duties. In this way, particularly in the rather exceptional circumstances of Singapore and Malaya, where one could point to a Chinese proletariat, the continuing importance of the Huashang pattern of emigration was not recognized. On the contrary, there was an over-emphasis on patriotic contributions and Chinese literacy at the expense of the strong economic base which the many kinds of Chinese entrepreneurs had built up during the first half of this century.

What seems to be clear now is that, when the Huaqiao pattern lost its dominance after the 1950s, it was again the Huashang pattern which sustained whatever migration there was out of China, Taiwan and Hong Kong. Even the emergence of the new pattern of Huayi remigration, which owed a great deal to the Huaqiao pattern of patriotic education and pride, was no less influenced by the unbroken successes of the Huashang and the confidence those successes gave to everyone of Chinese descent living overseas. The additional fact that foreign governments, notably those in Southeast Asia, strongly favoured the Huashang pattern over the aggressive Huaqiao pattern should not detract from the real contributions Chinese entrepreneurs made to the basic shapes of overseas Chinese communities everywhere.

I have to conclude therefore that, where the four patterns are concerned, the chronological picture is only a partial one. More accurately, the picture ought to be as follows:

The Huashang was and still is the basic pattern of emigration. This was strengthened for a while (in numbers especially) by the Huagong pattern. It continued to flourish under the qualitative changes offered by the Huaqiao pattern for about 50 years and benefited from, as well as contributed to the economic foundations of, that pattern. But now, in most places, the Huaqiao pattern is peripheral or subordinated to the growing strength of the Huashang pattern, which has now been highlighted again. The Huaqiao pattern survives as long as there are citizens of the PRC, Taiwan and holders of Hong Kong documents residing outside China, but it is unlikely that this pattern will ever be dominant again.

As for the new Huayi pattern, it is the by-product of the long history of Chinese migration, and had been greatly influenced by all three earlier patterns. What this means is that the success of earlier migrants of all kinds had made it easier for a pool of business and professionally qualified Chinese to re-migrate more freely to new and more congenial environments. In the future, however, this pattern will continue to depend largely on the basic Huashang pattern. I venture to suggest that, with notable specific exceptions, future Chinese migration will be based on the Huashang pattern and supplemented by the new Huayi pattern, with some features of the Huaqiao pattern surviving here and there.

II

The second part of this chapter will focus on the direction of future research on the history of Chinese migration in the light of the four patterns of migration described above. There are considerable possibilities but it will not be possible to be comprehensive. So only a few key points will be touched on here.

The first point is a general one which has already been mentioned above and elsewhere. Despite superficial similarities, there is a profound difference between Chinese migration to Southeast Asia and that to the countries of European settlement in the Americas and Australasia. This is a subject deserving detailed research and can only be briefly introduced here. One clue to that difference lies in the fact that the Huashang pattern was dominant in Southeast Asia from the beginning and the fact that that pattern has remained the main pattern to the present. In contrast, for the Americas and Australasia, it was the Huagong pattern that characterized early migration there. The Huagong numbers were great and led to open conflict with the working classes in these territories. This in turn led to strict immigration control advocated by people who claimed that there was a threat to their jobs. Most of the Huagong therefore returned to China, or went elsewhere. Those who remained turned to trade and tried to be Huashang in order to survive. But they had to start at the bottom as petty traders and were restricted by immigration laws which, although directed against Huagong, also hurt their chances of expanding their business with China.

It was the Huaqiao pattern in the twentieth century which saved the Chinese communities in the Americas (and to a lesser extent in Australasia). This pattern based on national pride and official protection found the warmest possible response among the small, impoverished, struggling, persecuted Chinese communities of Huagong origins. At the same time, it was accompanied by the recognition that their educated descendants could directly help to modernize China as patriotic Chinese now designated as Huaqiao. Thus the new Huaqiao pattern was a godsend to these Chinese. It gave them dignity and political purpose and it did not really matter whether they preferred Kang Youwei or Sun Yat-sen or even the Republican government in Peking. And then, to cap it all, when more and more students from China went to study in the United States and the local Chinese could see themselves as vital parts of a modernizing generation of intellectuals on whose performance the future of China was thought to depend, the position of the Chinese was secured. It is no wonder that, for generations of these descendants of Huagong, to call themselves Huaqiao was only natural and the name Huaqiao remains a badge of pride to this day.

In contrast, the Huaqiao pattern was not uniformly received in Southeast Asia with enthusiasm as it was in North America. We need more research to understand why this was so. For Southeast Asia, most documents in Chinese suggest that the Huaqiao pattern was no different there from elsewhere, but Western colonial and other local data often point to marked differences even within the region. Were these differences merely the result of different points of view, or did they arise from different local policies, or from real differences among various kinds of Chinese settlements in the region?

I would like to suggest that one factor in the difference was the long history of the Huashang pattern of migration and what that did for relations between the traders, especially the successful and potentially successful and upwardly mobile ones, and local colonial or native authorities and also local native communities. Where the Huagong pattern often led to ghettos of isolated Chinese groups, the Huashang pattern encouraged closer relations with officialdom to obtain maximum mutual benefits. Therefore, the new nationalistic Huaqiao pattern which gave purpose and self-respect to Huagong groups might bring less obvious benefits to the Huashang who already had subtle and profitable connections with local power holders.

I do not want to exaggerate this difference. In general, the Huashang pattern was not in conflict with the Huaqiao pattern of including professionals and other intellectuals. Difficulties arose largely because aggressive revolutionaries brought China politics to the region and came into conflict with local authorities — very often the same officials on whom the Huashang depended for their successes. The result was, some of the Huashang leaders shied away from the Huaqiao label and, in practice, supported the less turbulent and more strongly based Huashang pattern which they could control and which local officialdom accepted.

These differences between the Southeast Asian response and the North American response to the Huaqiao pattern of migration became even more marked after the end of World War II. Again, we need research into each of these responses in order to understand the differences. Even more interesting is how events in China, Taiwan and Hong Kong of the past forty years have influenced attitudes towards the concept of Huaqiao. On the one hand, the new Southeast Asian nations wanted no more Chinese immigrants, of whatever kind. On the other, the United States opened its doors to Taiwan Chinese students and began to liberalize its Chinese immigration quota. In this context, the Huaqiao pattern as supported by Taiwan was still acceptable; but of greater importance was the increasing significance of the ubiquitous Chinese trader all over the Anglo-American world. The centre of gravity for new Chinese migration shifted away totally from the Southeast Asian region to the Americas and Australasia and parts of Western Europe. But now there was a new pattern emerging: the re-migration, secondary or tertiary migration of Huayi. To mention some recent examples: Chinese from Papua New Guinea and East Timor to Australia; from Mauritius to Canada; from Malaysia to Britain and Australia; from the Philippines, Thailand and Korea to the United States, and so on.

I think I have said enough about the differences between Southeast Asia and North America to establish that we need fresh comparative research and that such research should be an exciting one. Let me now turn to two other obvious areas: the local districts in China which produced most of the migrants and to which many of them returned; and the countries and localities abroad which received most of the migrants over the past two centuries. For both these, there has been valuable research for several decades and many of the scholarly writings refer to the differences in policies and consequences following upon the introduction of the active and interventionist Huaqiao pattern of emigration. But there has not been enough attention given to the differences between the Huashang and Huagong, and between these two and the Huaqiao pattern.

In China, it is important to remind ourselves that the Huashang pattern was not limited to the southern provinces of Guangdong, Fujian and Guangxi. Many other provinces produced Huashang for Japan, Korea and Southeast Asia, even further west to India and a few to Europe. They include provinces like Zhejiang, Anhwei, Jiangsu, Shandong, Hubei and Yunnan and the great port cities of Shanghai and Tianjin, even Beijing itself. What remains to be done is a close examination of the different experiences of the Huashang from the dominant three southern provinces and those from elsewhere in China. For example, we would like to know if these experiences support the view that there was one basic Huashang pattern of migration. Also, if those from the three southern provinces were more likely or less likely to settle abroad than those from the north. And, if there was a significant difference between north and south in the proportion of Huashang who returned to China, why was this so?

These questions concern spatial differences. These differences could further vary or grow less over time, or grow less because of dramatic events like the large-scale migration of Huagong in the nineteenth century and the evolution of an active Huaqiao policy in the twentieth century. We would like to find out if the large numbers of Huagong from mainly Guangdong, and to a lesser extent Fujian, per- manently transformed the economy of these two provinces. Most coolies were engaged for short periods and most of them returned to China — what effects did this have? Many of them, after returning from one contract season, signed up for another — perhaps to differ- ent places as a mobile labour force. If so, their eventual return might not have unduly affected the labour market in China itself.

Even more challenging is to find out how the Huaqiao pattern was understood in the various provinces. Most research done so far has dealt with central government policies or Guomindang party policies and very little has been done to assess the effect of these new policies on actual relations between the migrants and their families at home in the provinces. On the one hand, one could argue that the new Huaqiao pattern of migration transformed someone like Chen Jiageng (Tan Kah Kee) from being a mere home-loving Huashang to a Huaqiao of national and high profile stature. In so doing, it also transformed the quality of Chen's contributions to southern Fukian and to succes- sive Chinese governments. On the other hand, it may well be that most Huashang simply continued to maintain their philanthropic contacts and property investments with their villages and counties. Why Chen Jiageng and the few others like him did what they did, and why most others might have been more comfortable with traditional *local* links, would be important topics for study and may even have relevance for the present.

The Huaqiao pattern this century raises many unresolved questions because it is a much more complex pattern than one of official protection and intervention. It had from the start several strands. It protected Huashang and Huagong who were already abroad. It also encouraged them to return to China — whether to help modernize the country or to fight for revolution. At the same time, it sponsored teachers and journalists to go out among the Chinese abroad, to make sure they remained loyal and patriotic. And it welcomed Huaqiao descendants to return to China to study and eventually serve the country. The new policies criticized localisms based on clan, dialect or county differences and the disunity among Huaqiao caused by them; instead, they encouraged Huaqiao to think and act in national terms. But the importance of strong village and county ties was acknowledged as essential factors in the new nationalism. And political divisions between major parties, the fierce and deadly rivalries over ideology and revolutionary methods and the factionalism among China's national leaders could not be hidden from the Huaqiao. What effects did these have? It must have been terribly confusing in the 1920s and 1930s for some Hokkiens in Java, for example, to hear that their village in Fujian had been overrun by warlord troops who turned out to be brigands from another province and who were then in turn thrown out by a set of local outlaws; and then, welcoming the Guomindang Northern Expedition (with soldiers mostly from Guangdong) only to find out later that the local garrison was now led by some former brigand leader who had led one of the gangs which terrorized their village a few years earlier. This kind of disorder and instability was also occurring elsewhere during those decades in Guangdong and Guangxi. Did these developments encourage Huaqiao to become cynical and lose faith in China's progress? Did they persuade some to settle down locally and never return to China? Moreover, if not the Huaqiao themselves, did China politics turn their children and grandchildren away from returning?

We badly need some objective and scientific research to answer these questions. If scholars are genuinely interested in the history of migration, especially the Huaqiao pattern that dominated the first half of this century, then we cannot be content with simple statements (repeated again and again) that all Huaqiao were patriotic, poor and exploited. It was all much more complex than that, and I believe also far more interesting.

I think the same could be said about the countries which received Chinese migrants and the changes in their policies which such immigration induced. Both native rulers and Western colonial governments in Southeast Asia welcomed Huashang from time to time and found that pattern of Chinese migration quite acceptable. Until the industrial revolution, there was no other pattern possible anyway. For other parts of the world, however, the end of African slavery brought the need for cheap labour from Asia, mainly from China and India. Hence Huagong found favour in areas where few Huashang had ever been.

The point is that there were times when Chinese, whether traders or labourers, were most welcome. But the welcome varied considerably from place to place, and, what was more important, Huagong were welcome only for short periods. Their arrival in large numbers was acceptable only when it was understood that most of them would leave. The ideal position for most governments was for Chinese labour to be brought in for a specific task for a given period and then sent home. Huashang, on the other hand, had opportunities to make themselves welcome for longer periods and even to make themselves indispensable for the country's development. This was so when the countries concerned were keen to see economic growth and thought Chinese entrepreneurship valuable to ensure that growth. In short, the Huagong pattern of migration could not endure whereas the Huashang pattern could create conditions for it to endure. How this was actually done deserves careful study.

What was quite unacceptable for most governments was the Huaqiao pattern, certainly the aggressively nationalistic and revolutionary features of it. These governments could not deny their Chinese residents the right to be protected by the Chinese government under international law, although they conceded this right with reluctance. But the Huaqiao pattern rarely ended there — nationalistic education and cultural revival often accompanied that protection and these most governments were obliged to control, sometimes with great severity. Thus the entrepreneurial, hardworking and law-abiding Chinese, who had previously been valued and admired, were often quickly transformed in the eyes of these foreign and colonial governments and the local peoples into chauvinists who might be agents for the Chinese government. The problem was not important where the Chinese numbers were small, but where large communities were found, the Huaqiao pattern of migration was regarded with fear and resentment. Such fear and resentment often fuelled the envy of Chinese successes which might have been dormant but now came to the surface.

There has been a lot of exaggeration and propaganda about the Huaqiao phenomenon, both from the Chinese and from the local governments, and it is not always easy to know whom to believe, especially when many writers and journalists wrote emotionally about the subject at the time. What we now need is careful, independent research by scholars who really want to get at the truth. To this end, a great deal will have to be done to persuade governments, especially in China, Taiwan and Southeast Asia, to open their local records to qualified historians. Fortunately, on this score, North American and Australasian archives are open and high standards of scholarship are now possible.

This brings me to an important area of research which has been most unevenly treated and by only a very few scholars. This is the broad area of Chinese society and culture overseas. It is a difficult subject to study and there are many ways to approach it. So there is no room for any false optimism about how we may go about doing the research. At the same time, because so little has been done so far, modest beginnings with small Chinese communities are in fact immediately possible.

Here the conventional historians have a harder time. Social and cultural documents concerning the life of merchants and labourers in the nineteenth century are very hard to come by. There were colonial and other official reports about the Chinese and these are helpful. But both native and Chinese writers and observers were rare and they tell us little that could fill out what the foreign reports have to tell. The sketches that we have of Huashang society and culture in Southeast Asia, for example, contrast sharply with the sketches of Huagong society and culture in Australasia and the Americas. But were they that different? Perhaps the differences were merely due to their occupational backgrounds, to differences between wealth and poverty. Or, they could have been largely due to local social and cultural conditions, to the differences between trading with natives and colonials on the one hand and working for white settlers on the other.

For the twentieth century, however, there is greater scope. The official record is fuller. There are dozens of newspapers for most countries. More people were literate and more was written down.

The Huaqiao pattern encouraged a degree of self-consciousness among the Chinese unknown before and literacy in Chinese among the local-born increased the audience for books, magazines and newspapers from China and encouraged local publications. Indeed, the rapid increase in Chinese social and cultural activities gave the impression that the local Chinese were being drawn away from both Western-colonial and native societies and cultures. But was this really true? We would like to know, if it was so, whether this was solely because of the nationalistic Huaqiao pattern of migration or whether local and colonial discriminatory policies played a major role in alienating the Chinese.

The conventional wisdom is that, before the 1850s or even before 1900, parts of the basic Huashang pattern of migration actually encouraged Chinese to mix freely with native and white colonial peoples alike. But after 1900, following new policies from China encouraging the Huaqiao pattern, the situation changed. Chineseness was thereafter measured against original cultural values in China; young Chinese were discouraged from going to schools other than those teaching in Chinese; and they were expected to use only textbooks published in China. But was this decisive in separating Chinese from other peoples? What about modern Western values and the rise of local nationalism and anti-colonialism? From this perspective, Chinese entrepreneurs were seen to have been in collusion with the European colonial powers and were equally resented by the local nationalists and anti-imperialists. We may be attributing too much change in the normal trading relations between local Chinese and native Southeast Asians to the new nationalistic policies from China. Those policies might after all have been merely a Chinese response to aggressive colonial and imperialist policies — a defensive response to protect the Chinese abroad from cynical Western policies. Again, we need to know more before we accept the conventional picture.

This brings us to contemporary times, to the society and culture of a new breed of Chinese in Southeast Asia. I refer to the descendants of Chinese, the local-born, and the new pattern of re-migration which may become more significant in the future. The society and culture of the ethnic Chinese, mostly with local nationality, of course, have roots in overseas Chinese history as a whole. They may be compared with that of the Babas and Peranakans and Lukchins who might have migrated from one Southeast Asian area to another in an age when boundaries were less formal or not yet fixed. But they are quite different in that they are not merely descendants from an earlier

Huashang pattern, but have either experienced the later Huagong and the Huaqiao patterns, or are descendants of coolies or patriotic Huaqiao. Some are the multiple products of all three patterns *plus* having been educated in a modern or Western cosmopolitan environment. They are those Chinese who have not assimilated to local values or even been acculturated by native nationalism. Instead, they have (perhaps by having been Huaqiao the generation before) turned more to the global modern culture of the professionals with their highly marketable skills.

Why have they done so? They are familiar with the Huaqiao pattern but have rejected that by becoming local nationals. They have experienced the new nationalism in their country of adoption but do not feel that they belong. They are often too Western to be comfortably Chinese and yet too Chinese to accept conditions where Chineseness is being penalized. This is a new phenomenon which evolved during the past three decades or so. We need to understand the nature of their society and culture. We want to know what prevents them from being content to merge with their new local identities. If they have become cultural Eurasians, as some of them have, we also want to know what makes them believe that it would be more satisfying to be Eurasian among Westerners than among Asians. Or perhaps they are really looking for somewhere where they and their families could still remain quietly Chinese in more tolerant circumstances.

There is research to be done here, not least by social and cultural historians. The Huayi has emerged as a recognizable group and their pattern of re-migration already has a history. What is yet uncertain is whether this pattern is also a transitional one. By this, I mean whether they might really be the Westernized Huaqiao who do not want to return to China but want to be Huaqiao again in countries which do not object to such Huaqiao. As this is part of living history still unfolding, it is likely that only by examining their social and cultural values while they are being changed can we hope to know the answer.

As must be obvious by now, there are no simple answers to the questions asked above. My suggestions have all been made in the spirit of stimulating further inquiry. What is offered, however, is the framework of *four* patterns of migration in which that inquiry might be made. But we must guard against using this framework too rigidly and must therefore remember that:

1. the **Huagong** pattern of emigration is gone and unlikely to be revived (the new Vietnamese Chinese refugees may look like coolie labour, but are really closer to the new re-migrant pattern);
2. the **Huaqiao** pattern survives but is now peripheral;
3. the **Huayi** pattern is new and its future still uncertain;
4. only the basic **Huashang** pattern remains — the foundation for Chinese migration from ancient times to the present, the most resilient pattern for us to study through the ages.

In concluding, let me say that I believe we need to know what the Huagong pattern contributed to migration history; what gave the Huaqiao pattern its strength and impact and why it weakened so rapidly; what produced the hybrid Huayi pattern and whether it has a future. But, unless we understand the powerful and indestructible Huashang pattern, we will not be able to present the full history of Chinese migration.

NOTE

1   The main points in this chapter were first made in a keynote lecture given at an international conference on Chinese Emigration held at the University of Hong Kong, December 14–16 1984. Given Professor Mackie's interest in Southeast Asian Chinese as entrepreneurs, I have revised the paper in order to dedicate it to him.

CHAPTER 2

Southeast Asian Huaqiao in Chinese History-Writing

THE NUMBER OF SCHOLARLY books and articles on the Chinese in Southeast Asia has increased so rapidly during this century that it would be useful to examine some of the trends in writing and put the results into some historical perspective. For example, there have been the early writings by Chinese in China and by various colonial officials of the region; then came writings by Southeast Asian Chinese themselves, whether in Chinese or in some local or colonial language; and more recently, the work of specialist scholars trained in social science disciplines, including the work of local scholars whether of Chinese descent or not. There is scope for a full-scale study of the whole range of historical works and it is hoped that the study will be attempted soon. This chapter is a preliminary outline and focuses on writings in Chinese, especially those which help to mark some important turning-points both in the history of the Chinese communities and in the writing of history itself.

I have focused on works in Chinese because they are directed to easily identified audiences and, although they reflect different interests at different times, including varying political positions, they do reflect some unity of purpose in trying to influence their Chinese readers in China and the Chinese educated in Southeast Asia. The majority of these works were published in China before the Second World War. Since 1949, many more were produced in Taiwan and Hong Kong and in the region, notably in Singapore, Jakarta, and Manila. In China, a number of historical studies were produced in the decade after 1955, but there followed a break of some fifteen years until 1979. Only during the past two years has interest revived, mainly at the Nanyang Research Institute of Hsia-men University in Amoy (Xiamen) and at the Institute of Southeast Asian History of Chung-shan (Sun Yat-sen) University in Canton (Guangzhou)[1]. As one might expect from the number of publication centres, the audiences for these writings were far from homogeneous and unchanging. On the contrary, there were enough changes in these audiences to make the writings sufficiently varied to be of considerable interest. Let me now outline the background of this history-writing before the Second World War and then examine some post-war trends and the major problems in dealing with Huaqiao history.

I

There are several landmarks in the growth of Chinese communities in Southeast Asia. Obviously, the coming of the Europeans to the region and to the China coast marked some new beginnings: a challenge to Chinese activities as well as fresh opportunities and different roles for more and more Chinese traders. These changes were reflected to some extent in various writings touching on the Chinese. Prior to the seventeenth century, the desultory writings in Chinese which dealt with Southeast Asia barely mentioned the activities of Chinese traders and sailors although it was clear that these activities were becoming increasingly significant from the late Song dynasty (960–1276) onwards. By the Ming dynasty, with the writings on the Cheng Ho expeditions of the fifteenth century, the quality of information on Southeast Asian and Indian Ocean ports had improved. More references to Chinese communities may be found and the work by Chang Hsieh, the *Tung-hsi yang-k'ao*, early in the seventeenth century is the most thorough of its kind. Similarly, Ch'en Lun-chiung's *Hai-kuo wen-chien lu* (eighteenth century) was a notable contribution to contemporary history. But partly because Chinese communities were relatively few and each of them still small, and partly because of the policy of the Ming dynasty prohibiting overseas travel, none of the early writings may be considered studies of the Southeast Asian Chinese but merely of countries of interest to China.[2] This remained true through most of the Qing dynasty well into the nineteenth century, even though Western writings clearly showed how many more Chinese had migrated during the eighteenth and nineteenth centuries. Indeed, by the middle of the nineteenth century, some Western colonial officials seem to have been better informed about the various Chinese communities around the region than Qing imperial officials themselves. The work of J.D. Vaughan, *The Manners and Customs of the Chinese of the Straits Settlements* (1879), for example, records more information about an overseas Chinese community than any earlier work in Chinese.

A new awareness had emerged in the mid-nineteenth century among various authorities about the size of the Chinese communities, about their wealth and potential influence as well as about the anomalies that surrounded what was soon to become a "Chinese problem". This awareness was to lead to a qualitative change in Chinese attitudes which also produced a different kind of historical writing about the Chinese abroad. The final recognition that something had to be done to outworn laws is worth noting. In 1893, the traditional ban on overseas travel was lifted. It had long been modified and defied and was quite ineffective and, by this time, the Qing government admitted that it was ridiculous. Still, this decision itself was not really as significant as it appears because the removal of the ban was something of a formality. What had probably been more important for the Chinese communities was the period between the foundation of Penang and that of Singapore (1786–1819). These were the first settlements where the Chinese were actively welcomed and where they were soon to achieve social and economic dominance. It could also be argued that the years after the opening of China by the British and especially the foundation of Hong Kong in 1842 were more important. I would not reject that idea although I am inclined to see the new waves of migration that followed the rise of Hong Kong as the climax of a development that had begun with the end of the eighteenth century.

But where writings about the Chinese are concerned, the change in the late eighteenth century was not significant, for while it led to more references to the number of Chinese abroad, it did not lead to changes in the nature of the writings themselves. For the latter to change, we would have to wait for the cumulative weight of numbers to bring about a dramatic shift in attitudes in China about these Chinese abroad and ultimately in the Overseas Chinese attitudes about themselves. This I believe did not come about until the end of the nineteenth century, during the period between 1895 and 1912. This shift can perhaps first be discerned in the brief accounts by some of the earliest foreign affairs experts to represent China abroad, especially in the reports by Kuo Sung-t'ao and Huang Tsun-hsien.[3] These began to paint a sympathetic picture of the Chinese who struggled for their livelihood under hostile circumstances and began to speak glowingly of those who were successful in acquiring modern technical and entrepreneurial skills. On the one hand, there had been growing shame at the way the Qing government did so little to help the victims of the extensive coolie trade or to prevent discrimination against Chinese in the new worlds of North America and Australasia. On the other, the government began to recognize the advantages of having Chinese overseas whose wealth and skills could be harnessed to the great task of modernizing China. The efforts of Tso Ping-lung, the first Consul in the Straits Settlements, and the development of the first Chinese newspaper in Southeast Asia, the *Lat Pau*, led to the publication of historical notes about the Chinese which showed increasing pride in Chinese achievements over the centuries.[4] Although all these writings were to gain influence among Qing official circles and were to lead to policy changes by the government in China towards Overseas Chinese, they were not in themselves markedly different in style, form, and even content from earlier writings like Wang Ta-hai's *Hai-tao i-chih* of the late eighteenth century, Hsieh Ch'ing-kao's *Hai-lu* of the early nineteenth, or the various short works and extracts of longer works collected in the *Hsiao-fang hu-chai yü-ti ts'ung-ch'ao* series published between 1891 and 1897. Even the later authors would have seen themselves as having mainly updated the information contained in Wei Yuan's authoritative *Hai-kuo t'u-chih* (completed in 1852) and to have written in the same grand tradition.[5]

The turning-point in historical writing about the Overseas Chinese did not come until after 1895, after the defeat of China by Japan, which quickly made the question of China's survival as a civilization a crucial one. I argue for *after* 1895 because 1895 itself was more important for China and too broad in all its ramifications to be specifically meaningful for the Chinese overseas. Also, clearly the turning-point had occurred *before* 1912 because, by that year, a number of dramatic steps had already been taken to legalize the position of the Chinese abroad and to define their legal status, most notably the Chinese Nationality Law of 1909. Furthermore, thousands of Overseas Chinese had, by 1912, been directly involved in activities for or against various political organizations which supported reform or revolution in China. The Overseas Chinese had even produced their first martyrs in 1910 in the abortive Huang-hua-kang uprising in Canton.

The key development among the Southeast Asian Chinese during the period 1895–1912 was obviously their willingness to involve themselves in Chinese politics to an increasing degree. This development did not arise from internal social and economic pressures in the region so much as direct political agitation by a handful of men who were forced to seek support for their cause ouside of China. I refer, of course, to Sun Yat-sen, K'ang Yu-wei, and their supporters who trav-

elled around Southeast Asia in the name of revolution or reform.
They aroused an intense concern for the future of China which was
reinforced by Western interest in a more modern and stable China
after the upheavals of the Boxer Rising of 1900 and by the measures
taken afterwards for constitutional and administrative reforms.

We would expect historical writing about the Overseas Chinese to
change during this decade. But what criteria should be used to measure the extent of the change in history-writing as distinct from a
turning-point in history? I suggest that the criteria be based upon the
dramatic shift in attitudes about such Chinese both in China and
among these communities abroad. And the most striking single
example of this shift lies in the increasing use of the concept of
Huaqiao, the Chinese sojourner, as a political term with strong emotional overtones. In particular, the coming together of this term with
that of *chih-min*, to colonize or colonization, totally transformed the
way the Chinese wrote about the Overseas Chinese.

As I have written elsewhere about the origins of the term Huaqiao
and the way it became the dominant term for all Chinese abroad, I
shall not repeat the arguments here. The key point is that *qiao* came
into use for the Chinese abroad only after it had been used to translate "temporary residence" for foreign officials in China in a series of
treaties beginning with the Sino-French Treaty of Tientsin in 1858;
and it was used to stress residence overseas that was official, approved, and protected. And it was not until the end of the century
that *qiao* was used as part of the noun *Huaqiao* meaning a Chinese
person or a Chinese community residing abroad.[6] What needs further
consideration is whether contemporary writers and later historians
saw the Huaqiao as comparable to the colonists that the Europeans
had encouraged and used to expand their overseas empires.

It would seem that two developments were occurring about the
same time. On the one hand, there was the growing awareness that
Chinese born overseas (for example, in the Straits Settlements) preferred to travel to China as British protected subjects because they
enjoyed the benefits of British consular protection. This protection
was contrasted to large-scale exploitation of Chinese contract labour
to Southeast Asia, the Americas, and other places where they received little if any protection from the Chinese government. Not
least, Chinese officials were increasingly impressed by the large
numbers of Chinese long resident in Southeast Asia who were still
recognizably Chinese and some of whom, because they felt discriminated against by Western colonial governments, would welcome

Chinese official recognition and protection. All this was to make the Chinese government face up to those aspects of international law, immigrant regulations, and colonial statutes pertinent to a new policy of active support of its subjects abroad.

On the other hand, improved understanding of the nature of Western expansion in Asia, Africa and the Americas led the Chinese to an appreciation of the concept of *chih-min* (to colonize) and *chih-min ti* (colony).[7] At first, the Chinese term had been *shu-kuo*, translating dependency or colony, which stressed the element of imperial control, suzerainty, or even sovereignty. It was not until close to the end of the century that the emphasis shifted to the settlers and colonists, and this was induced by their awareness of the sharp contrast between Western official support for colonization and Chinese non-support over the centuries for those Chinese who had been desperate enough or foolish enough to leave China. As long as Chinese official rhetoric still spoke of Western cultures in contemptuous terms, the connection between Huaqiao and *chih-min* could not be made. It was not really until China's defeat by Japan and after Chinese reformists had turned to Japanese writings on the West that the success of Western imperialism and colonial expansion came gradually to be openly admired. It is interesting, and I believe no coincidence, that the politicization of the term Huaqiao and the earliest published reference to the history of Chinese "colonists" in Southeast Asia appeared within a year of each other. First came the poem "Song of Revolution" (*Ko-ming Ko*), somewhat dubiously attributed to Chang Ping-lin, which was attached to Tsou Jung's *Ko-ming Chün* ("The Revolutionary Army") published in Shanghai in 1903.[8] Then in 1904 came the essay by Liang Ch'i-ch'ao entitled "Chung-kuo chih-min pa ta-wei-jen chuan" ("Biographies of the eight great men of Chinese colonization") published in *Hsin-min ts'ung-pao* in Yokohama. The eight were men who had been kings or rulers of Srivijaya (Palembang), Borneo (Pontianak), and Sunda and Yap Ah Loy, the pioneer settler of Selangor.[9]

In both cases, the writers were describing the Chinese in Southeast Asia. The author of "Song of Revolution" had obviously been impressed by the stories of enormously wealthy Huaqiao like Oei Tiong Ham in the Netherlands East Indies and enjoined them to stop their meaningless extravagance and use their fortunes to support the patriotic anti-Manchu cause. Liang Ch'i-ch'ao, however, dug deeper into Chinese historical records for the fragmentary references to successful Chinese in the Nanyang since the early fifteenth century (see also his biography of Cheng Ho published in the same journal later the same year). His ability to connect such Huaqiao with later Western colonists (chih-min) was enhanced by his own travels in Southeast Asia, Australia, and North America where he saw for himself the great difference between European admiration for their great colonizers and adventurers and total Chinese neglect of their own. Also, by this time, he and many other reformers and revolutionaries had digested the Japanese books praising Western colonization. Liang Ch'i-ch'ao began to feel that Huaqiao achievements should also be acclaimed, that the Chinese right to migrate and settle abroad be asserted, and that the well-established Chinese communities in the various ports and kingdoms of Southeast Asia over the centuries should be recognized as Chinese colonies.

Let me now return to the subject of history-writing. Liang Ch'i-ch'ao's essay did not claim to be a work of history. On the contrary, he was struck by the Western historical studies of men like Columbus, Clive and Livingstone and by the lack of studies of Chinese counterparts.

> We may well ask how many of our 400 million people have heard of the activities of our eight gentlemen. Let us not speak of activities, even their names have probably not been heard of. When I read the Foreign Countries chapters of *Ming Shih* and read of the four kings of Sri Vijaya, Borneo and Java, I was surprised and delighted and speechless with emotion. I could only sigh to see such great men of ours buried so deeply in worm-eaten texts; and two of their names have not even been recorded for posterity. I felt angry, fearful, ashamed, and hurriedly added what I have learnt of the achievement of four other gentlemen during the last hundred years.[10]

Liang ch'i-ch'ao was the most widely read and influential writer of his time and his essay was the first of several others during the next decade and may be described as the precursor of Huaqiao history. Of these, I do not need to say much about Hu Shao-nan's biographies of Huaqiao colonial leaders in *Tung-fang tsa-chih* (1910) or a similar work by Ya-hsia in *Ti-hsueh tsa-chih* (1913).[11]. Both are expanded versions of Liang Ch'i-ch'ao's essay which correct some of his serious mistakes but make other mistakes of their own. What deserves some attention is the first Huaqiao history to call itself such, that is, Hsi-huang cheng-yin's (pen-name of Yi Pen-hsi) *Nan-yang hua-ch'iao shih lueh* ("A short history of the Nanyang Chinese") published in *Min Pao* in Tokyo in 1910.[12]

Both the author and his friend Liu Sung-heng, who contributed an emotional preface and an equally passionate essay to the Chinese massacred by the Dutch at Batavia in 1741, had been to Java; both were anti-Manchu revolutionaries. Also, Yi Pen-hsi himself taught in a Chinese school in Semarang in 1906–08. The author admits that his history is largely about the Dutch and British possessions in the Malay archipelago and has relied on oral accounts as well as Chinese written sources. It consists of nine chapters plus an introduction and a conclusion. It openly compares Huaqiao with Western colonists and only regrets that Chinese colonization failed in Southeast Asia because of the anti-Chinese policies of the Manchu dynasty.

Yi Pen-hsi cannot be taken seriously today as an historian, but his history is important in so far as it was the first of its kind and was a clear development from Liang Ch'i-ch'ao's successful linking of Huaqiao with *chih-min*. Although the work was full of elementary errors which were largely corrected in later Chinese writings, it did set the pattern for history-writing on the Huaqiao for the next three or four decades. By this, I mean that it began with the earliest Han dynasty trading and tributary relations with Southeast Asia, assumed that most contacts showed that Huaqiao settled in the region, glorified the Cheng Ho expeditions and the achievements of Cheng Ch'eng-kung (Koxinga), and generally praised the Ming dynasty for its positive "colonial" policies while condemning the Qing dynasty for its negative attitudes towards the Huaqiao.[13] Yi Pen-hsi reflected the new nationalism that had been developing since the turn of the century. It was obviously gratifying to point to evidence that the Chinese had had overseas colonies from early times and to suggest that they now needed a more dynamic government that appreciated these achievements and was prepared to do something about protecting these colonies.

I suggest that this use of Huaqiao to imply colonists marked the first turning-point in historical writing about the Chinese in Southeast Asia. Some of the Huaqiao themselves accepted their new name with enthusiasm. On the whole, however, the keenest tended to be those who had recently arrived from China and especially those who were educated in the Chinese schools which had become increasingly prominent in the region. In particular, with the establishment of the Republic of China in 1912, the new textbooks introduced the new perspective fairly rapidly. By the time Chinese middle schools appeared in Southeast Asia, all history books had accepted the use of Huaqiao for communities of very well-established traditional Chinese "colonies" in the Southeast Asian region. The 1920s, just before and just after the Kuomintang victory over the warlords in 1927, saw a flood of books about the Huaqiao and the Nanyang which alarmed Western colonial powers and native political leaders alike throughout Southeast Asia. They are too many to mention here and deserve a fuller study on their own. The foundation of the Nanyang Research Institute at Chi-nan University in Shanghai, with its journal *Nanyang Yen-chiu* in 1928, was the climax of this powerful movement to involve the Chinese government more actively in Southeast Asian affairs.[14] The appearance of several works of history between 1927 and 1929 by scholars like Chang Hsiang-shih, Li Ch'ang-fu, and Wen Hsiung-fei marked the mature development of this particular kind of Chinese "colonial" history.[15] The two most authoritative histories of this genre were Liu Chi-hsuan and Shu Shih-ch'eng's *Chung-hua min-tsu t'o-chih Nan-yang shih* ("History of the Chinese people's opening up of the Nanyang") published in 1934 and Li Ch'ang-fu's *Chung-kuo chih-min shih* ("History of Chinese colonization") in 1937.[16] Both books are ambiguous about whether Huaqiao were migrants (*yi-min*) or colonists (*chih-min*) and argue that Chinese colonization was quite different from Western colonization. But they are both clear that *chih-min* was legitimate and justified and a matter of national pride and, therefore, Huaqiao should receive both official and public support.

II

Before I turn to examine some of the problems of writing Huaqiao history today, let me briefly outline the trends since 1945. I am specially interested in the extent to which scholars have turned away from the Huaqiao "colonial" history approach described above to one that may be described as multidimensional in recognizing the immense complexity of the subject. Two obvious points may be made immediately. Most historians have responded to the great changes in East and Southeast Asia over the last thirty-five years, and this response has influenced the kinds of histories they wrote. Also, as two Chinese governments emerged after 1949 in Peking and Taipei and independent centres publishing in Chinese survived in Hong Kong and Singapore, different viewpoints could be supported and each of them appealed to a different group of Chinese. Here one would have to distinguish at least the following: the nationalists whether pro-Taiwan or not; the communists whether inside or outside China; those of Chinese descent who wrote in Chinese but as citizens of one or another of the new Southeast Asian nations.

Bearing this in mind, one is struck immediately by the change in attitude towards the term *chih-min* for colony. Within the first five years after the war, largely because of extensive anti-colonial literature by Chinese and Southeast Asians alike, the term was discredited and virtually dropped altogether. Certainly, pro-Peking Chinese and local ethnic Chinese rejected it by 1950. Chinese nationalists in Taiwan and Hong Kong were more casual or insensitive and many new books until the mid-1950s allowed the term to be used. An example of this was Li Jui-hua's *Ma-lai-ya hua-ch'iao* published in Taipei in 1954 which still spoke of "the history of Malayan Chinese colonization".[17] Not surprisingly, it was the kind of book that the Federation of Malaya Government thought necessary to ban. After this, new Taiwan books were more circumspect and were content to use Huaqiao to cover everyone of Chinese descent overseas no matter what his or her nationality was. Adhering to the *jus sanguins* principle in China's nationality law, the Taiwan government felt justified under all circumstances to call everyone of Chinese blood a Huaqiao. And in so far as both the books by Liu and Shu in 1934 and by Li Ch'ang-fu in 1937 were still used and reprinted in 1971 and 1966 respectively, it is likely that many Chinese still accepted the strong link between Huaqiao and Chinese overseas colonies and all that the link implies.

But the term *chih-min* itself has been avoided since the mid-1950s. What is now interesting is the way the word Huaqiao is used in Taiwan. In the 1950s, in the various series produced by the Hai-wai (Overseas) Publishing Company in Taipei, more than half of the books were about Southeast Asia and most of these dealt with aspects of Huaqiao history.[18] Similary, the semi-official series of country-by-country Huaqiao studies produced in Taiwan under the general editorship of Chu Hsiu-hsia dealt mainly with Southeast Asia. The latter was continued into the 1960s and a revised edition of the key General Volume appeared in 1964.[19] In all of these, there was a strong emphasis on national pride in Huaqiao history and a concern to involve the Huaqiao in current anti-communist activities. But a fresh tone has crept into the writings in the 1970s. A good example may be found in the thoughtful and sophisticated articles by Chang Wen-yü (David W. Chang) collected in 1972 in his *Hua-jen she-hui yü Tung-nan-ya chu-kuo chih cheng-chih fa-chan* ("Chinese society and the political development of Southeast Asian nations").[20] These articles show a new sensitivity to the feelings of Southeast Asian national leaders and of local Chinese. They use Huaqiao sparingly, even in the passages about history, and introduce wherever possible terms like Huaren and Huayi now preferred within Southeast Asia itself. This new approach does not mean that the Taiwan Government will reject the term Huaqiao or that historians will follow suit, but it does suggest an awareness that Huaqiao had been too directly tied to involvements in China's politics, to matters concerning Chinese na-tionality-by-blood, to questions of an alien loyalty and patriotism, and even to the sinister idea of "once a Chinese, always a Chinese".

In contrast to the flood of publications about Huaqiao history and society from Taiwan, there has not been a great deal published about these subjects in China: indeed very little history before Chou En-lai went to Bandung in 1955 and then sporadically in 1956–59 and 1962–64, and almost nothing at all for the next fifteen years until 1979. The collected volumes published in 1979/80 by Hsia-men and Chung-shan universities both include articles first published in the 1950s and before 1964.[21] Even the very original work based on interviews with returned coolie labourers had been done first in 1963 and left in cold storage until 1979.[22] As for the scholarly articles that appeared during the decade after 1955, they seem either to introduce aspects of indige-nous history or to describe the Chinese in the region as being victims of colonial oppression. The common theme stressed was that the Chinese labouring classes and the indigenous peoples were both victims of history and therefore co-operated with each other in anti-colonial struggles. But the evidence for this co-operation was slim and the scholars seem to have been aware enough of this not to push the point too far.

In short, for different reasons and in different ways from Taiwan and Southeast Asia itself, political considerations have restricted scholarly work on Southeast Asia.and on the ethnic Chinese domi-ciled there. The Marxist analysis that was followed by all scholars who got into print spoke only of the unity of workers and peasants — of whatever ethnic origins — who would, at a particular moment of history, work with the national bourgeosie everywhere against colo-nialism. Therefore, the historians emphasized the class struggle and depicted local Chinese as generally sympathetic to revolutionary movements led by indigenous leaders. It was recognized that with the exception of British Malaya (now Singapore and West Malaysia), the Chinese did not have the numbers. There was no sizeable pro-letariat and least of all any peasantry to speak of anywhere else. Ironi-cally, in Malaya where the Chinese had the numbers and some of them dominated the communist movement, history has not shown the Malays as favouring communism at all.

Nevertheless, the historians in China did have the opportunity to avoid the conventional types of Huaqiao history and the Great Han chauvinism that often accompanied them. They could approach afresh the role of the Chinese in Southeast Asian history and did in fact begin to do so by translating historical writings by Southeast Asians themselves, notably the work of Sanusi Pané on Indonesia. In Volume 1 of the Chung-shan University collection, ten of the essays on modern Southeast Asian history (four on the Philippines, two on Burma, two on Thailand, and two on Malaysia-Indonesia) deal integrally with progressive indigenous movements and clearly recognize that if and when the Huaqiao were relevant, they were quite peripheral to the major developments.[23] Furthermore, in Volume 2 of the collection where four essays on Huaqiao from 1959 have been collected, two points of interest can be made. First, the stress on colonial exploitation of Chinese labour and the lack of a righteous *nationalist* tone mark a departure from earlier Huaqiao history; but all four essays are ambivalent whether they are about Southeast Asian or about a part of Chinese history. Second, it is interesting that of the fourteen essays on modern history collected, the four on Huaqiao were published in 1959 while the ten on Southeast Asian history itself were published in 1962–64. This fact suggests that there had been conscious efforts to direct the historians' attention to the region itself and leave the Huaqiao alone.[24]

This trend can also be seen in the growing interest in the returned Huaqiao as part of Chinese history. I have already mentioned the interviews with returned coolie labourers and the valuable data that were collected (both Hsia-men and Chung-shan universities published the report which was the result of collaborative work between the two institutions). Even more interesting has been the research done on Huaqiao industrial investments in China. The fieldwork was done in 1958/59 in twenty-three cities and countries in Kwangtung, Fukien, and Shanghai and four volumes of data have been collected, but the first study published by Lin Chin-chih has only just appeared in the Hsia-men University volume on Huaqiao.[25] Taken together with Wang Mu-heng's article, which attempts to argue that Indonesian and Huaqiao industry in the late nineteenth and early twentieth centuries together formed an integral part of the Indonesian economy and therefore of Indonesian history,[26] it would appear that the Chinese historians are, unlike in 1959, beginning to distinguish between that part of Huaqiao history which is Chinese and that which is

Southeast Asian. This attitude is in sharp contrast to that of most other historians who tend either to extend Chinese history to cover all Huaqiao activity in Southeast Asia (as many in Taiwan and Hong Kong still do) or, more recently, to domesticate most Huaqiao history as a part of Southeast Asian history (as most local historians of Chinese descent are attempting to do).

Let me now turn briefly to the locally domiciled historians writing in Chinese. A fresh start had been made with the formation of the Nan-yang Hsueh-hui (South Seas Society) in Singapore in 1940, the members consisting of both scholars from China and local scholars from all over the region who had studied in China. They wrote very much in the shadow of the Nanyang Research Institute of Chi-nan University in Shanghai, but two men in Singapore were outstanding in their dedication to scholarship. Tan Yeok Seong (Ch'en Yü-sung) was the local-born scholar highly sensitive to changes and developments in the region who encouraged the next generation to look more to the region's own Huaqiao sources and put together the finest single collection of historical materials. Hsü Yun-ts'iao came from China but adapted to local conditions and sought in his own way to bridge the gap between traditional Huaqiao history and the region's own history.[27] Then came the growth of Nanyang University in Singapore and this encouraged a new generation of scholars, mainly from Singapore, Malaysia, and Indonesia, to study Southeast Asian history itself and place the Huaqiao in context.

I shall not go into details about local scholarship. The work is uneven and now varies greatly in quality from country to country. Unquestionably, Singapore is alone in having produced its own historians writing in Chinese, but it is uncertain that they will be encouraged to produce significant scholarship about the place of Chinese communities in other countries in the region. The only point I wish to stress here is that these younger scholars are more open to the influence of local and Western scholarship about the region than those in China and Taiwan and are more likely to reassess the historic role of Huaqiao from a local, and not necessarily a Huaqiao, point of view. But they too are struggling with the term Huaqiao. They have tried to use alternative terms like Huaren, Huatsu, Huayi, and, for Singapore and Malaysia, *Hsing-Hua* and *Ma-Hua* (other prefixes varying with each country), but are not yet agreed which is the most suitable alternative.[28] Let me conclude by re-examining the term Huaqiao again in terms of the history-writing that is now being done and will still have to be done.

In one of the essays published in China in 1980 on investments in China by returned Overseas Chinese by Lin Chin-chih, it was said that "Huaqiao living abroad have had a history of two thousand years".[29] This reminded me of my response to the fine scholarly book by Ch'en Ching-ho entitled *Shih-liu shih-chi chih Fei-lu-pin hua-ch'iao* ("The Overseas Chinese in the Philippines during the sixteenth century") published in 1963 when I wondered whether it was appropriate to speak of Huaqiao as early as that when the Ming dynasty cared nothing for the Chinese overseas and still thought of them largely as criminals, pirates, smugglers, even potential rebels.[30] There was no question of recognition, support, or protection. Were they, therefore, Huaqiao? This had led me to examine more carefully the origins of the term and the way it has been used since it became popular at the turn of the twentieth century. There have been many alternatives suggested. *Yi-min* (migrants) is the most general, but it cannot apply to those who had settled down, in many cases for generations. *Chung-kuo jen* and Huaren are also general but would be used for all Chinese and do not indicate the person's location outside China. Huatsu (ethnic Chinese) is still new and not familiar in China and Taiwan, although *tsu* has long been used for the ethnic minorities in China as well as for Han Chinese. More specific terms by country (as in *Yin-Hua*, *Ma-Hua*, and *Fei-Hua* for Indonesia, Malaysia, and the Philippines) would not help if one wished to speak generally of the Chinese abroad; also, they would be anachronistic for periods when there were no countries called by such names. And, as for Huayi, which may be appropriate for more and more "descendants of Chinese", it could not really apply to those who were China-born and those who chose to be Chinese citizens.

In fact, when the term Huaqiao is used in its precise meaning of "the Chinese sojourner", indicating a Chinese national temporarily residing abroad, it can be a most useful one. It has been generally applied to those who have been leaving China and Taiwan since the late 1940s to reside abroad (especially North America and Japan). It can also be used to describe most Chinese from Hong Kong who have migrated to North America, Western Europe and Australasia during the past decades. But ethnic Chinese with foreign nationality who have identified with their country of adoption may not then be called Huaqiao and countries with large numbers of such Chinese, especially in Southeast Asia, have rightly insisted on the rejection of the term for their citizens of Chinese descent. And it may not be long before both China and Taiwan would be obliged to go along with this, especially following the promulgation of China's new Nationality Law in September 1980.[31]

But the problem still remains for the historians of Southeast Asian Chinese. Even if the true Huaqiao have become but the smallest of minorities in each Southeast Asian country, and even if historians hereafter might agree to stop referring to Huaqiao after each country had gained its independence, what of the periods before 1945 that historians wish to write about? There are many ambiguities here. But could we not argue that, before modern times and before the concept of nationality was introduced, everyone of Chinese descent or who identified himself as culturally Chinese could be called Huaqiao? Would it not be simpler if historians accepted Huaqiao retrospectively for periods before the late nineteenth century even though the term had not yet been invented? Why not Huaqiao in the Philippines in the sixteenth century? Why not two thousand years of Huaqiao history?

Ultimately, it would seem to me that one must confront the origins of the term, the political, legal and emotional overtones it acquired almost from the moment it came into use, the way it assured official protection to the Chinese abroad and the association it had with the idea of colonies and Western colonization policies. If these connotations are correct, how could it be said that the Chinese prior to the late nineteenth century were in any way Huaqiao? It would seem to be a distortion of history to imply China's appreciation of these Chinese and their communities abroad long before it happened. The fact that Huaqiao would be a convenient single word to describe an unusual phenomenon should not, I think, lead us to give a false and anachronistic impression of China's concern for Huaqiao before it became true.

I would like to suggest that there was a period when it would be correct to speak of Huaqiao in Southeast Asian history. This was the period from the end of the nineteenth century to the late 1940s when the Chinese government conferred rights and demanded duties from the Huaqiao, and most people of Chinese descent there seemed to have responded to a greater or lesser degree. I realize that this may be difficult to accept outside of the region and that, left on their own, historians in China and Taiwan would always find it difficult to think afresh on the matter of Huaqiao history. The term is too convenient and the dubious associations it has in the region mean little to them. Thus, throughout the 1960s and 1970s, China-born historians still used Huaqiao freely for all periods. But, increasingly, those born in the region (whether writing in Chinese, in Western, or in local national languages) have shied away from the term and even from the very idea of Huaqiao. They speak, of course, of the Chinese in various parts of the region and what they were like at various periods of history, but they do not insist that there had always been Huaqiao. There is, in general, greater care and sensitivity about the proper use of the term, at least for Southeast Asian history. Should they agree to adopt a consistent definition of Huaqiao that would enable them to speak of a Huaqiao period of about half a century, this could lead to a richer pluralistic understanding of different periods of the history of the Chinese and their descendants in Southeast Asia. It would be interesting to see, when that happens, whether historians in China and Taiwan would consider reviewing their own attitudes towards the writing of Huaqiao history.

NOTES

1 A party of Southeast Asianists from the Australian National University visited both these centres in September 1980 and received some of their publications. There are, in addition, small centres at Chi-nan (Jinan) University, also at Canton and at the Yunnan Historical Institute and other similar institutions in Kunming. A group of Southeast Asian language scholars at Peking University are associated with the Institute of South East Asian Studies (a joint institute of Peking University and the Academy of the Social Sciences in Peking) which plans to expand its activities into Southeast Asia. The revival of interest in Southeast Asian studies began with a conference in Amoy in 1978; this was followed by one in Kunming in 1980 and a third conference in Canton in 1982.

2 The best-known writings of this kind must begin with Chao Ju-kua, *Chu Fan Chih* (early 13th century), translated by F. Hirth and W.W. Rockhill (St. Petersburg, 1911); the best of the Cheng Ho-related books is that of Ma Huan, *Ying-yai sheng-lan* (early 15th century), translated by J.V.G. Mills (Cambridge, 1970). The most accessible edition of Chang Hsieh is that published in Shanghai, 1936 Ts'ung-shu chi-ch'eng edition); and that of Ch'en Lun-chiung is that of Taipei, 1958. None of these and other similar works devote special sections to the Chinese residing overseas.

3 Kuo Sung-t'ao *Kuo Shih-lang chou-shu* (Yang-chih shu-wu yi-chi edition 1892), vol. 12, 91-b; also see *Kuang-hsü ch'ao tung-hua lu*, Peking reprint 1958, pp. 298–99. Huang Tsun-hsien's famous letter of 1893 to Hsueh Fu-ch'eng may be found in Hsueh Fu-ch'eng Ch'üan-chi (*Yung-an ch'üan-chi*) Taipei 1963 reprint, vol. 3, Hai-wai wen-pien, 1, 18b–19a; see also *Kuang-hsü ch'ao tung-hua lu*, pp. 3241-242.

4 On Tso Ping-lung, see Tan Yeok Seong (Ch'en Yü-sung) "Tso Tzu-hsing ling-shih tui Hsin-chia-p'o hua-ch'iao ti kung-hsien", *Nanyang Hsueh-pao* 15/5 (June 1959),

pp. 12–21. For *Lat Pau*, see Chen Mong Hock, *The Early Chinese Newspaper of Singapore, 1881–1912* (Singapore, 1967), pp. 28ff; Tan Yeok Seong, *Nanyang ti-i pao-jen* (Singapore 1958), pp. 1–12. Also, Song Ong Siang, *One Hundred Years of the Chinese in Singapore* (Singapore, 1967), pp. 209–210. See also the work of Tso Ping-lung's friend, Li Chung-chueh, who visited him in Singapore in 1887 and later published his *Hsin-chia-p'o feng-t'u-chi* (1895), reprinted with annotations by Hsu Yun-ts'iao (Singapore, 1947).

5 For Wang Ta-hai, see Ong Tae-hae, *The Chinaman abroad*, trans. W.H. Medhurst (Shanghai, 1859). A modern edition of Hsieh Ch'ing-kao, with annotations by Feng Ch'eng-chun, was published in Shanghai in 1938. The Hsiao-fang hu-chai collections in three parts appeared in Shanghai between 1891 and 1897. Wei Yuan's great work was expanded during the 1840s; the 100-chuan edition was published in 1852.

6 "A note on the origins of *hua-ch'iao*", published in Lie Tek Tjeng (ed.), *Masalah-masalah International Masakini*, no. 7 (Jakarta, 1977) and reprinted in Wang Gungwu, *Community and Nation: Essays on Southeast Asia and the Chinese*. ASAA Monographs (Singapore, 1981).

Huaqiao (Hua ch'iao) as a noun may have begun in the 1880s. Ma Chien-chung and Wu Kuang-p'ei were both close to it when they wrote of *hua-shang ch'iao-yü che* and *hua-jen ch'iao-yü che* respectively during or after their visit to the Straits Settlements in 1881; see Ma's *Nan-hsing chi* (6b) and Wu's *Nan-hsing jih-chi* (5b); *Hsiao-fang hu-chai yü-ti ts'ung-ch'ao tsai-pu pien*, vol 10 (Shanghai, 1897). It had been thought that Huang Tsun-hsien was the first to use the term hua-ch'iao in 1893; *Nanyang nien-chien* (1951 kuei, p. 23, quoted in Kao Wei-lien, "Huang Kung-tu hsien-sheng chiu-jen Hsin-chia-p'o tsung-ling-shih k'ao". *Nanyang hsueh-pao* 11/2 (1955):1–16; and again quoted in Wu T'ien-jen, *Huang kung-tu hsien-sheng chuan-kao* (Hong Kong, 1972), pp. 116–17. But the original of the 1893 letter used *hua-min* and not hua-ch'iao, see *Hsueh Fu-ch'eng ch'üan-chi* and *Kuang-hsü ch'ao tung-hua lu* (note 3 above).

7 There was no serious discussion of the idea of *chih-min* in China except in the context of Social Darwinism, geopolitics, and imperialism (*ti-kuo chu-yi*) in Africa and the Pacific after 1895. The earliest notable study was Liang Ch'i-ch'ao's "Lun min-tsu ching-cheng chih ta-shih" in 1902; see Taipei reprint of *Hsin-min ts'ung-pao hui-pien hsü-k'an* (Chin-tai shih-liao ts'ung-shu hui-pien, series one), pp. 243–301, esp. p. 288. Two years later, Liang spoke of Huaqiao colonists in Southeast Asia; see note 9 below.

8 *Ko-ming chün* text and appendices in Tsou Jung, *The Revolutionary Army: A Chinese Nationalist Tract of 1903*, trans. John Lust (The Hague, 1968).

9 Text in Liang Ch'i-ch'ao, *Yin-ping shih chuan-chi*, vol. 3, no. 8 (Shanghai, 1936), vol. 3, no. 8, pp. 1–5.

10 *Yin-ping shih chuan-chi* 3/8: p. 4.

11 *Tung-fang tsa-chih* 7/12 (15 Dec. 1910): pp. 93–104; *Ti-hsueh tsa-chih* vol. 4, nos. 10–12:1a–4a, 1a–7a, and 1a–7b of Shuo-fu sections.

12 *Min Pao* (Minpao Magazine), nos. 25 and 26, pp. 1–35 and 1–40.

13 Later works modified this last point by admitting that the ban on overseas travel was introduced not by the Qing but early during the Ming dynasty; e.g., Li Ch'ang-fu, *Chung-kuo chih-min shih* (Shanghai, 1937), pp. 100–103.

14 *Nanyang Yen-chiu* continued publication until 1944, in 11 volumes. There were other influential journals like the *Ch'iao-wu yueh-pao* (1933–37) and the *Hua-ch'iao pan-yueh-k'an* (1932–36), but these were more political than scholarly.

15 Chang Hsiang-shih, *Hua-ch'iao chung-hsin chih Nan-yang* (Hai-k'ou, 1927); Li Ch'ang-fu's first version of *Nan-yang Hua-ch'iao shih* (Shanghai, 1929); Wen Hsiung-fei, *Nan-yang hua-ch'iao t'ung-shih* (Shanghai, 1929).

16 Liu and Shu's work was published in Nanking while Li's book appeared in Shanghai. Both were reprinted in Taipei, in 1971 and 1966 respectively.

17 Taipei, 1954, ch. 2. It also had a chapter on race relations (ch. 7), which may have been the main reason for its being banned in Malaya.

18 The two series of booklets of particular interest here were *Hua-ch'iao hai-wai k'ai-fa shih* (Overseas Huaqiao development history) *Hai-wai ming-jen chuan* (Famous Chinese abroad).

19 Hua-ch'iao chih Editorial Committee, *Hua-ch'iao chih: Tsung chih* (Taipei, 1954), rev. ed. 1964. The nine volumes for Southeast Asia were Vietnam (1958), Thailand (1959), Malaya (1959), Singapore (1960), Cambodia (1960), Indonesia (1961), Laos (1962), the Northern Borneo States (1963), and finally Burma (1967).

20 Taipei, 1972; esp. the essay "The Present Condition of the Southeast Asian Chinese", pp. 111–230, esp. the survey of the problems in defining Huaqiao, pp. 144–48.

21 From Hsia-men University: *Nanyang yen-chiu so chi-k'an* (collected essays), 1980, 2 vols. (I: Politics and Economics; II: History and Hua-ch'iao); *Tung-nan-ya shih lun-ts'ung* (Essays on Southeast Asian history), 1980; *K'ao-ku min-tsu lun-wen hsuan* (Selected essays on archaeology and ethnology), 1980; of the 35 essays collected, only five had been published in the 1950s. From Chung-shan University: *Tung-nan-ya li-shih lun-ts'ung* (Essays on Southeast Asian history), 1979, 2 vols. (I: History of the region; II: History of Chinese relations, including the Huaqiao in the region); and 22 essays collected had been previously published and seven had been published in the 1950s.

22 Liu Yü-tsun *et al.*, *Chu-tsai hua-kung fang-wen lu* (Chinese coolie labour: record of interviews), Guangzhou, 1979; also included in the History volume of *Nanyang yen-chiu so chi-k'an* in note 21 above.

23 Especially the three essays by Ho Chao-fa on the Philippines (first published in 1962 and 1964) and the three by Liu Yü-tsun on popular uprisings in the 1920s and 1930s in Indonesia, Burma, and Thailand (also published in 1962 and 1964).

24 Essays by Kuo Wei-pai on the economic role of the Chinese in the Malay States and Malaya; Chiang Hsing-tung on Dutch colonial exploitation of the Chinese; Li

Yung-hsi on Spanish policies and Ts'ai Hung-sheng on the coolie trade; all published in 1959.

25 Lin Chin-chih, "Chin-tai hua-ch'iao t'ou-tzu kuo-nei ch'i-yeh ti chi-ko wen-t'i", published first in *Chin-tai shih yen-chiu*, nos. 1 and 2 (1980), pp. 199–230 and 217–38, esp. footnotes 2 and 3 on p. 199 (no. 1, 1980).

26 Wang Mu-heng, "Shih-chiu shih-chi mo er-shih shih-chi ch'u Yin-tu-ni-hsi-ya min-tsu kung-yeh ho hua-ch'iao kung-yeh ti ch'an-sheng ho fa-chan" (The rise and development of pribumi and hua-ch'iao industry in Indonesia during the late 19th and early 20th centuries), pp. 108–16. Compare this with the more conventional approach found in another recent article, Ch'en Tsao-fu "Shih-chiu shih-chi yi-ch'ien Chung-kuo ho Yin-tu-ni-hsi-ya kuan-hsi k'ao-lueh" (Sino-Indonesian relations before the 19th century). *Li-shih yen-chiu*, no. 3 (1980), pp. 17–33.

27 For an account of the history of *Nanyang hsueh-pao* and a list of its contents, see Koh Soh Goh (Hsu Su-wu), *Nanyang Hsueh-hui yü Nanyang yen-chiu* (Singapore, 1977). I have singled out Tan Yeok Seong and Hsu Yun-ts'iao for mention but there were other dedicated scholars in Jakarta, Manila, Kuala Lumpur, and Bangkok who had a harder time to keep up scholarly work in Chinese.

28 A dedicated, though unorthodox, scholar, Fang Hsiu has produced the basis for a reassessment of pre-war literature in Chinese published in Malaysia and Singapore, *Ma-hua hsin wen-hsueh shih kao* (Singapore, 1962–65), in 3 volumes, available in an abbreviated English translation by Angus W. McDonald Jr., *Notes on the history of Malayan Chinese New Literature, 1920–1942* (Tokyo, 1977). Fang Hsiu's use of *Ma-Hua* is controversial and there are times when one wonders if *hua-ch'iao* is not more appropriate for his subject and for his period.

Huaren seems neutral and is now the most common, though since about 1970 in Singapore, Huatsu seems to have gained some popularity. It could mean "ethnic Chinese", using *tsu* in the same way that China uses it for "minority nationalities". I am uneasy about the usage, as I am also unhappy that Huatsu (*kazoku*) in Japanese means nobility or aristocracy. This could just be misleading in some contexts.

29 Lin Chin-chih (see note 25), no. 1 (1980), p. 200.

30 Ch'en Ching-ho's book was published by the New Asia Research Institute in Hong Kong in 1963, and was translated into English as *The Chinese Community in the Sixteenth Century Philippines* (Tokyo, 1968).

31 An unofficial translation appeared in *Beijing Review* 40, 6 Oct, 1980.

CHAPTER 3

Ming Foreign Relations: Southeast Asia

THE RULERS OF MING China would not have recognized the region known today as Southeast Asia (see map, p. 72). They considered the archipelago east of Brunei (modern Borneo) part of the Eastern Oceans, while all other coastal states were considered part of the Western Oceans, which for long periods also included countries bordering on the Indian Ocean. The states which comprised what is now modern Burma, Laos, and northern Thailand were grouped quite differently from the rest.

Of course, the view from the imperial capital at Nanking or Peking was always sinocentric. Foreign countries had no meaningful existence unless their rulers had a relationship with the emperor of China. Such factors as the country's distance from the capital, whether the country shared a border with the empire or not, and whether it was important to the empire's defence were also deemed significant. There were also technical differences: countries which sent missions through Ch'üan-chou in Fukien were distinguished from countries entering through Canton in Kwangtung; and overland missions from beyond the provinces of Kwangsi and Yunnan were different again. The general principles of foreign relations that the Chinese court continually emphasized notwithstanding, what remained most important in determining foreign policy towards Southeast Asia were the political conditions that prevailed at different times during the dynasty.

During the first sixty years of Ming rule, Yuan precedents and lessons learned from Yuan policies were decisive in shaping foreign policy; so too were the attitudes and fears of the new elites from Central China who had founded the Ming, particularly in respect of the Mongols. Along the coast, problems of piracy and maritime trade led to restrictions on travel. There were problems with Vietnam and Champa and with the relations between those two countries. The conquest of Yunnan (until 1382, still controlled by the Mongolian Prince of Liang)[1] and troubles along the southwestern borders with Burma and Laos also shaped foreign policy. Finally, there were the expeditions of the eunuch admiral Cheng Ho (1371–1433) and the impact they had on Southeast Asia. After about 1435, the court gradually lost interest in the south. When the imperial capital was moved to Peking in the early fifteenth century, contacts with countries in Southeast Asia and beyond became infrequent. Except for a few decades during the sixteenth century when Japanese, assisted by Chinese pirates, raided along the South Chinese coast, the focus of foreign policy was entirely on northern defences. The arrival of the Europeans added a new dimension to maritime trade, but did little to change attitudes towards foreign relations with the countries of the south.

Ming records clearly reflect the court's concentration on relations with Southeast Asia up to the middle of the fifteenth century. The reign of the first emperor saw the encouragement of formal tributary relations, but also attempts to limit the extent of foreign contacts. During the Yung-lo reign, however, a new flurry of activity was recorded. The secondary literature also supports this picture. Modern scholarship on the first sixty years of the dynasty has been enriched by the almost universal interest in Cheng Ho's naval expeditions through Southeast Asia to the coasts of the Indian Ocean. In addition, the Ming invasion and administration of Vietnam for twenty years has added volumes to the sources and to secondary writings. After the 1430s, however, the primary sources are relatively silent about relationships with the southern kingdoms. Foreign merchants and traders on the China coast looked for their counterparts in Kwangtung and Fukien, but these contacts were only occasionally recorded when they posed a threat to impartial interests or infringed on established policies.

Early Ming Policies

The first Ming emperor was particularly concerned about the lessons to be learned from the Yuan dynasty's policies. The Mongols had attacked the southwestern kingdom of Ta-li from eastern Tibet and had threatened Vietnam as part of their preparations for the conquest of the Southern Song dynasty. After having conquered the Song, they demanded submission from the rulers of Vietnam, Burma, the Shan-Lao-Tai states,[2] Champa and even Java. When these rulers did not respond with sufficient respect, the Mongols invaded their countries. Although these aggressive policies were abandoned after the death of the emperor Khubilai (r. 1260–94), the Yuan policy of encouraging maritime trade did not appeal to the founder of the Ming dynasty. Private trade was uncontrolled and became intermingled with the tributary trade of the court. This, in his view, had given rise to the unrest and instability along the coastal frontiers that he inherited with his throne.

Yuan policies towards the southern kingdoms were predicated on the assumption that the dynasty faced no threats along its northern frontiers. The Yuan rulers could afford to threaten these southern rulers and to extend their power as far south as was feasible. The first Ming emperor found himself in the opposite position; he faced danger from the north.[3] He needed to secure his southern and coastal frontiers so that he could concentrate on pacifying the great Mongolian-Turkic confederations to the north and on defending the long northern border between western Manchuria and eastern Tibet. He could not afford to fight his southern neighbours at the same time.

From this point of view, the strategic position of the Ming dynasty was comparable to that of the Han, Tang and Song dynasties. The first Ming emperor's advisors urged him to look to the historical record of these earlier dynasties for solutions. He had been persuaded to look to the past for models for most aspects of his empire-building, and his policies towards the south were no exception. He revived the earlier sinocentric rhetoric of foreign relations and many of the ancient ceremonies that his Han, Tang and Song predecessors had used for dealing with tribute missions from vassal states. His policies differed markedly from those of the Yuan in that he avoided displays of force, demands for submission, and attempts to assert indirect control over vassal states. His emphasis was on symbolic acknowledgement of China's cosmological centrality and his legitimate succession to power.

However, there was a clear awareness that conditions under the Ming dynasty differed from those that had prevailed under earlier dynasties. Unlike the Han emperors Kao-tsu (r. 206–195 BC) and Wu-ti (r. 140–87 BC), the first Ming emperor inherited a South China that was already populous and plagued by serious problems of coastal defence. Unlike the first Tang emperor and his famous son, T'ai-tsung (r. 626–649), the first Ming emperor was not an aristocratic professional soldier from the northwest who moved easily and confidently among the nomadic horsemen from the steppes and their fierce tribal leaders. For him, the steppes remained alien and hostile. And unlike the Chao brothers who founded the Song dynasty, he controlled the whole length of the Great Wall line. The Ming dynasty was never handicapped as the Song dynasty had been by having its greatest enemies entrenched on Chinese territory. Therefore, the first Ming emperor did not depend entirely on earlier models and had to be innovative in his defence plans and foreign policies, even towards his peaceful southern neighbours. He had to evaluate, almost from first principles, how to deal with overland neighbours in the south-west beyond Kwangsi and Yunnan and overseas neighbours whose ships could enter the ports of Kwangtung and Fukien.

His first communications with the southern kingdoms were sent early in 1369 and were essentially announcements of his victory over the Mongols and of the establishment of a legitimate new dynasty.[4] It is noteworthy that this proclamation was sent to Korea and Vietnam on the same day and then a month later to Champa, Java, South India and Japan. By that time, Champa had already sent its first mission to China, being the first state in Southeast Asia to do so. Also, it was discovered that the last Javanese envoy to the Yuan court was still in Fukien when the Yuan dynasty fell, and the Ming envoy to Java escorted him home. Vietnam responded quickly, but its king died soon after sending a mission to the Ming court. The emperor was solicitous and, after observing a ritual period of mourning, confirmed the deceased monarch's nephew as the successor.

In all these cases, the stress was on tradition; normal relations were resumed, it was claimed, after a century of aberration under the rule of the Mongolian Yuan dynasty. The key features of Ming foreign policy in this period were the use of an established, conventional rhetoric and the restoration of proper rituals: these included the presentation of tributary gifts and the bestowal of imperial gifts in return, the enfeoffment of foreign kings, and even gifts of the new Ming calendar. The rituals were elaborate but did not demand actual submission to imperial control. Degrees of symbolic submission were later worked out in detail, but even these took account of what the Ming court thought were conventions acceptable to the rulers receiving and sending envoys. Yet there was at least one new feature which went beyond Tang and Song practice in Southeast Asia. The first Ming emperor introduced the practice of registering the rivers and mountains of Vietnam and Champa (together with those of Korea) and sacrificing to their spirits together with those of rivers and mountains within China, and this practice was later extended further south in Southeast Asia and then west to Sri Lanka. Although merely symbolic and introduced for the apparently benevolent reason of wishing to ensure the longevity and security of these kings and the lasting prosperity of their lands, the registration and the sacrifices did imply a measure of cosmic, imperial responsibility over these lands which had never been so clearly claimed before.[5]

Behind the rituals, however, was a reality which could not be disguised by the rhetoric of harmony and prosperity. There was continual fighting between Vietnam and Champa; there was still a Mongolian prince governing Yunnan and considerable unrest among the tribal principalities along its borders; and there were political upheavals among the countries in the region of the Java Sea and the Straits of Malacca. The first Ming emperor soon discovered that he had to become involved in the first and the second of these conflicts, and his empire was eventually touched by the ramifications of the third conflict.

Indeed, for the rest of the Ming period, the region now called Southeast Asia posed at least four different problems for the Ming court, each of which determined certain aspects of the dynasty's foreign relations in the south. They may be summarized as follows.

First, the relations between Vietnam and Champa, which ended in the Vietnamese conquest of Champa, developed into hostile relations with Cambodia and later rivalry with Thailand. Although these conflicts took place away from Vietnam's borders with China, they nevertheless influenced Ming China's policies overseas.

Second, there were special problems in China's relations with Vietnam. These problems were related to the first point, but largely concerned the frontiers between the two countries as well as Vietnam's policies towards tribal territories to its west and to Ming China's south. The failure to absorb Vietnam into the empire was an event of great significance in the history of mainland Southeast Asia.

Third, the Ming empire's maritime activities, both military and commercial, involved the littoral states of the South China Sea, from Luzon to Thailand and the Champa ports; but they also involved countries beyond the Straits of Malacca and, for a short period in the early fifteenth century, brought various states bordering on the Indian Ocean as far west as Arabia and East Africa into close contact. This connection also brought Indian, Persian, and Arab traders to China as part of official missions and later opened the way for the new commercial and political activities of the Portuguese, the Spanish, and the Dutch along the southeast coast.

Fourth, the Ming court claimed to govern the southwestern states in modern Burma and Laos, as it governed the province of Yunnan, through aboriginal offices (*t'u-ssu*). This administration system was a legacy of the Yuan, which was established when the Mongols incorporated the Nanchao kingdom of Ta-li into their empire as an imperial province. One development that occurred just before the Ming dynasty was founded was significant. Along with the Vietnamese and Burmans, the ancestors of the modern Thai had also been expanding towards the south. The kingdom of Ayuthia was founded in 1350. It stretched down the Menam valley and combined the Hsien (Syam or Sukhbothai) state of the north with the ancient Lo-ho (Lopburi) state in the south to form a kingdom known as Hsien-lo in Chinese records.

The region of Southeast Asia only became the object of imperial policy in China following Mongolian emperor Khubilai's expeditions against Ta-li, Burma, Vietnam, Champa and Java. This dramatic series of events left the region with the shared experience of a power which had never been exerted so extensively in the south before and awakened the kingdoms there to the problem of living with a powerful and potentially aggressive China as their neighbour. Thus, a new Chinese emperor, like the founder of the Ming dynasty, who could defeat the Mongols, was a person to be treated with respect. It is in this context that the first Ming emperor's letters to Southeast Asian rulers should be read.

The first Ming emperor's initiatives to seek his neighbours' acknowledgement of his legitimacy may be contrasted with his desire to limit severely all foreign contacts. The limits imposed were justified in Confucian terms, but the practical reasons were more important. The first Ming emperor believed in tight centralized control over all matters pertaining to relations beyond the borders of his empire. While his main concern was the security of his dynastic house and his empire, he was nonetheless anxious to control all foreign trade so as to ensure that trading along sensitive frontiers would not disturb the law and order of his realm: hence, the primacy of the formal relations with foreign rulers and the ban on private commerce. This policy did not mean that trading abroad was impossible; it simply made it illegal, secret, and largely unrecorded. The commercial aspects of foreign relations need not concern us here; this chapter will focus on the workings of the Ming imperial system as it applied to China's Southeast Asian neighbours.

The immediate purpose behind sending imperial messengers to

Southeast Asia with news of the first Ming emperor's accession was to sort out quickly which countries wanted close relations with China and which did not, which were dependent and friendly and which were potentially hostile. It soon became clear that, unlike the early Mongolian rulers of the Yuan dynasty, the first Ming emperor was less interested in ritual submission to the Son of Heaven than in a formal acknowledgement of his new dynasty. He concentrated his efforts on a relatively small sphere of influence and consistently tried to restrict the number of tribute missions by adhering to the classical ideal of one mission every three years for neighbouring countries and one mission every generation for the rest. He encouraged attention to three aspects of such relations: sensitivity to the need to demonstrate adequate respect for the Son of Heaven; quickness in responding to border troubles; and wariness of any linkage between foreign powers and domestic politics. On two other aspects of foreign relations, he laid down explicit policies: countries overseas were not to be attacked; and tribute relations were not to be undertaken for profit and were not to be conflated with private maritime trade.

In all these policies, the emperor was innovative and indeed laid the foundations for Chinese relations with Southeast Asian countries for the next five centuries. The innovative aspects of his foreign policy must be explained. His sensitivity about respect for the Son of Heaven appeared conventional, yet his acts were not routine or ritualistic. A sense of moral and political purpose lay behind the missions to and from China. This sense of moral purpose is most evident in the various missions dispatched to Vietnam, a country itself very sensitive to questions of independence and self-respect after a century of delicate relations with the Mongolian rulers of the Yuan dynasty. The first Ming emperor's reign coincided with some troublesome decades for the Trãn dynastic house. The first two missions he sent to Vietnam in 1369 arrived while a violent succession dispute was taking place. The Trãn emperor Du-ton had just died and the adopted son of his deceased eldest brother was set on the throne. With great care and elaborate ceremonies, the Ming court officially recognized this succession. Less than a year later, the newly installed emperor was dethroned and executed. The Ming court was not informed of this. Instead, the new ruler, Nghe-ton, tried to deceive the first Ming emperor, who was understandably incensed when the truth was finally revealed.

The Ming court refused to recognize Nghe-ton. When Nghe-ton gave up his throne two years later to his younger brother Due-ton, tributary relations were resumed. But relations remained cool as long as Nghe-ton ruled behind the scenes; and neither Due-ton nor his son, Phe-de, sought a patent of enfeoffment from the Ming emperor. When Phe-de was in turn removed and killed by his cousin, Lê Qui-ly, the first Ming emperor became even more suspicious and hostile. By 1393 he was again rejecting tribute missions sent by the Vietnamese court. Only the disputes along the empire's border with Vietnam led to the resumption of diplomatic relations during the last three years of the Hung-wu reign (1396–98), and these relations were far from friendly. What angered the emperor most was that this series of usurpations made a mockery of his acts of recognition and enfeoffment, which he saw as the basis of secure relationships. As he put it, when informed of Nghe-ton's death in 1396, more than a year after the event:

> If we send a mission to show we share the bereavement, that would be supporting the rebellions and conceding to bandits. When others hear of this later, would they not imitate him and would not evil plots then abound? This does not conform with China's principles in dealing with foreign countries.[6]

The unilateral resumption of diplomatic relations with Vietnam in 1395 illustrates the first Ming emperor's readiness to respond quickly to border troubles. When Lung-chou tribesmen rebelled along the southernmost borders of Kwangsi, two missions led by senior envoys were sent to Vietnam. The finer points of tributary protocol were put aside when the problems were seen as serious. In comparison, an earlier dispute in 1381 along the same border was less serious; the emperor angrily ordered the authorities in Kwangsi province to turn back all Vietnamese missions in the future, but in fact one was accepted in the following year.[7]

The first Ming emperor clearly distinguished between alertness about the security of his borders and involvement in the troubles of his neighbours. Imperial correspondence regarding the attacks and counter-attacks between Vietnam and Champa make interesting reading. The emperor was unwilling to take sides in this bitter quarrel; five times during the 1370s, he appealed to both parties to stop fighting. Even when Vietnam was out of favour and Champa had regular access to the Ming court, the emperor never wavered in his principle of strict impartiality. However, where the security of the empire was concerned, the response was different. When the Ming forces needed grain supplies during the campaign in Yunnan in 1384,

Vietnam was expected to send the provisions up the Red River to the border. And when supplies were again needed to crush the Lungchou rebels on the Kwangsi border in 1395, Vietnam was expected to deliver supplies to the nearest Ming garrisons. Vietnam could not remain neutral when the Ming court was engaged in pacifying frontier regions close to Vietnam's borders.

Even more sensitive was the question of relations between foreign rulers and Ming officials. Two examples will suffice to illustrate the emperor's concern about this subject. The first is related to Vietnam, which had long been defiant about its right to be a southern empire equal to China and which was proud of its record of survival against Mongolian coercion. The battle of wills was established at the start, with the Ming emperor determined to assert his superiority and not allow any challenge to his supreme position in the universe or to the hierarchical relationships it was his duty to maintain. The strictest protocol was insisted upon. When the official sent to enfeoff the king of Vietnam found that the king had just died, he refused to enter the country to anoint the deceased king's successor. The Vietnamese were forced to report the king's death and to request formal recognition of his demise from the Ming emperor himself.

Having put Vietnam in its place, the emperor lavished praise on Ming envoys who had refused to accept any gifts from the Vietnamese ruler, even at the risk of offending him. This both underlined the principle that the emperor and not his officials conducted foreign relations, and illustrated the inferior status of Vietnam, which could only offer tribute but not bestow gifts, even to Chinese envoys. Indeed, Vietnam's determination to assert some degree of equality in foreign relations was a source of tension with China during the following decades. The Ministry of Rites devised ever more elaborate ceremonies for the reception of Vietnam's tribute envoys at the Ming court and for the reception of Ming envoys sent from the court to Vietnam; this reached a point where the Ming emperor had to restrain the ministry from going too far. At the same time, Vietnam was pressured to forgo annual missions and to follow instead the traditional practice of dispatching a mission once every three years like Champa, Cambodia and Siam. A further sign of imperial disfavour may be found in a decision made in 1383 to send official tallies used to establish a Ming envoy's credentials to Champa, Cambodia and Siam, but not to Vietnam.[8]

The second notable example concerns relations with San-fo-ch'i kuo (Srivijaya) or the Malay world around eastern and central Suma-

tra and the Malay peninsula. Professor O. W. Wolters has examined
the background to this Malay connection and has offered a new
explanation of the events of the 1370s and late 1390s that affected
Ming relations with the Malays.[9] His explanation underscores the
first Ming emperor's ignorance of and lack of interest in the finer
points of politics in maritime Southeast Asia. It also underscores the
complexities of the relationships between sovereigns and vassals in
the region, which the Ming court failed to appreciate. How these local
struggles for trade and legitimacy might have involved Ming officials
and how they led the first Ming emperor to make humiliating errors
and cause the death of his envoys at the hands of the Javanese have
been persuasively explained. Even if Ming officials had not been
plotting with these foreign rulers, their failure to save the emperor
from error aroused his suspicions about them. In particular, he sus-
pected his powerful prime minister, Hu Wei-yung, who was also
subsequently accused of having had clandestine relations with the
Japanese and with those responsible for the piracy along the whole
length of the China coast. The fate of the Ning-po commandant, Lin
Hsien, accused of serving as the link between Hu Wei-yung and the
Japanese confirmed the emperor's suspicions about officials interfering in foreign relations. Relations with foreigners had to be   abso-
lutely formal and tightly controlled.[10]

Obviously, from the emperor's point of view, tributary relations
were not to be conducted for profit. What does need to be emphasized is the emperor's explicit policy of refraining from aggression
against overseas countries. This striking new feature of an entirely
defensive policy towards countries to the south and east cannot be
overemphasized. It not only confirmed the past practices of the Han,
Tang and Song empires and rejected those of the Mongolian emperor
Khubilai, but also established an important doctrine of Ming foreign
policy.

Even more significant was the fact that this policy was first enunciated in 1371 and then embodied in the first emperor's *Tsu hsün lu*
(Ancestral injunctions) promulgated in 1373 and, after revisions,
reaffirmed in detail towards the end of his reign in the final version
of the *Huang Ming tsu hsün*. It was one of the few basic policies from
which the first Ming emperor never deviated. It was such an extraordinary declaration of policy that it deserves to be quoted in full.
The key passage is found in the 1373 version of his instructions to his
descendants:

The overseas foreign countries like An-nan [Vietnam], Champa, Korea, Siam, Liu-ch'iu [the Ryūkyū islands], [the countries of the] Western Oceans [South India] and Eastern Oceans [Japan] and the various small countries of the southern *man* [barbarians] are separated from us by mountains and seas and far away in a corner. Their lands would not produce enough for us to maintain them; their peoples would not usefully serve us if incorporated [into the empire]. If they were so unrealistic as to disturb our borders, it would be unfortunate for them. If they gave us no trouble and we moved troops to fight them unnecessarily, it would be unfortunate for us. I am concerned that future generations might abuse China's wealth and power and covet the military glories of the moment to send armies into the field without reason and cause a loss of life. May they be sharply reminded that this is forbidden. As for the *hu* and *jung* barbarians who threaten China in the north and west, they are always a danger along our frontiers. Good generals must be picked and soldiers trained to prepare carefully against them. [11]

This passage from the opening section of the *Ancestral injunctions* is retained in the final revised version of 1395. Additions and changes to the later version of this text are of interest, and one was probably important. In the earlier versions, this passage was the last item in the section, whereas in the final version, this injunction had been advanced to the position of the fourth most important injunction.

In addition, fifteen countries were designated countries "not to be invaded". To the three countries in Southeast Asia listed above, seven more were added: Cambodia, Samudra-Pasai (northern Sumatra), Java, Pahang, Pai-hua (Battak or West Java), San-fo-ch'i (Srivijaya or Palembang in central and southern Sumatra), and Brunei (Borneo). The inclusion of the last four countries is significant; all four were probably vassals of the Majapahit empire of Java. What is interesting is that the emperor had been aware since 1371 that Brunei was a vassal state of Java and probably since 1378 that Srivijaya was as well. Yet he insisted on keeping both kingdoms on the list as late as 1395 and did not publicly acknowledge Srivijaya as Java's vassal until 1397.

In the later version, the emperor also discriminated between these countries and indicated that only Cambodia and Siam had untroubled relations with the Ming empire. Vietnam was not favoured and was restricted to a mission once every three years. Champa and the rest of the southern countries had deceived the emperor by including private traders in their tributary mission; these missions had to be reminded to desist from such deceptions several times between 1375 and 1379 before the practice was stopped. Clearly, the emperor was aware that trade was the primary purpose behind dispatching tribute missions to China, but he wanted foreign rulers to be circumspect about it. Finally, the specific reference to "overseas" countries and the mention of "the various small countries of the southern *man* was omitted. In listing by name the fifteen countries not to be invaded, this final version was more precise than the earlier version, although not necessarily more accurate in reflecting the political realities in the region. Whether the omission of "overseas" was deliberate is less certain; the omission did allow Korea and Vietnam to be included in the list, and the emperor was certainly aware that both countries could be invaded by land routes.

The Ming court also established diplomatic relations with countries to the south that could be reached by land routes. The first Ming emperor had known of foreign countries beyond Yunnan from the records of the Yuan court. In 1371, when he was sending missions in every direction, he probably sent a mission to travel to Burma via Vietnam. This mission was obstructed by a Cham invasion of Vietnam and failed to reach Burma after spending more than two years in Vietnam. During this time three of the four envoys died. In 1373, the sole survivor returned.[12] As a result, no other effort was made to contact Burma, although the emperor thought that Burma was the most powerful state beyond Vietnam and probably wanted it to ally with him against the Mongolian administration still in control of Yunnan. Whether the first Ming emperor would have incorporated Yunnan into the empire if it had not been under the control of a defiant Mongolian prince is difficult to know. Certainly the fact that Yunnan was still under Mongolian control made it imperative for the emperor to attack it sooner or later. After the successful invasion in 1382, the Yuan policy of appointing central officials to rule over the various ethnic groups in the region was modified; the system of aboriginal offices (*t'u-ssu*) was extended beyond the empire's borders, and local rulers or chiefs were confirmed as imperial commissioners of various grades to rule at least nominally on the emperor's behalf. In this way, a system of appointments was instituted which blurred the distinction between foreign vassals and autonomous territories which were beyond direct imperial control. Thus, the creation of a number of Shan-Lao-Tai territories led to the curious situation of having the ruler of Hsien-lo (Ayuthia or Siam) recognized as a king (*kuo wang*), but not any of the Shan-Lao-Tai, Burman, or Mon rulers. The latter were merely given the military title of pacification commissioner and were regarded as being more directly subordinate to Ming rule.[13]

The most significant change in foreign policy during this period was the Ming court's decision not to recognize Burma as a kingdom (*kuo*). This decision resulted from the Ming policy of encouraging indirect rule, while simultaneously diminishing the status of local rulers in southwest China. After the conquest of Yunnan, this policy was also confirmed for territories further south. In 1393, after contact had finally been re-established through the principality of Chiengmai (nominally a Ming pacification commission), Burma sent an envoy to China. In 1394, the ruler at Ava was appointed pacification commissioner for his territory. There was no discussion of restoring Burma to the status of a kingdom. The Ming court realized that since the Mongolian destruction of the Burmese kingdom at Pagan, various Shan states had been formed (even the Ava kingdom was ruled by a branch of the Shan royal house) and the once great Burmese kingdom had become fragmented.

The Ming court continued the policy of keeping these states divided and weak. As the Ming emperor saw it, the Maw Shan state of Lu-ch'uan was the most powerful and threatening of these principalities.[14] It was within striking distance of Ta-li and controlled large tracts of territory beyond the Salween River. It was also trying to destroy Ava and to unify the other Shan states under its leadership. Consequently, a few years after the conquest of Yunnan, the emperor acted to contain this state and to break its power. The Ming court had already established three Shan-Tai pacification commissioners, the other two being Ch'e-li (Sipsong Banna and areas in Yunnan, Burma, and Laos around it) and Chiengmai (Pa-pai). Chiengmai had provided the first diplomatic link with the Burma court at Ava; the conferral of titles on Ava's Shan ruler was another step in the policy to contain the Maw Shan state. After 1402, it was left to the first emperor's son, the Yung-lo emperor, to complete the fragmentation of the old Burmese kingdom by raising two more Shan states bordering on Lu-ch'uan to the status of pacification commissions. But the Yung-lo emperor was the architect of a more aggressive policy, one that his father would not have approved of.

Policies under the Yung-lo Emperor

The founder of the dynasty had laid down a framework for his successors' foreign policies and had specified in such detail what they had to do that foreign relations thereafter might have been expected to have adhered closely to his instructions, but this did not happen. The first emperor's successor and grandson, the Chien-wen emperor, was overthrown by his uncle. The usurper, the Yung-lo emperor, felt the need to legitimize his accession as thoroughly as his father had, and that included implementing an aggressive foreign policy on all fronts. His most radical policies concerned relations with Southeast Asia and the countries bordering on the Indian Ocean. His most renowned policy was the dispatch of immense naval expeditions under the eunuch admiral Cheng Ho. During the Yung-lo reign, tense relations between Vietnam and Champa were over-shadowed by the growing tensions between Vietnam and China. Even relations with the Shan-Lao-Tai states to the south of Yunnan were affected by the aggressive imperial policy to dominate Vietnam, while all other overseas relations were eclipsed by the grand voyages to the Western Oceans. The developments that occurred during this reign may best be understood by first considering the invasion of Vietnam and then Cheng Ho's naval expeditions, and examining the far-reaching ramifications of each.

On the surface, the Yung-lo emperor simply reaffirmed his father's policies: no private contact with foreigners; no private foreign trade; and no trading or other relations outside a carefully regulated tributary system. In practice, he was more demanding, more aggressive, and more willing than his father had been to intervene and to threaten when people (either Chinese adventurers or foreign rulers) did not do what he expected them to do. This belligerence might have resulted from his insecurity towards his imperial relatives, for whom his usurpation remained a stigma. It might also have come about owing to his attitude towards the use of force. He was a great soldier and believed that many problems could be solved by military means. His relations with Vietnam illustrate this position particularly well. When the new ruler of Vietnam, who had failed to gain recognition from the Yung-lo emperor's nephew in 1400, again asked to be recognized as the legitimate successor of the defunct Trần dynastic house, the emperor responded with caution. His father had been unhappy about a series of usurpations that had taken place since 1370; none of the rulers since that time had satisfied Ming officials' inquiries about their legitimacy.

VIETNAM

The Yung-lo emperor followed his father's policy in seeking to confirm the legitimacy of the Vietnamese king. When his officials assured him that the ruler was a relative of the Trần house who had been chosen as the new ruler, he was content to confirm him "king" of An-nan. Then, to his great annoyance, a few months later he discovered that the man was a usurper and a regicide. The same thing had happened thirty years earlier, when his father had been deceived and manipulated in the interest of Vietnamese court politics. The Yung-lo emperor had also insisted on verifying the new Vietnamese king's claim and had again been deceived. The sole remaining descendant of the Trần line was then found and returned to Vietnam to be king, but he was murdered on his arrival. The Yung-lo emperor had pledged his support to the now defunct Trần house; his outrage at the Vietnamese usurper's treachery was so great that he immediately ordered a full-scale invasion of Vietnam. He was perfectly aware that Vietnam was on his father's list of countries "never to be invaded", but he believed that there was sufficient provocation in this instance to override the *Ancestral injunctions*. The usurper simply could not be allowed to go unpunished. Perhaps he was also aware that there were questions about his own legitimacy. He certainly could not permit it to be said that he was not the strong supporter of a legitimate ruling house.

A large expeditionary army consisting of units from more than ten provinces was dispatched to Vietnam. This expedition may be compared with the armies sent by the Yung-lo emperor's father into Yunnan twenty-five years earlier. The main armies passed through Kwangsi; one army came down the Red River from Yunnan itself; and other units were sent by sea routes. The initial successes of the campaign came swiftly. The main difference between the conquest of Yunnan and this campaign was that the Vietnamese had by this time become a fairly homogeneous state with a sophisticated administrative system based on the Chinese model. Vietnam had a distinct cultural identity and the resources to resist becoming incorporated into a Chinese empire.[15]

The superficial similarities between Vietnam and China led the emperor to make an unfortunate decision. Not content with overthrowing the usurper, he decided that Vietnam was sufficiently like China for it to be reorganized as a Chinese province. The Trần dynastic house had no legitimate claimants and the Chinese emperor thought he could establish historic territorial rights on the basis of boundaries established under the Han dynasty almost 1,500 years earlier. Thus came about the fateful decision to destroy the kingdom and to administer it centrally from Nanking.

Another reason behind this policy was the Vietnamese claim that theirs was an empire equal to Ming China. When its capital was taken and "imperial" Vietnamese records and documents were found, these were taken as further evidence of the Vietnamese court's presumption and duplicity. While the Yung-lo emperor was justified in believing that the Vietnamese were accustomed to being ruled in a Chinese imperial style, he failed to see that his cultural assumptions were opposed by something akin to cultural nationalism. The fact that this proto-nationalism had been expressed in Chinese cultural terms was particularly misleading.

The war in Vietnam, the failure to hold it after twenty years of fighting and occupation, and the amazing success of Lê Loi's guerrilla war tactics belong properly to the history of China and of Vietnam, and the details need not concern us here.[16] What is relevant is what China's failure in Vietnam meant for its relations with other countries in Southeast Asia. Vietnam's two neighbours were drawn into the conflict. Champa, Vietnam's perennial enemy and a loyal vassal of China which depended on China to hold the Vietnamese back, found that having Ming China as a neighbour was even more uncomfortable than having the smaller Vietnamese kingdom as a neighbour. The Cham rulers were forced to send troops and supplies to support the Ming occupation, but they soon found that Ming officials insisted on the same claims the Vietnamese had made on lands which the Chams had also claimed. When the Ming took these territories, Champa had nowhere to turn.

Even more significant was the final outcome of the war. Before the Yung-lo emperor ordered the invasion of Vietnam, Chinese authority was backed by enormous military potential which the Vietnamese had no wish to test. An admonition from the Ming emperor was a useful deterrent. But when the war went badly after initial victories and when the Ming armies failed again and again to crush the Vietnamese "rebels", that authority lost its deterrent force. Champa was in the end confounded by three developments: its own anger at the cupidity of Chinese soldiers and officials; its growing respect for Lê Loi's resistance; and finally its alarm at China's defeat and the emergence of a much more powerful and united Vietnamese nation. The end result, the weakening of Ming authority over Vietnam for the remainder of the dynasty, sealed the fate of Champa. Champa's attempts to restore the status quo ante, when it was a power equal to Vietnam, were disastrous; and there was no authority left in Ming exhortations to restrain the Vietnamese when the opportunity came to destroy Champa a few decades later.[17]

The invasion of Vietnam had repercussions among other peoples in mainland Southeast Asia as well. The Chams, emboldened by China's invasion and occupation of their ancient enemy, Vietnam, attacked Cambodia. For a while, Cambodia was being threatened from two sides, for Ayuthia (Siam) to the west also continued to expand at its expense. And for the only time during the Ming dynasty, Cambodia successfully sought Chinese help to restrain the Chams. But after the Chinese retreat from Vietnam, it was Vietnam and not China that restrained and finally destroyed the Chams.

More interesting was the role of Laos during the Ming occupation of Vietnam. It was one of several similar Shan-Lao-Pai principalities south of Yunnan, and its ruler was a loyal pacification commissioner who had been confirmed in his position by the Yung-lo emperor. Laos had emerged as a result of Khmer efforts to keep the various Tai chieftains divided in order to stop the expansion of Ayuthia. Ming policy, for different reasons, supported fragmentation along the empire's southwestern borders; and the Ming court recognized Laos in the same way that it had acknowledged Ch'e-li (Sibsong Banna), Pa-pai (Chiengmai), Lu-ch'uan (the Maw Shans) and several other principalities.

Laos was content to survive through diplomacy, dealing with Cambodia to its south, Vietnam to its west and distant China beyond the minor tribal confederacies to its north. But when Vietnam came under Chinese rule, its position was less secure. Defeated Vietnamese forces, unwilling to escape south to seek help from their traditional enemies in Champa, preferred to take refuge in Laos. The ruler in Laos was not prepared to take sides in the war. He had not wished to have Ming China as a neighbour and probably sympathized with the widespread Vietnamese hostility against Chinese rule. At the same time, he did not want to anger the Ming court. Thus, when asked not to support the Vietnamese, he discouraged Vietnamese "rebels" from making Laos their base for anti-Ming resistance, but he probably also anticipated that it was the Vietnamese his country would have to live with in the long run, so he took care not to arouse Vietnamese hostility towards Laos.

All the states bordering the province of Yunnan felt the impact of the invasion of Vietnam. That province provided large armies for the campaign, not only for the initial invasion, but also for some of the efforts to crush Vietnamese resistance. By 1428, Vietnamese counter-attacks up the Red River to the Yunnan border had made clear the limits of Chinese and Vietnamese power in southeastern Yunnan. The small numbers of minority tribesmen in that area must have been awed by both powers and submitted to whichever was the stronger in their neighbourhood; but the two large principalities (Laos and Sibsong Banna) that shared borders with both protagonists weighed their futures between the powers and took great care to maintain their independence. Certainly as long as the Yung-lo emperor was on the throne and showed a willingness to resort to force, all the states bordering on Yunnan found it wise to keep their peace.

The Yung-lo emperor did not, of course, depend solely on threats and force. He systematically continued his predecessor's policy of fragmenting the potentially powerful states in the southwest and appointed at least five new pacification commissioners, largely to break the power of the Maw Shans of Lu-ch'uan and to check the future growth of Burmese power. And he pursued two different policies towards Ayuthia (Siam): on the seas, he restrained south-ward expansion down the Malay peninsula towards Malacca; on land, however, he did not oppose military activities northward against the Burmese, the Cambodians, and the Shan-Lao-Tai states. In short, the invasion of Vietnam alerted all the states contiguous with Ming China's southern borders that China was prepared to use force. But, perhaps more important in the long run, it also showed that China had neither the will nor the capacity to conquer and hold territory in the south. Its defeat in Vietnam and the Lê dynasty's diplomatic skill in keeping China at bay thereafter were important lessons for all the other states in mainland Southeast Asia. The case of Vietnam showed that it was possible to satisfy Chinese pride while maintaining politi-cal independence.

CHENG HO'S NAVAL EXPEDITIONS

The Yung-lo emperor's aggressive policy towards Vietnam had a counterpart in Cheng Ho's naval expeditions to the Indian Ocean. First, both policies directly contravened the first emperor's explicit injunction against dissipating military force in the south. Second, both undertakings enhanced the Yung-lo emperor's pride and pres-tige at great cost and without economic benefits or long-term political advantages. Finally, by the end of the Yung-lo emperor's reign, both undertakings had become increasingly burdensome and were clearly not in the empire's interest. The transfer of the capital to Peking in 1419 and the Yung-lo emperor's final desperate personal campaigns to mitigate the far more serious threat from the Mongols in the north changed the focus of foreign policy. It is not surprising that the campaigns against Vietnam and the naval expeditions were both abandoned when his grandson found the imperial coffers bare and the northern borders threatened.

Why then did the Yung-lo emperor launch these naval expeditions to Southeast Asia and India and later extend them further west to Arabia and East Africa? It was certainly related to his usurpation and his desire for universal legitimation. His announced intention to find his predecessor and nephew, the Chien-wen emperor, who was rumoured to have escaped abroad, might have been no more than a public justification to overcome his father's prohibition against military action overseas; but his need to appear as a great and legitimate emperor before all his half-brothers and nephews, before the generals and officials who knew he was a usurper, and indeed before all his subjects, led him to seek endorsements from all the foreign rulers his navies could reach. This display of force was also related to his confidence as a soldier, his military success against the Mongols, and his acquisition of a Mongolian view of power and policy from the northern perspective of his new capital at Peking. Hence, the idea that he should send a naval force to ascertain the strength of Timur at Samarkand, who was mounting a campaign against China, was not as bizarre as it might seem, although that too may have been emphasized in order to overcome his father's prohibition against overseas adventures.

Finally, the expeditions and his efforts to persuade all foreign rulers to send tribute missions to him was related to the imperial policy on trade that his father had initiated. The Yung-lo emperor knew that most tribute missions would not come to China if there were no profits to be made, so he had to make these missions worthwhile. I will focus here on the political and international aspects of the spectacular show of force engendered by the expedition.

Altogether, seven expeditions were sent across the Indian Ocean in 1405, 1407, 1409, 1413, 1417, 1421, and 1431. The largest consisted of over 300 ships of various sizes (including 62 large treasure ships) and over 27,000 men; even the smallest expedition had a fleet of between 40 and 50 ships. The first three expeditions went as far as the west coast of India; the fourth went further, crossing to the Persian Gulf; the fifth and the seventh expeditions visited the east coast of Africa.

They were very successful voyages from the point of view of the Yung-lo emperor and his admirals; at least two kingdoms in Southeast Asia, Malacca and Samudra-Pasai (North Sumatra), benefited directly from this display of power. The expeditions were discontinued after 1433 and the spectacular performance was never repeated; in the end, they left no permanent mark on the thirty or so "countries" visited. As J.V.G. Mills rightly says, "the great expeditions . . . remained isolated *tours de force*, mere exploits".[18] There were, of course, other lesser missions preceding and contemporary with Cheng Ho's expeditions. Each would normally have been worth noting, especially the side trips Cheng Ho's entourage made to Bengal, Siam and East Java, and the special missions to Brunei, Sulu and other islands in the Philippines. Taken together with the whole range of Chinese activity in Southeast Asia, the great expeditions were significant. They certainly impressed the maritime states of Southeast Asia with China's wealth and power, and the increase in trade between these states and the China coast continued thereafter.

In so far as the Yung-lo emperor tried to create a new framework for overseas foreign relations, one that was based on a regular and overwhelming naval presence and predicated on new attitudes about active intervention, three points became clear. First, this policy was too expensive: it had led to two decades of war in Vietnam and innumerable missions to and from the region followed by generous if patronizing hospitality and gifts. If the policy had been supported by expanded private enterprise in an open economic system, all kinds of benefits might have flowed on to the peoples who lived along the major transportation routes. The cumulative benefits to the economy as a whole might have created sufficient wealth to pay the costs of the missions. But, given the conservative Confucian opinion that the ideal state and society should operate on a limited rural base and that this policy had just been fully and faithfully implemented only a generation earlier, the Ming treasury could not afford such new expenses for long.

Second, the new commitments in the south endangered the northern defences. The peace that the Yung-lo emperor had achieved in northern and Central Asia after the death of Timur did not last long. He soon went back to Peking, his old military base, and was off again on campaigns beyond the Great Wall line. The decision to move the capital to Peking, itself an enormously expensive proposition, was only the beginning of a new awareness that displays of power in the north were essential, while such displays in the south were not. The truth behind this is manifest in the inherent contradiction in Yung-lo's last decision to send Cheng Ho to Southeast Asia while preparing, at the age of sixty-four, to go on yet another personal campaign against the Mongols.

Finally, the traditional tribute system was never meant to support active international politics. It had been evolved over centuries to encourage regular but minimal foreign relations, to provide an instrument for imperial defence policy, and to satisfy some of the trading requirements of foreign rulers and Chinese merchants. In sum, the Yung-lo emperor's new activism was actually built on his father's reorganized foreign policy system, which had been carefully restructured to limit further foreign contacts. The use of that same system to pursue interventionalist goals suggests that the Yung-lo emperor's ambition ran far ahead of his understanding of the nature of traditional foreign relations with China's Southeast Asian neighbours. He clearly wanted to elicit signs of respect from the smaller and weaker states in the south; but he could not, and was unwilling to, change the basis of China's foreign relations in a creative way. More money, power and ceremony applied in the same old way was simply bound to fail. It is not surprising, then, that his more conventional grandson, backed by civil officials loyal to Confucian principles as well as to the first emperor's specific injunctions, decided to reverse the Yung-lo emperor's policies within a few years of his death. He decided to end the war in Vietnam and concluded that the great naval expedition of 1431–33 would have to be the last.

During the next two centuries, there were no further Chinese adventures in Southeast Asia. It may be said that there was a return to the first emperor's policy of non-intervention; but it is probably more accurate to say, especially after 1449, when the Mongols captured the Ming emperor and might have taken Peking, that the Ming state was never again confident about the security of its northern frontiers and was thereafter too weak to embark on expeditions beyond its southern borders. Apart from some border troubles with the Maw Shan tribes and Vietnam, and later with Burma and other Shan states, no military forces were sent anywhere near Southeast Asia again. Regular foreign relations continued with a limited number of southern kingdoms, notably Champa until it was destroyed by the Vietnamese, various rulers of Java to the end of the fifteenth century, and Malacca until it fell to the Portuguese in 1511. Only the mainland kingdoms of Vietnam, Ayuthia, Laos, Burma and various Shan-Tai states had continuous and not always harmonious relations with the

Ming court to the end.

Overseas Trade

From the point of view of Ming China's overseas trade, a major turning point came soon after 1500 with the arrival of the Portuguese at Malacca, in the Moluccas and finally off the coast of China.[19] This was the beginning of the period when Western traders, armed and aggressive, undermined Muslim trading power, whether Arab, Persian or Indian, and indirectly encouraged the development of Chinese and Japanese private trade in Southeast Asia. Thus, the history of Ming overseas trade can be divided fairly equally between the first half of the dynasty, when it was largely dominated by tributary trading, and the second half, when local and Japanese competition and cooperation with Western armed traders off the China coasts became the norm. There are, however, some problems of interpretation which affect the way changes during the Ming have been presented. Lo Hsiang-lin offered the following periodization of the history of Ming overseas trade and foreign relations: 1368–1404; 1405–1433; 1434–1510; 1511–1618; 1619–1661.[20] This division takes developments both in foreign relations and in trade into account; but, if Ming foreign relations are examined more closely, there is no need for such fine divisions. Aside from a short period of aberration in 1402–35, the first Ming emperor's policies remained in effect for the rest of the dynasty. Nevertheless, there were important differences between the period preceding the reign of the Cheng-te emperor (1505–21) and the period following it which need to be pointed out.

First, once the dynasty saw that the imminent dangers to its survival were centred in the north, northwest and northeast, relations with southern kingdoms became increasingly ritualistic and peripheral. The Ming dynasty might not have been strong enough to assert its authority in the south — as was clearly seen in its unwillingness to save Champa from Vietnam and to help Malacca against the Portuguese — but it was stable and confident enough not to need legitimation of any kind. Tributary missions no longer had the aura they had had under the Hung-wu and Yung-lo emperors. Relations with countries to the south had become expensive and dreary rituals without any real benefits to the dynasty. Thus, tribute missions from overseas virtually had come to an end by about 1500. Of the few that still came, several were dealt with at the southern ports and not encouraged to travel north to present tribute to the emperor.

The second difference follows from the first. With the growing meaninglessness of the tribute missions, Ming officials turned a blind eye to the coming of the Portuguese. Despite the awareness that Portugal was a considerable naval power that had vanquished Malacca, a nominal vassal of the Ming court, there was no serious attempt to use the tributary system for one of the key functions it had been devised to serve. Tributary ceremonies together with profitable trading opportunities had helped the Ming court control its neighbours and safeguard its borders. By the time of the Cheng-te reign, the court had lost interest in this instrument of control and had come to treat tribute missions as commercial visits with no political significance.[21] Hence, the Ming court's failure to notice how rapidly the region had begun to change after the arrival of the Europeans, especially after the Spanish, the Dutch, and the English joined the Portuguese to reshape the map of South and Southeast Asia.

Even more important was a third development: the increasing importance of trade in the Ming economy as a whole. The trade in luxury goods alone was stimulated by the activities of the court itself through its thousands of eunuch procurers and the extensive requirements of members of the imperial family throughout China. Although private trade was never officially encouraged, its growth was tolerated, and the need to import certain foreign goods was acknowledged. However, the retention of early Ming policies towards overseas trade and the lack of new institutions to deal with later developments led to severe disruptions along the China coast. The more the Ming officials tried to restrict foreign contacts to one or two ports, the greater the strain placed on local and foreign entrepreneurs who sought each other out. Thus, for long periods after the Cheng-te reign, serious trade and foreign policy issues which could have been resolved by paying closer attention to the details of foreign relations and to the variety of existing trading networks were reduced to questions about how to improve coastal defence and how to repulse widespread and large-scale attacks by pirates.

These pirates comprised an altogether new breed. In contrast to the relatively peaceful groups of Arab, Persian, Hindu and Muslim traders of South and Southeast Asia, the combination of Portuguese naval forces, Japanese freebooters and the burgeoning class of Chinese dependent on overseas and coastal trade created a violent and explosive mixture.[22] It is a measure of Ming complacency that for over 150 years no attempt was made to review the system of foreign relations established in the late fourteenth century, even though regional and global conditions had changed beyond recognition during the interim. The system had by then lost its capacity to monitor the extent of those changes. Thus, in terms of foreign relations overseas, the tributary system of regulated trade became ritualized and then nominal and finally ineffective.

Overland Relations with Southeast Asia

However, where Ming China's honour, its security, and its cultural superiority were concerned, the system was more useful. This was particularly true of China's overland relations with Southeast Asia. The most striking examples include the wars and border disputes involving the Shan-Tai states on the Yunnan border, Vietnam, and Burma. Although these conflicts occurred at different times between the middle of the fifteenth century and the end of the sixteenth century, they reflect the basic stability of the Ming state. Despite the danger to Peking in 1449 and the considerable military pressures on the northeastern borders during the 1590s, the tributary system continued to work adequately for the southern borders, even though the court employed the same rhetoric, institutions and techniques to control "barbarians" that had been in use since 1368.

Although Ming forces suffered a disastrous defeat in Vietnam in the 1420s, followed by the consequent loss of Chinese authority among the Shan-Tai principalities and states south of K'un-ming and Ta-li, the dynasty coped with rebellion and border disturbances very well. The first test of power and diplomacy was played out with the Maw Shan chiefs west of the Salween River. The first Ming emperor had tamed the most powerful Maw Shan leader in 1387 and then after 1398 carved up the large state of Lu-ch'uan (P'ing-mien) into eight small territories. His son, the Yung-lo emperor, fragmented the state further by establishing two of the territories as pacification commissions, thereby raising them to the same status as Lu-ch'uan, and openly used these two tribes to check the power of Lu-ch'uan. This policy had the unfortunate consequence of exposing the whole fragmented southwest region to the depredations of the ruler at Ava and prepared the way for future Burmese domination of all the Shan states on the Ming border.

The re-emergence of the Maw Shan chieftains of Lu-ch'uan followed the withdrawal of Ming armies from Vietnam in 1427. Knowing that the Ming court was in no condition to fight on the Yunnan border, the Maw Shan tribes became increasingly ambitious during the next few years. After 1436 their armies began to invade the border counties of central Yunnan, reaching as far as Yung-ch'ang and Ching-tung. Throughout this period, neither tributary diplomacy nor the administrative mechanisms of the aboriginal offices system could prevent war. When the imperial forces won some victories along the northwestern frontiers, strong voices were raised in favour of sending a full-scale expeditionary army to Lu-ch'uan in 1440. However, a measure of the futility of war in this remote southwestern corner of the empire is revealed in the fact that the campaigns dragged on for nearly a decade without a decisive victory. The Ming court had to call in support from all southern and western provinces and seek help from Burma and other Shan rivals of Lu-ch'uan before the rebellion was finally crushed. It even promised the land of Lu-ch'uan to any tribal leader who could deliver the heads of the Maw Shan leaders. However, when the Burmese succeeded in doing so, the Ming court withdrew its offer.[23]

On all counts, the war had disastrous consequences for the Ming state: it disrupted the economies of all the southwestern provinces involved in sending men and supplies to fight a war of attrition against a small tribal state; and it cost the Ming court the respect of its tribal allies on the border, who saw how inept and wasteful Ming armies were. Moreover, it drew commanders, officers, men and other resources from the north where they might have been vital to the defence of the northern borders. It is significant that the end of the Lu-ch'uan campaigns early in 1449 was followed immediately by extensive tribal uprisings and other revolts in five provinces south of the Yangtse River, and by the spectacular defeats later in the year which virtually destroyed the imperial armies in the north and led to the capture of the emperor himself by the Mongols.

The year 1449 was a turning point in the history of the dynasty. The Ming court had barely recovered from the disasters in Vietnam when it became involved in the costly and unnecessary wars on the Shan-Burma border. Thereafter, Ming China never again sent large armies to fight beyond its southern borders. The dynasty was fortunate to have survived these campaigns. There was subsequently no doubt that the gravest threat to dynastic security came from the Mongols just north of Peking. The south had to be better managed through tributary rhetoric and diplomatic manoeuvres: war could not be counted on even as a last resort. Thus, the relations with Vietnam and Burma for the next two centuries were dominated by high-flown and reassuring rhetoric mixed with a few feeble threats.

Soldiers appeared from time to time, but the scale of fighting was kept down to the levels appropriate to these two relatively minor powers, both of which were clever enough never to challenge the Ming empire's power directly.

Relations with Vietnam provide a useful illustration of how important the tributary framework was in ensuring peace in the south. Two examples will suffice: one concerns the reign of the Lê ruler Thanh-ton (1460–97), and the other concerns the beginning and end of the Mac regime in northern Vietnam (1537–97). Under Thanh-ton, two related events put the Ming tributary system to the test.[24] The first was the final destruction of the Cham kingdom in 1471 and the other the invasion of Laos between 1479 and 1481. The demise of Champa forty-five years after China's defeat in Vietnam was certainly related to the Ming occupation of Vietnam. Before the Ming invasion in 1406, the two states of Champa and Vietnam had been evenly matched for some three centuries. Even the Mongolian invasion of both countries at the end of the thirteenth century had not upset that balance. An invasion of Champa by Vietnam was followed by a counter-invasion of Vietnam by Champa. This happened over and again, and China's role as moderator was relatively easy. Admonition of the invader and exhortation against retaliation was enough as long as each attack was indecisive and expensive in men and goods. China's successful invasion in 1406, however, resulted in a tighter administration of Vietnam which the Lê dynasty inherited and expanded. It also led to a unified resistance movement that strengthened the Vietnamese armies and gave them a new confidence. Most important, China's defeat in 1426–27 destroyed China's credibility as a chastiser of the defiant and the rebellious.

The Vietnamese were now certain that Ming China would not invade again if tributary procedures were followed and the Chinese court did not lose face. Moreover, the reaffirmation of Confucianism as a state ideology led to the restoration of Vietnam's own tributary system. Tai and other tribal minorities to the west had already been designated by Vietnam as pacification commission territories on the Chinese aboriginal offices model. Vietnam had become so adept at managing its tributary relationship with China that it also became very skilled at dealing with its neighbours as its own tributary states.

The crucial test of Vietnamese power came first against Champa and then against the states in the interior (Laos, Chiengmai and Sibsong Banna). After destroying Champa in 1417, Vietnam informed the Ming court that the fall of Champa's ruling house had come about as a result of civil war. A new Cham court was created in the southern corner of what was left of Champa; its puppet king paid tribute to Vietnam, while another candidate for the Cham throne sought the Ming court's intervention. During the next four decades, the exchanges between this Cham claimant and the Chinese court, and between China and Vietnam taxed the tributary system to its limit.

These exchanges illustrate that when China was weak and did not want to resort to the use of force, the language and institutions of the tributary system provided an elaborate way for the court to maintain its myth of superiority and its image as protector of the weak against the strong. The evasions, the rationalizations, and the specious arguments of officials reluctant to support a loser fill the records. The result was never in doubt, and both the Vietnamese and Chinese courts probably realized this throughout the four decades of discussions. Champa was finished as a power; its lands had been absorbed, and China and Vietnam could go on indefinitely exchanging Confucian niceties over the question of responsibility. Meanwhile, Vietnam sent missions to China which the court considered tribute missions; the Ming court enfeoffed the Vietnamese ruler as the "king" of An-nan, while the Vietnamese used a rhetoric which placed their court on equal footing with the Ming empire. The Cham pretender paid tribute both to Vietnam and to China. A great deal of tension and resentment was diverted into rituals, proclamations and commentaries. Everything was arranged so that the Chinese tributary system appeared to be what was restraining the Vietnamese and pacifying the Chams; this satisfied the Ming court's sense of moral superiority and thus kept the peace for over four decades.

Thanh-ton's other expansionist effort was less successful, but it throws light on the diplomatic aspects of the Chinese aboriginal offices system. Thanh-ton invaded Laos and other Tai tribal territories in 1479. The Vietnamese had noted during the Ming occupation of Vietnam that the ruler of Laos held Chinese titles and supported Chinese efforts to suppress Vietnamese resistance. Thanh-ton's grandfather, Lê Loi, had been unable to find secure refuge in Laos during his efforts to free Vietnam from Ming occupation forces. Later, the Lê court also realized that Laos was expanding its authority over Tai peoples who had previously acknowledged Vietnam's suzerainty and had regularly paid tribute to Vietnam. Thus, the campaigns to reassert Vietnam's authority over the Tai tribes led to the invasion of Laos. Luang Prabang was captured and its ruler killed. When one of the ruler's sons escaped to Chiengmai (nominally a Ming tributary state), Vietnam tried to enlist Sibsong Banna, a Chinese pacification commission, to help invade Chiengmai. In turn, Ming border officials warned Sibsong Banna not to become involved in this struggle. Chiengmai, on the other hand, sided with Laos to drive off the Vietnamese army, and the Ming court rewarded Chiengmai for its loyalty. The Vietnamese denied that Laos had been attacked; they insisted that they did not even know where Chiengmai was and suggested that Chinese officials had been misinformed. Ming officials, however, thought they saw a pattern in Thanh-ton's aggressive behaviour: excuses made when raiding across the border into Kwangsi and Yunnan were compared with those made to attack and kill in Laos, and a prince of Laos was hurriedly confirmed as the country's new ruler.

Thanh-ton's armies did not return to the Mekong valley. He had regained control over his immediate tribal neighbours and had secured Vietnam's western borders. Laos, Chiengmai and Sibsong Banna did not pursue the matter any further, and the Ming emperor was content to send Thanh-ton an admonitory letter reminding him of his Confucian obligations.

There are several remarkable features to this affair. First, Ming China was aware that Vietnam had established its own aboriginal offices system along its northern and western borders and did not object to that arrangement. In this way, the Ming court conceded a higher status to monarchical states like Vietnam and Champa than to the ten southern pacification commissions, including Laos and Burma. Yet China also knew that such a monarchy might be nominal. Only China's formal recognition of the "king" of Champa after 1471 prevented Champa from being seen as what it was, a vassal state of Vietnam, weaker by far than Laos, Chiengmai and Sibsong Banna, which had the relatively low status of pacification commissions. The latter three did not, in fact, depend on China, certainly never in the way that Champa continued to rely on Chinese assistance. Finally, and most remarkable, was the fact that there were no references to the numerous wars which Chiengmai and Laos fought with Ayuthia (Siam). This was not because the Chinese did not know how aggressive Ayuthia was. On the contrary, China had to warn Ayuthia against attacking Malacca, Sumatra and Champa. But a sharp line seems to have been drawn to separate Ayuthia, a foreign country (*wai kuo*), from the Shan-Tai pacification commissions.

It is not clear whether the Chinese simply did not know or did not care about Siamese aggression, or whether regular Siamese tributary missions had focused the court's attention so successfully on their activities overseas that the Ming court never looked at Siam as a possible threat to the peace of Ming China's southern borders. In light of the Ming court's concern about Vietnam's invasion of Laos, it is astonishing that the Chinese said nothing about Siamese attacks and so little about the Burmese conquest of Chiengmai (not to mention Ayuthia) and several invasions of Laos during the sixteenth century. This certainly confirms that, while there was a considerable blurring of the distinctions between aboriginal offices and foreign countries on the Southeast Asian mainland, this was not the case for Vietnam. Vietnam was the closest foreign state to the areas of South China administered by the Ming government. Vietnam had defeated the Ming armies, and it had modelled its state system directly on the Chinese administrative system. Vietnam was a special case: the tributary system was not always an appropriate mechanism for the conduct of foreign relations with Vietnam.

During the sixteenth century, Vietnam was weakened once more by internal dissension, and China, invited to intervene, did not hesitate to aggravate the internecine strife. Yet, when all parties subscribed to the same values and were skilled in the use of the same rhetoric and institutions of tribute diplomacy, the outcome was far from simple. As before, China and Vietnam went to the brink of war. This time, however, war was averted when the Mac usurpers submitted themselves to the Ming; Vietnam's status in the tribute system was reduced from that of a monarchy to a superior form of pacification commission (*tu-t'ung shih ssu*).[25] Vietnam officially remained in this position until the end of the dynasty, even though the Mac house was overthrown and the Lê house was restored in 1592.

While Vietnam was a much-reduced force during the sixteenth century, the Burmese under Tabinshweti and Bayinnang had become the major force in mainland Southeast Asia. The contrast between Burma and Vietnam during this period is interesting. The weaker Vietnam had not been reduced to the status of an aboriginal office because it was administered not by barbarian chieftains, but by Confucian literati. Yet powerful Burma was not even treated as a foreign country, as Ayuthia had always been. Despite the fact that by the second half of the sixteenth century Burma was one of the most powerful countries in mainland Southeast Asia, it was still registered as an aboriginal office under the jurisdiction of the governor of Yunnan. This anomaly became even more clear when, at the height of its power, Burma had subjugated Ayuthia and almost all the pacification commissions to the south of the Yunnan border.[26]

China's system of foreign relations remained unchanged throughout the Ming, and this obscured the magnitude of the political and economic changes in Southeast Asia over the course of three centuries. The failure to grasp the significance of the arrival of European powers in the South China Sea and along the China coast was matched by the failure to see that the extension of the aboriginal office system beyond Yunnan could not indefinitely prevent the consolidation of powerful states and could not ultimately ensure China's control over them.

The spectacular success of the Burmese under Tabinshweti and Bayinnang totally overshadowed the small-scale expansions by the Vietnamese. Only the earlier aggression of Ayuthia was comparable. The fact was, Ming China witnessed the thrust of three major forces — the Thai, the Vietnamese and the Burmese — southward down the valleys and along the coast of mainland Southeast Asia. Did the dynasty's mixed system of tributary states, aboriginal offices and pacification commissions help it understand what was going on in the region? It is difficult to see how it could have. Vietnam was a former part of China practising a familiar Confucian style of government and was therefore unique. The kingdom of Ayuthia seemed to have become removed from its Shan-Tai-Lao links and was mainly seen as a maritime power stretching down the Malay peninsula into insular Southeast Asia; it was active east of China in the Ryūkyūs, Korea and Japan.

And as far as Burma was concerned, any understanding of its political role was hampered by describing it as a superior kind of aboriginal office subject to the jurisdiction of the governor of Yunnan, even after its resurgence in the 1540s. Indeed, surviving Ming records about Burma reveal this all too clearly. Apart from a few hints that it had Mon and Siamese neighbours and was in touch with the Portuguese to its south, Burma appeared to the Ming court as a recalcitrant and surprisingly powerful aboriginal power against which the rest of the aboriginal powers could form defensive alliances of various kinds and varying strengths. It is extraordinary to see the grand reunification of Burma during the sixteenth century depicted in Ming records as a number of troublesome border incidents on particular stretches of the Irrawaddy and the Salween rivers (with occasional alarms along the Mekong River as well). This was the region where Chu Yu-lang, the last claimant to the Ming throne, finally escaped when his armies were defeated in Kwangsi and Kweichow.[27] When he fled from Yunnan in 1659, his only hope of survival was to take refuge in Burma. It was no doubt an act of desperation. Although this last claimant to the throne had resided for many years in Kwangsi and Hunan, it is doubtful whether he knew what kind of state Burma was. He would have had to depend on the governor of Yunnan for advice. If he thought Burma was just another aboriginal office with doubtful loyalties towards the Ming emperor instead of the powerful foreign state it was, then clearly the absolute and unchanging system for controlling China's foreign neighbours was as misleading to Ming contemporaries as it remains today for students of Chinese history.

S.E. ASIA AND CHINA

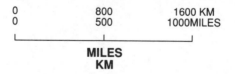

| 0 | 800 | 1600 KM |
| 0 | 500 | 1000MILES |

MILES
KM

BIBLIOGRAPHIC NOTE

Traditional Chinese historians from the Han to the Qing dynasties have described the tributary relationship as at the core of China's defence, trade and diplomacy with foreign countries. They have therefore written fully about the workings of the tributary system of foreign relations, from its early origins in the Han to its heyday under the Tang and then to its final restrictive form during the Ming and Qing dynasties. They were less interested, however, in the foreign states themselves, except when these kingdoms and principalities challenged the system and threatened the security of the empire. Thus, the bulk of traditional sources and scholarly writings about China's foreign relations concern the powerful nomadic states or confederations on the northern and western land borders. Kingdoms in Southeast Asia which rarely gave any trouble to the Chinese emperors attracted little attention.

Nevertheless, official histories have almost continuously provided reports on tributary relations with various states in Southeast Asia since the Han dynasty. By the Ming dynasty, more was known about the region than ever before. And the preservation of the *Veritable Records* of eleven Ming emperors has meant that we have even more detailed information about such relations. These records clearly are the most important source for this essay. Between 1959 and 1968, the materials in these *Veritable Records* pertaining to Southeast Asia were collected and the Nanking edition collated with the Taipei edition. They were then published in Chiu Ling-yeong *et al*, *Ming shih-lu chung chih Tung-nan-ya shih-liao* (vol. I, 1968; vol. II, 1976). Also important has been the *Ming Shih* and several Ming compilations like Ch'en Tzu-lung, *Huang Ming ching-shih wen-pien* and Chang Lu, *Huang Ming chih-shu*.

Various Ming works on foreign countries provide material not found in the *VR* and *Ming Shih*. These are Ma Huan, *Ying-yai sheng-lan*; Fei Hsin, *Hsing-ch'a sheng-lan*; Yen Ts'ung-chien, *Shu-yü chou-tzu lu*; and Shen Mao-shang, *Ssu-i kuang-chi*. More specialized but particularly useful for this essay have been the following: For Vietnam materials, the newly collated and composite edition of *Ta Yueh shih-chi ch'uan-shu* (*Dai Việt su k'y toàn thu*) by Ngô Si Liên and edited by Ch'en Ching-ho, published in 3 volumes by the University of Tokyo in 1984–86; and Chang Ching-shin, *Yü Chiao chi*. For mainland Southeast Asia beyond Yunnan, Li Yuan-yang, *Yun-nan t'ung-chih*; T'ien Ju-ch'eng, *Yen-chiao chi-wen*; and especially helpful, Ch'ien Ku-hsun, *Pai I Chuan*, as reconstructed and annotated by Chiang Ying-liang and published in Kunming in 1980. For materials on the Portuguese and other Europeans, Chang Hsieh, *Tung-hsi Yang K'ao*; the annotated editions of *Ming shih Fo-lang-chi chuan* by Chang Wei-hua (1934) and Tai I-hsuan (1984); and the pioneer study by Chang T'ien-tse, *Sino-Portuguese Trade from 1514 to 1644* (1934).

Modern scholarship about China's foreign relations also paid attention to the tributary system. It really began when European powers challenged that system successfully in the nineteenth century. At that time, the Chinese response to this threat from the West was to try to place the powers in a traditional context, as can be seen in the last great Chinese work compiled within the framework, Wei Yuan's *Hai-kuo t'u-chih* (1842–52). And because the Europeans had come by sea and were already in control of a large part of Southeast Asia, what Wei Yuan saw reflected a changing perspective on the region. This makes an interesting contrast to the Ming and early Qing understanding of Southeast Asia; see Jane Kate Leonard's study, *Wei Yuan and China's Rediscovery of the Maritime World* (1984).

European and American scholars who worked in Southeast Asia and China were immediately fascinated by China's traditional relations with Southeast Asia. Some of the earliest scholarly writings on this subject were by sinologists like W.P. Groeneveldt, P. Pelliot, F. Hirth and W.W. Rockhill. They in turn influenced Japanese scholars like J. Kuwabara and T. Fujita and, later, Chinese scholars like Chang Hsing-lang and Feng Ch'eng-chun. But much of their work concerned China's knowledge of Southeast Asia prior to the arrival of the Europeans, rather than any systematic study of the nature of China's foreign relations. The first full study of the tributary system from the outside came only with the pioneer study by J.K. Fairbank and S.Y. Teng, "On the Ch'ing Tributary System" (1941). And it was this work that led the present author to pursue a similar topic with special reference to early Chinese relations (for the thousand years or so before the Song dynasty) with Southeast Asian coastal states. That work, *The Nanhai Trade*, completed in 1954, provided the background to the study of Song, Yuan and Ming relations with the region. The study went on to focus on the strictly controlled Ming tributary system during the first two reigns of the Ming founder and his son, the Hung-wu and the Yung-lo reigns. (See Bibliography for essays published in 1964, 1968 and 1970.) These essays provide much of the detailed references for the analysis offered here.

But the present essay goes beyond the earlier three in two respects:

it extends the study to mainland Southeast Asian states on China's land borders and it takes the story beyond 1424 to the second half of the sixteenth century. The work of earlier scholars have again been useful, that of the Marquis d'Hervey de Saint-Denys and P. Pelliot, followed by that G.E. Harvey and G.H. Luce. More recently, the work of C.P. FitzGerald, *The Southern Expansion of the Chinese People* (1972) is an important contribution to the understanding of the respective fates of Vietnam and the Yunnan tribal principalities. The present author has also compared the northern and southern border-states under the Song which makes a useful contrast to developments under the Ming ("The Rhetoric of a Lesser Empire", 1983).

Finally, a note on recent scholarship in China, on the mainland and in Taiwan. Most socialist historians on the mainland are unhappy with the emphasis on sinocentrism and the tributary system as the focus of China's traditional foreign relations. They see the institutions, rituals and rhetoric associated with tribute as extensions of a feudal structure supported only by the imperial houses and their Confucian mandarins. They were never expressions of Han Chinese superiority over neighbouring peoples. In their view, Chinese foreign relations should be studied through the policies devised for national defence and orderly trading between countries. Hence, for most of the past four decades, studies on Ming relations with Southeast Asia have concentrated on shipping technology, navigation skills and the rise of the great southern ports; maritime trade and the coastal merchant class; and defence arrangements against piracy. More recently, there has been a revival of interest in the political significance of Admiral Cheng Ho's naval expeditions and in the new overseas Chinese communities emerging in various Southeast Asian cities and ports. But there is no attempt to consider the role and importance of the tributary system as the basis of China's relations with the countries of the region.

The scholars in Taiwan share the interest in shipping and navigation, in trade and defence, in Admiral Cheng Ho and in the Overseas Chinese. But they have not been shy to study Southeast Asian states in the context of tributary relationships. The leading scholar in China's foreign relations was Fang Hao, but more specifically on the Ming, there is the work of Chang I-shan and Ts'ao Yung-ho. Particularly noteworthy are essays (originally published in 1974 and 1976) on the use of the tributary system by Ming emperors, collected in Chang's *Tung-nan-ya shih yen-chiu* (1980).

As for the mainland states on China's land borders, very few

Chinese scholars have paid them much attention. Three books, however, are useful. They are Wang P'o-leng, *Chung Mien kuan-hsi shih* (1941); Hsieh I-tse *et al*, *Ming tai t'u-ssu chih-tu* (1968) and Fang Kuo-yü *Chung-kuo hsi-nan li-shih ti-li kâo-shih* (2 vols, 1987).

NOTES

1 For the Ming conquest of Yunnan, see Langlois, "The Hung-wu reign", *The Cambridge History of China*, vol. 7, pp. 143–146.

2 I have used Shan-Lao-Tai states to describe kingdoms or tribal territories in Burma, Laos, northern Thailand and Yunnan that were not under the control of Ayuthia (that is, Hsien-lo or Siam). For the rulers of Ayuthia, I have used Thai or Siamese. Strictly speaking, Tai is now used for speakers of the Tai language in Yunnan, but during the Ming, the line between the Tai, the Shan and the Lao was not too clear. Nevertheless, it would be clearer if I used Thai only for those who ruled Ayuthia or were ruled by Ayuthia.

3 For a fuller analysis of the first Ming emperor's policies, see Wang Gungwu, "Early Ming Relations with Southeast Asia: a background essay", in John K. Fairbank (ed.), *The Chinese World Order: Traditional China's Foreign Relations*, (Cambridge, Mass., 1968), pp. 34–36, 50–53.

4 *MSL, T'ai-tsu shih-lu*, pp. 36–47.

5 *MSL, T'ai-tsu shih-lu*, pp. 47, 48

6 *MSL, T'ai-tsu shih-lu*, p. 244.

7 *MS*, 321, pp. 8309–8311; also Chiu Ling-yeong *et al*, *Ming shih-lu chung chih Tung-nan-ya shih-liao*, vol. I (Hong Kong, 1968) pp. 3, 7, 15, 17, 25, 28, 30, 35, 41, 48, 50–51, 56, 60–64.

8 The Ming view of the relationship is drawn from *MSL* and *MS* (see note 7 above). It is interesting to compare it with the Vietnamese view presented in *Ta Yueh shih-chi ch' üan-shu (Dai Việt su k'y toan thu)* by Ngô Si Liên, edited by Ch'en Ching-ho (Tokyo, 1984), vol. I, p. 436–470. Also see John K. Whitmore, *Vietnam, Hô Qu'y Ly, and the Ming (1371–1421)*, Yale Southeast Asia Series, New Haven, 1985, pp. 16–36.

9 See O.W. Wolters, *The fall of Srivijaya in Malay History (Ithaca, 1970)*, and *Early Indonesian Commerce: A Study of the Origins of Srivijaya* (Ithaca, N.Y., 1967).

10 On Hu Wei-yung's treason, see J. Langlois, "The Hung-wu reign, 1368–1398", in F.U. Mote and D.C. Twitchett, ed., *The Cambridge History of China*, Vol. 7, *The Ming Dynasty*, Part 1 (Cambridge, 1988), pp. 137–42.

11 Ming T'ai-tsu, *Huang Ming Tsu-hsün lu* (1373), rpt. in *Ming-ch'ao k'ai-kuo wen-hsien*, III, pp. 1686–1687. Cf. the final revised version of 1395, *Tsu-hsün*, III, pp. 1588–1591. This explicit policy about "the various small countries of the *man* and *i* overseas

separated from us by mountains and seas and far away in a corner" was first enunciated on 30 October (*hsin-wei* in the 9th month), 1371; see *T'ai-tsu pao-hsün* (Preface dated 1418), collected in Lü Pen and others, *Huang Ming pao-hsün*, edition of 1602, ch. 6 "Yu I Ti".

12 *MSL, T'ai-tsu shih-lu*, p. 86; Chiu Ling-yeong *et al, Ming shih-lu chung chih Tung-nan-ya shih-liao, vol.* I, p. 18.

13 *MS*, 313–315, chapters on the *t'u-ssu* of Yunnan. Although the ruler at Ava became "Mien-tien pacification commissioner" in 1394, Ming T'ai-tsu, *T'ai-tsu shih-lu*, 242 and 244, still speaks of Mien kuo wang, "the King of Mien" for years 1395 and 1396. In all the later *shih-lu*, Burma is called "Mien-tien", and never a kingdom.

14 See Ch'ien Ku-hsun, *Pai I Chuan*, annotated by Chiang Ying-liang (Kunming, 1980) provides the fullest account of the Maw Shan state. A briefer version is in *MS*, 314, pp. 8111–8114.

15 Wang Gungwu, "China and Southeast Asia, 1402–1424", in Jerome Ch'en and Nicholas Tarling (eds.), *Studies in the Social History of China and Southeast Asia: essays in memory of Victor Purcell* (Cambridge, 1970), pp. 381–383; Wang Gungwu, "Chang Fu" and "Huang Fu", in DMB, pp. 64–67, 653–656. See also C.P. FitzGerald, *The Southern Expansion of the Chinese People* (New York, 1972), for an extended discussion about Vietnamese national identity in contrast to the peoples of Nan Chao and Ta-li in Yunnan.

16 See John K. Whitmore, *Vietnam, Hô Qu'yly and the Ming (1371–1421)* (New Haven, 1985); and *The Cambridge History of China*, Vol. 7, Part I, pp. 229–31, 289–91.

17 On the history of Champa, see G. Maspero, *Le Royaume de Champa* (Paris, 1928). Also *MS*, 324, pp. 8383–8393.

18 J.V.G. Mills, trans. *Ma Huan, Ying-yai sheng-lan: The Overall Survey of the Ocean's Shores* [1433], (Cambridge, 1970), p. 34.

19 See Chang Wei-hua, *Ming-shih Fo-lang-chi Lü-sung Ho-lan I-ta-li-ya ssu chuan chu-shih* (Beijing, 1934); Chang T'ien-tse, *Sino-Portuguese Trade from 1514 to 1644* (Leiden, 1934, rpt. N.Y. 1973). A recent annotated edition by Tai I-hsuan, *Ming shih Fo-lang-chi chuan chien-cheng* (Beijing, 1984) contains some new materials.

20 Preface by Lo Hsiang-lin to Chiu Ling-yeong *et al, Ming shih-lu chung chih Tung-nan-ya shih-liao* (Hong Kong, 1968), vol. I, pp. 2–26.

21 It is interesting to note the sharp contrast between the amount of *shih-lu* material on Southeast Asia before and after 1487 in Chiu Ling-yeong *et al.* (note 20 above): 444 pages from the 120 years between 1368 and 1487, and only 100 pages for the 136 years between 1487 and 1623.

22 Two recent studies have highlighted the importance of trade in the 16th century: Lin Jen-ch'uan, *Ming mo Ch'ing ch'u ssu-jen hai-shang mao-i* (Shanghai, 1987) and Chang Tseng-hsin, *Ming chi tung-nan Chung-kuo ti hai-shang huo-tung*, vol. I (Taipei, 1988). The most accessible Western-language work is So Kwan-wai, *Japanese Piracy in Ming China during the 16th Century* (East Lansing, 1965).

23 *MS*, 314, pp. 8111–8123; 315, 8129–8155. A slightly fuller account may be found in Yen Ts'ung-chien, *Shy-yü chou-tzu lu* (Ku-kong po-wu yuan edition, Beijing, 1930) 9, pp. 12a–31b. See also G.E. Harvey, *History of Burma from the earliest times to 1824* (London, 1925) and Wang P'o-leng, *Chung Mien kuan-hsi shih* (Ch'angsha, 1941).

24 *MS*, 321, pp. 8327–8337. The *shih-lu* material is collected in Chiu Ling-yeong *et al*, *Ming shih-lu chung chih Tung-nan-ya shih-liao*, vol. II (Hong Kong, 1976), pp. 398–438. For the Vietnamese view, see *Ta Yueh shih-chi ch'uan-shu* (*Dai Viêt sủ k´y toàn thú*) by Ngô Si Liên, vol. II (Tokyo, 1985), pp. 639–710.

25 Charles Hucker, *A Dictionary of Official Titles in Imperial China* (Stanford, 1985), p. 545 suggests the *tu-t'ung* is a military title equivalent to Campaign Commander. This title, however, was not regularly used during the Ming. Where Vietnam's status here was being demoted, I suggest that the context was one comparable to that of the Burmese and Shan-Tai-Lao *hsuan-fu* or *hsuan-wei shih* (pacification commissioner) but higher. Therefore, I think "a superior form of pacification commission" would be appropriate.

26 On Burma's rise to power in this period, see G.E. Harvey, *A History of Burma from the Earliest Times to 1824*, (London, 1925). Also see D.G.E. Hall, *A History of Southeast Asia*, 4th edition (London, 1981), pp. 287–295.

27 See Struve, "The Southern Ming", *The Cambridge History of China*, vol. 7, pp. 706–710.

CHAPTER 4

Merchants without Empires: The Hokkien Sojourning Communities

CHINESE MERCHANTS HAVE LONG struggled against the orthodox Confucian view that they should be at the bottom of the socio-political scale. The agrarian empire was established by force of arms and run by a centralized bureaucracy. This empire soon developed strict controls over the sources of mercantile wealth and thereafter kept merchant families on the defensive. The underlying principle was that such families should not be allowed to use commercial wealth to acquire political power either directly through official appointments or indirectly through high social status. And as the mandarin state evolved through the centuries, military families also were ultimately excluded from political power, except during times of dynastic crises. The mandarins, selected largely from literati with or without landed wealth, became the embodiment of imperial authority and legitimacy. Merchants could not hope to challenge such a state structure. All they could hope for was to get some of the mandarins to collaborate in the acquisition of commercial wealth and to educate some members of their families to reach literati status and help to protect their enterprises.

Behind this overall framework, however, there were countervailing trends. For the first thousand years, from the Han to the Tang dynasties (from roughly the second century BC to the ninth century AD), the major pressures against mandarin power came from military families seeking to erect feudal structures. Merchants had no place in this struggle; their lowly status placed them with the artisans, even though their skills with money in an increasingly cash-based economy made them useful agents to powerful families from time to time. After the tenth century, when no military aristocracy was possible any more within China, the literati route to power was supreme and firmly established. But this opened up a different trend, creating a meritocracy in which wealth could and did play an important role, which encouraged entrepreneurship and the emerging mercantile class. Thus the Song dynasty (980–1276), and especially the Southern Song during the twelfth and thirteenth centuries, offered opportunities to merchants to create wealth to increase the imperial revenues and, at the same time, strive for upward social mobility.[1] But the wealth was never allowed to be independent of the mandarinate. It was always contingent on its value to the court and its links with officialdom, preferably through family members who had made the transition to literati status.

It was in this context of a new role for merchants that maritime trade became important in the southeastern coastal provinces of China after the tenth century. This chapter explores the nature of Chinese merchant communities through their activities overseas. Given the background of discrimination, what can we learn from those who were more daring and enterprising and who sought their wealth in areas outside mandarin control? Among the most active of them were the merchants of south Fujian, better known as the Hokkiens.[2] The first part of the chapter will describe the background of their maritime activities, especially the trading conditions before the end of the sixteenth century. The second will concentrate on two of their communities: one in Manila from the 1570s and the other in Nagasaki after 1600. From their experience, it may become clear why the Chinese did not develop strong networks and organizations of the kind that had emerged in Europe by the seventeenth century. The Hokkiens also provide a contrast with the merchant communities in Europe, which fared better in a variety of small contending states that needed and supported them in their overseas trade. There is also the difference between merchants barely tolerated by a centralized empire and those whose rulers and governments used them for their imperial cause. When merchants could extract favourable conditions from kings and aristocrats, they could hope eventually to gain control of the governments themselves. A mandarinate that believed that the successful state was dependent on a peaceful and prolific peasantry would question the function of profit and mercantile wealth. And despised merchant communities excluded from political power could hardly expect to build merchant empires of their own.

Chinese Maritime Activities before 1500

Long-distance overseas trade for the Chinese was no different than for other trading peoples. It required advanced shipping technology, large capital investment, and some degree of official protection to ensure continuity and profitability for those who specialized in it. For China, the technology for coastal trading over relatively long distances, that is, from the coasts of the Korean peninsula down to those of Indo-China and the Malay peninsula, had been available from ancient times. We know little about private investment, but we have ample material about the trade supported by imperial and provincial governments, either by sending their own missions overseas or by encouraging foreign merchants (official or otherwise) to come regularly to Chinese ports. By the Tang dynasty, foreign merchants were numerous enough to form communities in Guangzhou (Canton). And during the first half of the tenth century, with the establishment of independent kingdoms in the Guangdong and Fujian provinces, the Nan Han and the Min respectively, more foreign traders (many still seen as representing official missions from their rulers) frequented their ports, notably Fuzhou and Quanzhou in addition to Guangzhou. Although the two kingdoms lasted only fifty to sixty years, they laid the foundations for economic growth, notably, the opening of new lands, population increase, and the rise of local trade and industry, which made the two provinces of increasing importance to the Song dynasty.[3]

Becoming an independent kingdom during the tenth century was a major turning point in Fujian's history. For the first time, Fujian was developed not for China but for itself. And clearly, maritime trade was essential for its future prosperity. It was no accident that Quanzhou took over from Fuzhou as the leading port. It had the better harbour, the Hokkiens had less agricultural land than the people of the Min valley to their north, and their two prefectures of Quanzhou and Zhangzhou were "frontier" territories further from direct interference by court and provincial mandarins. Thus maritime trade began to flourish, and it grew even more rapidly when the Southern Song treasury after 1127 enjoyed the revenues from foreign trade collected at the Maritime Trade Commission in Quanzhou.[4]

Despite its growing importance, the trade and the merchants who controlled it were never clearly described in contemporary records. The revival of Confucian orthodoxy, among other things, reaffirmed the lowly position of the merchant. Fujian chroniclers and literati were much prouder of their successes in imperial examinations, their share of high posts in the Song court at Hangzhou, and, not least, the fact that some of the great Neo-Confucian thinkers of the time, including the greatest of them, Zhu Xi himself, were products of the province. The province's contribution to the Song economy and to imperial finances through maritime trade and the taxes collected at its ports, in contrast, was downplayed. And as for its merchants, sailors, and their enterprises, there is only the most meagre information.[5] The most extensive information we have concerns official approval and the treatment of foreign merchants.

Maritime trade depended on official support, if not sponsorship. This was particularly true at the larger ports, where trade commissioners and customs officials were posted. With official acquiescence some of the wealthy and powerful families at such ports would provide the capital for oceangoing ships and invest in their cargo. The risks were great but so were the profits when each merchant fleet returned. Lesser trading families as well as skilled artisans who produced marketable goods would also join the enterprise. In time, the successes encouraged the merchant classes in smaller ports also to invest in ships for the overseas trade. Thus, radiating out of the port of Quanzhou itself, for example, would have been a chain of minor ports like Anhai and Yuegang, which, by the following Yuan and Ming dynasties, became centres themselves for maritime trade. These lesser centres, being even further away from official supervision, allowed their traders to act more freely and adventurously in the expanding trade. It also meant that an increasing number of coastal communities in Fujian (and to a lesser extent in Guangdong and Zhejiang) became directly involved in maritime enterprises.[6] Hence the extension of maritime skills and technology between the twelfth and fifteenth centuries, which made possible the Mongol Yuan naval invasions of Japan and Java towards the end of the thirteenth century and the even more extraordinary expeditions of Admiral Cheng Ho to the Indian Ocean at the beginning of the fifteenth. In both cases, official approval of private maritime trade paid off when the fleets and the shipbuilders and the captains and the navigators could be turned to such spectacular ventures.

The treatment of foreign trading communities living in Quanzhou and elsewhere was based on laws first devised for imperial capitals like Changan and Loyang, where foreign merchants had first come overland to China a thousand years earlier. These laws had protected the overland merchants and they applied equally to the overseas merchants who came to the southern ports. It can also be assumed that Chinese practices were influenced by practices elsewhere in Asia, that they were modified in China with experience, and that they in turn had influenced practices elsewhere. Thus non-Chinese quarters for different foreign merchant communities were officially recognized, and they had their own formally chosen leaders, and their own community centres, markets, and places of worship.[7] Special Chinese officials and interpreters were appointed to deal with each of these quarters. Over the centuries, a pattern of rights and duties evolved in China that was probably similar in other foreign merchant communities elsewhere in Asia. In this way, Chinese merchants who aspired to trade overseas would know more or less what to expect when they went abroad and when they themselves sought to establish their own communities there. Perhaps the only difference was that the Chinese merchants who went to the ports of smaller kingdoms or fiefdoms in Southeast Asia and Japan often had the chance to negotiate with kings or nobles or powerful chiefs directly for their trading and residential rights. In contrast, foreign merchants in China were supposed to deal with commissioners sent by the court but were more likely to face lowly provincial or local Chinese officials who implemented elaborate and irksome administrative rules if they were not suitably bribed.

It is within this background that Fujian and, especially, the port of Quanzhou became the major centre for foreign merchants during the thirteenth and fourteenth centuries. Fujian merchants developed their maritime skills in a relatively free, officially backed trading atmosphere. They were taxed and supervised but otherwise unrestricted. This encouraged them to set out to trade with every intention of returning after each voyage, not to stay abroad unless they really had to, and never to remain away from home for long. If small numbers were left behind in a foreign port, they were sent there as agents for enterprises that sent ships out from China regularly, probably every year. Thus they were really sojourners temporarily residing abroad on behalf of their families or their employers. But as the trade expanded and the numbers of sojourners grew, small communities emerged, and there is evidence that they were to be found (together with some Guangdong traders) in the major ports of Champa (later part of Vietnam), Cambodia, Sumatra, and Java by this period.[8] Not surprisingly, some of the sojourners elected to settle, marrying local women and producing progeny to carry on the trading connections with China or simply to become local traders in their own right. The sojourner communities often performed valuable services for the local economy, and for that they seemed to have received favourable treatment. Unfortunately, the little evidence available is fragmentary and indirect, and no description of these merchants as communities exists.

It is also not clear whether the sojourners who returned regularly to China also married local women and left their descendants behind to become assimilated members of the local community. If they did, there would not have been settled *Chinese* merchant communities overseas. Instead, there would only have been sojourner communities, that is, communities consisting of a continuous series of sojourners and providing shelters for accommodating new sets of sojourners. The first two clear references to overseas merchant communities date to early in the fifteenth century, a period when imperial policy on maritime trade had drastically changed. The change had come between the end of the Yuan (1368) and during the reign of the first Ming emperor (1368–98).[9] The new policy restricted all maritime trade to foreign tributary missions and banned overseas travel for all Chinese — hence, these two merchant communities abroad. One was on the northeast coast of Java, and the other was at Palembang (Sumatra). The former is described as Muslim, probably sinicized Muslims of foreign origin who had settled in Quanzhou (or other Chinese ports) and who had been forced by the change in Ming policy to shift their operations to Java after 1368. The latter consisted of natives of Guangdong and Fujian. They could have been descendants of Chinese sojourners who had regularly traded at Palembang, but more likely they were victims of the new Ming policy, forced to remain abroad because they had defied the trade bans and gone overseas. They were not part of a settled Chinese community but were members of armed, illegal (if not piratical) trading fleets who had seized Palembang in order to defend themselves when they found they were unable to return to China. It is likely that there were other similar communities elsewhere in Southeast Asia at this time: in Champa, in Siam (Ayuthia), on the Malay peninsula, in the Sulu archipelago, and on the coasts of Borneo, where there had been a thriving China trade during the fourteenth century, but no descriptions of such communities are available. The point to be made here is that a different kind of Chinese merchant community could have arisen from a sudden change of imperial policy.

Ming policy for the first hundred years was aimed at stopping *private* overseas trade. Whatever justifiable strategic reasons the Chinese government had for this policy, the consequences for Quanzhou and Fujian merchants in this trade were calamitous. Instead of the supervised trade that had made Quanzhou great, an elaborate machinery for registering and checking all tribute-bearing missions from western, southern, and Southeast Asia was created in Guangzhou. These missions and their merchandise were then normally escorted overland to the capital, first at Nanjing and later at Beijing, and they were showered with imperial gifts and returned overland to Guangzhou. Quanzhou and the Fujian ports were largely bypassed. Instead of foreign traders, these ports saw only imperial garrisons, who built new walled forts and manned coastal flotillas to arrest illegal shipping, fight off pirates (both foreign and Chinese), and prevent smuggling. The consolation, however, was that the policy brought peace and stability to the provinces and consequently a different kind of economic growth.[10]

The policy also produced one unexpected result. The number of Chinese traders who resided abroad only temporarily was drastically cut at the end of the fourteenth century. But for those who were abroad and had failed to return to China immediately as well as those who defied the bans and continued to trade overseas and had to prolong their stay indefinitely, the policy ensured that they formed more stable communities and even settled down permanently. And as long as the bans were strictly enforced, fewer Chinese traded abroad but more of those already abroad were forced to organize themselves in communities there. It was in this atmosphere that Admiral Cheng Ho and his navy set forth on their great voyages between 1405 and 1433. When these expeditions came to an end and it was decided never to send any more out again, they had, paradoxically, educated many more Chinese about the trading opportunities overseas at a time when private trade was being destroyed and future generations of those who were drawn to trade privately overseas were being intimidated.

The port of Quanzhou was seriously affected by the neglect of foreign merchants and by the virtual end of Chinese overseas activity. It never regained its former greatness as a port. But the merchant classes of Fujian turned to other enterprises.[11] During the century of relative stability, their attention turned to cash crops like sugar, tea, indigo, timber, fruits, and even cotton. They produced better-quality textiles, silks and porcelain and encouraged the development of other crafts and manufactured goods. They improved the salt and fishing industry and, in particular, developed a network of trading connections in the neighbouring provinces both by land and by sea. The coastal Hokkiens (including the people in the fishing ports of Xinghua and Fuqing to the north) did not lose their skills in shipbuilding and navigation. They deepened, in fact, their experience of maritime trade up and down the whole coast of China and up the great Yangtse river into the interior of central China. They joined increasingly large and active groups of merchants in Guangdong, Zhejiang, Jiangsu, and even Anhui, to organize private trade within China. Their main strength, however, was that they were most at home at sea, because the sea provided them with their best access to all the great markets of China. They also depended most on the sea because their coastal plains were narrow and their agricultural land limited; when their population began to grow rapidly, they were forced to turn to the sea to transport the grain they needed to buy from the grain markets of the Yangtse and Pearl river deltas. This also meant, of course, that whenever the overseas trade bans were laxly enforced or partially lifted or when local officials were prepared to turn a blind eye to Hokkien traditional maritime activity, there was never any shortage of people able and willing to reach out to markets overseas.[12]

The isolationist policy of the Ming was, in fact, impossible to sustain. Its very success in curtailing lawlessness along the China coasts brought rapid economic growth and consequently also population growth. This in turn increased the pressure on coastal Chinese, and especially the Hokkiens, to look at the great profits to be made in overseas trade and seek ways to get round the trade bans. Furthermore, the prosperity of China encouraged more foreign traders to come, and more and more of them were frustrated by the pretence of being tribute-bearing missions. They too sought every possible means, with the connivance of those local officials who became increasingly tempted to condone private trade, to broaden their opportunities to trade directly with ports other than the highly bureaucratic Guangzhou, where their missions were forced to register. Chinese merchants already abroad in foreign ports were ready to help and often served as the representatives of foreign rulers or as interpreters coming to China with their missions. Others, especially the experienced but bypassed Hokkien sailors and traders, secretly went out to trade with, and perhaps even join, the small merchant communities already formed in Southeast Asian ports. Thus, despite the bans and the increased risks of trading overseas during the fifteenth century, small Chinese merchant communities abroad survived, for example, at ports like Malacca, Bantam, Brunei and Sulu and perhaps also in the Ryukyu Islands and Kyushu. Thus, before the arrival of the Europeans, a chain of small port communities of Chinese traders was servicing a thriving trade that many people in eastern and Southeast

Asia were actively seeking to expand.[13]

We have no details about these communities and what they were like. Because they were not legitimate in the eyes of China, no official accounts are available, and the Chinese sojourners themselves were either illiterate or too discreet to record anything. Their better-educated counterparts in ports in China who supported them were unable to admit publicly to their profitable involvement with this trade. Hence we begin to have a fuller picture of these communities only when first the Portuguese, then the Spanish, the Dutch, the Japanese, and finally the Chinese themselves (when Ming policy was all but abandoned after 1567) left us descriptions of some of the notable ones in Faifo, Malacca, Patani, Hirado, Nagasaki, Manila, Bantam and Batavia.[14]

Chinese Maritime Activities after 1500

Until the end of the sixteenth century, it is doubtful whether any of the Chinese communities was more than a few hundred in number. Of course, a few hundred Chinese males who married locally and brought their children up as Chinese could quickly increase the number to thousands. But apart from Manila in the 1590s, this probably did not happen before the seventeenth century. The Chinese males were mainly sojourners, who did not plan to stay long, or if they intermarried, they allowed their children to assimilate to the indigenous people. The exception of Manila is an interesting one. Unlike the Portuguese, who had conquered well-established city-ports like Goa and Malacca and had access to rich hinterlands and technically advanced native populations, the Spanish in the Philippines settled on an undeveloped chain of islands on the frontiers of sophisticated, "oriental" civilizations. Fortunately for them in the 1560s and 1570s, the Muslims they met were weak and cut off from stronger Muslim allies by the Portuguese, and neither the Japanese nor the Chinese were interested in territory. It quickly became clear to the handful of Spanish officials, priests and soldiers that if they wanted to defend and develop what they had, they needed to expand the China trade and, what was more, they needed Chinese ships, traders and skilled artisans to build up Manila as a great maritime centre and help speed up Spanish control of the islands. Thus they welcomed the coming of Chinese traders as no one in the region had ever welcomed them before. In less than thirty years, the Chinese population reached some ten thousand, perhaps more if the mixed-blood descendants were all counted.[15] This was the first truly large Chinese community overseas and easily the largest one in the sixteenth century.

During the seventeenth century, another large Chinese merchant community was to be found in Batavia, which eventually became much larger than that in Manila. Again, this was the result of deliberate Dutch policy, which sought to gain a total monopoly of eastern and southeastern Asian trade through making use of the Chinese trading networks already established throughout the Malay archipelago, the Indo-China coasts and Japan. The Dutch were much stronger than the Spanish and more determined to expand quickly. They welcomed Chinese co-operation and tried to woo them wherever possible away from the Portuguese and the Spanish. In that way, a Dutch-supported chain of Chinese communities grew up between Batavia and areas like the Moluccas to the east, Siam to the north, and China and Japan to the northeast. When the Portuguese were driven out of Malacca and the Moluccas and confined to Macao, the Dutch in Batavia, like the Spanish in Manila, controlled the largest Chinese communities in Southeast Asia and used them to strengthen their own maritime empires. It is no coincidence that they both also felt threatened by the numbers of Chinese attracted to their two cities, and both tried to control their Chinese very carefully. During the next 150 years, whenever the Spanish felt threatened by the Chinese in Manila, they massacred them, and in Batavia, a major bloodletting occurred in 1740. The Spanish felt specially vulnerable because their dependence on the Chinese was greater, their forces were weaker, and the homeland of the vigorous Hokkiens of Zhangzhou and Quanzhou was close by. But even with their great navies, the Dutch had to be careful to check the potential power of their Chinese allies. They could not afford to relax with large Chinese communities living in their empire, and an especially large one on their doorstep in Batavia.[16]

MANILA

Two Hokkien communities, those in Manila and Nagasaki, deserve more attention here. The first is one that rose out of a dramatic demand for Chinese traders by a European power, and the other is a basically Asian development influenced by the European presence.

The story of the rise of a large Chinese community in Manila cannot be separated from Spanish policy, but it first began, on the one hand, as an extension of traditional Hokkien trade in the archipelago, reaching out from Brunei to Sulu, and, on the other, as a response to new trading developments on the Fujian coast following the arrival of the Portuguese early in the sixteenth century. As a natural extension of their trading efforts, the Chinese established a new sea route to Luzon via Taiwan and the Babuyan Islands. This shortened the journey considerably and gave the Zhangzhou and Quanzhou people a decisive advantage over other Chinese in the Philippines trade that they never lost. Thereafter, regular voyages to specific ports in Luzon–Mindoro and in Mindanao and Sulu were normal. This new route was in no way spectacular, however, and was clearly subordinate in importance to the major trading routes to the richer ports of the western end of the South China Sea. With the arrival of the Portuguese and the ramifications of increased trade on the China coasts, however, Hokkien trading fortunes took a surprising turn.

The Portuguese arrived at the time when the Ming trade policy had all but broken down.[17] Unofficial trade by Chinese and foreigners alike had outstripped trade through tribute. Thus when officials in Guangdong rejected the Portuguese because they were outside the tribute system and the Portuguese decided to trade anyway, using force if necessary, the impact on the Hokkiens in particular was considerable. Restless Hokkien traders were ready to seek out the Portuguese who sailed past their ports. The trade was illegal, but ineffectual officials did little to stop it. When it continued to grow and became a source of conflict and disorder with the Portuguese and their allies, some earnest imperial officials finally sought to enforce the trade bans with vigour. The uproar this created led to widespread resistance among the local Hokkien notables secretly involved in this overseas trade and among Japanese and other illegal traders. And because this coincided with virtual anarchy in Japan following a series of civil wars when many Japanese ronin were available for hire, the resistance took the form of a series of Sino-Japanese attacks on the south China coast that lasted from 1550 to 1570. Four coastal provinces were under continuous attack, especially between 1552 and 1565. Although the Ming forces eventually won, the lesson was learned, and the maritime trade bans were lifted in 1567.[18] This coincided with the arrival of the Spanish in the Philippines and was only five years before the Spanish settlement of Manila.

The prospects for a profitable relationship between these Spanish and the Hokkiens recently freed from heavy trading restrictions were good from the start. It was significant that the 150 or so Chinese whom the Spanish found in the Manila area when they first arrived were eager for the trade. This augured well for the future, and indeed the Hokkiens came in large numbers over the next three decades. As for the formation of a merchant community, which is well attested in several sources, the description in Zhang Xie's *Dongxi Yang Kao* (1617) sums it up well:

> The Chinese who visit Luzon are consequently many. They often stayed on and did not return, and this was called *yadong*. They stayed together in the *Jiannei* [the Parian] to make their living, and their numbers gradually rose to several tens of thousands. One hears that some cut their hair and produced sons and grandsons there [that is, converted to Christianity or took to foreign ways, married local women, and established their families there].[19]

The Chinese settlement in Manila remained nevertheless a dependent and an uneasy one for both the Spanish and the Chinese. This was in part due to the conditions on the China coast in the aftermath of the era of "Japanese" pirates. There were several major pirate bands still harassing Chinese coastal officials, and one under Lin Feng (Limahong) sailed south to try to capture Manila in 1574–75. Lin Feng nearly succeeded and the Spanish were painfully reminded of how precarious their position still was. But they also learned something else about the Ming empire. Ming coastal officials offered to help destroy Lin Feng's forces and were actually grateful for the Spanish success. Two groups of Ming officials visited Manila, and the second actually brought imperial approval for the Spanish to trade in China. More significantly, they showed no interest in the Chinese merchant community there. The clear message to the Spanish was that the Chinese trading abroad were really on their own and could be used to further Spanish interests in the China trade as well as their own enterprises in Southeast Asia. At the same time, as these Chinese became increasingly numerous, they had to be carefully contained in their own quarters. A special area, the Parian, was marked out for them in 1582 (this was moved several times during the next 200 years, but the principle of controlling non-Catholic Chinese remained the same). The trade in silks for silver in the 1580s had become particularly profitable, and about twenty ships were coming from Fujian each year. These numbers rose to over thirty by 1600, and three years later, the number of Chinese who chose to remain in Luzon had exceeded 25,000. In 1603 Spanish suspicion and fear of these Chinese led to a dispute that ended with most of the Chinese being killed. Of the survivors, reputedly about 500 retured to China and only 500 others remained. Hokkien gazetteers and genealogies report this tragedy with particular poignancy.[20]

Despite the many references to the Chinese in Spanish writings of this period, there are few details about how the Chinese merchant community in the Parian was organized. We are told the major traders were those selling silks and other textiles; others sold porcelain, and yet others food, furniture, tools and personal services. Other important skills represented included tailoring and printing. But most of the Chinese opened shops and bought and sold with great success. Increasing numbers of them converted to Catholicism and married local women, and they were allowed to live outside the Parian. Among them and their children were found the trusted leaders who dealt with Spanish authorities on behalf of the community. Some of these trusted Chinese were even allowed to live among the Spanish within Manila fort.[21]

But it was hardly a stable Chinese community. After the 1603 massacre, the numbers were drastically reduced to about 500. Surprisingly, it did not take long for more Hokkien ships to arrive with more traders and for the numbers to rise again. Within another two decades, the total in the Philippines had reached 30,000. The policy was to allow no more than 6,000 to stay in Manila, but in practice, this had been ignored, and it is estimated that there were at least 20,000 in the Parian by 1621. Also, by this time, a clear distinction had been made between sojourning Chinese in closed areas like the Parian and converted Catholic Chinese, who were permitted to live among the "Indios" if they wanted to. And for the rest of the century, the numbers continued to fluctuate as Spanish policy changed from time to time, especially in response to the uncertainties of Chinese politics between 1620 and 1684. The Spanish learned to live with a limited number of Chinese ships arriving from China. Also, their own Chinese mestizo community had grown steadily to handle the China trade. Thus the Chinese community in Manila and elsewhere in the Philippines changed in nature. It had become divided into two related but different communities: a sojourning community and a transitional one that had become a localized community of mestizos (of part-Chinese descent), many of whom concentrated on the trade with the Chinese sojourners from their ancestral homes in Fujian, but whose descendants were on the way to becoming future Filipinos.[22]

The sojourners, the non-Catholic Chinese, were controlled by a Spanish "governor," but the Parian also had its own "headmen", who acted as intermediaries. We know nothing about how the various trades were organized. Elsewhere, one centre of community life was always the temple, whether to Tian Hou, the goddess of sailors, or Guan Yu, the deity preferred by merchants, or both (often joined later by Buddha or the compassionate Guanyin). Because of the several massacres and because the Parian was moved several times, there are no relics of early temples in Manila nor even any record of them having been there. The Spanish sources, on which much of our information depends, focus so much on the China–Mexico trade, on the Chinese threats to Spanish authority, and on the potential conversion of the Chinese to Catholicism that they do not mention what institutions the Chinese themselves used to provide solidarity or further their business efforts. It was not until the eighteenth century that secret societies, guilds and dialect group associations became common. In any case, because the Chinese were almost all natives of Quanzhou or Zhangzhou, such organizations were probably not essential.[23]

The records suggest that the sojourners in the Parian were housed in a few streets of wooden buildings that were grouped according to the major trades or around clan, village or county origins, with perhaps one building serving as a temple to Tian Hou and Guan Yu and small altars scattered in other buildings. The Catholic Chinese (not more than 10–15% of the Chinese population during the early seventeenth century), especially those who were married, lived around the churches in Binondo and neighbouring suburbs. In 1687 we hear of the Gremio de Chinos de Binondo (a town council) headed by ten Chinese captains and five mestizo captains. But by the middle of the eighteenth century, the mestizos were numerous enough to have broken away from the sojourners. The impression given is certainly one where the Spanish controlled most of the population through a policy of church guidance, leaving the various groups of Chinese free to organize themselves in their own way whenever they wanted to or to bribe the officials to allow them to do so.[24]

NAGASAKI

In sharp contrast to the community in Manila, the Chinese sojourners who went to trade in Japan at the end of the sixteenth century did not have to deal with an insecure but expansionist Western power. Instead, they could benefit from the long historical and cultural links between China and Japan. Nevertheless, these links had not been continuous or even predictable, and the traders on both sides were often victims of the variable policies of two proud imperial governments. For example, the growing trade during the Song dynasty was cut off by the ambitions of Kublai Khan (the emperor Khubilai) at the end of the thirteenth century when he twice attempted to invade Japan. Later, when Ming policy confined foreign trade to tribute missions, Japan rejected the idea of a subordinate relationship, however nominal that was. And Japanese pirates and smugglers at the end of the fourteenth and the beginning of the fifteenth century worsened relations to the point that it was increasingly difficult for Chinese traders to travel safely to Japan, much less to support any sojourning community there. It did not make it any easier that this was also a period when Japan was in the grips of civil war. As the various feudal lords fought bitterly to defend their territories, political anarchy made regular trading relationships impossible. All the same, the interests of the lords in Kyushu, the ports of which were closer to the southern Chinese provinces and more accessible to enterprising Chinese, did keep an unofficial trade alive. Their own ships and traders began to go beyond China and find their way to various ports of Southeast Asia. Indeed, private connections with Chinese merchants, again notably with those of south Fujian, developed further. They had become so close that when the Chinese trade bans were vigorously enforced in the middle of the sixteenth century, the Japanese and Chinese merchants who were directly affected joined forces to raid the Chinese coasts. For these raids, they used the offshore islands of Zhejiang and Fujian, but the port bases from which they organized their major attacks were in the Kyushu group of islands.[25] Many of these ports are reported to have had sojourning Chinese, but there is no evidence of a community before the seventeenth century.

It is not known how much these continuous raids on the China coast over two and a half decades satisfied commercial needs. The records emphasize the destruction of property, including cultivated fields and coastal industries and the terrible loss of lives; and not least, they describe the very expensive efforts by leading Ming generals to crush these pirate bands and drive them back to Japan. There is little doubt that many Chinese, either individually or in small groups, escaped to Japanese ports and sojourned or settled there, and others, together with their Japanese comrades, travelled south to sojourn in various ports in Vietnam (now including Cham ports), Luzon, Patani, Bantam and Malacca.[26] Of significance was the fact that the "Japanese" were not forgiven by the Ming. When the trading bans were lifted in 1567, the ban on trading with Japan remained in force. This meant that the Chinese sojourning in Japan could not return to China, nor could Japanese merchants trade directly with China. Thus the Hokkiens, whose enthusiasm for the illegal private trade had caused the bans to have been reinforced in the first place and whose fervent and desperate pleas had led to their being relaxed in 1567, were not able to benefit where the rich Japan trade was concerned. Instead, the main beneficiaries were the Portuguese, who used their newly created Macao base to carry the China–Japan trade both ways. And Hokkien traders had to be content to ally with and depend on Portuguese captains and join with the Portuguese in their small but successful trading and missionary centres in Japanese ports.[27]

Early in the seventeenth century, there was an excellent example of this indirect trade with Japan. The Nan'an (in Quanzhou) adventurer Zheng Zhilong, father of Koxinga (Zheng Chenggong), went to join his maternal uncle in Macao, became a Catholic convert, and accompanied the Macao fleet to Kyushu. At Hirado, he worked for the very successful Hokkien merchant Li Dan (Captain Andrea Ditties), married a Japanese wife, and when Li Dan died, took over his commercial and maritime empire. Clearly, there must already have been a small Hokkien community at Hirado. Another Hokkien, named Yan Siqi, was said to have started life there as a tailor and eventually made enough of a fortune to lead his own maritime empire before Zheng Zhilong arrived. And there is evidence of other small groups of Chinese traders and adventurers at several ports in the neighbourhood of Nagasaki and in Nagasaki itself.[28]

The Dutch arrived in Kyushu early in the seventeenth century, soon after the new shogun, Tokugawa Ieyasu, had reunified Japan under his control. He was quick to recognize that there were great profits in the China trade. Instead of leaving that trade to Portuguese–Dutch rivalry, he decided that Japanese merchants should recruit Chinese to help them. A new system of trading permits was introduced to cut down on the European dominance of the trade. And it was during this period that Li Dan and Zheng Zhilong built up their maritime forces and the island of Taiwan was opened up as a useful trading base by the Chinese and then by the Dutch and the Spanish. During the 1620s, the trade of Macao, Manila, Yuegang in Zhangzhou (which replaced Quanzhou as the port of the Hokkiens during the sixteenth century), Xiamen (or Amoy, which was emerging as the new Hokkien port of the seventeenth century under the influence of Zheng Zhilong), Taiwan and Kyushu was no longer a trade for small merchants. The arrival of the Europeans had established a new scale of long-distance trade, with their respective royal houses supporting the Portuguese and the Spanish and with official collective backing for the Dutch East India Company. The shogun's response of providing central support for Japanese merchants was a realistic one.[29] Only the Chinese — and here I refer especially to the peripheral Hokkiens in the southeast corner of a weakening Ming empire — received no official support. Zheng Zhilong held his large maritime forces together by military and diplomatic skill, through successful trading, and, not least, by the support of his large family and his devoted Hokkien countrymen.

The situation remained fluid in Kyushu until the period of Ieyasu's grandson, when Japanese internal politics led to a full closed-door policy. Foreign relations of all kinds were ended, the Portuguese and their trading fleets were sent away, and by 1641 only one port, Nagasaki, was kept open and that only to Chinese and Dutch ships. The story of Nagasaki, the fishing village that grew in importance because of the Portuguese trading and missionary efforts of the 1570s, is a remarkable one that has often been told. The Chinese, including Chinese Catholics in the service of the Portuguese, took an active part in that development. By 1602 there is evidence of a small community of Hokkiens, and they remained the most significant group of Chinese there for the rest of the seventeenth century. It is possible to distinguish three periods of growth and decline for this small Hokkien community. The first lasted from the 1580s to 1635, when they were the strongest. During the second, from 1635 to 1688, the Hokkiens did well because they had their own naval forces while other Chinese from Fuzhou, Ningbo, and the Yangtse delta were weakened because their home bases were more severely affected by the unrest in China between the fall of the Ming and the consolidation of Qing power. After 1688, the number of Chinese at Nagasaki declined, and the Hokkiens became much more interested in peopling Taiwan and various ports in Southeast Asia.[30]

The Tokugawa were increasingly anti-Catholic after 1600 and wanted Chinese who were willing to demonstrate that they were not Catholic. Hence the first phase of the sojourning community in Nagasaki was marked by an open commitment of the Chinese to Buddhism, something not expected of them elsewhere.[31] The Hokkiens were not alone here but in 1602 were the first to use a local Buddhist temple as their official meeting place. Their competitors from Jiangsu and Zhekiang went further in 1623 and established the Xingfu (or Nanking) Temple. This led the Hokkiens soon after, in 1628, to build their own, the Fuji (or Zhangzhou) Temple. And the next year, the third group, from Fuzhou, built their own, the Chongfu (or Fuzhou) Temple. In this way, they cut themselves off from the Portuguese and their Japanese and Chinese converts (including other Hokkiens converted by the Spanish in Manila) and became the favoured foreign traders in Nagasaki. Later, in 1641, when the Dutch were forced to move from Hirado to Deshima, the artificial island that confined their activities at Nagasaki, it was obvious that the "Buddhist" Chinese were given favoured treatment. Indeed, the Chinese were not confined to the neighbourhoods of their respective temples in the town itself but were allowed to live freely among the Japanese merchant families who traded with them. However, it may be assumed that each of the three subcommunities did use their own temples as meeting places and social and welfare centres as well as places for religious activity to confirm their subethnic solidarity.[32] Unfortunately, we do not know if the temples were ever used to further their business ambitions or played any part in the successes achieved by people like Li Dan and Zheng Zhilong.

For the second period, Zheng Zhilong and his son Koxinga ensured that Hokkiens dominated whatever trade there was between Nagasaki, Xiamen and Taiwan (and sundry other Chinese and Southeast Asian ports). More clearly than in any other period, the Zheng fleets controlled something like a maritime empire. They were helped by the Qing policy of moving coastal populations inland. This policy lasted for over twenty years (1661–81) and left the Zheng family with little competition during its declining years. During this period, the Nagasaki authorities began to supervise the Chinese more closely and took a keen interest in their social and political activities, but the Chinese were still relatively free to live among the Japanese. As for the refugees who were loyal to the Ming and escaped to Japan, they found favour by choosing to assimilate (*guihua*) and were never classified with the numerous sojourning Hokkiens. The climax came for the community, however, when the Zheng "empire" collapsed and Taiwan fell in 1683 to the Qing navy and the coastal population was allowed to go to sea again. By 1687 more than 100 ships had arrived from China. Suddenly, the pressure of these numbers was seen as too great. The Nagasaki authorities decided to limit the number of ships and also to build a Chinese quarter for the Chinese. With the rounding up of all Chinese in 1689 and forcing them to live in a restricted area, like the Dutch at Deshima, a new era began.[33]

From 1688 to the middle of the nineteenth century, the Chinese in

Nagasaki were confined to an enclosed and guarded "China town". This area was controlled by the Japanese, and in 1708, 96 staff were employed there, whereas 134 had been appointed to keep the Dutch in Deshima. Also, 250 staff were employed in the (Foreign Affairs) office for the Chinese, compared with 138 staff employed to deal with the Dutch. Among the Chinese themselves, the Hokkiens still stood out despite the fact that fewer Hokkiens looked to the Nagasaki trade in the eighteenth century. In 1708, of the 167 interpreters for various Chinese dialects, 101 were trained for the Quanzhou (Hokkien or Xiamen) dialect.[34]

Conclusion

The Hokkiens have been the focus of this essay because they were the majority of the overseas traders between the thirteenth and eighteenth centuries. They were also the most successful. They emerged as a coherent trading force on the China coast earlier than the Portuguese did on the European coast. Their earlier success was due to official support under the Song and the Yuan emperors, just as Portuguese achievements depended on royal encouragement from the start. But when Ming imperial policy changed and official help was withdrawn after 1368, the Hokkiens persisted outside the law and survived on their own. They needed the skills of Hokkien shipbuilders and captains, the capital of wealthy clansmen who had made their fortunes in China's internal trade, and their literati relatives to speak for them and even protect some of their illegal activities. And they needed their families and village networks to provide the personnel. They also had to bribe corrupt officials at home and co-operate with foreign officials and merchants overseas. Despite all these efforts and their geographical advantages and their long-time knowledge of the Southeast Asian region, the Hokkiens were hard-pressed to compete with the officially sponsored and armed Portuguese.

As for the Spanish, the Hokkien advantage should have been even greater. The Philippine Islands were close by, the seas in between well-traversed, and the Hokkien merchants far more numerous than the Spanish. Furthermore, the Spanish were at the weaker end of a vast empire and restricted by hostile Portuguese and Moro shipping. The Hokkien communities in Luzon should have been able to hold their own, if not dominate political and economic affairs. But this did not happen. Instead, the Hokkiens, abandoned by Chinese officials, chose a low profile as sojourning merchants. They were helpless against Spanish imperial power and, in fact, many became instruments of Spanish expansion. On the other hand, the communities in the Philippines contributed greatly to the Chinese economy. Their successful trade brought vast amounts of silver into China and their enterprises introduced New World crops like the potato, maize, groundnuts and tobacco, which were to transform subsistence agriculture all over their home province.[35]

The Dutch, like the Hokkiens and the Portuguese, lived on the edge of a continent and similarly faced the dangers and opportunities of the sea. Unlike the Portuguese, theirs was not a trade supported by their royal house but was backed by a chartered company. The company was organizationally modern and better adapted to the needs of an emerging bourgeois class. And unlike the Hokkiens, the Dutch had official support and legal and political protection. Their vessels, armed in the name of the Dutch East India Company, were also sanctioned by the monarch. Even in Nagasaki, when no foreign group was in control and the Chinese were theoretically equal with the Dutch, the Dutch had the advantage over the Chinese because they dealt with the shogun's officials as representatives of a foreign state. Whether the shoguns were impressed or not, the Dutch were continually able to remind them that their company had royal recognition and that they could negotiate on their king's behalf. The Hokkiens could make no such claims. They could only seek the best possible arrangement that they could get, and they could get only what their hosts thought they deserved. Whether in Manila or Nagasaki, the Hokkiens could not compete with the colonists, priests and soldiers of the Spanish Crown or with the well-armed servants of a state-supported chartered company. They were lowly provincial merchants remote from the Chinese court. They had to live by their wits, cultivate the fine art of risk-taking, and, at the crunch, could count only on their family–village system and strong local Hokkien loyalties to help them through hard times.[36]

The successes and failures of the Hokkiens can be easily exaggerated. What stands out from their story in Manila and in Nagasaki is that their trading activities were greatly stimulated by the European presence and that they could, in terms of entrepreneurship and daring, do everything that the various Europeans could do. But they were helpless to produce the necessary institutional changes in China to match European or even Japanese power. They were never the instruments of any effort by Ming or Qing authorities to build merchant empires; nor could they hope to get mandarin or ideological support for any innovative efforts of their own. Eventually, they had to be content to become participants, even supporting agents, in the merchant empires that their counterparts from smaller states with state-backed organizations were able to build. In such indirect ways Chinese merchant communities contributed to the growth of the world economy. The extent of that contribution will have to be the subject of future study.

NOTES

1 Mark Elvin, *The Pattern of the Chinese Past* (Stanford, 1973), pt. 2 and chap. 14 (pt. 3).

2 Shiba Yoshinobu, "Sodai ni okeru Fukken shonin to sono shakai keizai teki haikei" (Fujian merchants in the Song and their socio-economic background), *Wada Hakase koki kinen Toyoshi ronso* (Studies in oriental history in honour of the seventieth birthday of Dr. Wada), (Tokyo, 1960).

3 Wang Gungwu, "The Nanhai Trade", *Journal of the Malayan Branch, Royal Asiatic Society*, 31/2 (1958): pp. 1–135; Edward Schafer, *The Empire of Min* (Tokyo, 1959).

4 Shiba Yoshinobu, *Sodai Shogyo shi kenkyu* (Commerce and society in Song China), (Tokyo, 1968); Mark Elvin has published a translation, Ann Arbor, 1970.

5 This is most marked in the voluminous gazetteers of Fujian, for example, those of Quanzhou and Zhangzhou prefectures and those of Haicheng, Jinjiang, and Longxi counties of the Qianlong period (late eighteenth century).

6 *Anhai Zhi* (Jinjiang, 1983); and the essays in *Yuegang yanjiu lunwenji* published by the Xiamen Branch of the Fujian Historical Society, 1983.

7 Kuwabara Jitsuzo, "On P'u Shou-keng", *Memoirs of the Research Department of the Toyo Bunko*, 2 (1928): pp. 1–79.

8 Zhou Daguan (Chou Ta-kuan), *Zhenla fengtuji*, trans. Paul Pelliot, in *Bulletin de l'Ecole Francaise d'Extrême-Orient*, 2 (1902): pp. 123–77; see Ch'en Cheng-hsiang, *Zhenla fengtuji yanjiu* (Hong Kong, 1975).

9 Ma Huan, *Ying-yai Sheng-lan: The Overall Survey of the Ocean's Shores* (1433), trans. and ed. J.V.G. Mills (Cambridge, 1970); Wang Gungwu, "Early Ming Relations with Southeast Asia: A Background Essay", in *The Chinese World Order*, ed. John K. Fairbank (Cambridge, Mass., 1968), pp. 34–62.

10 Zhu Weigan, *Fujian Shigao*, vol. 2 (Fuzhou, 1986), pt. 6, chap. 17.

11 Evelyn S. Rawski, *Agricultural Change and the Peasant Economy of South China* (Cambridge, Mass., 1972).

12 Zhang Weihua, *Mingdai Haiwai maoyi jianlun* (Shanghai, 1956); Lin Renchuan,

Mingmo Qingchu siren laishang maoyi (Shanghai, 1987); Ng Chin-keong, "Gentry-Merchants and Peasant-Peddlers — The Response of Southern Fukienese to Offshore Trading Opportunities, 1522–66", *Journal of Nanyang University* 7 (1973–74): pp. 161–175.

13 Evidence scattered throughout the Ming Veritable Records has been collected in two volumes: *Ming Shilu Zhong Zhi Dongnanya Shihliao*, ed. Zhao Lingyang *et al.*, (Hong Kong, 1968, 1976).

14 M.A.P. Meilink-Roelofsz, *Asian Trade and European Influence in the Indonesian Archipelago between 1500 and about 1630* (The Hague, 1962); Yanai Kenji, *Nagasaki* (Tokyo, 1966); Chingho A. Chen, *Historical Notes on Hôi-An (Faifo)* (Carbondale, 1974).

15 Ch'en T'ai-min, *Chung-Fei kuan-hsi yü Fei-lü-pin Hua-ch'iao* (Hong Kong, 1985), draws fully on the rich materials translated in E.H. Blair and J.A. Robertson, *The Philippine Islands, 1493–1898*, 55 vols. (Cleveland, 1903–07). An excellent brief account is Ch'en Ching-ho, *The Chinese Community in Sixteenth-Century Philippines* (Tokyo, 1968).

16 Susan Abeyasekere, *Jakarta: A History* (Singapore, 1987), chap. 1, pp. 3–47; L. Blussé, "Batavia, 1619–1740: The Rise and Fall of a Chinese Colonial Town," *Journal of Southeast Asian Studies* 12 (1981): pp. 159–178.

17 Chang Tien-tse, *Sino-Portuguese Trade from 1514 to 1644* (Leiden, 1934).

18 Kwan-wai So, *Japanese Piracy in Ming China during the Sixteenth Century* (East Lansing, 1975); also Chen Mouheng, *Mingdai Wokou Kaolue* (Beijing, 1957).

19 Zhang Xie, *Dongxi Yang Kao* (Cheng-chung reprint, Taipei, 1962), p. 174.

20 *Anhai Zhi*, pp. 144–152, outlines some notable references to this tragedy.

21 Alfonso Felix, Jr. (ed.), *The Chinese in the Philippines, 1570–1770* (Manila, 1966), I, using mainly materials in Blair and Robertson, *Philippine Islands.*

22 Edgar Wickberg, *The Chinese in Philippine Life, 1850–1898* (New Haven, 1965), pp. 3–41.

23 Temples, however, were essential. No thorough study is available on those in Manila, but Claudine Salmon and Denys Lombard, *Les Chinois de Jakarta: Temples et Vie Collective* (Paris, 1977), demonstrates how vital they were for Chinese communities overseas.

24 Felix, *Chinese in the Philippines;* Wickberg, *Chinese in Philippine Life.*

25 Kwan-wai So, *Japanese Piracy;* Yamawaki Teijiro, *Nukeni, sakoku jitai no mitsuboeki* (The Smuggling Trade during the Age of Isolation) (Tokyo, 1965).

26 Kawashima Genjiro, *Tokugawa shoki no Kaigai boekika* (Tokyo, 1917).

27 C.R. Boxer *The Great Ship from Amacon: Annals of Macao and the Old Japan Trade, 1555–1640* (Lisbon, 1959); C.R. Boxer, *Fidalgos in the Far East* (The Hague, 1948); George Bryan Souza, *The Survival of Empire: Portuguese Trade and Society in China and the South China Sea, 1630–1754* (New York, 1986).

28 J.E. Wills, Jr., "Maritime China from Wang Chih to Shih Lang: Themes in Peripheral History," in J.D. Spence and J.E. Wills, Jr. (eds.), *From Ming to Ch'ing: Conquest, Region, and Continuity in Seventeenth Century China* (New Haven, 1979).

29 Murakami Naojiro, *Boeki shijo no Hirado* (Hirado in commercial history) (Tokyo, 1917); Nagasaki shi yakusho, *Nagasaki shi shi: tsuko boeki hen, Toyo shokoku bo* (History of Nagasaki City: Trade and Transport, Volume on Eastern Ocean) (Nagasaki, 1938).

30 *Kai hentai* (Changing Conditions of Chinese and Barbarians), Toyo Bunko series no. 15, vol. 1 (Tokyo, 1958); Yamawaki Teijiro, *Nagasaki no Tojin boeki* (The Chinese Trade of Nagasaki) (Tokyo, 1964).

31 Yamamoto Noritsuna, *Nagasaki Tojin Yashiki* (The Chinese Quarter of Nagasaki) (Tokyo, 1983), pp. 146–93.

32 Yamawaki, *Nagasaki no Tojin boeki.*

33 The literature on Zheng Chenggong in now vast; see two recent collections published in China, especially *Zheng Chenggong yanjiu lunwenxuan, Xuji* (Fuzhou, 1984). On the Chinese quarter, see Yamamoto, *Nagasaki Tojin Yashiki*, pp. 197–207.

34 Nakamura Tadashi and Nakada Yasunao (eds.), *Kiyo Gundan* (Various Talks on Nagasaki) (Tokyo, 1974), pp. 263–303.

35 Rawski, *Agricultural Change*; Zhu Weigan, *Fujian Shigao*, vol. 2.

36 Ng Chin-keong, *Trade and Society: The Amoy Network on the China Coast 1683–1735* (Singapore, 1983); Tien Ju-kang, "Causes of the Decline in China's Overseas Trade between the Fifteenth and Eighteenth Centuries", *Papers on Far Eastern History* 25 (1982): pp. 31–44.

CHAPTER 5

Song-Yuan-Ming Relations with Southeast Asia: Some Comparisons

CHINESE RELATIONS WITH SOUTHEAST Asia can be traced back some 2,000 years. During this long period, it would appear that changes in the nature of relations with the region were minimal and, when there were changes, they occurred so gradually that they have rarely been considered significant. But there were times when the changes were striking. The last decades of the Southern Song, the Mongol Yuan and the early decades of the Ming formed such a period. The following is an attempt to explain the changes and assess their importance.

The major relevant events during the 200 years between the second half of the thirteenth century and the first half of the fifteenth century are well enough known. An outline of a few of them, however, will be useful to illustrate the main changes in China-Southeast Asian relations during these two centuries. The question to begin with is what did Southeast Asia look like to the Southern Song, the Yuan and the early Ming rulers? The question of perspective is important. Southeast Asia probably looked different from Hangzhou, the Southern Song capital, as compared with the view from Peking during the Yuan and that from Nanking during the early Ming. This may be called "the imperial view", since one would expect such a view from the imperial capital and one might also expect that view to change when the location of the capital was shifted. But there were also other important perspectives, for example, from different key trading cities and ports from which relations of any kind were conducted. Perhaps the best example of these was the view from Quanzhou during the Southern Song and the Yuan.

Song Relations with Southeast Asia

We could begin with the point of view of the compiler of *Zhu Fan Zhi* at the beginning of the thirteenth century. It is assumed that the text of the work as we have it today has not been unduly changed and does represent what the various *fan*-states and cities looked like to Zhao Rugua and all those who used this important work for the next 200 years. What is immediately clear is that the compiler, holding office at Quanzhou, starts out with a maritime and commercial perspective. Therefore, the fact that he opens with a brief description of Jiaozhi (North Vietnam today) is not for the conventional reason that Vietnam was the southern kingdom with the closest historical connection with China, but because, as he puts it,

> Each year it sends tribute, but the country does not trade [with the Song]. It is listed first here only because one starts with the nearest one to us.

He then proceeds quickly to Champa, of which he provides a much more detailed account. After Champa, the work follows the Indo-China coast down to Cambodia and the Malay peninsula and also covers in some detail key parts of Sumatra and Java. In between, however, he inserts a brief reference to Pagan (Burma), which is included probably because he thought Pagan had sent a tribute mission together with Srivijaya (Sumatra) and Dashi (Arabia) in the year 1004 AD. The reference seems to have come from an earlier work, the *Lingwai daida* (twelfth century), so Chao Ju-kua probably did know that Pagan was not near the various maritime states he had mentioned but was, as clearly stated in the *Lingwai daida*, reached by going south from the kingdom of Dali (modern Yunnan). He would also have known that the Southern Song had no official contact with Dali and the only trade with that kingdom was conducted overland through western Kwangsi and had nothing whatsoever to do with Quanzhou.

This puzzling reference to Pagan in *Zhu Fan Zhi* is mentioned not to stress the fact that Zhao Rugua had not travelled overseas himself and thus had a poor idea of the Southeast Asian region, but to draw attention to the residual "imperial view" of the Northern Song which survived in Southern Song works like the *Lingwai daida*, which Zhao Rugua used, and which is also found elsewhere in the *Zhu Fan Zhi*. It is an interesting contrast that he bypassed Vietnam for not being a trading state but included Pagan when there was no mention of even a possibility of a trading connection. This reminds us that the "imperial view" was understandably never very far away from a Chinese official's mind even when he expressly says he was concentrating on trading relations and indeed uses half his book to describe foreign commercial products.

The perspective from Quanzhou clearly puts the emphasis on the South China Sea-Indian Ocean littoral states. After Java-Sumatra, the twenty or so states and ports of India, the Middle East and East Africa are mentioned. And this reflects the dominance of Muslim traders of Arab-Persian and Indian origins in the trading relations that China had with Southeast Asia during this period. Zhao Rugua claimed to have obtained much information about foreign countries from the traders at Quanzhou. Clearly his main informants were those from India and West Asia. Indeed, even the eastern extension of this trade, which reached Brunei and the Philippines, seems to have been described to him by the same traders. Significantly, that eastern trade did not come directly to Quanzhou but indirectly via Champa, another confirmation that it had been opened up from western Southeast Asia (Champa and Java-Sumatra) via western Borneo and not by the Fujian traders themselves.

Also of some interest is the way Zhao Rugua added Silla (Korea) and Woguo (Japan) at the very end of his list. According to convention, these two would have appeared first in Chinese accounts of foreign countries. But he not only puts them last but calls them by somewhat anachronistic names: Silla had been conquered by Gaoli (Korea) nearly 300 years earlier and Jih-pen had become the common name for Japan even earlier than that. Again, it would appear that he used Silla and Woguo because these were still employed as the names for Korea and Japan in Arabic.

In short, what we seem to have is a picture of Southeast Asia seen from the perspective of Chinese traders at Quanzhou who depended on the West Asian merchants for their information, a far cry from the "imperial" view during the Song. Indeed, we may well ask if there was an imperial view of Southeast Asia from Hangzhou in the thirteenth century. We simply do not have the sources to piece together such a view for the reigns of the last Southern Song emperors, even for the long reign of Lizong (1224–64). But it is unlikely that that view would coincide with that of Zhao Rugua or Quanzhou. Much more likely was a perspective which placed the greatest emphasis on relations with the Mongols, whom the Song had tried to use to destroy the Jurchen Jin dynasty. These former allies soon turned out to be far more dangerous enemies than the Jurchens had ever been. Also, more weight would have been given to trading relations with states like Korea and Japan whose traders came directly to the Hangzhou region and whose proximity to North China would have had political importance as well. Similarly, overland trading relations with the Chinese in the north and various non-Han tribal states in the west and northwest of Sichuan, and even those bordering on the kingdoms of Dali and Annan (Vietnam), would have been part of an imperial view. Precisely how that view would include Southeast Asia is not clear. It would be reasonable to expect that Southeast Asia had no political significance in that imperial perspective, but was merely a region through which the Muslim traders came and whose rich natural products the Muslim traders brought to China and where Chinese goods found a good market. That is to say, the region's trade with China was a rich source of revenue for the Southern Song government and thus the region really impinged on the economic rather than the political consciousness of the officials at Hangzhou.

How peculiar was this to the last decades of the Southern Song? After all, the Tang, the southern kingdoms of Min and Nan Han during the Five Dynasties period, and even the Northern Song, had all acknowledged the economic benefits of Southeast Asian trade. The major differences, at the height of Tang and Northern Song, were twofold. Firstly, there were regular "diplomatic" relations through tributary missions, even though many of the missions were sent for largely commercial reasons. The Southern Song seemed to have admitted it did not have the power to command any kind of tributary mission to come to Hangzhou. Secondly, the Tang did control key parts of Vietnam as its "protectorate" and managed to maintain an active diplomatic and military role on the Yunnan-Sichuan border, and even fought the Nan Zhao kingdom over the control of Vietnam during the ninth century. But the Tang had been weakening since the middle of the eighth century and its imperial view of the south had become increasingly rhetorical by the ninth century. When the dynasty fell and the Vietnamese fought successfully for their independence, a major change had already occurred in China's relations with the south. But it took the Northern Song more than a century to accept that the change (i.e., Vietnam's independence) was not a temporary one.

No less important was the increasing distance between imperial China and the southwest region, especially Yunnan, which the kingdom of Dali had taken over from the last rulers of Nan Zhao. By the eleventh century, the relationship here was also mainly commercial. The Song abandoned the diplomatic and military roles of the Tang in the face of far greater problems in North China (within the Great

Wall) than the Tang had to deal with. And with further defeats in North China and the fall of Kaifeng, the Southern Song was simply in no position to support even the attenuated imperial view of the Northern Song. From the middle of the twelfth century, it was defensively seeking to survive and Southeast Asia's main claim to attention rested with the trading profits which the Hangzhou government could count on. This position may be compared to that faced by the Nan Han and the Min kingdoms in South China during the tenth century but neither of those could be said to have had any real claims to having had an imperial view. Southern Song did and therefore its perspective on Southeast Asia was peculiar to an imperial power which had its back increasingly to the wall and which saw Southeast Asia as being useful only for its economic benefits.

Dali and Vietnam were directly responsible for the first change the Mongols made to the history of relations between China and Southeast Asia. This occurred even before their conquest of the Southern Song. In 1253–57, the Mongols made their first move to outflank the Song armies fighting in Sichuan, and elsewhere in North-Central China, by marching through Eastern Tibet just west of Sichuan, crossing the Jinsha River (upper reaches of the Yangtse) into Yunnan, and conquering the kingdom of Dali. They then consolidated their control over the various tribal principalities and incorporated most of Yunnan as prefectures and counties in a new province. The move also brought the Mongols to the borders of Vietnam and the borders of the Southern Song provinces of Tongzhuan and Guangnan West. Although these conquests did not lead immediately to total conquest by the Mongols as the Southern Song survived for another twenty years, the consequences for Chinese relations with Southeast Asia were profound. Yunnan became permanently part of the Chinese empire and direct control of Yunnan laid the foundation for a new kind of political and economic relationship with China's overland neighbours in modern Southeast Asia.

Yuan Relations with Southeast Asia

The Mongols ruled over South China for 92 years after 1276 (and over Yunnan for over 130 years). There were several obvious differences between the Yuan dynasty and its predecessors where Southeast Asia was concerned. Control of Yunnan was one. The resumption of efforts to conquer Vietnam (not attempted by the Song since the mid-eleventh century) was another. Even more significant were the wars fought along the whole stretch of the land borders between Yunnan and the various kinds of Tai peoples (in modern Laos, Burma and Thailand) and the Burmans. There was also the exceptional attempt to conquer Champa, the key trading state for the maritime relations between China and the littoral states of the South China Sea. Control of the Song navy enabled the Mongols to contemplate military conquests overseas and led to the expeditions against Champa, Japan and Java. Although none of them was successful, the one against Java in 1293 introduced a Chinese imperial naval force into Southeast Asia, something the region had not seen since the early seventh century.

But what, if anything, did these obvious changes do to Yuan China's view of Southeast Asia? There were three major works of the Yuan period that dealt directly with Southeast Asia and a large part of two of them have survived: the *Zhenla fengtu zhi* of Zhou Daguan (early fourteenth century) and Wang Dayuan's *Daoyi zhilue* (mid-fourteenth century). Only fragments of the third, the earliest work, the *Dade Nanhai lu* by Chen Dazhen (late thirteenth century) have survived but the other two provide enough information for a few interesting comparisons to be made.

Zhou Daguan's work is invaluable for the study of thirteenth-century Angkor and Khmer society, and it is a remarkable work of ethnography and travel reporting. But what is of particular concern to us is that he was part of an official mission. There were several earlier ones to Champa and another to Siam at about the same time. His book provides a very detailed picture of what a mission left in a foreign country for a year was able to do. What is more, it confirms that the Yuan did have an imperial view of the region in a way the bare official records fail to convey. Such an imperial view would include an interest in details of state and society well beyond what was needed for commercial purposes. Indeed, at least half the observations Zhou Daguan made could have had political, diplomatic and military significance. Furthermore, it also reminds us of how imperfect official records were for the Yuan, since Zhou Daguan's mission of 1296–97 does not seem to have been recorded in the Yuan archives and we would have no knowledge of this mission at all were it not for his book.

The second work was based on personal experiences. Wang Dayuan used Quanzhou as his base for five years when he made a series of voyages that took him through Southeast Asia to the Indian Ocean ports, and then, a few years later, for another three years during which he travelled mainly in Southeast Asia. This was probably in the 1330s and the author of one of the prefaces to his book noted that Chinese traders who travelled in Southeast Asia after the Mongol expeditions to Java in 1293 were treated with respect and therefore were able to learn a great deal about the region. The other preface also stressed the point that Wang Dayuan made himself throughout the book, that he only wrote about what he actually saw. There are two notable points about this private travel record. First, it was concerned far less with countries and governments than with ports, commercial products and local customs. Second, he began with the eastern archipelago (including Taiwan and the Philippines) and devoted slightly more than half his book to Southeast Asia. The book is totally devoid of the West Asian flavour found in Zhao Rugua's book. On the other hand, because Wang Dayuan had only his own commercial interests in mind, his observations on each place he visited were rather flat and there is little evidence that he was aware of the relative importance of the ports and countries described. Two striking exceptions are the references to Cambodia and Java. He was clearly impressed by what he saw of Angkor and by the power and wealth, and law and order, of the Majapahit empire. But of the latter, whereas he noted that the Yuan had sent a mission there and influenced the Javanese to be respectful towards China, he failed to note that the expedition had been a failure. He even got the mission's date wrong by over four years. Nevertheless, Wang Dayuan's freedom to travel and his record of the more than 100 places described or mentioned suggest that there might have been something of a "Pax Mongolica" for Muslim and Chinese traders in Southeast Asia and the Indian Ocean comparable to that in North-Central West Asia.

Neither of the two books mentioned above is part of the official record. The official sources that have survived show that the perspective from Quanzhou, whether seen through West Asian eyes (as in *Zhu Fan Zhi*) or Chinese eyes (as in *Daoyi zhilue*), did not coincide with the newly emerging imperial view which even officials at Zhaozhou had come to embrace in the fourteenth century. This is admirably summed up in the postscript (*houxa*) to Wang Dayuan's book, as follows:

> Imperial Yuan consolidated its authority to reach out to the most distant lands. Its physical extent has never been heard of in the past. The several tens of thousands of countries (*guo*) among the island barbarians (*yi*) across the seas all offer tribute of gifts to fulfil their loyal duty. They come scaling the mountains and crossing the oceans

to trade. As for China's traders who go forth among the different courts and various territories, they travel as if between east and west prefectures [of China].

The imperial view was expressed in universalist terms, but these terms were also the conventional ones used at the beginning of each great dynasty, as they had been during the first decades of the Tang and the Northern Song. That they were absent during the last decades of the Southern Song was understandable. Rulers who were beleaguered by end-of-dynasty problems were in no position to employ rhetoric which was blatantly meaningless and hollow. Thus the return of the imperial view under Kublai Khan (the emperor Khubilai) was not in itself significant. What was really new where Southeast Asia was concerned was the political situation. The powerful Mongol armies in South China had none of the fears of enemies at the northern borders that every Han Chinese dynasty had had. They were therefore more free to advance militarily into Southeast Asia than any other previous dynasty. Their alliance with West Asian Muslims in North-Central Asia was now extended to Muslim traders linking Quanzhou with the whole of maritime Asia. And, in addition, they could also use the naval power built up by the Southern Song if they wanted to. Thus, for nearly a century, there was gathered in South China ports more military power that could be employed to realize the imperial vision of that region than Southeast Asia had ever known.

Furthermore, it was an imperial view uninhibited by Confucian reservations about the place and role of merchants. It was a view that endorsed the commercial perspectives with no difficulty at all. The Quanzhou perspective, in other words, was no longer an alternative and more realistic view, but an essential part of this new imperial view which the Monguls had forged together by using their own faith in their greatness to reinvigorate the inspiring rhetoric of the Han-Tang-Song empires. By so doing, it removed the old Chinese reluctance to advance aggressively southwards and thus opened Southeast Asia to a new naked power which could be used in support of peaceful trade dominated by the friends of the Mongol Yuan house.

If that power had been solely directed seawards, it would have lacked conviction with a China that had always been a continental power. But there was an overland factor that made this imperial view more real for Southeast Asia. This was the Mongol march through

Eastern Tibet (their influence on the Tibetans is yet another story) into Yunnan. The conquest of the Dali kingdom opened up that whole area for Chinese settlement, for Mongol armies to garrison, and for new diplomatic and military initiatives to be taken overland with the land-locked states of Southeast Asia. And these gains were permanent and totally changed the nature of Chinese-Southeast Asian relations overland via Yunnan till the present day. Hereafter, there would not only be an imperial view that could be re-stated at the beginning of a new and powerful dynasty but, in addition, a continuous Kunming view of overland Southeast Asia that would be more stable and firm than any maritime view from Quanzhou and Guangzhou (and later, Shanghai and Amoy) could ever be.

Ming Relations with Southeast Asia

By the end of the Yuan dynasty, an equilibrium had been achieved in China-Southeast Asian relations. The Mongols, after some spectacular successes and failures in the south during the last decades of the thirteenth century, had settled down to receiving tribute from the region in the context of a profitable trade. Indeed, the emphasis had clearly shifted from political domination to commercial concern and Wang Dayuan's work probably depicts the harmony and stability that existed for foreign and Chinese merchants accurately.

Thus, when that peace in the south was broken by the fall of the Yuan after decades of rebellion and fierce fighting in Central China, the countries and traders in Southeast Asia must have wondered what kind of imperial view would replace that of the Yuan. As one would expect, the main rhetoric of a newly empowered dynasty was not very different from that of its predecessor. The Ming founder, the emperor Hung-wu, was particularly concerned about the lessons to be learnt from the Yuan and was quick to turn to the histories of the Han, Tang and Song for models of proper Chinese rule which had to be restored. There was no doubt that the imperial view, the claims and the rhetoric, had to be reaffirmed. But where Southeast Asia was concerned, the Mongols had not hesitated to use force. Conquering the kingdom of Dali in Yunnan, invading Vietnam, Burma, the Shan and Tai states, Champa and even Java, were all done to ensure that Yuan authority was feared and respected. Afterwards, no aggressiveness was necessary, because the message it had brought had been understood. Maritime trade for friendly foreign merchants on the Chinese coast could thereafter be protected. But there was a feature of this private trade which did not appeal to Hung-wu and some of his orthodox Confucian advisers. They favoured the restoration of tributary relations, but were anxious about the consequences of mixing these relations with uncontrolled foreign trade. Having had to fight many groups of maritime traders off the coasts of Jiangsu and Zhejiang, they came to believe that unfettered private trade had led to unrest and insecurity along the coastal frontiers of the new empire.

The policies of the Mongols towards their Southeast Asian neighbours were predicated upon having safe northern frontiers. The Yuan could afford to threaten these southern rulers and seek to extend its power as far as was feasible. The Ming founder had a position which was exactly the reverse. As with so many Chinese dynasties, there was danger from the north. He needed to secure his southern and coastal frontiers so that he could concentrate on pacifying the great Mongol-Turk confederations and defending the long border between Western Manchuria and Eastern Tibet. This was the strategic position that underlined his imperial view of Southeast Asia. It was a view drawn from the study of Han, Tang and Song historical experiences. And he went a long way to revive the grand language and ancient ceremonies that those earlier dynasties had used for dealing with tribute-bearing missions from vassal-states. But he was not content with that because he was aware that conditions in his time were markedly different from those earlier on. Unlike the Han, Tang and Song founders, he inherited a South China that was already populous and trade-oriented and threatened by serious problems of coastal defence. He also inherited an independent neighbour in Vietnam, now stronger and even more determined to defend its independence after its dangerous encounters with the Mongols. Furthermore, he inherited the problems of the new province of Yunnan, with its numerous minorities and the complex administrative and political relationships with the various tribal principalities. This province had become strategically vital to his empire because he could not forget how vulnerable the Southern Song had become when the Mongols seized Yunnan by going south from Eastern Tibet. Nor could he escape the ramifications of having to deal with a region closely linked with mainland Southeast Asia and thus with neighbours now sharing a long border with the Ming empire.

Thus, a new imperial view was evolving in the Ming capital at Nanking. It was one which sought to stress that it was restoring tradition and normalcy after a century of aberration under the Mongol Yuan. The key features of this normalcy were the use of established conventional rhetoric and the restoration of proper rituals. These included personalizing the relationship between rulers through tributary presentation and the emperor's gifts in return; the enfeoffment of foreign kings and chiefs and even gifts of the Ming calendar. The rituals were elaborate but did not demand actual submission to imperial control as the Yuan had insisted upon. Degrees of symbolic submission were worked out in detail, but even these took account of what the Ming court thought were acceptable to the rulers receiving and sending envoys. All these went beyond Han, Tang and Song practice in Southeast Asia. Probably the most striking was the registration of the rivers and mountains of Vietnam and Champa (together with those of Korea) and the practice of sacrificing to their spirits together with those of rivers and mountains within China. This practice was later extended further south in Southeast Asia and even westwards to South Asia. Although merely symbolic and introduced for the apparently benevolent reason of wishing to ensure longevity and security for the kings and prosperity for their lands forever, the registration and the sacrifices did imply a measure of cosmic (and imperial) responsibility over these lands which had never been so clearly defined before.

This new imperial view of Southeast Asia was different from the Yuan in that there was no display of force, no demand for submission, no attempt even to assert indirect control. Nor was there any encouragement of private maritime trade. On the contrary, the Ming founder wanted to control all trade officially by placing it under the revised tributary system. The imperial view emphasized the symbolic acknowledgement of China's cosmological centrality and the legitimacy of the Ming founder's succession to the authority of the great dynasties of China.

Nevertheless, behind this view was a reality in Southeast Asia which could not be disguised in the rhetoric of harmony and prosperity. There was continual fighting between Vietnam and Champa; there was considerable unrest among the tribal principalities bordering on Yunnan; and there were political upheavals among the countries in the region of the Java Sea and the Straits of Malacca. The emperor Hung-wu soon discovered that he had to be involved in the first and the second of these and that his empire would feel the ramifications of the third. And indeed, for the rest of the Ming period, Southeast Asia posed at least four separate problems which affected the Ming imperial view of the region. These are as follows:

1. The relations between Vietnam and Champa, ending in the conquest of Champa by the former and developing into hostile relations with Cambodia and rivalry later on with Thailand. Although these concerned Vietnam's own foreign relations, how the Ming emperors viewed these developments is a measure of their imperial view of Southeast Asia.

2. The special problem of China's overland relations with Vietnam. This is related to the above, but focuses on the land frontiers between the two as well as Vietnam's policies towards tribal territories to its west and to China's south. The key historical fact underlying this special problem was the failure of the Ming to absorb Vietnam into the empire early in the fifteenth century, an event of great significance to the history of mainland Southeast Asia.

3. The maritime connection, both naval and commercial, involving the littoral states of the South China Sea, from Luzon in the Philippines clockwise to Thailand and the Champa ports, but also going beyond the Malacca Straits and, for a short period, including various states of the Indian Ocean as far west as Arabia and East Africa. This connection can be traced back to the Arab-Persian and Indian traders of the Southern Song and Yuan periods, but following the Cheng Ho expeditions of 1405–33, it was more and more dominated by the Chinese who had become deeply involved in trading directly with the increasingly prosperous kingdoms of Southeast Asia itself and less interested in the trade of the Indian Ocean. It was not until the sixteenth century that the Europeans began to bring Indian Ocean commercial needs to the China coast again.

4. The southwestern tribal states in modern Burma, Laos and the province of Yunnan to which the Ming extended its policy of *t'u-ssu* (local commissions or tribal principalities). This was a legacy of the Yuan, but one new development which started just before the Ming was founded was significant. In addition to the southward-expanding Vietnamese and Burmans, some of the ancestors of the modern Thais had also been moving south. The kingdom of Ayuthia founded in 1350 down the Menan Valley and

combining the Hsien (Syam or Sukhothai) of the north with the ancient state Lohu (Lopburi) became Xianlo in Chinese records. Its special relations with Ming China provided something of a link between the maritime and overland concerns of the Ming which were gradually to unfold.

The outline of the Ming imperial view of Southeast Asia above underscores the fact that the active tributary policies adopted by emperor Hung-wu and the naval expeditions ordered by his son, emperor Yung-lo, left little room for any other perspective of the region. Indeed, one might expect that the view from Guangzhou. (Canton) or from Quanzhou was different but, unlike with the Southern Song *Zhu Fan Zhi* and the Yuan *Daoyi zhilue* there were no early Ming writings which reflect the perspective from one of its great port-cities in the south. On the contrary, all records pertaining to Southeast Asia for the first sixty years of the Ming were either official or the writings of those who had accompanied Cheng Ho on some of his voyages. The most valuable was clearly the material from the archives which was included in the *Veritable Records* of the first two reigns and other imperial collections. But perhaps more interesting for commercial and naval information were the surviving works arising from the Cheng Ho expeditions, the *Yingyai Shenglan* of Ma Huan, the *Xingcha Shenglan* of Fei Xin, the *Xiyang fanguo zhi* of Gong Zhen. (One might add some of the later derivations of the sixteenth century, like the *Xiyang chaogong dianhi* of Huang Shengtseng, and the relevant materials collected in *Chouhai tubian* of Zheng Rozeng.) None of them, as one might expect, reflects any other perspective than that of the official one — the imperial view from Nanking and the Yangtse delta (until the capital moved to Peking in 1421). And it was not until the seventeenth century that we once again find a work that clearly reflects a local perspective, that of South China. This is Chang Xie's *Dongxiyang kao* and it reflects the various policy changes during the second half of the sixteenth century when private maritime trade reasserted itself. This occurred after the Portuguese had arrived off the coast of South China and after the raids of Japanese and Chinese pirates had rendered the earlier policy which prohibited trade unpopular and totally unrealistic. And then, for the first time in Ming writings, we find a view of Southeast Asia which did not simply reproduce the official line stipulating the need for all relations to be conducted via the tributary system.

Conclusion

It is obvious that the flurry of activities involving Southeast Asia during the first sixty years of the Ming was a sharp contrast to the sixty years of the Yuan after the death of Kublai Khan. Similarly, the forty years from Kublai Khan's involvement in Yunnan to his expedition to Java was totally different from the first forty years of the Southern Song. Did these differences merely represent the ups and downs of dynastic cycles? They seem to have gone beyond that and the Mongols and emperor Hung-wu respectively contributed permanent features to the China-Southeast Asia relationship which had lasting consequences. They both revived an imperial view of Southeast Asia but in new and different ways. The Mongols stressed the power elements in imperial rhetoric by successive use of force. Their incorporation of Yunnan within the imperial boundaries totally changed the shape of Southeast Asia in the eyes of future Chinese emperors. But their imperial view remained one that was tolerant of independent commercial developments, even of dominance of the China-Southeast Asian trading connection by West Asian Muslim merchants. It is a grander and more pluralist imperial view that owed its cosmopolitan nature to its strong military base and the Mongols exuded the confidence of people who had conquered half of the world. In contrast, the Ming house of Central Chinese peasant origins pulled back from such a grandiose perspective and sought only a Chinese imperial view. It was not only narrower in its sinocentric starting point. It was even narrower than the imperial perspective of the Tang and the Song in that it was hostile to any form of private relationship between Chinese and foreigners, and that included maritime trade outside the tributary system. Thus the Ming imperial view of Southeast Asia was one which sought direct control and restricted foreign travel. This view also separated overseas relations from overland ones and thus saw Southeast Asia as essentially two unrelated sub-regions, with a loose link through a special relationship with Vietnam.

Let me conclude with the most distinctive difference in imperial view between the Ming and the Yuan. This lies in the Ming founder's explicit policy of not attacking countries across the seas.[1] This striking new feature of an entirely defensive policy towards countries to the south and east cannot be over-emphasized. It not only rejected the policy of Kublai Khan, but was actually raised to a major doctrine in Ming dynastic policy. Even more significant was the fact that it was first ennunciated in 1371 and then included in the *Tsu-hsün Lu* (Ancestral Injunctions) promulgated in 1373 and, after revisions, reaffirmed in detail in the final version of the *Huang Ming Tsu-hsün* towards the end of the Ming founder's reign. It was one of the few basic policies from which Hung-wu never wavered. Its significance for China-Southeast Asia relations is obvious. Although there are echoes of similar sentiments made by Tang and Song rulers about not conquering territories which are useless to China, it was in this context an extraordinary declaration of policy that deserves to be quoted in full. The key passage is found in the 1373 version of the instructions to his descendants (the final version of about 1395 lists seven more countries in Southeast Asia: Cambodia, Samudra-Pasai, Java, Pahang, Pai-hua in West Java, Srivijaya and Brunei):

> The overseas foreign countries like An-nan [Vietnam], Champa, Korea, Siam, Liu-ch'iu [the Ryukyus islands], the [countries of the] Western Oceans [South India] and Eastern Oceans [Japan] and the various small countries of the southern *man* [barbarians] are separated from us by mountains and seas and far away in a corner. Their lands would not produce enough for us to maintain them; their peoples would not usefully serve us if incorporated [into the empire]. If they were so unrealistic as to disturb our borders, it would be unfortunate for them. If they gave us no trouble and we moved troops to fight them unnecessarily, it would be unfortunate for us. I am concerned that future generations might abuse China's wealth and power and covet the military glories of the moment to send armies into the field without reason and cause a loss of life. May they be sharply reminded that this is forbidden. As for the *hu* and *jung* barbarians who threaten China in the north and west, they are always a danger along our frontiers. Good generals must be picked and soldiers trained to prepare carefully against them.

Note

1 See also Chapter 3 of this book "Ming Foreign Relations: Southeast Asia", pp. 50–52,

CHAPTER 6

"Public" and "Private" Overseas Trade in Chinese History

CHINA'S OVERSEAS TRADE WITH South and Southeast Asia began under imperial patronage if we are to believe the records of the Former Han dynasty (206 BC–9 AD). It seems to have been a special interest of the emperor's inner court and was soon to appear as a function of the inter-ruler relations which historians have called the tributary system. Such a picture was further enlarged when the official historians began to record all foreign relations and gave much more emphasis to the tributary aspects of these relations without clear reference to their connections with trade.

Largely because of this lack of clarity, it has been easy to assume that, since trade was one of the functions of tribute, tribute was mainly disguised trade. This, however, does not mean that there was no trade before there was tribute, nor that there was little other trade than that disguised as tribute. On the contrary, there was far more trade outside the tributary system than within it.[1] This was certainly the experience of the Europeans on the China Coast after the sixteenth century, and there is considerable evidence to show how this happened in the seventeenth and eighteenth centuries, the last two centuries when the tributary system could still be said to have been functioning. Much more difficult have been our efforts to calculate the nature and extent of trade before the sixteenth century.

Before we begin, we must dispose of the myth that there was no demand for maritime trade in China. This myth has been fostered by Chinese officialdom and perpetuated in official writings. It has done a great deal to prevent historians from understanding the various kinds of demands which underlay foreign trade for the Chinese. We must also guard against the common view that China never changed. According to this view, Confucian officials decried trade during the Han dynasty and this remained true of all Confucian officials throughout the imperial period. Hence the fact that imperial bureaucrats confirmed from time to time that China did not need maritime trade was often taken to mean that there was really no demand for such trade.

In order to help us examine this demand and have some idea of the nature of the trade, it is helpful for us to recognize two levels of maritime trade. At one level, it was carried out directly by the emperor's court or by the government and, at the other, it was locally encouraged with or without the knowledge of the court. The first could be described as a "public" and the second as "private" trade.

Let me point to some example which would justify the distinction. For example, the earliest reference in the *Han Shu* clearly relates to a "public" trade which palace eunuchs handled by "the buying of bright pearls, opaque glass, rare stones and strange objects, taking with them gold and various fine silks to offer in exchange for them".[2] Similarly, with the opening of South China from the Wu kingdom (220–280 AD) to the Southern Dynasties (420–589 AD), there were considerably more reports of missions bringing tribute goods from South and Southeast Asia. For this period, there have been recorderd at least 116 missions. In other words there was an average of one mission every three years for nearly 370 years. Or, if we take only the Southern Dynasties period of 170 years there was an average of one mission every $1^1/_2$ years.[3] There was obviously a strong element of "public" trade in these missions, although the convention was to list the goods which came as gifts to the Chinese emperors. It is important to note that most of the gifts had something to do with the rise of Buddhism in Southeast Asia and the growing interest in that religion throughout South China during these centuries. That this was a form of "public" trade is clear if a comparison is made with the objects of Buddhist worship, the spices and the drugs needed for the monasteries and temples in China. For the "private" trade, it was already the practice for port officials and local traders to purchase from and sell to foreign merchants who arrived at the China coast.[4]

This distinction was equally marked for the following Sui-Tang (589–906) and Five Dynasties (907–959) periods. In fact, the trade became obviously "private" with a subsidiary "public" sector to satisfy the demands at the northern capitals of Ch'ang-an and Lo-yang. While there are no trade figures for comparison, the importance of the Bureau of Shipping Trade and the large number of anecdotes about foreign traders, especially Persian, Arab and Indians for these centuries, make it clear that it was "private" trade which kept the ports going and supplied the regional demand for medicines and condiments.[5]

With the Song (960–1276) and the Mongol Yuan (1276–1368) dynasties, "private" trade became even more dominant. In fact, for long periods of the twelfth, thirteenth and fourteenth centuries, there was nothing much that could be associated with "public" trade at all.[6] The distinction is nevertheless important because of the way these latter centuries contrast with the first few decades of the Ming dynasty (1368–1644). The Ming founder's decision to enforce strict control over overseas travel led him to encourage "public" trade for the prestige and other benefits this had for the court. This posed problems both to the private traders whose movements were restricted and to the central government where Confucian officialdom was quite unprepared to commit public funds for such a trade unless it was dressed in appropriate ways.[7]

This leads me to show how this distinction between "public" and "private" trade is meaningful to help us explain some of the fluctuations in trading patterns. For example, because of the attitude of Confucian bureaucrats towards trade in general and foreign trade in particular, it is possible to link trading developments to the power of Confucians at the court, the degree of central control over coastal affairs, the changing ideology of Confucianism itself and the changing structure of the Confucian bureaucratic elite.

Let me begin with the proposition that "public" trade was rarely developed because Confucian practice was expected to stand in opposition to the extravagance of the emperors, their favourites and their eunuchs. And therefore maritime trade with South and Southeast Asia was particularly vulnerable because it was mainly in luxury goods.

Parallel to this proposition is one that points to the growth of the "private" trade at the ports and local and provincial centres nearby, and ultimately also at the metropolitan capitals themselves. This was related to the fact that local officials or central officials posted far from the capital did not have to play strictly Confucian roles outside of the ceremonial affairs of their office. Such officials could, therefore, participate in maritime trade directly or indirectly as long as they maintained the minimum of care and decorum.

To examine the two propositions, I suggest that a number of comparisons be made of different periods of Chinese history up to the eighteenth century. The following four periods are meaningful for the reasons I shall explain below:

1. Before the fifth century AD;
2. Fifth to eighth centuries;
3. Ninth to fourteenth centuries;
4. Fourteenth (after 1368) to eighteenth centuries.

As for the basis of comparisons useful to this study, the following may be made:

a. Demand for maritime trade. This was closely related to the growth of population along the coasts, the rise of markets and urban areas and the intensification of internal trade. It depended on improvements in land, river and coastal communications and also on consumer sophistication leading to an interest in exotic and luxury goods. With increasing sophistication, what might appear luxuries of one period would have become necessities of the next.

b. Surplus wealth for investment and risk-taking. This depended initially on the productivity of the countryside, on new crops, new techniques of drainage and irrigation and new lands being brought under cultivation. The rise of productivity over the increase in population might be indicated by the use of surplus wealth in commerce and industry. Ultimately, investment and risk-taking depended on opportunities and these varied from one area to another, but the opportunities should improve from period to period.

c. Credit and financial institutions. This was a much later development and certainly depended on the first two: a considerable demand for trade and a sizable surplus wealth for this trade to be profitable on a large scale and over a long period of time. Initially, it was a question of reliable money; later, it depended on the development from coinage to various kinds of drafts and promissory notes and more flexible forms of currency. How secure the credit and financial institutions were at each period and in each place depended on specific political and economic conditions.

d. Technological advances. This underlay all internal communications and farming and industrial techniques, but particularly relevant was the question of shipping and sailing technology. As all technical advances are interdependent and progressive, each stage of development has to be preceded by necessary advances in an earlier period. It is important to be reminded that the needs of war have always been a factor in technological advances and that shipping and sailing technique are closely linked with military needs.

e. Political stability. The relative dangers of internal rebellions and external invasions also varied from period to period and area to area. As external dangers on the Chinese land frontiers far surpassed those on the sea frontiers, it was the dangers from within which were particularly important where maritime trade was concerned. Only when dynastic changes were determined by external attacks were external events relevant.

f. Confucian attitudes. There are two aspects relevant to overseas trade: the attitudes towards trade and their importance in the social fabric and the imperial economy and the attitudes towards the role of government and bureaucrats in trade. Both underwent little change in theory but were sufficiently elastic in practice for very different policies to emerge from time to time.

With these six main factors in mind, let me return to the four periods mentioned earlier and examine the factors in terms of developments in maritime trade for each period.

1. PERIOD I — BEFORE THE FIFTH CENTURY AD

Although there had been a rise in population in South and Southeastern China during the third and fourth centuries, there were no significant changes in trading conditions. All demand for trade was still centred on the metropolitan areas in the north and the lines of communication between north and south were limited and primitive. Apart from the Canton and Hanoi regions, where flourishing trading communities may be found, there were no important markets between the southern coasts and the few key river ports of the Yangtse region. Coastal traffic to the mouth of the Yangtse was known but that did not constitute a major trading route.

The north had produced considerable surplus wealth for investment and risk-taking, but there is little evidence of any interest in using this wealth south of the Yangtse. Opportunities for profit in farming, mining and industry in the north were sufficient and neither public nor private enterprises were yet able to exhaust them. And for the limited needs of internal northern trade, simple money-lending arrangements seem to have served their purpose. There were no notable developments in credit institutions to meet long-term and large-scale needs.[8]

As for technological advances, developments in shipping along the southern and southeastern coasts, particularly the shipping of what must have been Yueh peoples of the Kwangtung and Tongking areas, prove that coastal ships were plentiful and communications important but it is doubtful if ocean-going vessels were needed regularly. The important fact is that the techniques were there and such vessels could be provided when they were needed as when the Chu Ying and K'ang T'ai expedition was sent out to Southeast Asia in the middle of the third century AD.[9]

Political stability throughout the empire was rare for the two and a half centuries after the Later Han rebellions in the second half of the second century AD. South China was cut off several times from the north and there could not have developed any economic dependence on the richer northern provinces which could have assisted the growth of maritime trade. This lack of stability and of mutual commercial reliance may be used to explain the lack of progress in the economic development of South China.

Finally, Confucian attitudes were not relevant during this early period although Confucianism was the dominant state ideology for most of the period after the second century BC. The important factors of demand, investment and credit institutions not being present, it can only be argued that these factors had in some ways been obstructed in their growth by Confucian attitudes. But that is a different problem and need not trouble us here.

2. PERIOD II — FIFTH TO EIGHTH CENTURIES

The population increase in South China during this period has been frequently noted. More significant, however, was the growth during this period of market towns throughout Central China which were to provide vital trading links between north and south in the centuries to follow. Land and river communications improved noticeably, and the spectacular Grand Canal of the early seventh century linking the Yangtse and the Yellow Rivers was a turning point in the history of commerce in China. In addition, the advent of Buddhism throughout China introduced many new demands and some of these could only be met by increased trading relation with South and Southeast Asia.

Similarly, the peopling of the south led to the opening of new lands, the cultivation of new crops and the introduction of advanced agricultural techniques from the north. It is possible to speak of the limited growth of surplus wealth on the new frontiers of the south, but these frontier lands were still so full of investment opportunities that there was no need for the surplus to be invested in the riskier overseas trade. All that can be said is that trade followed the extension of imperial administration and reached out towards the remoter regions of South China itself.[10]

Despite the new surpluses and the new investment opportunities in trade, the preoccupation was still with agriculture. Simple credit arrangements still appeared adequate, and although there were many experiments in new credit institutions, especially through the growing needs of the large number of Buddhist monasteries, none of the developments was significant enough to encourage the long-term risks of overseas trade.[11]

Technological advances were notable in agriculture, but again were not really relevant to overseas trade as long as demand and investment possibilities were still limited. There is more evidence of overseas shipping facilities, but the arguments for Chinese, as distinct from Southeast Asian, Indian or Arab shipping, are not convincing. It would appear that overseas trade was still largely conducted in non-Chinese vessels.

As for political stability, the first half of this period was an unstable one in South China when compared with the Great Peace of the early Tang dynasty up to 755. Here the comparison may not be all that important, for the records suggest that there was enough stability in the southern "empires" of Liu Sung (420–479), Liang (502–557) and even Ch'en (557–589) for a flourishing trade to develop. What is more important was that South China, as an imperial and administrative entity during the period of the north-south division, had the opportunity to grow into an economic unit with its own markets and trading needs. Some of these needs could only be met through foreign trade and all that was necessary was a modicum of political order accompanied by the freedom to trade. It was a period when Confucianism was out of favour and insignificant and Confucian attitudes played no part in inhibiting economic growth and overseas trade. If overseas trade did not develop more impressively, this was the result of broader economic and political considerations.[12]

3. PERIOD III — NINTH TO FOURTEENTH CENTURIES (BEFORE 1368).

From the point of view of social and economic change, this was a most important period. The rate of increase of population in South China advanced rapidly, especially during the period of the late Tang and the Southern Kingdoms in the ninth and tenth centuries and during the Southern Song (1127–1276). Important markets grew up all along the coasts south of the Yangtse mouth and in the interior, along the several major routes into Kwangsi, Hunan, Anhwei and

Hupeh provinces. In every way, demand for goods increased, and so did the purchasing power of a much larger urban class. Consequently the growth in trade, both internal and external, went on steadily. By the Southern Song, it can be said that consumer sophistication had reached a point when luxuries of an earlier period became necessities of the period.

The consequent increase in surplus wealth for investment and risk-taking does not need elaboration here. This is evident in the widening range of products which became commercialized. Opportunities for investment also increased, and, although most of them were in land, agriculture, cash crops and small-scale industries like printing, textiles and dyes, there was encouragement from the provincial and local (and during the Southern Song, even imperial) authorities to invest in foreign trade.[13]

Also, for the first time, adequate credit and financial institutions appeared. The development of varieties of promissory notes to the point when paper currency replaced most forms of coinage during the Yuan dynasty show the degree of financial sophistication of the governments, the traders and the common people. What inhibited the full development of modern banking and credit facilities, however, was the lack of a legal and political framework which protected wealth from the state itself and some of its rapacious officials.[14]

With the appearance of most of the preconditions for a flourishing foreign trade, technological improvements came quickly to provide the Chinese with some of the most advanced ocean-going vessels in the world at that time. This phenomenon confirms that technological problems were not a factor in inhibiting the growth of maritime trade. Once that trade was needed and capital was available, technology provided no serious difficulties.[15]

On the other hand, political stability and Confucian attitudes were important factors. The south was relatively stable throughout the period, and, except for the change of dynasties at the end of the Tang and at the end of Southern Song, it experienced virtually no disruption of overseas trade. The defence of the northern land frontiers of the empire, however, was a serious drain on the wealth of the country and the badly-devised, rather crude and often arbitrary commercial taxes collected by the imperial officials were a serious obstacle to the flowering of commercial capitalism. This was related to Confucian attitudes about the relationship between the imperial state and the merchant classes, although it does not mean that Confucianism stood in the way of trade. It is necessary to make this distinction because

Confucian officials often encouraged, and even directly participated in commercial activities. But their conception of social and political relationships precluded them from emphasizing the economic benefits of trade and this, in the long run, especially after the appearance of Neo-Confucianism and the recovery of Confucian dominance during the Song was a restraining factor where rational calculations of trade were concerned.[16]

4. PERIOD IV — FOURTEENTH (AFTER 1368) TO EIGHTEENTH CENTURIES

By 1368, the Chinese had achieved almost all the preconditions for a flourishing trade both within and outside the empire. It can easily be shown that there was demand for maritime trade, there was the surplus wealth for investment and risk-taking, there were credit and financial institutions albeit still lacking in security, there were the technical skills for seafaring and there was political stability. It may be pointed out that only in the framework of government and in the attitudes of the officials and the Confucian elite who sustained that framework were there obstructions in the path of the natural growth of a major mercantilist power.

Herein lies one of the most perplexing questions for the historians of China. Is this a sufficient explanation why China did not become a major mercantilist power after the fifteenth century? Are we to conclude that, were it not for the Confucian view of man and his world which guided Chinese imperial governments, China would have become such a power from that time on? This obviously does not fit in with our examination of the three earlier periods, where Confucian views and the nature of the imperial government did not prevent, nor did they determine, the growth of maritime trade. Yet, with the foundation of the Ming, there was a bid for maritime dominance of Asian water, and there were unprecedented successes, only to be followed by a deliberate policy to restrict maritime trade and foreign relations in South and Southeast Asia. So sharp was the shift in policy after 1435 that no one since has seriously regarded China as a sea power.[17]

I would like to suggest that Confucianism in the neo-orthodox form of the Ming and Qing periods was a major factor, not because a Confucian bureaucracy with political power really controlled every aspect of a country's development, but because the form of government it supported determined many crucial aspects of economic and technological change. In particular, I refer to the principles of government by moral example which minimized the importance of legal protection of wealth and property and failed to protect the credit and financial institutions necessary for large-scale and long-term investments. These must have had repercussions on the accumulation of surplus wealth and the range of trading activities. And in so far as such a government determined almost all priorities, it must also have dictated what technological advances were necessary and what were not.

In this way, Confucian attitudes may be seen to qualify all the preconditions for a flourishing maritime trade. They did not interfere at early periods, partly because they were not so dominant as they became after 1368 but also partly because the maritime trade had not reached a point where its further growth would have challenged the accepted view of the Confucian state. Instead, the Confucian officials preferred to restrict the demand for foreign goods and merely allow private traders to continue to meet the needs which could not be satisfied from within. And, despite the change of circumstances accompanying western incursions into South and Southeast Asia during the sixteenth, seventeenth and eighteenth centuries, this was the policy the Chinese government maintained.

Two other points may also be made. One concerns the insecurity of the Chinese land frontiers and official preoccupation with their defence. This led to the move of the Ming capital from Nanking to Peking and the abandonment of active interest in maritime trade. China's geography remains a vital factor and governments, whether Confucian or otherwise, could hardly have ignored it. The second is that, by 1368, and certainly after 1700, the Chinese economy may have passed the point of no return when its productivity is measured against the rise in population. Without major changes in agricultural, commercial, industrial and managerial techniques, the time had probably passed for an easy transition from an agricultural to a mercantilist economy. The Confucian bureaucrats might have sensed this and wrongly concluded that salvation lay in the ideal road back to a more glorious past.

Let me now return to my earlier distinctions of "public" and "private" trade and examine the distinctions in terms of the periods covered above. My two propositions that "public" trade was determined by Confucian ideas of good government and that "private" trade flourished at the ports far from the metropolis because officials did not have to play strictly Confucian roles both need to be qualified. Both varied according to period and place. For the first proposition, it has to be qualified by the statement that Confucian ideas of good government were not predominant during most of the centuries before 1368, and even when they were, as in the Southern Song, they were modified by the southern and coastal location of its capital at Lin-an and its consequently different needs. As for the second proposition, it is modified by the fact that "private" trade did develop according to economic and rational needs and did not become constrained by Confucian attitudes until after 1368, and especially after 1435, when the political centre thereafter remained in the north. Only after that could "private" trade be related to the roles the local and provincial officials along the coasts were prepared to play.

If we take the question further, the survey above of the periods would also suggest that the earlier Confucianism was not an important factor in either "public" or "private" trade. For both Periods I and II, Confucianism was not obtrusive and did not directly affect the nature of both "public" and "private" trade nor its rate of growth. Confucianism only became important again during the second half of Period III, as Neo-Confucianism. With the rise of Neo-Confucianism, "public" trade almost disappeared and "private" trade was left to develop up to such a level as it was thought to contradict and threaten the ideals of the Confucian system. If this is a correct appraisal of the function of Confucianism in the history of Chinese maritime trade, then it would suggest that the extraordinary developments of 1368–1435 which have puzzled historians for so long must be taken as indeed extraordinary. In other words, the maritime power as exhibited during those 65 years or so should not be seen as the natural outcome of China's political and economic history which was arrested by unprogressive Confucian bureaucrats but as an exceptional phenomenon which lasted as long as the emperors Hung-wu (1368–98) and Yung-lo (1402–24) were alive and which fizzled out once the traditional state was permitted to regain its equilibrium.[18]

NOTES

1 The evidence for this is overwhelming for the late Tang and Five Dynasties period, the Southern Song and Yuan periods and the centuries after 1435. See F. Hirth and W.W. Rockhill, *Chau Ju-kua* (St. Petersburg, 1911); W.W. Rockhill, "Notes on the relations and trade of China", in *T'oung Pao*, XV and XVI, 1914–15; Chang Tien-tse, *Sino-Portuguese Trade from 1514 to 1644* (Leiden, 1934); G.F. Hourani, *Arab Seafaring* (Princeton, 1951).

2 *Han Shu*, 28B, 27B. (The *Po-na pen* edition has been used for all dynastic histories.)

3 Wang Gungwu, "The Nanhai Trade", in *Journal of the Malaysian Branch Royal Asiatic Society*, vol. XXXI, pt. 2, June 1958, pp. 31–61, 118–123.

4 *Chin Shu*, 33, 12a; 37, 4b; 90, 9b; 97, 9b–10a. *Sung Shu*, 97, 29b. *Nan Ch'i Shu*, 31, 6b; 32, 2a. *Liang Shu*, 33, 2b–3a.

5 Wang Gungwu, "The Nanhai Trade", pp. 71–112.

6 F. Hirth and W.W. Rockhill, *Chau Ju-kua*, and W.W. Rockhill, "Notes on the relations and trade of China". Throughout the Southern Song and the Yuan, tribute from overseas was negligible, while references to the range and variety of maritime trade were plentiful.

7 Wang Gungwu, "Early Ming Relations with Southeast Asia", in J. K. Fairbank (éd.), *The Chinese World Order* (Cambridge, Mass., 1968), pp. 34–62.

8 N.L. Swann, *Food and Money in Ancient China* (Princeton, 1950); Yang Lien-Sheng, *Money and Credit in China* (Cambridge, Mass., 1952); H. Bielenstein, "The Census of China during the period 2–742 A.D.", in *Bulletin of the Museum of Far Eastern Antiquities*, XIX, 1947, pp. 125–163; E. Balazs, *Le traité économique du "Souei-Chou"* (Leiden, 1953); Wang Gungwu, "The Nanhai Trade", pp. 16–45. Particularly relevant are chuans 24A–B and 28A–B of *Han Shu*, chuans 109–113 of *Hou Han Shu* and chuan 26 of *Chin Shu*.

9 Wang Gungwu, "The Nanhai Trade", p. 33.

10 H. Bielenstein, "The Census of China"; E. Balazs, *Le traité économique*; Wang Gungwu, "The Nanhai Trade".

11 Yang Lien-Sheng, *Money and Credit in China*, and J. Gernet, *Les aspects économiques du Bouddhisme dans la société chinoise du Ve au Xe siècle* (Saigon, 1956).

12 Wang Gungwu, "The Nanhai Trade", pp. 46–89. The formal Confucian codes of the early Tang do not appear to have affected questions of maritime trade in the southern ports in any way. The Bureau of Shipping Trade was controlled by eunuchs and the inner court and the officials in the south were expected to protect the trade; T'ao Hsi-Sheng and Chü Ch'ing-Yuan, *T'ang-tai Ching-shi Shih* (Shanghai, 1936), pp. 76–80.

13 *Chiu T'ang Shu*, chuans 38–41; *Hsin T'ang Shu*, chuans 37–43B; Wu Jen-ch'en, *Shih-kuo ch'un-chiu*, 1793 edition; Kato Shigeshi, "On the Hang or the Associations of Merchants in China", in *Memoirs of the Research Department of the Tōyō Bunko*, IX, 1936, pp. 45–83; J. Gernet, *Daily Life in China on the eve of the Mongol Invasion*, tr. H.M. Wright, (London, 1962); P. Wheatley, "Geographical Notes on some Commodities involved in Sung Maritime Trade", in *Journal of the Malayan Branch Royal Asiatic Society*, vol. 32, pt. 2, 1959.

14 Yang Lien-Sheng, *Money and Credit in China*, pp. 51–67; E. Balazs, "The Birth of Capitalism in China", in *Chinese Civilisation and Bureaucracy* (Yale University Press: New Haven, 1964), pp. 34–54.

15 Lo Jung-Pang, "The Emergence of China as a Sea Power during the Late Sung and Early Yuan Periods", in *Far Eastern Quarterly*, XIV, 1954–55, pp. 489–503.

16 Kato Shigeshi, *Shina Keizaishi Kosho* (Tokyo, vol. 1, 1952), pp. 299–379; vol. II, 1953, pp. 176–221. Also E. Balazs, "The Birth of Capitalism in China".

17 Lo Jung-Pang, "The Decline of the Early Ming Navy", in *Oriens Extremus*, V, 1958–59, pp. 149–168.

18 Almost without exception, scholars have studied the great expeditions of 1405–35 as extraordinary events in Chinese history. The emphasis, however, has been on the reasons why they were begun by emperor Yung-lo and why they were ended by Confucian bureaucrats. I have suggested elsewhere that we must look more closely at emperor Hung-wu's policies and that we should consider his reign and that of his son as innovative, even revolutionary, for Chinese history. The abandonment of their policies may, therefore, be seen as a result of restoration of standard practices or return to conformity. Wang Gungwu, *Early Ming Relations with Southeast Asia*; and "The Opening of relations between China and Malacca, 1403–1405", in J. Bastin et R. Roolvink (eds.), *Malayan and Indonesian Studies* (Oxford, 1964), pp. 87–104.

CHAPTER 7

Political Chinese: Their Contribution to Modern Southeast Asian History

I

THE GREATER PART OF the literature on the Overseas Chinese in Southeast Asia describes their economic successes and contributions. A small part has touched on their customs and festivals, their social structure and their kinship system. Very little, however, has been written about their attitudes towards politics and this is usually negative: claiming that is, either that the Chinese are non-political or that they form a serious political threat as a potential fifth column for either Chinese nationalism or Chinese communism. There are good reasons why the literature divides itself in this way. Chinese economic power is visible and considerable; Chinese culture is strange and resilient; and Chinese politics either negligible or underground, and thus difficult to assess. In this chapter, I shall not attempt to deny the justice of the well-accepted views of Overseas Chinese economics, society and politics. The distribution of attention is not in itself important. What is important is that the Chinese have had to live in continually changing contexts in Southeast Asia and I want to show that Chinese groups are not static communities with firm and indestructible characteristics; they are not obliged to remain the same and make the same kind of contributions no matter what goes on around them; they are mobile and dynamic enough to act as agents of change. This is necessary to understand before any useful effort can be made to assess the Chinese contribution to complex processes like modernization in Southeast Asia.

This paper is a preliminary effort at showing why Overseas Chinese are in a state of flux today, why this state is not new, why this state does not agree with them and also why it may be a purely transitional stage in a continuous effort to, achieve more stable conditions for their children to live in. I have chosen to discuss these problems in terms of politics because politics can be more volatile and more susceptible to radical change. It may not be as deep as social and cultural change, nor as fundamental as economic innovation, but political change is easier to respond to and the responses are easier to trace. It is also easier to periodize and the periods easier for a historian to characterize. Moreover, the Chinese are alike in many ways, but not in their attitudes towards political change. In this, they divide more readily and are easier to group. By tackling this easier task first, I hope to show that similar questions are worth asking about social and economic change and that the answers these produce would provide a sound basis for evaluating the role of the Chinese in the modernization of Southeast Asia.

Let me begin by distinguishing the three major elements in Southeast Asia's political history. The most obvious element is European imperialism — the gradual beginning, the period of ascendancy and the latest period of withdrawal. The second is indigenous polities — the many layers of tradition which can be further divided in their earlier periods of gestation and consolidation, the era of colonial rule and the most recent glories of national independence. The third is the unassimilated Chinese minorities — their traditional trade, the period of Sino-European symbiosis and the present adjustment to nationalist politics. The periods mentioned here may be more subtly identified, and it may be found that none of them can be made to coincide, or, they may be more broadly generalized and it is found that each of the periods overlap to a considerable extent. The important common feature of all the periods, however, is that they imply political change and it is this political change I shall focus on here in order to evaluate the Chinese contribution.

Thus I hope to show Chinese awareness of politics in a non-Chinese environment by tracing their efforts to fit themselves into indigenous politics, into colonial situations whether mixed with indigenous institutions or not, and into post-independence power structures. In so doing, I have also to keep in mind the Chinese variables themselves, that is, the response to radical political changes in China from empire to republic to the two-China dilemma. This is not to say that I am taking *all* variables into account. In a true state of flux, it would be futile to take *all* variables into account, and reprehensible to pretend that this can be done. All I am attempting to do here is to take the main obvious political variables and seek to identify the range of contributions the Chinese have made to modern Southeast Asian history which have not been found significant in the past. I am aware that Thailand had a different experience with the

European powers, and Mainland Southeast Asian politics have been somewhat different from politics in Island Southeast Asia, especially where the Chinese minorities are concerned. But there seems to be enough in common in all the countries for me to offer the broad generalizations below.

This is not the place to enter into the controversy as to what is politics and what is not. The Chinese experience has never been comparable to that in democratic politics, but within a basically authoritarian tradition, it ranged from community leadership to a share in national and international power and this is so wide an area that it would be surprising if some of the Chinese overseas were not passionately interested in some aspects of it. What is important is to determine what groups of Chinese were involved in which level of politics and how significant this type of activity was in enabling them to contribute to Southeast Asian history. For this purpose, I have suggested that, *at all times* among the Overseas Chinese, three major groups can be distinguished by their political interests and activities. These are as follows:

Group A, which is predominantly concerned with Chinese national politics and its international ramifications;

Group B, which is principally concerned with community politics wherever it may be;

Group C, which is drawn into the politics of non-Chinese hierarchies, whether indigenous or colonial or nationalist.

As this paper is concerned with modern Southeast Asia, I shall not discuss here the validity of this grouping earlier than for the nineteenth century. It is, in any case, enough to begin with the nineteenth century because, during the past 150 years, the region has experienced the change from traditional politics to colonial administrations to nationalist politics and we can observe all three groups of Chinese living under and adapting to these different political conditions.

II

The accepted picture of the Chinese during the first stage, during most of the nineteenth century, is that they were completely non-political, concerned only with trade and livelihood and anxious to stay out of political life of all kinds. This, of course, is at best partially true and in some areas, quite inaccurate. In fact, all three groups existed even then. The communities were still small and mainly transient; most of the Chinese were illiterate and survival was not always easy. There are few reliable documents detailing the whole range of Chinese activities with most merely repeating that they were industrious and clever. Yet there is enough for us to perceive that Group B was the main group, concerned primarily with community leadership, status and influence; and that Group A existed although it tended to keep close organizational links with China through secret societies and their anti-Manchu, even anti-establishment, sentiments; and that there was a very small Group C, some of them assimilated Baba or Peranakan etc., whose main function was to maintain a political dialogue with indigenous rulers and their aristocratic officials. The line between A and B groups, and that between B and C groups, was not always clear, and there were vigorous B group leaders to be found who wore several caps at one time or another, occasionally aspiring to political ties with the local rulers and aristo-crats, and at other times retaining a place in the secret society hierar-chies. But already some degree of division was discernible and also some degree of rivalry. All three types produced leaders who sought power, rank and respectability within the Chinese community. Group B leaders had, on the whole, the easiest task. They wooed the com-munity directly by commercial success, they bought its respect with great wealth; they bought their ranks and titles from the Qing empire and thus outshone their Group A rivals whose China politics were often dangerous; and they sometimes strengthened their local positions by buying the services of lesser Group C Chinese who had successfully ingratiated themselves with the native rulers and officials.

The existence of the three types gives us a picture of the Chinese which has appeared contradictory from the start. Group B, in particu-lar, provided the impression of opportunism, the lack of any concept of political loyalty, the fence-sitting and double insurance image which has persisted to this day. Group A provided the picture of the sinister and proud Chinese, of the "once a Chinese, always a Chinese" school, idealistic and patriotic in their own mysterious way but definitely ungrateful for any help and advantage given to them by any non-Chinese. As for Group C, they seemed reasonable enough, adaptable and accommodating, even pliable, virtually offering to assimilate if they could be given certain privileges and guarantees.

How can it be said that the politics of these Chinese groups con-tributed anything to modern Southeast Asian history? At this first stage, it seems they contributed very little. It is extremely difficult to assess to what extent Chinese secret societies stimulated indigenous societies of a similar nature and undermined feudal loyalties. It is even more difficult to say that Group B Chinese corrupted native politics by their use of far greater wealth than the local aristocracies and common people had ever seen. What is clearer is that, with the extension everywhere of European commercial enterprise and imperial rivalry, this group of Chinese contributed towards the weakening of local economic, and consequently political, power and made the task of European conquest a little easier. But this was probably related to the rivalry among the Chinese themselves. When Group B noted Group A's links with China and Group C's favours from the native rulers, they probably saw much to gain by seeking special relations with European administrative and judicial powers. As for Group C, they contributed some skills in enabling the ruler to know and influence, if not directly control, the Chinese trading community. Their close associations with the local hierarchies might have helped to maintain harmonious racial relations and thus keep the peace, but they probably contributed most when they intermarried and their families became the new members of officialdom and, therefore, firm and able supporters of well-established political institutions in which they had acquired an abiding interest.

During the second stage — primarily the last years of the nineteenth and the first half of the twentieth century — the picture is still mainly that of non-political Chinese actively making money for themselves but being harassed by political agitators who had either been sent out from China to collect money or had escaped from their political failures within China itself. This picture is even less accurate than the accepted picture of the Chinese during the first stage. The Chinese communities were now much larger and settled, they were mainly urban, and their composition was changing rapidly. The number of successful merchants had increased, the number of educated rose in leaps and bounds whether in Chinese or in colonial schools, and there were also new groups of literate Chinese arriving in the region, especially in the 1920s and 1930s. Furthermore, we are no longer dependent on a few outside observers for scanty descriptions of the communities. Chinese newspapers and magazines appeared in greater numbers, and they clearly reflected the increasing attention paid to political affairs in China as well as in the local Chinese communities in various parts of Southeast Asia. Literacy in the colonial or the indigenous languages also led to growing interest in the politics of colonialism and Southeast Asian nationalism.

Thus the three groups became more sharply defined. Group B remained the largest group, but its leaders no longer dominated the community's affairs. Group A was growing, largely through the migration of the more literate Chinese and through the growth of the local Chinese-educated. The secret societies which had earlier provided some slight political links with China gave way to new organizations which openly supported the anti-dynastic movements in China. These, in turn, following the 1911 revolution, grew into self-conscious political parties organized along the lines of the Kuomintang and later the Chinese communist party. The decisive factors in the growing strength of Group A were the deep resentments at having been humiliated for several decades, the feeling that China and the Chinese were about to rise again and the ideological frameworks that both the nationalists and the communists were able to provide. The group shared the excitement of a rejuvenating China and tried to convey this to all Overseas Chinese through their writings, their speeches and the conversations in every coffee shop in Southeast Asia. They felt that a greater loyalty now claimed them and directed their energies towards politics in China and even rationalized their stay abroad as one of the ways in which wealth could be accumulated to help China's development in trade, industry, and power.

That they were able to feel this way was, of course, largely due to the modernization of both China and Southeast Asia. The imperialist powers had forged strong communication links between the Chinese ports and their bases in Southeast Asia. The conveniences of faster and safer shipping, cable and telephone connections, and the ubiquitous international news agencies all helped to bring the Overseas Chinese closer to China and China closer to the region. And as contact became more and more direct, Group A's advantages in gaining for themselves status, respectability and even fame among the Chinese also grew.

At the same time, the modern colonial regimes were also stronger than ever and quickly learnt how to deal with the large Chinese minorities. Group A political agitators were unwelcome. They disrupted the routines that most Overseas Chinese were known to prefer in their trading activities, and ideological rivalry among different groups and nationalists and between nationalists and communists clearly endangered the peace. Thus the colonial governments, with or without the agreement of surviving indigenous rulers, sometimes sought to encourage Chinese loyalty towards the states under which the Chinese lived. In short, they favoured the small Group C Chinese by honouring their leaders, rewarding their services with titles and appointing some of them to minor posts in the government. Colonial education, in particular, was the means to channel some Chinese energies towards successful colonial administration.

For the Group C Chinese leaders, their main function was still the same as during the first stage: it was to maintain a political dialogue with the ruling officials largely on behalf of their own section of the community and to help these officials understand the problems of the Chinese as a whole. This was a most difficult role under conditions in which colonial control was still being extended and Chinese nationalism was intensifying its appeal to the Overseas Chinese. It is by no means clear what variety of reasons moved Group C Chinese to identify with the European or mixed European-indigenous governments; certainly some were self-seeking, and others had no choice because they were no longer Chinese-speaking, but there is evidence that many were simply grateful to their adopted lands and wanted to make their permanent homes there. For the latter, there was a new-found loyalty, in some cases to benevolent paternalism, in others to political principles like the rule of law and rational bureaucracy, and in some others to the relatively modern way of life appearing in the urban centres of the region. Whatever the reason, Group C Chinese were drawn to local politics, largely to the politics of increasing their influence in the colonial governments, but some of them, following the rise of indigenous nationalist movements, also to the politics of anti-colonialism and anti-imperialism.

But while, on the whole, Group C Chinese got on well in local politics, their position in the larger Chinese community was ambiguous. The other sections of the community sometimes found them useful and did not hesitate to use them when they could, but more often, Groups A and B were uneasy about Chinese identifying too much with non-Chinese and even went so far as to vilify those who were thought to have gone too far in their apparent rejection of their Chineseness. Partly for this reason, though also partly because meaningful friendships with Europeans or indigenous Southeast Asians were far from easy, Group C remained small, and marginal members of the group have been known to fall back into the larger Group B or even to convert to an intense Chinese nationalism.

Thus in this second period, there was a vigorous and aggressive Group A increasingly proud of a new China, republican and progressive, and a quiet and accommodating Group C tentatively seeking to become part of the colonial or indigenous establishment. In between was still the large body of Group B Chinese, seemingly non-political because they were not openly engaged in either local politics or the politics of China. Yet here was political life too. They continued to organize effectively to meet the needs of an increasingly complex situation. Their traditional clan and guild associations were not always adequate to protect their interests, and they formed modern pressure groups to ensure good relations with their own respective colonial governments as well as with the governments of neighbour-ing areas with which many of them traded. At the same time, they were willing to join in patriotic efforts to keep themselves respectable in the eyes of Group A Chinese and their own friends and relatives in China, but only as long as their own involvement did not endanger their respectability before the local ruling officials. Furthermore, they had to be watchful of the political factions among Group A Chinese which tried to dominate their traditional spheres of influence and infiltrate their organizations. Thus, although no longer dominant in Chinese affairs as they had been, Group B Chinese had to exercise considerable political skill to keep both their Chinese credentials and their manoeuvrability in an alien environment. They were the group which formed the reservoir from the margins of which many young Chinese flowed one way into Group A political commitments and many flowed the other way into Group C aspirations in local politics. The strength of all three groups varied from country to country depending on the policies of colonial governments, and varied from time to time depending on the remarkable events in China, but there were times during this second period when the white heat of Chinese nationalism and the dubious legitimacy of European colonialism drove them all together and momentarily gave them a sense of unity as a Chinese community and even made many believe that there was truly a community of Nanyang Chinese.

Again, one may ask if the politics of these Chinese groups contri-buted anything to this second stage of modern Southeast Asian history. Colonial historians have often noted the usefulness of the Chinese as middlemen in trade, but usually dismiss the possibility of a Chinese contribution to Southeast Asian government and politics. Yet the very fact that there were Chinese minorities almost every-where in the region when the Europeans set up their governments and that these minorities all became larger during the period of colonial rule warns us not to accept this simple picture. As historian E.H. Carr says, "numbers count in history", and they count because they carry political weight.

The Europeans arrived in Southeast Asia as several rival groups dealing with many more rival groups of indigenous powers. Through a process of elimination, each group of Europeans successfully delimited the indigenous powers which each would have had to deal with through either treaty rights or conquests. But more often than not, they found Chinese minorities which were clearly distinguishable from the indigenous peoples and who were also difficult to eliminate. These minorities demanded attention largely because they had their skills, their capital and their energy to offer. And almost everywhere, the Europeans soon found it useful to consider the Chinese as a separate variable in their political calculations. The Chinese could be frightened into helping the Europeans against recalcitrant natives, and the Chinese could also be pointed to as the real threat to the native well-being which the Europeans claimed they were there to protect. Also, by successfully isolating natives from Chinese, in some cases clearly for political reasons, the Europeans confirmed the Chinese in their traditional economic skills and thus encouraged their modernization while confining the indigenous peoples to their traditional arts and slowing down their modernization. This, of course, is not a direct Chinese contribution, but that the Europeans were on the whole successful in adopting such policies was in no small measure due to Chinese attitudes and values and the implicit assumption of Chinese superiority over the Southeast Asian peoples. Such attitudes and values have had political relevance and certainly affected the political style and atmosphere in the region during the colonial period.

The Chinese contribution was less remarkable in the modernization of political institutions. Here the main work was certainly that of colonial administrators who either transplanted their institutions from their home countries and their other colonies or accepted and modified indigenous institutions and the practices of other colonial empires. Still, it should be noted that the growth in strength of Group A Chinese was seen as a threat, and this caused colonial governments to devise subtler means of isolating and restraining their activities and brought refinements particularly to the institutions of law and order and to those of the communications media. Also, such a threat led to compromises in regulations and policies which could help to keep the Group B Chinese majority happy and contented, and such compromises did affect the supremacy of some key institutions like political representation and aspects of judicial and fiscal practice.

These compromise measures were often later confirmed by the presence of loyal and reliable Group C Chinese who had learnt to operate most of the new and changing institutions from within.

A third major area of influence was a direct Chinese contribution to ideology, not because nationalism was Chinese or that capitalism, socialism and communism were Chinese, but because the Chinese played a role in stimulating some kinds of nationalism, some kinds of capitalism, and also some kinds of socialism and communism in several countries. In each case, it is possible to show that Group A Chinese aroused some of the violence in Indonesian and Malay nationalism which often affected *all* Chinese; that Group B Chinese were responsible for some of the peculiar features of capitalism and anti-communism in Thailand and the Philippines; and that both Group A and Group C Chinese helped to shape the socialism and communism in Malaya and Singapore before World War II. The picture, however, does not become clear until the third period in modern Southeast Asian history, the years since 1945.

III

The third stage since 1945 is still evolving and it is too early to say how the various groups of Chinese will divide in the decades to come. Nor can we reliably estimate the contribution of political Chinese to the region's post-war history. A great deal more has yet to unfold before that can be done. What is useful here is to trace the ways the three groups changed from the second stage to the third and how they readjusted themselves to the first two decades of national independence and colonial withdrawal as well as to the rise of communist China. From this, we can better appreciate the significance of certain trends in the second stage and this in turn should help us to understand what is happening today. Also, by examining developments in this third stage, we can more sharply define some of the contributions the Chinese have already made to the modernization of Southeast Asia.

The most notable developments among the political Chinese since 1945 have been the gradual erosion of Group A aggressiveness and enthusiasm, the reversion of many Group A Chinese to Group B caution and community solidarity, and the erratic but marked growth in the members of Group C Chinese trying hard to identify with their countries of adoption.

The political importance of the Chinese in post-war Southeast Asia was quickly recognized. The late Victor Purcell was able to begin exploring this subject even before the war ended, and there has never been any doubt ever since his major study *The Chinese in Southeast Asia* appeared in 1949 that the Chinese communities would have a political role in the region. There were, from the start, two widely accepted views about them. The first concerned the Chinese as an external threat, a potential fifth column for China. Before 1949, they were seen as possible agents for a powerful nationalist China asserting itself in the region; and after 1949, they were seen as possible subversive elements who would be tempted to work for international communism on behalf of the Peking regime. The second view concerned the internal threat in several countries if Chinese economic power was allowed to be the basis of an unsettling and irrepressible political power. This view was a contradictory one because those who saw it also picture the Chinese as greedy irresponsible capitalists who regrettably owe no political loyalty to the new nations beyond that to the profits a show of loyalty may produce. It is a view which was responsible for much confusion in policies towards the Chinese. Some governments try to make the Chinese feel more loyal and more committed to local political affairs and, at the same time, want the Chinese to make merely economic contributions which would not have political repercussions.

Both the views of the Chinese as external and internal threats are inaccurate. They are derived from a dim perception of the Chinese being Group A types on the one hand and of their being Group C types on the other, without any recognition that the two groups represent Chinese at the two extreme ends of the spectrum. What is also not appreciated is that neither of these groups is a stable and unchanging one and that the majority of the Chinese belong to Group B whose primary political activity is defensive and status-oriented. There have been some among these who have been converted to Group A idealism or atavism; others have been disillusioned enough to return to the main community fold. There have been some who have chosen to accept Group C identification with local political aspirations and there have been others among them who have also been disillusioned enough to return to the main community.

Thus when we compare the post-1945 situation to that before the war, we can observe considerable mobility between groups and the considerable increase in political alertness which the Chinese displayed from time to time. Group A responsiveness to events in China had become marked after 1900, supporting the nationalist revolution after 1911, breaking up into political factions in the 1920s and organizing United Front activities during the Sino-Japanese War. After 1945, they experienced a brief spell of nationalist revivalism and then a longer spell of enthusiasm for communist China which was often a thinly-disguised form of "Great Han Chauvinism". During the 1970s, much of the passion abated and there has been some agonizing reappraisals, but a small core of the group has certainly survived. Their rationale for rejecting Group B for their "passivism" and Group C for "selling out" is no longer directed to the present but towards the future. It is based on a perception of the future in which China will in time be the dominant power in Southeast Asia. Group A now realize that they may not as yet be able to act on their convictions, but they see no reason why they should not stay on the side of history and prepare themselves, often quietly and unobtrusively for the sake of their families and friends, to be on the winning side. They are the only group which could still be accurately called "Overseas Chinese" ("Huaqiao"). In their respective countries, they are considered "chauvinists" if they are not known to have progressive views and "communists" if they make no secret of their Maoist leanings.

Group B Chinese had also been increasingly aware of events in China before 1945 and continued for a while after 1945 to hope that a strong China would help them in their work and livelihood overseas. Unlike Group A, however, they had traditional doubts about the limits of China's power and about the relevance of China's politics for themselves. Their reservations proved to be justified in time when Southeast Asian nationalism affected them far more directly and forcefully, and they were obliged to reconsider their former hesitation about being involved in local politics. Many went so far as to join Group C Chinese to try and consolidate their positions in their respective countries. But, on the whole, there is ample evidence that Group B remains the majority in most countries. Where there have been defections to Group C, there has also been some augmentation from Group A. Their numbers have remained large because they too are politically conscious and may be seen as being more realistic or hard-headed than either Group A or Group C Chinese. They too have their perception of the future of Southeast Asia. They expect China's influence in the region to grow, but also expect that the new nations genuinely want their independence and that China (whether Peking or Taipei) knows this and would not want to challenge that new nationalism, certainly not for the sake of the Overseas Chinese. In short, they see that the status quo of legitimate new nations in

Southeast Asia will continue and that the only thing they can do is to try and fit themselves into the respective national frameworks as best they can. At the same time, they are not prepared to go as far as Group C Chinese and run the risk of seeing their children assimilated and the Chinese community disintegrated. Although they appear resigned to being more or less cut off from the mainstream of Chinese history, they still wish to stay Chinese in their culture and language and preserve not merely their lives, their families and their properties but, to some extent, also their identity as an economic community. They are normally prepared to call themselves Huaren instead of Huaqiao, but see themselves as Malaysian Chinese (*Ma-Hua*), Thai Chinese (*Tai-Hua*), Indonesian Chinese (*Yin-Hua*) and so on, rather than as Malaysians, Thais and Indonesians, or as sojourners (e.g., *Ma-ch'iao, T'ai-ch'iao, Yin-Ch'iao*).

As for Group C Chinese, many of them had long turned their backs on China since the nineteenth century, some because they had long realized that Overseas Chinese could not count on help from China and must fend for themselves by moving first towards indigenous and then colonial governments, and others because, through sustained contact, they were happier in the local political environment in which they felt they could find their place. Thus the events in China immediately before the war in 1937–41 and those immediately after in 1945–49 did not greatly affect them. On the whole, they opposed the Japanese during the war, but their loyalty (apart from in Thailand) was more to the European colonial cause than to the Chinese anti-Japanese one. But like the other two groups, they faced radical post-war changes. While Group A were excited by the rise of communist China and Group B feared the growing strength of indigenous nationalism, the main part of Group C Chinese had to switch their loyalty from the colonial Europeans to the nationalist anti-colonial cause. This was, in fact, a most trying kind of adjustment and Group C nearly disintegrated at the height of the nationalist struggles just prior to independence. On the one hand, there were many loyal "colonials" who, when faced with the inevitable withdrawal of the imperial powers, preferred to leave and seek a home in the metropolitan country when they could. There were a few others who chose to turn to the larger Group B community rather than accept a nationalism they did not trust. Thus the initial reaction to the transition "from empire to nation" was a reduction in the size of Group C. However, after independence, where the new nations settled down a little, many former members returned to the Group and many more from Group B found it possible to accept the new order. In many cases then, Group C Chinese in the post-war period contained at least three layers: the original core of Group C Chinese who could trace back two or more generations in the group without a break; the new-comers into the group who were keen to establish their credentials as loyal nationals; and the older members who returned to the group when they found that, after all, they were more comfortable with the local nationalists than with the larger Chinese community.

Group C Chinese have their own perception of the future of Southeast Asia. They see the new nationalism as inevitable and natural, even just and desirable, and want to be part of it wherever possible. To them, it is unlikely that China, communist or otherwise, will dominate the region, nor would they want China to. Most of them know no Chinese, rarely speak even their own dialects and are much more at home in the native languages of their countries, or in the former colonial languages, or both. They are physically of the Chinese "race", but see little point in struggling to revert to being Chinese when it is possible and advantageous to go forward and become socially and politically superior nationals of their adopted countries. They accept the constitutional and political framework of their countries as workable, and believe that they can be politically integrated, if not fully assimilated, into the national community. Many in the group would not normally call themselves Chinese, but Malaysians, Thais, Indonesians, etc. At most, they would add, "of Chinese descent". In their respective countries, the indigenous nationals may still have some reservations about them, but would nevertheless grace them with names like *national* Chinese, loyal and trustworthy Chinese, even *good* Chinese.

I have already noted that it is premature to assess the Chinese contribution to the third stage of modern Southeast Asian history itself. The developments during the third stage have been outlined above mainly to enable us to better understand what has changed among the political Chinese during the past few decades and also to help us assess the Chinese contribution to the last hundred years of Southeast Asian history. I felt it necessary to come forward to the present because it gives us perspective for the crucial, formative decades before 1941.

In concluding, let me return to the contributions of political style, institutions and ideology I discussed briefly above. In political style, post-1945 changes among the Chinese increased the fear that the large Chinese minorities would seriously hamper the transition to independent new nations. The fact that the indigenous nationalists also found that Chinese skills, energy and capital were vital affected their political calculations. The new national leaders found that the colonial double-handed formula for dealing with the Chinese could be adapted to their own use. There were certainly enough Group C and Group B Chinese who could be frightened into co-operation and support by the threat of unleashing extremist racists against them if the new regime failed; and the Group A and most of Group B Chinese could still be pointed to as serious threats to true independence which only the new national leaders could keep down. More serious were residual Chinese attitudes of superiority and the economic and educational advantages that urbanized Chinese had over the mainly rural indigenous peoples. Against the first, there were efforts to humble the Chinese and put them in their place; against the latter, there had to be campaigns to weight policies for the benefit of the less educated and the less skilled, very often by encouraging the nationals to be better than the Chinese while putting pressure on the Chinese to be less dynamic and less aggressive. Under no circumstances were the Chinese to be allowed to use their economic strength to achieve any real power. Such concerns were in some cases fully justified, but they did produce negative effects on many levels of government and did affect the political style of the successful nationalists. The ruling elites inherited much of the national, modern paternalist style of the colonial elites, but there was the occasional innovation. The spirit of "divide and rule" which permeated colonial theory and practice from time to time was extended to subtler efforts to keep the Chinese communities divided from within, and this was achieved largely by means which could be summed up in terms of the three Chinese groups above, as follows: isolate Group A Chinese, slowly encourage the growth of Group C, and provide Group B with just enough incentives to remain active, prosperous and content.

The heritage of administrative, legal and political institutions in the new Southeast Asian nations was even more markedly colonial, and the presence of the Chinese did make it more difficult to have this heritage rejected or seriously modified. Most of the institutions already had in-built arrangements to make it easier to control the Chinese. They varied from police powers to the rule of law, from educational structures to political representation, and they were used to cope with not only external world-wide pressures for modernization but also the pressures of having modernized or rapidly modernizing Chinese communities *within* the countries themselves. Here it must be emphasized that political modernization relates closely to economic modernization, and with the European colonial elite gone or leaving, it was the Chinese advances in commerce and industry which kept up the pace. As a result, all three groups of Chinese were keeping the pressure on for innovation and forward-planning in the three respective fields of security, economic development and political participation.

Finally, the contribution to ideology. Events since 1945 have confirmed that the Chinese have aroused some of the violence in indigenous nationalism, moulded certain features of capitalism and anti-communism and also determined the place of socialism and communism in some Southeast Asia countries. I have already noted how these were foreshadowed in the pre-war decades. What had been less obvious earlier on and only recently apparent has been the effect the large Chinese minorities have had on the ideology of race, both on racism and on racial tolerance. Superficially, this is not surprising; there had been warnings about racial troubles well before the colonial withdrawal. But one major condition had changed. Empires depend on racial tolerance but small nation-states find it much more difficult to avoid racism. And indeed this heritage from the West of the nation-state, and all its assumptions, myths and rituals, has put Southeast Asians and Chinese alike greatly on the defensive. The sanctity of national oneness is difficult enough to live with in the best of circumstances, where the nationals share the same language, culture, religion, history and political ideals. The presence of aliens and alien concepts of race, taken together with marked differences in language, culture, religion and wealth, must demand considerable willingness to compromise, unusual skill in political juggling and exceptional humanity. In Southeast Asia, the prolonged presence of large Chinese minorities has encouraged everyone to feel racial while thinking tolerantly. This had already been a Chinese contribution to the Southeast Asian experiences of race, but it was muted as long as an Asian solidarity against European colonial elites was possible, and it was manageable where the Chinese have fully accepted the indigenous religion. In the post-war situation, when more nations than ever before have problems with race, we need not wonder that Southeast Asia should also be troubled by it. What is noteworthy is that there has been a Chinese contribution towards both racism and racial tolerance and there will almost certainly be future contributions.

I began by saying that the Chinese are changeable and that Southeast Asia has been changed, that political changes are the most easily noticed and that the Chinese are politically alert enough to respond to them. By concentrating on the political Chinese, all three groups of them, adjusting themselves to changing historical conditions, I have emphasized specific contributions the Chinese minorities have made to the region. This is not to claim that such contributions were the most important. It does, however, point to the possibility of starting a fuller inquiry into an aspect of Southeast Asian history which has been written about but frequently misunderstood.

CHAPTER 8

Lu Xun, Lim Boon Keng and Confucianism

THIS IS A SHORT essay drawn from an unfinished study of Lu Xun in south China. The topic appeals to me for a number of reasons. Lim Boon Keng (1869–1957) was a Singaporean from an earlier phase of Singapore's interest in Confucianism. As a modern doctor-reformer-entrepreneur, he was invited in 1921 at the age of fifty-two by his friend and admirer Tan Kah Kee (1874–1961) to give up his interests in Singapore to be president of Xiamen (Amoy) University (i.e., Xiada).[1] His role as president has not received much attention outside the alumni and some Singapore friends and admirers. In China, it has only been because Lu Xun (1881–1936) had taught at the university for a few months in 1926–27 that many writers have remembered Lim Boon Keng. Their references, however, have not been flattering and most of them have dismissed him with a few words about his earnest efforts in support of Confucianism. Contemporary politics in China has led to both Lu Xun and Tan Kah Kee being praised as models for the Chinese people while Lim Boon Keng, saddled with his "Confucian" image, has drawn harsh judgements. It would seem that he can only hope now for more forgiving treatment from his fellow Singaporeans.[2]

The story behind this short essay began within days of Lu Xun's arrival at Xiamen (Amoy) on Saturday 4 September 1926.[3] On the following Wednesday, one of the students called on Lu Xun to talk about the university and its future. The student recalls telling him that the university president (Lim Boon Keng) was someone who advocated "returning to the ancients" (*fugu*), "respect for Confucius" (*zun Kong*) and forced all students to use classical and not modern Chinese.[4] We do not know if the student really told Lu Xun about the president so soon after his arrival, because Lu Xun left no record of this conversation. If he was told, I would assume that he was surprised, because his friend Lin Yutang, who had invited him to the university, and the other colleagues who had met him on arrival or taken him out to lunch before he met the student, were unlikely to have told him about Lim Boon Keng's favourite subjects. They knew his strong views well enough not to want to upset him. What they could not keep from him was the fact that the university was inefficient and the president slow to sign contracts even for some who had arrived a couple of weeks before. But at this stage, only the third evening after his arrival when he recorded his first complaint, he did not blame the president but the Edinburgh-educated acting secretary to the president, Sun Guiding, also the professor of education.[5]

Whatever he thought, he did not let one student's views disturb him. He had other things on his mind: the isolation of the campus, his inability to communicate with the native Hokkien people, his problems with food and other necessities of life, the lack of congenial and stimulating friends, the extended warm weather to which he was not accustomed after fourteen years in Beijing (not to say a typhoon on his sixth day at Xiada), his increasing loneliness, and most of all, his growing awareness that the Institute of Sinology (*Guoxue yuan*) which had brought him to this cultural desert was unlikely to get off the ground.[6] What irritated him much more was the fact that there were so many supporters of his old Beijing enemies around, some recruited as he had been, by Lin Yutang, but others gathered together by the historian Gu Jiegang.[7] Lu Xun felt that, as admirers of Chen Yuan and Hu Shi, they formed a clique of elitist opportunists, the same kind of people as those in Beijing who looked down their noses at Lu Xun's writings but really did not themselves know much. He was so irritated by one in particular that he sent in his letter of resignation from the institute within three weeks of arrival. Only Lin Yutang's appeal led him to withdraw it soon after.[8] As this happened only four days after the academic year started on 20 September, it was hardly the best of starts.

About this time, his thoughts about Xiamen were ominous. As he looked around, he confessed he was not easily moved by the beauties of nature. What caught his attention were a few relics of Zheng Chenggong (Koxinga) and his resistance against the Manchus. He found unforgettable the remains of a wall nearby which was said to have been built by Zheng Chenggong. It struck him forcibly that, apart from the island of Taiwan, Xiamen represented the last bit of China to fall to the Manchus. And when he thought about the fall of Taiwan in 1683, he recalled that that was also the year when the Kangxi emperor ordered a new imperial edition of the Thirteen

Classics and the Twenty-one Histories.[9] He then added:

> As for today, some of our citizens are only too anxious to read the
> Classics. The imperial edition of the Twenty-one Histories has be-
> come some kind of treasure. The collectors of antiques and old books
> are willing to pay the highest prices to purchase them and store them
> to be later handed down to their descendants. But Zheng Chenggong's
> wall is left to stand alone. I hear that the sand at the base of the wall
> has been taken away and sold to someone on Gulangyu Island oppo-
> site us and that this is about to endanger the base of the wall. Early
> one morning, I saw several small ships weighted low in the water
> and with their sails up moving towards Gulangyu. I suppose they
> were our sand-trading friends.

The message was clear enough: the heroic past was neglected in
favour of a meaningless "love of the ancient". But he himself was not
sentimental about relics. What he missed most, after the turbulent
and exciting years in Beijing, were interesting people, lively debate,
something or someone to set his thoughts going again and inspire
him to write. Instead, writing up his lecture notes for his students —
the history of Chinese literature — he had to read "China's old
books" every day until there was not a thought in his head.[10]

His views about the modern versus the traditional had long been
clear during the intense debates of the May Fourth Movement. It is
not clear if Lim Boon Keng knew much about Lu Xun's anti-establishment writings before he arrived at Xiamen. There is no evidence that
he was familiar with what was going on in intellectual circles in
China. He was probably not aware of the deep disagreements between Lu Xun and most of the notable scholars he had recruited to
the Institute of Sinology for Xiamen University.[11] If he was, he might
have thought little of them because the announcement of the new
institute created quite a stir in the national dailies and led some of
them to comment that the university showed foresight and discrimination and predict its future greatness. Indeed, for some, obtaining
the services of Lu Xun was something of a coup and the news did
attract students who were admirers of his literary works as well as his
modernist and unorthodox views.[12] Perhaps Lim Boon Keng simply
trusted his fellow-native of Zhangzhou, Lin Yutang, who was a close
friend and former colleague of Lu Xun's when they were both involved in the troubles at the Women's Normal University at Beijing.[13]
The pro-Confucian president probably did not know that he had
recruited an anti-Confucian with the sharpest pen in China. Bearing
this in mind, conflict between Lim Boon Keng and Lu Xun was

probably inevitable and this came to the surface during the first half of October, less than six weeks after Lu Xun's arrival.

It could have begun as early as Sunday 3 October when Lim Boon Keng called for a grand ceremony commemorating the birthday of Confucius and gave what amounted to a Sunday sermon. He had declared Saturday 2 October a holiday and, on Sunday, brought the whole university to gather in the Great Hall. He then spoke on the subject "Are the Teachings of Confucius applicable today?" Incredibly, he spoke in English with his acting university secretary, the professor of chemistry, as his interpreter. He was conscious of the anomaly and explained that his "Mandarin" was not good enough and he was concerned to get his point across accurately.[14] Lu Xun, as far as we know, did not attend the meeting. It seems unlikely that he did not know of the meeting — apparently, some 400 staff and students were present and that meant just about everyone on campus. He would have at least known that the meeting was written up fully in the *Xiada Weekly*, the university's news organ, on 9 October.[15] Yet there is no mention of the meeting anywhere in his diary and his several letters of this period. He has left us no barbed comments as he was wont to do when anything irritated him, and it is hard to imagine that this performance did not do that. Perhaps he was trying to practice what he told Xu Guangping he was doing the night after the meeting, "I have now adopted a closed-door policy, to have as little to do with, and to say as little as possible to, all the staff here."[16]

Lim Boon Keng was forthright in his faith in Confucianism. The summary of his remarks is revealing (and, in a different context today, also interesting):[17]

> To find the answer to the question, we must first know the value of the true meaning of Confucius' teaching, what its basic goal was. If we understand that, then we will have no difficulty with the question. My own views are mainly the following three:
>
> 1. Confucius' idea of religion and philosophy. There are many scholars of the new learning in China today, who have been gradually influenced by Western culture to believe that Confucianism is not a religion.[18] This idea has become dominant from 1849 to this day and repeated unquestioningly by so many. The reason for this view is that Confucian books very rarely speak of the supernatural, therefore they may only be considered as excellent texts for moral teachings. In fact, such a view is grossly mistaken. It ignores the fact that Confucian doctrines emphasise the practical and should not be compared with those which use the weird and fantastic to deceive

people into believing. As for Confucian philosophy, it not only examines in depth everything that is manifested in contemporary state and society but also profoundly explores and explains the meaning of past experiences in order to establish a set of consistent principles. That is why Confucian doctrines have been truly indestructible through the ages.

2. Morality. Confucian morality begins with the family and reaches out to the society, the country and to all under Heaven through the basic concept of *xiao* (filial piety). Now countries in the West are appreciative of this moral principle. For example, recent ideologies derived from ideas like universal love and so on all start from the family.[19] Thus the basic moral precepts in Confucianism in our country are really superior to those in other countries. Furthermore, these doctrines can be practised by everyone, not like those which consist only of hollow words.

3. Political Affairs. We Chinese are most dissatisfied with this aspect of Confucianism. But this is not because we really know Confucius. In Confucius' time, what was meant by the doctrine of "respect the ruler" was completely different from the "imperialism" that people oppose and reject today. Let us look at what our gentle Mencius said: "Let us value the common people!" This sums up in a phrase the key to Confucian ideas about politics. Also, the basic goal of leading the world to the perfect society (*Datong* or Great Harmony) is surely applicable today.[20]

From the above three points, my question today "Are the Teachings of Confucius applicable today?" is largely answered.

What did Lu Xun make of all this? Clearly he would have been unimpressed. But his thoughts were elsewhere, so all he said about Lim Boon Keng's views was that he was a "respecter of Confucius" (*zun Kong*).[21] But he was more unhappy about how the president ran the new Institute of Sinology, how slow he was to issue contracts to new staff, how unhelpful he was to his dean of Arts, Lin Yutang, how he failed to keep the new director and allowed the institute to be dominated by one clique of traditionalists hostile to Lu Xun.[22] Lu Xun had attended the institute's first business meeting on 18 September and noted the ambitious plans which struck him as being dominated by a crude productivity yardstick, "like feeding cows with good grass so that more milk could be squeezed out".[23] He was also caustic about the president's publishing plans for the institute. He doubted Lim Boon Keng's sincerity because, as he said, when he produced his manuscript on ancient stories to show how ready he was to show "productivity", it came to nothing.[24]

It was in this atmosphere of great promise on paper and stringent financial control by Lim Boon Keng that the institute was officially opened on National Day, 10 October, with considerable fanfare.[25] Lu Xun was present but really had nothing to say about Lim Boon Keng's earnest justifications for such an institute and the backing he had received from the university's founder, Tan Kah Kee, for Chinese traditional studies. He commented instead on the National Day fireworks and the evening's entertainment. Concerning the institute, he was simply irritated by what he saw as the meanness, the lack of style, the pathetic self-satisfaction of ignorant provincials being deceived by some mediocre performers. He did not directly say so, but his description of what he and his colleagues had to do to put up an "instant" antiquities exhibition on the cheap points to his views on the hollowness in the president's claims for the institute.[26]

But Lu Xun did not forget what Lim Boon Keng said about Chinese traditional studies at the official opening. When he was asked to give the weekly address to the whole university four days later (14 October), he spoke for half an hour and deliberately chose to give the opposite message. His topic was "Study fewer Chinese books, Be a busybody."[27] One of his students recalled what Lu Xun said.[28] He said that although he was in Xiamen to teach Chinese studies and should therefore be advising everyone to study the ancient books, his experience in Beijing with those who advocated classical studies and his concern for those in Xiamen who embraced the *Guwen Guanzhi* anthology of classical essays fervently had led him to think: "instead of reading more ancient books, it would be better to read less!" Of late, he said, the voices calling for "returning to the ancients" in order to save China had become louder. But most of the people who advocated this had ulterior motives. They wanted people to read the Classics so that they would become filial sons and obedient citizens. They boasted of their skills in the Classics and their mastery of Chinese civilization. But how many had used the *Analects* to persuade foreign soldiers not to shoot Chinese people during the May Thirtieth Affair (1925),[29] how many had used the curses in the *Book of Changes* to sink the Japanese ships (off Tianjin) which led to the 18 March (1926) tragedy when some 200 people were killed and wounded?[30]

He went on to add, to save China, it might be better for the time being to read fewer Chinese books: to read fewer of such books might cause your literary style to suffer a little. But to read more might cause more harm at least in three ways: the more you read, the weaker your will to act; the more you read, the more cautious you would become; the more you read, the more confused you would be about what was right and wrong. This was not to ask you not to read. It was good to like to read, but not "dead books" which had little application; not to read yourself stupid but to care for worldly matters; and not to read yourselves to death, but also to look after your health. There were good books and bad books; books that could be believed and those that could not be believed. As the ancients said, "to believe everything you read in books, it would be better not to have books". That, he explained, was said in the context of the accuracy of historical fact. Here he was speaking of the realm of ideas in the ancient classics: Read fewer of such ancient Chinese books for the time being. If you had to read them, then do not forget to be discriminating and critical, to reject the dross and accept only what was good in them.

This contrary message was clearly directed against Lim Boon Keng's platitudes about respect for the Confucian classics and was an open challenge to the very institute Lu Xun was appointed to and Lim Boon Keng was so proud of. But Lu Xun gave the appearance of tempering his message with another insight in the second half of his talk. This second comment saved the president's face and made it possible to have Lu Xun's talk half-recorded in the *Xiada Weekly*. And the fact that only the second half was summarized and published and no mention was made of the first suggests how much Lim Boon Keng was hurt by Lu Xun's call to read fewer ancient Chinese books. What Lu Xun thought about this omission is not on record, but clearly the younger members of his audience who remembered how they clapped enthusiastically at the first message never forgot the treatment this message received. That this message was left out while the second was set out at some length was not the kind of behaviour they could respect the university for.

That second message brought out another aspect of Lu Xun's impression of Lim Boon Keng, which is interesting. The message was summarized as follows in the university's weekly organ:

People do not like busybodies because the word "busy-ness" suggests stirring up trouble. In fact, this should not be so. I think China today needs more busybodies. All matters need busybodies to weed out the old, to bring forth the new and thus gradually make progress. For example, Columbus's discovery of the New Continent, Nansen's explorations of the Arctic and the various discoveries made by scientists — they are all achievements made by busybodies. And this university, for example. Originally, it was no more than a piece of waste land. Erecting buildings and admitting students is in fact another case of "busy-ness." Thus I think that busybodies should not be faulted.

I notice that our sports field is often full of people and the Chinese reading room in the library is often full. That is a good sign. But there are very few readers of the newspapers and magazines in the Western languages reading room — as if they are not important. That is the result of not knowing how to be a busybody. It may not matter much if these Western newspapers and magazines are not read, but to look at them after class could really increase your general knowledge. So I hope you will all pay attention whenever you can to all kinds of knowledge. . . .

Of course, different people have ideas and face circumstances that are different. I would not advise everyone to be great busybodies, but why not taste some little "busy-ness." For example, whenever you meet with matters that need a little correction, a little improvement, you could do something. Even in such small things, constant attention to them is not without benefit. And even if you cannot do anything, then let us not join the common mocking and scolding of busybodies, especially those busybodies who fail.[31]

This message met with Lim Boon Keng's approval. As a doctor with a fine training in modern science in Edinburgh, he would greatly appreciate what Lu Xun was trying to say. But apparently when Lim Boon Keng totally agreed with Lu Xun and said that Tan Kah Kee, the university's founder, was one such busybody when he invested so much of his fortune in education, Lu Xun was amazed that he did not see how that contradicted his profound respect for Confucius. Lu Xun added, "This place is just like that, a lot of confused nonsense!"[32]

Nothing, of course, is so clear-cut. Tan Kah Kee, the busybody whom Lu Xun was prepared to praise, was, according to Lim Boon Keng, also the man who supported the emphasis on Chinese classical studies and who believed that Chinese studies and modern science should be given equal weight. And indeed, Tan Kah Kee had a modern practical side that was truly refreshing for China at the time. With his own paltry village education in the Classics, he had gone out in the world and learnt to value the science, technology and business institutions of the West.[33] It was he who invited his friend Lim Boon Keng, a modern man of science and entrepreneurship, to give up everything in Singapore and help him build Xiamen University. Both agreed that the university should educate a new generation of Chinese who would have all the modern skills while still projecting the best in Chinese civilization. It was perhaps tragic that Lu Xun, the epitome of the outraged traditional scholar in revolt against the corruptions of the past, saw himself on one side and saw Lim Boon Keng as a cultural parvenu supported by a well-meaning but insensitive millionaire on the other. In between, and probably at the heart of the division between the two men, were Lim Boon Keng's efforts to revive Confucianism.

Lu Xun stayed for another three months at Xiamen University and became increasingly disillusioned with the place.[34] Only the students with keen literary interests gave him some happy moments.[35] Soon after his talk on 14 October, he began thinking of cutting short his two-year contract to one and then sought to leave even sooner. An offer of appointment to the new "revolutionary" Zhongshan (Sun Yat-sen) University in Guangzhou (backed by the victorious Guomindang) as dean of the Arts Faculty clinched it and he decided to leave. Lin Yutang and others tried to dissuade him, even Lim Boon Keng, and most of his students were specially disappointed at his decision.[36] The story of Lu Xun's later disgust at the way the Institute of Sinology was run and with what he managed to do during the remaining months before his departure for Guangzhou deserves fuller treatment. For this brief essay, Lu Xun's own picture of how it all ended will suffice. This is found in the third of his Xiamen letters which he wrote on 31 December 1926 and the letter he wrote on board the ship taking him to Guangzhou dated 16 January 1927, both written for publication in the weekly, *Yusi*.

In his December letter, he speaks of the president twice, the first time in the context of publishing a couple of scholarly collections and the second when the president wanted to invite the dean of Sciences as adviser to the institute. On the first occasion, he said:

> Later when budget cuts were made, (Lin) Yutang argued strenuously against them. It appeared that the president then said, if you have manuscripts ready for publication, you only have to bring them out and they will be printed immediately. Therefore, I brought out my manuscript ("Guxiaoshuo Goucheng"). This was placed before him for about at most ten minutes and then returned to me. Nothing more was heard about the matter. The result proved no more than that I had a manuscript and was not bluffing. I then decided to forget about the idea of publishing "Guxiaoshuo Goucheng" and also reduce my period of stay from one year to half a year. . . .[37]

On the second:

> The day before we had a meeting and found that even the institute's weekly nearly stopped publication. But the president wanted to add another adviser, for example, people like the dean of Science[38] as advisers, because we needed to make friendly contacts. I really don't understand the customs here in Xiamen. Why would the study of Chinese classics harm our relations with people like the dean of Science, so much so we need an adviser's rope to tie us together? I know nothing about the art of making friendly contacts. The Institute director, Shen Jianshi, has already resigned. So I decided also to leave.[39]

In the January letter, he speaks of his resignation and why people thought he was leaving. He had resigned for reasons of health, which everyone knew was only an excuse. The students obviously thought the university had pushed him out. The letter says:[40]

> I do not know how it happened, but the students eventually organised a Reform the University Movement and their first demand was that the president should sack the university secretary, Dr Liu Shuqi.[41]

> I understand that three years ago, there was a similar sort of (student) unrest. The result was a total defeat for the students who then went to found Daxia University in Shanghai.[42] I do not know how the president defended himself on that occasion. This time he said that my resignation had nothing to do with Dr Liu, but was the result of my being squeezed out in the struggle between the Hu Shi faction and the Lu Xun faction. This comment was published in the Gulangyu daily *Min Zhong* and has already been denounced. But some colleagues remained greatly agitated and asked questions at a meeting. The president's reply was very straightforward: I never made such a comment. . . .[43]

> The president, Dr Lin Wenqing (Lim Boon Keng), is a Chinese of British nationality who cannot avoid speaking of Confucius whenever he opens his mouth. He once wrote a book about the religion of Confucianism, but I regret I have forgotten its title.[44] I gather he also has an autobiography written in English which the Commercial Press (in Shanghai) is about to publish.[45] At present, he is doing a study on "Human Races." He has really treated me very well and has invited me to dinner several times. He has even given me two farewell dinners. The "squeezed out theory" has now been set aside, but what I heard the day before yesterday was that he has been propagating the view that I did not come to Xiamen to teach but to create trouble. That is why I did not even resign from my position in Beijing.[46]

Lu Xun then went on to predict that, now that he had left, his sins would become even worse and followed that with an account of how his talk in November at Jimei School (Chip Bee School) annoyed the principal Ye Yuan. This school, founded by Tan Kah Kee, was closely linked with Xiamen University and can be said to reflect a similar policy laid down by Tan Kah Kee, who trusted and supported Ye Yuan as much as he trusted and supported Lim Boon Keng. Lu Xun adds that Ye Yuan also says that the student agitation at Jimei School had been caused by what Lu Xun was preaching.[47]

Thus ended Lu Xun's four months and twelve days in Xiamen. But, as I have suggested, the last three months were mainly the playing out of what was already there within the first six weeks. By the time Lu Xun gave his assembly address on 14 October, a combination of factors had made his original plan of staying two years at Xiamen University almost impossible. Among these factors, Lim Boon Keng's Confucianism was minor but symptomatic. I shall end with some reflections on this.

First, there is no question that Lim Boon Keng was obsessive about his Confucianism. He had been writing on the subject for thirty years and was a great believer in the idea that it provided the moral and religious beliefs which complemented Western scientific values. What is also clear is that these views, which he had developed during the late nineteenth century, and which were confirmed and perhaps strengthened by people like Kang Youwei who visited Singapore during the first decade of the twentieth, remained more or less unchanged until he took up the presidency of Xiamen University.[48] This was probably not his fault. Greater thinkers in China had held aloof from the modernizations clamoured for by the supporters of the May Fourth Movement. Even some of the pioneers of Western ideas in China had reacted in the 1920s against what they thought were excesses. And among Lim Boon Keng's Western friends, including some well-known Western scholars, were many who were afraid of the calls for revolution, of both nationalism and communism, and who advocated the preservation of China's glorious traditions. And, not least, his friend who founded Xiamen University shared his concerns and entrusted the whole question of traditional Chinese studies to his judgement.[49]

What has not emerged from the Lu Xun materials, and from those who have been writing about Lu Xun's stay in Xiamen,[50] is the fact that Lim Boon Keng at this time was vigorously engaged in trying to build an engineering school and eventually a school of medicine. Also, of all the academic staff appointed to the university at this time, the great majority of them were in the sciences and social sciences. And in the humanities, there were not only foreign scholars like Paul Demiéville and Gustav Ecke and as many foreign-trained teachers as those educated in China there, but also as many courses on foreign languages as on the Chinese language.[51] If anything, one would expect criticism that the university did not emphasize traditional Chinese studies enough. Thus, establishing the Institute of Sinology could be interpreted as Lim Boon Keng's attempt to remedy that lack. Yet it was precisely this institute, the part of the university which employed Lu Xun, that was the focus of his anger and disillusionment. Of course, from the materials available, we could argue that the real cause of Lu Xun's anger was not Lim Boon Keng's Confucianism but his failure to make more of Chinese studies, to understand what that institute meant to the younger generation and to give it more support. Instead, Lim Boon Keng left so much to the group of traditionalists who only wanted to please him and never appreciated the aspirations of the students for a new kind of humanist studies. Given the authoritarian structure of the university, this failure would also be related to the starting-point of Lim Boon Keng's *guoxue*, the reaffirmation of Confucian values, which Lu Xun identified (and he might have been quite right here) as the real reason why the institute could have no future.[52]

After his experiences in Beijing, Lu Xun's negative views about Confucianism in its contemporary archaic forms are understandable. His lack of sympathy for the university, for its founder and for its president, who was a modern man with a fine scientific background, however, is less easy to explain. It would seem, in retrospect, that Lu Xun had not departed from the traditional Chinese literatus' contempt for the uncultured, self-made rich man who was perceived as using his wealth to make a memorial to himself.[53] He certainly had no sympathy for what it meant for someone like Lim Boon Keng to be born in a British colony and educated in the West and who still hankered for Chinese learning and wanted to identify with China. What was clear to Lu Xun was that this Chinese "outsider" had a limited knowledge of the traditional classics but was trying to dictate what young Chinese should know and do. And what particularly angered him was that people whom he considered were charlatans and who belonged to factions hostile to him personally were pandering to Lim Boon Keng's reactionary ideas.[54] As a result, there seemed to have been no opportunity for a dialogue between two essentially modern men: Lu Xun, the native-born Chinese who grasped the critical importance of modernity from within; and Lim Boon Keng, the Western-educated and foreign-born Chinese who thought he needed the Confucian cloak of respectability to legitimize the extent he wanted China to be transformed by science and technology. Without a dialogue to bridge the gulf in their respective backgrounds, it is no wonder that their brief encounter was such a futile one.

NOTES

1 Chen Yusong, "Lin Wenqing lun" (Essay on Lim Boon Keng), *Nanyang Xuebao*, vol.19, nos.1/2, (1965): p. 132, says that Lim Boon Keng had been called out of retirement, but from all accounts, he was still very active in public affairs in Singapore. By "retirement", Chen Yusong probably meant that he no longer held any official position in China or in the Straits Settlements, nor was he practising medicine. But he still had considerable banking and commercial interests.

2 When Lim Boon Keng died on 1 January 1957, he was mourned by many in Singapore, especially by the members of the China Society; see Chen Weilung, "Lin Wengqing boshi zhuanlue" (A short biography of Lim Boon Keng), *Annual of the China Society* (1957): pp. 71–73; and *Lin Wengqing boshi dansheng bainian jiniankan* (Commemorative Volume on the hundredth anniversary of Dr Lim Boon Keng's birth) (Singapore, 1973). Since then, there has been an extensive study of Lim Boon Keng's ideas by Lee Guan Kin (Li Yuanjin), "Lin Wenqing di Sixiang: Zhongxi wenhua di huiliu yu maodun" (MA thesis, Nanyang University, 1974), now in press.

3 There is a recent study by Ye Zhongling, "Lu Xun he Lin Wengqing zai Xiada di yichang chongtu", *Renwen yu shehui koxue lunwenji* 4 (1984): pp. 109–114. Lu Xun's diaries are invaluable. I have used the excellent annotated edition collected in the *Lu Xun Quanji* (Complete works of Lu Xun), 16 vols (hereafter *Complete works*) (Beijing, 1981), vols 14 and 15. For 4 September, *Complete Works* 14: p. 615.

4 This was Yu Nianyuan, a student who had come from Qingdao University. Also known as Yu Di, he wrote about this meeting thirty years later, "Huiyi Lu Xun xiansheng zai Xiamen Daxue", *Wenyi Yuebao*, 10 October 1956, reprinted in *Lu Xun huiyi lu* (Shanghai, 1979). Lu Xun's diary merely notes that he had come to visit him on the 8th, *Complete Works*, 14: p. 615.

5 Letter to Xu Shoushang, dated 7 September, *Complete Works*, 11: p. 480. According to the University Gazette for 1926–27 (*Xiada Bugao*), Sun Guiding was the professor of social psychology and head of education, and also head of philosophy. He is listed as having an education doctorate from Edinburgh University, Lim Boon Keng's alma mater, and is clearly someone Lim Boon Keng trusted. He represented Lim Boon Keng at the important Overseas Chinese Education Conference organized by Jinan University in Shanghai in 1930; see *Report* of that conference (Shanghai, 1930): pp. 14–32.

6 These views emerge from his early letters, most notably those to Xu Guangping, *Liangdi shu, Complete Works*, 11: pp. 105, 114–117, 118–121. Similar views, sometimes even more strongly expressed, are also found in his letters to Xu Shoushang, Wei Suyuan and Zhang Tingqian, *Complete Works*, 11: pp. 480–490. Also, see Chuan-dao, *He Lu Xun xiangchu di rizi* (Chengdu, 1979), pp. 50–64.

7 Letters to Xu Guangping, dated 20 and 25 September, *Complete Works*, 11: pp. 118–121, 125–128.

8 He resigned from the institute on 24 September. This is vividly described in his letter to Xu Guangping, posted on the 27th; Diary, *Complete Works*, 14: p. 617; *Liangdi shu*, 11: p. 126. Five days later, he was forced to withdraw his resignation by Lin Yutang; *Complete Works* 11: p. 133.

9 "Letter from Xiamen" dated 23 September and first published in the first issue of Xiamen monthly called *Boting*, edited by the Xiada students who formed the Yangyang Literary Society under Lu Xun's guidance. One of the editors was Yu Nianyuan (see note 4 above). The issue was undated but probably appeared in December 1926. This open letter was the only one in which he wrote about Xiamen in an affectionate, almost romantic, way. He did this for his Xiamen students and for a local audience; *Complete Works, Huagaiji xubian*, 3: pp. 369–371.

10 Letter to Wei Shuyuan, Wei Congwu, Li Jiye, dated 4 October; *Complete Works*, 11: pp. 483–484.

11 His early writings in the *Xin Qingnian* from 1918 and in various literary supplements of newspapers show his distaste for any restorationist of *fugu* views. In the six volumes of his work published before he arrived in Xiamen, at least three included essays of biting sarcasm about contemporary traditionalism and there were numerous references to his arguments with a faction of Western-educated scholars in Beijing. But it is likely that Lim Boon Keng was impressed by his fame as a writer and his scholarly *Brief History of Chinese Fiction* rather than by his radical opinions. He should, however, have been pleased (if he noticed it) that Lu Xun was an admirer of Qu Yuan. He was himself a great admirer and had started on a translation from *Li Sao*, and would have approved of Lu Xun's choice of the quotation from *Li Sao* in lieu of a preface to *Panghuang*, the volume of stories published in Beijing in August 1926, a few weeks before Lu Xun arrived in Xiamen. The sentiment of having been banished to the wilderness, of course, was probably on his mind when he was forced to leave Beijing to go to Xiamen. In his words a few years later, "Escaping from Beijing and hiding in Xiamen", his creative instincts dried up and, while in Xiamen, he was only able to write up some legends, fairy tales, historical anecdotes and some reminiscences; "Preface to Collected Works", dated 14 December 1932, in *Nanqiang Beidiaoji, Complete Works*, 4: p. 456.

12 Between June and August 1926, reports in *Shenbao* and *Shishi Xinbao* were favourable towards Xiada's plans for expansion, and reported on the appointment of Lu Xun (Zhou Shuren). For an extract from *Shishi Xinbao*, 4 August 1926, see *Complete Works*, 3: p. 396, note 6. Also see Zhou Zhi, "Lu Xun shi zhenyang zoudi, (16 January 1927)", in *Beixin* (Shanghai), 23 and 29 January 1927, reprinted in "Lu Xun

zai Xiamen ziliao xuanbian", a collection of documents concerning Lu Xun's period at Xiamen, published in *Lu Xun Yanjiu ziliao* (Beijing, 1977), 2: pp. 283–287. Other writings which touch on this subject are Ai Fei, *Lu Xun yu Qingnian* (Taiyuan, 1978), pp. 18–20; Chen Mengshao, *Lu Xun zai Xiamen* (Beijing, 1954); Xu Guangping, *Xinwei di jinian* (Beijing 1951), pp. 61–72.

13 They became close friends in 1925 when they were colleagues at Women's Normal University and where Lin Yutang was dean of studies. They did not always agree, but there was considerable respect and some affection between the two men; for example, Lin Yutang's views on "fair play" in *Yusi* 57, 14 December 1925 and Lu Xun's reply which he wrote two weeks later, later republished in *Fen, Complete Works*, 1: pp. 270–277. A few months later, in March 1926, both their names appeared in a list of those to be arrested which was circulating in Beijing — Lin was no.17 and Lu Xun was no.21 — and Lu Xun comments on this list in April 1926; in *Eryi ji*, Appendix, *Complete Works*, 3: pp. 575–581. In May 1926, Lin Yutang was recruited by Lim Boon Keng and in June, he in turn persuaded Lu Xun to come to Xiamen; diary entry, *Complete Works*, 14: p. 606; see also his letter to Li Bingzhong, dated 17 June, where he intimates that he was planning to leave Beijing and go south; *Complete Works*, 11: p. 468.

14 *Xiada Zhoukan* 158 (9 October 1926). The acting university secretary was Professor Liu Shuqi (see note 38 below).

15 *Xiada Zhoukan* 158 (9 October 1926).

16 *Complete Works*, 11: p. 140.

17 *Xiada Zhoukan* 158 (9 October 1926). This text of Lim Boon Keng's speech is quoted in "Lu Xun zai Xiamen ziliao xuanbiao", in *Lu Xun yanjiu zilao* (note 12), pp. 294–295.

18 This is an interesting point, but it is far from clear that it was Western culture that influenced the Chinese to think that Confucianism is not a religion. Among the literati, the distinction between *rujiao* (Confucian Teaching) and other *jiao* (teachings) had long been made, and it was difficult to equate Confucius with Buddha and the various popular *shen*. In that context, the literati usually held *rujiao* to be above the others. It merely took Western scholars to confirm what these literati already believed — that Confucius was not a god or a prophet, but a great and wise teacher.

19 I do not know what he had in mind. If the stress were on universal love, that would be the very opposite of the particularism of family relationships — and strictly hierarchical even within those relationships.

20 It is puzzling how Lim Boon Keng could have compared "respect the ruler" (*zunjun*) with "imperialism" (*diguo zhuyi*). Obviously the two are not the same, and there is no suggestion that to reject "imperialism" is connected in any way with not respecting the ruler. As for *Datong*, this harks back to the strong influence of Kang Youwei on Lim Boon Keng when he was still a young man; Lee Guan Kin, "Lin Wenqing di Sixiang."

21 He concluded this the night after Lim Boon Keng's speech, letter to Xu Guangping, dated 4 October, *Complete Works*, 11: p. 141.

22 Lu Xun was critical of the institute almost from the start, but did not always blame Lim Boon Keng for poor leadership. He also thought the director of studies, Shen Jianshi, was weak and irresponsible and was not impressed with his friend Liu Yutang's administrative skills. Much of his anger was directed against Gu Jiegang and the people he brought from Beijing. See his letters; *Complete Works*, 11: pp. 119–120, 126, 133–135, 140–142, 484–485, 489–490, 503–505.

23 Letters to Xu Guangping, 4 October, *Complete Works*, 11: p. 141.

24 "Xiamen tongxin (3)", in *Huagaiji xubian*, *Complete Works*, 3: p. 394.

25 *Xiada Zhoukan* 159 (16 October 1926). It reports on the exhibition of Lu Xun's collection of Six Dynasties-Sui-Tang rubbings.

26 Letters to Xu Guangping, 4 and 16 October, *Complete Works*, 11: pp. 141 and 157.

27 The first half of the topic was similar to his reply to *Jingbao* (Beijing) Supplement on 21 February 1925, on recommending books for youth to read, "Qingnian bidushu". He offered no titles of books, but filled in remarks to the effect that he thought the young people of China should read fewer Chinese books but more foreign books; republished in *Huagaiji*, *Complete Works*, 3: p. 12. On that occasion, he was severely criticized and had to elaborate on this point in three notable replies in the same Supplement on 3 and 8 March, and 3 April 1925; these were collected and published in *Jiwaiji shiyi* only after his death (in 1938); *Complete Works*, 7: pp. 248–251, 252–260, 263–265 (which include the texts of the letters objecting to what he said). The second part of his 1926 Xiamen talk, "Be a busy-body", however, represented his more recent thinking.

28 Yu Di, "Huiyi Lu Xun Xiansheng zai Xiamen Daxue" (see note 4 above) who recalls the talk thirty years later and his version may not be accurate. It is likely, however, that he would have checked his recollections with Lu Xun's 1925 re-marks and replies. I have included this version here because it is succinct and the main thrust of the argument is true to Lu Xun's views and comes out more clearly here than in his three replies.

29 R. W. Rigby, *The May 30 Movement* (Canberra, 1980), esp. pp. 108–111, for some comments on Lu Xun's reactions.

30 This refers to Duan Qirui's shooting on 18 March 1926 at demonstrators who protested against the arrival of the Japanese squadron off the coast of Tianjin.

31 *Xiada Zhoukan* 168 (23 October 1926); the text is quoted in "Lu Xun zai Xiamen ziliao xuanbian", in *Lu Xun yanjiu ziliao* (note 12 above), pp. 291–292. Lu Xun refers to this in his letter to Xu Guangping, dated 16 October, *Complete Works*, 11: p. 185, and note 5.

32 Letter to Xu Guangping, *Complete Works*, 11: p. 158.

33 There is now a growing literature on Tan Kah Kee (Chen Jiageng). On his contri-butions to education, see the brief statement in Wang Zengbing and Yu Gang,

Chen Jiageng xinxueji (Fujian jiaoyu chubanshe, 1981), pp. 15–44. For details, see Yong Ching Fatt, *Tan Kah Kee: The Making of an Overseas Chinese Legend* (Oxford University Press: Singapore, 1987).

34 It should be noted, however, that during these months he wrote several fine stories and essays and collected some of his best work from earlier periods for publication, notably some stories later collected in *Zhaohua xishi* and the two collections *Fen* and *Huagaiji xubian*. He also completed his manuscript, "Guxiaoshuo Gouchen", but the university failed to publish it. Cao Juren, in his sensitive biography of Lu Xun, claims that the months in Xiamen were very fruitful, and I agree, but it is not clear that he did the editing of his *Yecao* in Xiamen; *Lu Xun pingzhuan* (Hong Kong, 1961), p. 91.

35 Unfortunately, their literary talents did not impress him; letters to Xu Guangping, *Complete Works*, 11: pp. 212 and 226.

36 The offer was received on 11 November; *Diary, Complete Works*, 14: p. 623. But he hesitated a few days before deciding to leave; letters to Xu Guangping, *Complete Works*, 11: pp. 204 and 211. Within a few days, however, the news of his going to Guangzhou had spread and Lin Yutang tried hard to dissuade him from going. Financial problems at the institute, however, made Lin Yutang's work increasingly difficult. Lu Xun eventually persuaded Lin Yutang to seek Lim Boon Keng's permission to let him break his contract and leave by the end of the year, *Complete Works*, 11: pp. 215 and 221. Later, some of his students used his departure to organize demonstrations against the university and these became serious in January 1927, leading to considerable disruption of the university, *Complete Works*, 11: pp. 261, 262, 268–269, 274–276.

37 "Xiamen tongxin (3)", *Huagaiji xubian, Complete Works*, 3: pp. 393–395.

38 This was Liu Shuqi, professor of chemistry, a graduate of Michigan University who obtained his doctorate in chemical engineering from Columbia University.

39 This is not accurate; Shen Jianshi had left Xiamen in October, more than two months before these meetings about financial cuts. Lu Xun had received the Zhongshan University offer by mid-November and was determined to go if he were allowed to break his two-year contract; note the question about his contract in an interview given on 15 December 1926, in *Xiasheng Daily*, 15 January 1927, reprinted in *Lu Xun yanjiu ziliao* (note 12 above), pp. 270–273.

40 "Haishang tongxin", *Huagaiji xubian, Complete Works*, 3: pp. 398–401.

41 See note 38. Because the institute was short of space, it had borrowed the third floor of the Biology Building to be its exhibition room and library. Professor Liu, as dean of science, had asked to have the rooms of the third floor returned. It was later thought that he was responsible for getting Lu Xun so angry that Lu Xun resigned; *Complete Works*, 3: p. 402, note 5. Another report said that it was Professor Liu's expensive equipment, purchased from Britain and the United States, which led Lim Boon Keng to try to cut the institute's funds; but what has been seen to be more important are Lim Boon Keng's *fugu* ("restore the ancient") policies and Lu Xun's fierce opposition to them. That has been identified as the main source of

conflict between the two men; "Lu Xun zai Xiamen ziliao xuanbiao", in *Lu Xun yanjiu ziliao*, (note 12 above), p. 276.

42 *Complete Works*, 3: p. 402, note 6.

43 Lu Xun obviously believed that Lim Boon Keng did say what was published (and later denied) in *Min Zhong*. We have no way of determining the truth of this matter. There were so many rumours about why Lu Xun resigned that it cannot be assumed that *Min Zhong*'s report was accurate. By that time, Lu Xun was too angry to care.

44 This was Lim Boon Keng's *Kongjiao dagang* (Outline of the Confucian Religion), published in Chinese, but consisting largely of translations from his essays published in the *Straits Chinese Magazine* and presented to the Straits Philosophical Society, Singapore. I have not seen a copy and there does not seem to be one at the Singapore National Library. In a recent biographical entry in *Zhuanji wenxue* (Taibei), vol.34, no.6 (June 1979): p. 146, the book is listed as one in *English*, which suggests that no one there has seen it. It would appear that Lu Xun and his colleagues had not seen the book. He says here that he had forgotten the title, but it is likely that he was too contemptuous of Lim Boon Keng to bother to remember. At an interview given a month earlier to Li Shuzhen and published in *Xiasheng Daily*, 15 January 1927 (the day before Lu Xun wrote this letter on board ship on the 16th), Lu Xun is quoted as saying, "He (Lim Boon Keng) calls himself a Confucius-believer and had once written a book called 'Kong shenmo gang' (Kong I-do-not-know-what gang)". His friend Sun Fuyuan added, "Wasn't it *Kongjiao dagang*? That . . . ," and both looked at each other and laughed; reprinted in "Lu Xun zai Xiamen ziliao xuanbiao", in *Lu Xun yanjiu ziliao*, pp. 270–273.

45 There is no such autobiography. What the Commercial Press (Shanghai) published in 1927 was *Tragedies of Eastern Life: an Introduction to the Problems of Social Psychology*, which was an attempt at fiction drawn from stories of the Malays, Chinese and British in British Malaya. It has a strong ethical tone which is summed up in Lim Boon Keng's preface thus: "That there is the possibility of any good in the race of Aholybab proves the innateness of goodness in Man, however sunken in degradation, and affords an incentive to the highest efforts to rescue the victims of a cruel and heartless traffic, stupidly tolerated by civilized governments in the Far East."

46 By this time, rumours were circulating and the atmosphere was tense. Lu Xun was so hostile towards Xiamen University and its president that he was prepared to believe anything that put Lim Boon Keng in a bad light. There is no corroborative evidence to suggest that Lim Boon Keng actually said anything like that. There is, however, Lu Xun's diary to confirm that Lim Boon Keng called on him on 4 January and gave him two farewell lunches on the 9th and 13th; *Complete Works*, 14: pp. 638–639. The lunches could not have been very enjoyable: the students had seen Lu Xun on 2 January and, after failing to persuade him to stay, had organized a general meeting on 7 January to protest against the university and ask for radical reforms in the system; letter to Xu Guangping, 6 January and note 2, *Complete Works*, 11: pp. 268–270.

47 "Haishang tongxin", *Complete Works*, 3: p. 400. Between Lim Boon Keng and Ye Yuan, they would have given Tan Kah Kee a rather poor impression of Lu Xun. The unfortunate developments did not trouble Tan Kah Kee much, because he was in far greater difficulties trying to save his industrial enterprises in Singapore and Malaya and finding funds for both the Jimei schools and Xiamen University; see Yong Ching Fatt, *Tan Kah Kee*, chapter 4; and Chen Bisheng and Yang Guozhen, *Chen Jiageng zhuan* (Fuzhou, 1981), pp. 36–41.

48 This is brought out clearly in Lee Guan Kin's work (note 2 above).

49 Tan Yeok Seong, *Tan Kah Kee, the Towkay, a case study of Overseas Chinese Leadership and Pang Power* (Xiamen University Alumni in Southeast Asia: Singapore, 1969), quoted in Lee Guan Kin, p. 83.

50 All those who have written on this topic in China had nothing but rude things to say about Lim Boon Keng. Only those outside China and the alumni of Xiamen University have been relatively kind.

51 See *Xiada Bugao* for 1926–27 and 1928–29 for a list of academic staff and details of their educational backgrounds; also issues of *Xiada Zhoukan* nos.120–170 (1925–26) and nos.171–180 (November 1927–28).

52 In various letters to Xu Guangping between September 1926 and January 1927. *Complete Works*, 11: pp. 118–276.

53 This was certainly the view of one of Lu Xun's admiring students who wrote about Lu Xun's departure from Xiamen; Zhuo Zhi, "Lu Xun shi zeyang zoudi", *Beixin* (Shanghai), 29 January 1927, reprinted in "Lu Xun zai Xiamen ziliao xuanbian", *Lu Xun yanjiu ziliao* (1977), 2: pp. 283–287. For the story (probably apocryphal) about Lu Xun's contempt for Lim Boon Keng's continual praise for Tan Kah Kee's financial contributions and sacrifices and his offer of "liangmao qian" (twenty cents), see Hong Sisi's efforts to explain that away; preface to Wang Zengbing and Yu Gang, *Chen Jiageng xingxueji*, pp. 1–4.

54 Lu Xun's hostility towards his colleagues in the institute who were recruited from Beijing, especially those admirers of Chen Yuan and Hu Shi whom he believed were recruited by Gu Jiegang, is well-known and a little mystifying, even embarrassing to many admirers of both Lu Xun and Gu Jiegang. It was indeed a pity that these men contributed to Lu Xian's opinion of Lim Boon Keng as a mean, dictatorial and benighted charlatan who was also a bit of a fool. Particularly tragic for Lim Boon Keng was the fact that Lu Xun's departure was closely followed by that of Gu Jiegang, also for Zhongshan University at Guangzhou (Canton); see the letters between Lu Xun and Gu Jiegang in July 1927, and published in *Sanxianji* (1932); *Complete Works*, 4: pp. 39–40.

CHAPTER 9

The Chinese as Immigrants and Settlers: Singapore

IMMIGRATION AS AN HISTORICAL phenomenon has existed for thousands of years, but the concept of the immigrant is relatively new. The reason for this is that travel, trading between distant places and the actual movement of peoples were never clearly distinguished before modern times. It was assumed that people who travelled in search of work or in search of trade returned home after a period of time. But even if there was intermarriage and families stayed behind in foreign lands, this was regarded as perfectly natural. There was no idea that someone who arrived on an alien shore, for whatever purpose, was an immigrant as we understand it today.

This is important for our understanding of the early years of Singapore under the British flag. Singapore had been there long before the British arrived and people had moved in and out of Singapore for a long time. They included Chinese visitors, traders as well as cultivators. In that context, it would be difficult to say that any of them were immigrants. This was certainly true for the first few decades of Singapore after 1819, for Singapore was no more than one of many islands in the Malay archipelago and a part of the larger Malay world consisting of the Malay peninsula, Sumatra and extending to Java and Borneo. At that time, many Chinese and other people moved freely around the waters of the Straits of Malacca, the Java Sea and the South China Sea.

What was different was that the British established Singapore as a free port and this attracted people who were tired of paying onerous and arbitrary taxes elsewhere. Thus Singapore, following in the footsteps of Penang, the original free port, was a magnet and the Chinese were merely one of many groups of people attracted there. These Chinese came from the Malay peninsula, from the Riau-Lingga archipelago, from Bangka-Biliton, and from the Sumatran Coast, in quick response to the foundation of another free port.

Three types of Chinese moved into Singapore very quickly. The first were those who were accustomed to British and Dutch administration, who knew what European laws and trading arrangements would mean. These came mainly from Malacca and Penang and included others who were dealing with the Dutch in various parts of the archipelago. The second group were those who had experience with various parts of the Malay and Thai world and understood the subtleties of local customs. This second group, many of whom were several generations old in the region, were familiar with the problems of dealing with local rulers and were also invaluable to the British and Dutch administrators and merchants who needed their expertise to assist in their trading activities. Although they had lived under native rulers up to this point, they quickly adapted to British rule in Singapore.

The third group were probably the most interesting because they were relatively new to the region and came fresh to British rule directly from China. Most of them came from the southern counties of Fujian but there were also those from the Teochiu-speaking areas and also some who spoke Cantonese and Hakka. But it would be wrong to overemphasize their newness to the region. Most of them would have come because of some connections with relatives who had been trading in the region for decades. They would have come from villages and towns in southern China which had had long connections with the trade of Southeast Asia. So these newcomers from China were probably not totally unfamiliar with conditions in the region and, with the help of their families and business connections, knew what to expect and could quickly adapt to the new conditions of Singapore.

Thus most of the Chinese who arrived in Singapore during its first decade under the British were no strangers to the region. Sir Stamford Raffles and his successors were quick to appreciate that these Chinese could provide the expertise needed to get Singapore off the ground. These early arrivals, whether from within the region or from China, were traders or the descendants of traders or were related to traders and eager to learn to become successful traders themselves. Although there were many artisans and farmers amongst the new arrivals, they came to the region primarily to trade in the broadest sense of the word. Whether they were artisans with skills to produce goods for sale or cultivators who grew cash crops for trading purposes, they were effectively aspiring and potential merchants. This basic pattern of Chinese involvement in Southeast Asia, as traders or aspiring traders, had been present for nearly a thousand years. It is unlikely that anyone in the 1820s and 30s in Singapore could have expected the major changes in this pattern which were about to take place.

The most important change after the 1840s was the increase in numbers of Chinese leaving China for Southeast Asia and elsewhere in the world. This was a massive movement and certainly not peculiar to the area around Singapore. Nevertheless, its effect on Singapore was probably greater than anywhere else. For one thing, it led to larger numbers of Chinese arriving to work in Singapore or using Singapore as a base for relocation elsewhere in the Malay archipelago, creating both business and employment possibilities for this great entrepôt centre through a new trade in Chinese labour. It is important to remember that Singapore was not special or isolated in any way. It was a key destination for Chinese migration and of extreme importance because of its excellent location. For several decades, from the 1850s onwards, increasingly more Chinese came to or passed through Singapore each year.

The explanation for this is too complex for my purposes here. There were push factors from China as Western penetration after the Treaty of Nanking and the cession of Hong Kong and other treaty ports opened up south China in a totally different way from before. That penetration had disrupted the economy of south China and led to considerable hardship for many Chinese of the lower classes. It certainly contributed towards unrest and ultimately the great rebellions of the 1850s, in particular the Taiping Rebellion. Although the rebellions were eventually put down, the impact on south China and the resultant emigration of Chinese from the two provinces of Kwangtung and Fujian was remarkable. As for the pull factors, the main ones derived from Western expansion in the Far East following the Industrial Revolution in Europe, the growing Southeast Asian markets, and the increasing demand for labour in tin mines and various kinds of plantations. The qualitative change in economic and trading conditions in the region led to a rapid growth in the demand for cheap labour which the Chinese in the region were able to supply by bringing in their own countrymen in increasingly large numbers. The position of Singapore ensured that it became the recipient of the largest number of new Chinese who, on the one hand, swelled the labour supply and enabled the settled Chinese there to become richer and more successful, and on the other, provided a new reservoir of entrepreneurial talent and the next generation of merchants for Singapore. It is a measure of the stability of British rule in the settlement, and in particular their control over the economic growth of Singapore, that the original settled Chinese families were able to hang on to economic power alongside their British counterparts for at least another generation. And it was not until the end of the nineteenth century that the fresh blood from China was able to claim an increasingly large share of the Singapore economy.

Until about 1900, the character of Chinese immigrant society in Singapore was determined by those who already knew the region or who were related to people who knew the region, all of whom could readily be useful to the British. And while there may have been differences in their style of business activity, in their proximity to Europeans, in the way the Europeans trusted them or not, in their familiarity with Chinese customs as compared with British law, the fact remains that the Chinese community served British interests almost as well as their own Chinese interests. As long as most of the Chinese who arrived in Singapore had previous local connections, both the British and the local Chinese knew precisely what to do. The picture changed only when many more thousands of Chinese arrived who did not have trading connections of any kind. They had come as unskilled labour prepared to work hard in the hope of earning enough to send money back or to save enough money and return home to help their families. These late arrivals with no local connections would naturally turn to the various societies which were ready to organize them to help them survive. As their numbers grew, they threatened not only the authority of the British but also the authority of the local Chinese leaders. There came a time when the British officials and the upper-class Chinese settlers had to combine their efforts to keep the increasing numbers of new Chinese under control. It is a measure of the skill of the British authorities in Singapore and the co-operation they received from the local Chinese leaders that this threat was kept in check. Through such co-operation, the leading families and businesses in the colony were able to harness these new human resources to their mutual interests. In return, the new immigrants readily learnt from the settled Chinese and benefited richly from the sound foundation their predecessors had laid. By the end of the nineteenth century, a synthesis of old and new was poised to create a new kind of overseas Chinese society.

Adaptability to Change

While these changes were taking place in the nineteenth century, the key feature that can be attributed to the Chinese immigrants was their adaptability. I shall now focus on the nature of that adaptability. Adaptability is a controversial concept. For some it represents changeability and lack of loyalty or principle. For others it is a form of resilience, a strong survival instinct and an excellent defence mechanism against hostile elements. It would probably be true to say that the Chinese have components of all these characteristics when we describe them as adaptable. Certainly when Singapore came under British rule in 1819, the Chinese who first went there were adaptable in the sense that they were opportunistic and ready to change masters if new conditions promised better opportunities to make a living. Their adaptability represented a realistic approach towards authority as an instrument for trade.

Most of these Chinese could be compared with those who had moved quickly to Penang when Penang was founded and who were able to survive the changes in administration in Malacca — from the Dutch to the British, back to the Dutch, and then back again to the British after 1824. They also included those Chinese who could thrive under local Malay rulers, whether in Kedah, Kelantan or Trengganu, in Riau or Deli (Medan), in West Borneo or Brunei. In particular, there were those who knew the sultanates of Johore, Selangor and Perak very well. They would also include some Chinese who had lived under Dutch rule in Java or under the Thai Kings in Bangkok or Malay rulers in southern Thailand. They observed the code of the trader, going where there was money to be made, moving on when conditions changed and better opportunities were offered elsewhere. They were prepared to settle if settling down was financially worth their while, or if settling down ensured upward social mobility, which in turn guaranteed better economic prospects. Their loyalty was to trading opportunity, to those who traded fairly with them, and to stable regimes which protected their concerns. To that end they were Chinese merchants, not loyal to any single government or any single empire. Their loyalty was to their businesses linked with their kinship groups and their villages back in China. Of course, there was local support for their activities; organizations associated with their temples, and various kinds of societies, some secret and some open, also provided protection. Moreover, and above all, there were the local authorities, whether Malay, Thai, British or Dutch, to whom they turned for official recognition.

From that point of view, there was never any permanent loyalty to Singapore as a place of settlement, but mainly to Singapore as a thriving entrepôt and profitable trading centre. As long as the British offered superior terms for that trade, the Chinese could be loyal to the British, and indeed many of them were. Thus it made no difference, so long as it was British, whether the Straits Settlements was ruled from India or whether it became a separate colony directly responsible to London. Nor did it matter greatly how the British and the Dutch divided the Malay world for their respective purposes. Nor even how the British and the various Malay rulers worked out how they should rule over various troubled areas. Indeed, throughout the nineteenth century, the Chinese in the Straits Settlements moved freely into the Malay states under the umbrella of British protection and, if they did not have that, they moved under Malay protection and supported Malay rulers in their local disputes. Only when it became clear that the British had superior business arrangements and offered better legal protection and were administratively more efficient did the shift of loyalty away from local rulers and their nobles to British officials become unambiguous. Thus, as British rule became stronger, the Chinese adapted to British needs and British ways and turned increasingly away from local types of rule. Indeed, by the end of the century most Chinese had shifted from a Malay-language-based trading system to one that had become increasingly Anglo-Chinese.

The older settled Chinese of the Straits Settlements, who spoke Malay and became increasingly fluent in English, strengthened their dominant positions by assisting the British in their trading activities. Similarly, as the British became clearly the most powerful of the European powers in the area, those Chinese under British rule became increasingly appreciative of that power and of the relatively liberal and benign administration which the British provided compared with that of the Dutch, the Spanish and the French. Certainly those born in the region and known locally as Baba Chinese, who were English educated and worked closely with the British, came to believe that they were fortunate to live under the British. British citizenship and protection became increasingly meaningful and they came to value their connection with Britain, even to the extent of placing British interests above those of China, certainly the China of the declining Manchu dynasty.

This kind of adaptability was certainly a virtue from the point of view of the Chinese community itself. From the point of view of others, however, especially the local rulers and aristocrats who had found the Chinese useful and charming before, this was opportunism. As they observed the Chinese turn away from local cultures and interests in favour of alien styles of behaviour and business methods, Chinese adaptability became something suspicious and increasingly contemptible. In short, as trading interests became more dependent on modern power structures, the Chinese came to be seen as a people lacking in political loyalties. This was not only the case as far as the British and native ruling officials were concerned, but also the case as far as allegiance to China was concerned. As long as the Qing dynasty was weak and unable to protect them and indeed rejected them once they left the shores of China, any loyalty to China was itself tenuous. And of course, for most of the time, it was irrelevant since China exercised no influence over any part of Southeast Asia. The only real link with China was to families in their home villages and to that end, good relations had to be maintained with Chinese officials. It was also necessary to maintain the use of Chinese language and such cultural links as would enable them to fit in well when they eventually returned to China or if they should send their children to study in China.

A major test of loyalty occurred when the first Chinese Consul (later Consul General) was sent to Singapore. Welcomed by the Chinese in great style, relations with these Consuls were cordial, even intimate, and the cultural aspects of their activities and the extent to which the Consuls could assist families in China was gradually appreciated. This was even more so when official Qing policy changed after 1893 towards all Overseas Chinese who wanted to return to China. No longer were they threatened with punishment. On the contrary, they were told that all past restrictions were lifted, which further served to strengthen official links between Chinese traders and Chinese mandarins in China and also encouraged female emigration to Southeast Asia on a large scale.

The key to all this, of course, was not that the Overseas Chinese felt differently about the Manchu rulers of China than before. As southern Chinese, they remained anti-Manchu in spirit. This was reflected very clearly in the secret societies in South China and their branches in Southeast Asia. But in so far as they saw the declining Qing dynasty modifying its policies in response to the challenge of the West, and to the extent that these modified policies gave them status and access to trading opportunities in China, they recognized that an important historic change had occurred. Their basic trading instincts were aroused by China's changing policy towards merchants in general. By the end of nineteenth century, it had become clear that the status of merchants had risen in China. Overseas Chinese who had made their fortunes through trade were now welcome to invest in industries and other entrepreneurial activities in China. Their children were welcome to study there and any who had been educated abroad were also welcome to take part in the new policies for the development of China. In this atmosphere, the loyalties of the Chinese in Singapore were sorely tested. It is remarkable that during this transition period between the 1890s and before 1911 with the fall of Qing dynasty, many Chinese managed to remain loyal to the British and others were able to be loyal both to Britain and to China and saw no conflict in having such dual loyalties.

Nevertheless, this was a transitional period. Two developments led to major changes. The first indicated a change in attitude as the new Chinese immigrants at and after the turn of the century became more aware of changes in China and were thus more willing to be actively involved in China's affairs. The second important development also reflected changes in China. A new generation of intellectuals and scholars were asking for reforms and even for revolution. These people were influenced by Western ideas no less than the younger Chinese in Singapore educated in Western schools. They were attracted to the progressive ideas which were being disseminated throughout the Far East. They responded to the increasing concern for China's survival and wished for the regeneration of China through new ideas and institutions. Whether they were more literate in Chinese or in English, they recognized that sooner or later their attachments to China could no longer be limited to mere concern for their families in their home villages, but had to widen to include the national salvation of China.

The biggest test therefore was how adaptable the Chinese were to the new forces of nationalism. A kind of sinocentric consciousness had been in existence among the Chinese for hundreds of years, but the nationalism of the West that inspired younger generations of Chinese to respond to China's fate at the end of the century was to arouse them in quite unexpected ways. It was only a matter of time before those who were loyal to the British were increasingly seen by the majority as being disloyal to their Chinese cultural heritage. The indifference to Western values among newcomers from China was gradually turned into a rejection and even hostility against being ruled over by British officials and being subjected to laws which they did not fully understand.

Of course the test was not only for the Chinese alone. It was also a test for the British. How to retain the loyalties of the Chinese in Singapore had become a more serious problem at the turn of the century than it had been during the nineteenth century. The British had to reflect on the future of Singapore where 70% of the population was now Chinese. The prosperity of Singapore had become more dependent on these Chinese. Having them settle down and changing their attitudes towards mobility, adaptability and loyalty was now a major issue on the agenda. One of the key battlefields was education. As more Chinese women came south and more Chinese remained in Singapore, the number of the local-born rose steadily and their education became a major problem for both the British and the Chinese community leaders. To the new Chinese, the solution lay in building more Chinese schools. With such schools, the dilution of Chinese culture by English education would stop and there would be a return of loyalty to China. However, the British saw this as a threat and actively sought to persuade the Chinese to settle in Singapore and turn away from aggressive anti-British nationalism. English education was expanded to counter the growth in numbers of Chinese schools. By the turn of the century there was more interest in education under governor Sir Cecil Clementi Smith and the calls for higher education, first through the medical college and then later on through education for teachers and young officials for the Straits Settlements, began to arouse sympathetic response. Similarly, the Chinese community sought to extend their schools and improve the quality of Chinese education. The period from the turn of the century to the beginning of World War II was one of intense competition between those who argued for a Chinese community loyal to the Straits Settlements and those who wanted to restore all Chinese to a deep pride in China. It could be described as efforts to change the concept of adaptability among the Chinese. The original adaptability had been based upon the best trading conditions one could find. This made the Chinese willing to move and reluctant to commit themselves to any particular regime. The new kind of adaptability stressed flexible responses to changing conditions in one place and was based on loyalty to that place. The ability of the Chinese to change from the one kind of adaptability to another was the most interesting development of the twentieth century.

The Chinese as Settlers

It would be true to say that during the nineteenth century the major-

ity of the Chinese in Singapore did not settle permanently but returned home or moved on to other places in Southeast Asia. Because
of this, it is often assumed that the Chinese cared so much for their
home villages in China that they very rarely settled outside China
and, if they did, they were forced to do so because of special circumstances. But clearly this was not true if we examine the whole picture
of the Chinese in Southeast Asia. There is ample evidence that they
settled in Java, in Thailand, in various parts of Sumatra and neighbouring islands, in Penang, in Trengganu, in West Borneo, in the
Philippines and elsewhere. And we have already noted that many of
those who had settled in the region also moved to Singapore when
opportunities for expansion and employment appeared. Indeed, those
who came to Singapore from the neighbourhood (people who had
settled in the neighbourhood decades if not centuries earlier), were
all too ready to settle down in Singapore if their businesses were
successful. And there is ample evidence that a large proportion of
those who came from the neighbourhood had decided to settle down
in Singapore within a few years of their arrival. Hence by the middle
of the century, we can speak of hundreds of settled families, including those who had come from China and either intermarried with the
settled families, or entered into business partnerships with them. For
those who knew Southeast Asia, there seemed to have been no great
reluctance to settle down. Thus the picture of the Chinese as immigrants must be tempered with another picture of the Chinese as
settlers though this did not mean that they never re-migrated.

The story of the Chinese in Singapore as settlers can be periodized
in the following way. Firstly, the Chinese merchants or traders, the
Huashang, as settlers. These were the stalwarts of the Overseas Chinese. They knew the region, they traded successfully and they made
their homes wherever their trade led them. These were the settlers of
the period from 1819 to the end of the century. They remained the
dominant group of settlers perhaps even into the twentieth century.

The second group were the labourers or coolies, the Huagong, who
arrived during the second half of the nineteenth century. Their main
significance was that they came in large numbers, although for the
main part they came for short periods and many failed, became
destitute and were sent home. The more successful ones, however,
returned with their savings to help their families back in China.
Nevertheless, amongst them were a number who remained, having
married locally or having lifted themselves above their labouring
status and turned successfully to trade. Again, for most of them it

was their ability to establish a trade, and therefore own property, which was the first step towards settling down. Included amongst them were many artisans who were able to use their skills to establish businesses. Amongst them also were partly literate or semi-literate people who used their writing skills either to work for Chinese businesses or to go into business for themselves. Sooner or later, the two main reasons for settling were success in business and the acquisition of a family. This second group of Chinese only began to settle in Singapore towards the end of the century, but they settled down in larger numbers throughout the first half of the twentieth century. The reasons for this included the changing British policy which encouraged people to stay, the conditions in China which discouraged them from returning and encouraged the successful ones to stay on in Southeast Asia.

The third period has been the hardest to identify and has been hard for some historians to accept. This is the period of the Huaqiao. This term which has been translated into English as "Overseas Chinese", meaning Chinese who are temporarily living abroad, came into use very late in the nineteenth century. It only came into widespread use during the first decade of the twentieth century. But it gained currency very quickly because the term was used by the Chinese Government and by all the various political parties active in seeking overseas Chinese support for their political activities in China. As a result, the term superseded all other terms for the Chinese abroad and came to acquire a political significance which all the earlier terms for the Chinese abroad had never had. The key point about the term Huaqiao is that it was immediately applied to everyone of Chinese descent, however many generations their ancestors had been outside China. In this way, the very use of the term was inimical to the idea of settlement. It challenged the possibility of anyone of Chinese descent ever having any other loyalty than that towards China. It put considerable pressure on all those who had acquired local citizenship to reconsider their positions. It went further than that and made it imperative for everyone of Chinese descent to seek to restore their full Chinese status as soon as possible. The term Huaqiao became closely linked with the expanding emotions about the Chinese nation and the new republican state which all patriotic Chinese were called upon to support. And so powerful was the way the term was used in Singapore and elsewhere in Southeast Asia that it virtually eliminated the growing sentiment towards local loyalties which had been developing through the nineteenth century. By the beginning of World

War II, local loyalties had become suspect as identification with China had become increasingly necessary. Indeed the upsurge of patriotic sentiment during periods when China was invaded or in any way humiliated by foreign powers had become so strong that all the colonial powers as well as native rulers began to develop genuine fears, deep-seated fears, about the ambitions of China and its Overseas Chinese. In this context, settlement had acquired a more sinister significance. Settlement had almost become a kind of colonization of Southeast Asia by Chinese to be ultimately backed by Chinese power once Chinese nationalism had created a rich and strong China. These were not merely fears among the non-Chinese and Western colonial governments but sentiments encouraged by some of the patriotic Chinese themselves.

This Huaqiao period from the turn of the century to about the 1950s was, however, an ambiguous one. On the one hand, it seemed to encourage all Chinese eventually to return to China, and in some cases to return to China as soon as possible, especially those with skills to offer China in its task of modernization. On the other hand, it implied that those who settled were also doing the right thing, provided they offered their wealth and skills for industrialization and investment in China itself. By the 1920s there was a strong undercurrent of anti-colonialism and anti-Western values which led some Chinese to support local nationalist movements to drive out colonial powers from Southeast Asia. There were some Chinese, ideologically anti-colonial (not only from amongst those who had migrated from China but also amongst educated Chinese in Southeast Asia), who felt obliged to join with all Asian anti-colonial forces against the European powers.

Thus the Huaqiao period was a very complex one in which no clear view of what settlement actually meant can be deduced. Historically, the Chinese were settling down in Southeast Asia in larger numbers. And yet, psychologically, the very nature of that settlement was being modified by ambivalent feelings of loyalty and patriotism which created doubts in everyone's minds as to whether the Chinese would ever settle. Partly as a result of this confusion, it is not possible even for Singapore, where perhaps larger numbers of Chinese had indeed made their homes, to be sure that the majority of them had truly settled permanently.

It is important to remind ourselves that it was external events which changed the picture for the region and, most of all, events in China in the twentieth century. The fall of the Guomindang and the victory of the Chinese Communist Party further aggravated the complexities for the Chinese in Southeast Asia. When they themselves became part of a global ideological struggle between communism and the forces against communism, the Chinese abroad had their options considerably reduced. The thousands who did make their choice after 1949 and returned to China became a mere trickle by 1960. What was significant now for them was the strength of indigenous nationalisms in the new nation states of Southeast Asia. Here Singapore was a complete exception. When its attempt to be part of Malaysia failed in 1965 and it became independent as the Republic of Singapore, a completely new kind of future was put before the Chinese there. For the first time in the history of the Chinese in Southeast Asia, there was every reason for one group of Chinese to settle.

Singapore's remarkable success has truly turned immigrants into settlers and has ensured that those of Chinese descent among its citizens have a home to live and die for. These Chinese settlers, unlike most of their ancestors who came to Singapore in earlier times, are determined to change the image of the Chinese as opportunistic transients. It is still too soon to determine whether they will succeed. It will not be easy to convince their suspicious neighbours that they have fully escaped from their history and that, whatever economic and geopolitical problems the region may have to face in the future, they are in Singapore to stay. What is more, they will also have to prove that they stay as "Singaporeans". For them, as the majority people of Singapore, ancestral cultural values will only remain useful for social intercourse and business purposes. For them, whatever links remain between Singapore and China would have to be on the same basis as those between Singapore and any other country.

PART II

Contemporary Themes

CHAPTER 10

The Culture of Chinese Merchants

ONE OF THE SPECTACULAR discoveries of the West during the past two decades has been the East Asian entrepreneurs, whether Japanese, Chinese or Korean. In an age when international trade is playing a larger role than ever before in world economic development, attention has been increasingly focused on this group of East Asians and many efforts have been made to explain how they have become so successful. How these entrepreneurs adapted so quickly to modern trade and mastered the methods and skills needed to build business empires on several continents have aroused admiration. What is often forgotten is that modern Chinese entrepreneurs, like their counterparts in South Asia, the Middle East and the Mediterranean, have evolved from traditional merchants and they have been around for a very long time. As merchants, they have been active in East and Southeast Asia for much longer than the Japanese and the Koreans.

This has prompted many questions. For example, were the traditional Chinese merchants different from the Indians, the Arabs and the Europeans (or Franks, as they used to be called) of their time? And then, are they all that different from each other today? Are they more, or less successful? And how do they compare with the Japanese and the Koreans and even, how do all these East Asian merchants compare with North Americans and West Europeans now? The questions are intriguing, but I believe it is premature to attempt comparisons while we are still struggling to understand how the Chinese merchants and entrepreneurs evolved from their traditional limited roles to their present extended ones. The changes cannot be divorced from Chinese interactions with merchants elsewhere, but it is not so much the interactions that concern me. What I would like to pursue is the question why, given their early start, from at least as early as the twelfth century, Chinese merchants had not fully participated, as others had done elsewhere, in transforming their country from a traditional to a modern state.

It is now well known that entrepreneurs have played a significant role in the economic development of modern countries and that the kind and level of entrepreneurial activity has influenced each country's progress. If the Chinese merchants were entrepreneurial, why were they not more successful as the instruments of progress for China? Attention has been drawn lately to East Asian Confucian values as a potent factor in the development of "the dragons", big and small, in the area (see Chapter 14). These values originated with the Chinese and were carried by Chinese merchants everywhere from the past to the present. Yet, a satisfactory explanation has continued to elude us as to why the Chinese merchants have done well but never well enough to be really significant in the world in commerce, least of all in their own country, China. In the hope of understanding more, I turn to their cultural values to ask what aspects of their culture made them distinctive, and helped them succeed but also constrained them.

This chapter is in two halves. The first seeks to identify what that culture was like within China and how it might have helped or obstructed enterprises there during the past few centuries. The second will show the same culture and its value to the Chinese merchants who traded in Southeast Asia and elsewhere. This is not, of course, a history of Chinese business, nor does it suggest that cultural factors will explain business successes in either the past or the present. But, by outlining the main features of merchant culture in modern history, I hope to show that within China, merchant culture was elusive and hard to define, but among Chinese abroad, it took shape as an identifiably *Chinese* merchant culture and thus its role there in supporting business activities has been much clearer. I use the term , *Huashang wenhua*, to identify this merchant culture outside China. I would argue that closer attention should be paid to the different ways merchant culture functioned within and outside China.

What do I mean by the culture of merchants? We all speak of Chinese civilization or Chinese culture. By using such terms we seek to identify elements which make that civilization or culture distinctive. But we also recognize regional cultures within China and we can tell the difference between literati or elite culture and, say, peasant culture. It is in the latter sense that I explore what might constitute the culture of merchants, whether Chinese, Arab or European. There is such a thing as a merchant culture that can be found among all those who trade and do business with each other — such as the respect for contracts, whether verbal or legal, the taking of certain risks in ventures and so on. I would also suggest that there were separate identifiable elements peculiar to merchants from China.

It is well known that Confucian social and political philosophy placed the merchant at the bottom of a four-tier social structure, beneath the literati, the peasant and the artisan. This was endorsed and reinforced in the laws made by the Qin-Han imperial bureaucracy two thousand years ago. And merchants have remained officially, and in the eyes of most Chinese people, in that lowly social position until modern times. This was unique to China. Merchants were lowly in Hindu culture, but never at the bottom of the heap. They were more respected in the Christian and Muslim worlds and even had access to political power, especially in small trading cities beyond the direct control of royal or imperial officials, cities such as Venice or Genoa.

In practice, successful Chinese merchants did overcome their social inferiority to some extent, especially from the Song dynasty down to the early years of this century, when wealth became more important as a criterion of merit and success. But this was achieved at a price. Higher social status was attained only by those who rejected their merchant origins and identified with the elite culture of the literati. They did so in at least three ways: they sought official titles and bought them whenever they could. They also bought land, both urban and rural, and tried to emulate the lifestyle of the literati-gentry and they educated their sons in the hope that they could pass examinations and move up to become members of the literati in their own right.

As a result, until very recent times, there were no successful merchants to articulate the secrets of their success, those qualities of merchant values that helped them make their fortunes. On the contrary, they were intent upon showing that their values were little different from those of the literati. Only poverty and lack of educational opportunities had forced them to start in trade and, modestly, they would suggest that only good luck, hard work, stoic endurance and the virtues of a family system approved of by the Confucian literati lifted them up above others who had started in the same way. Thus, even those who succeeded in business would echo the literati in the view that there was only culture as expounded by the literati; below them the vast majority of Chinese had little or no culture. It would not have occurred to the merchants that some of their values, attitudes or behaviour were different from the dominant Confucian culture.

We can understand why successful merchants made no claims for having this culture. It was not prudent to do so in a literati-dominated world of powerful mandarins. It would have been foolish for an upwardly mobile group to draw attention to themselves by proclaiming values different from the others. What intimidated them most were the philosophical arguments, confirmed repeatedly by every dynasty, that placed them at the bottom of society. Even though that disadvantage could be overcome in practice, its psychological effects, the effect on their self-esteem and on the legitimacy of their values, were exceedingly burdensome. It gave them little pride in their achievements and in the class they were unable to acknowledge since the object of success was to get out of it quickly and the test of true success was to have their descendants join the literati.

What then constitutes merchant culture in China? How do we give a name to something that its most successful representatives either denied or belittled themselves? I suggest that we can discern the shape of such a merchant culture through the traits associated with commerce and through merchant attitudes towards trading methods and the use of wealth, as well as through their relations with other Chinese social groups or classes. These are less clear within China and therefore more difficult to describe. Outside China these traits seem more easily identifiable. I shall deal with the latter in the second half of the chapter and concentrate firstly on the more difficult traits within China.

The Chinese Merchant within China

Within China, the difficulty lies in the negative stereotype images which many Chinese had, and still have, about merchants. Merchants appear to them to be cunning, greedy and uncouth. Even the most successful merchants were often objects of pity or mirth, if not the targets of ridicule and literary satire. Such views were not confined to literati and intellectuals. Well-to-do peasants and skilled workers or artisans would share them as well, happy to know that the merchants were socially inferior to them. But no one ever denied the usefulness of merchants. Confucius and philosophers of other persuasions all acknowledged their value to society as facilitators of necessary trade, with their ability to provide and transport goods that were in demand, to balance any unevenness in distribution and even offer credit services to the poorest as well as to the most powerful. And for their work, and the risks they were prepared to take, they deserved appropriate rewards. Provided they knew their place and did not seek to change the approved social and political structure, they were allowed to cultivate those qualities needed for merchants to go on being useful to their betters.

My thesis is that as they had to operate in the most difficult conditions of any group in China, they became the most flexible and most skilled in learning how to grasp opportunities for profit-making.

This was the framework within which Chinese merchants operated. They kept a sharp eye on the mandarins and literati to guard against disapproval, but also kept their links with the peasantry and the artisan class from whom they obtained the goods for trade. They recognized that, on a small scale, peasants and artisans also traded in what they produced and were potentially partners if not competitors. Indeed, from the Song dynasty to the nineteenth century, with the growth of marketing centres and towns, an urban merchant class developed consisting mainly of small professional traders who had begun to enjoy their intermediate position between the literati and the rural majority. This class eventually consisted of at least three groups:

a) the sons or descendants of merchant families, the nucleus of the merchant "class";
b) the poorer artisans and peasants who turned to trade and through their entrepreneurial talents helped them form this new urban class; and
c) the lesser kin of literati families who abandoned official or teaching careers and turned to commerce for their livelihood.

With this background it would not be surprising that the culture they espoused was eclectic. Of course they shared some common Confucian values of Chinese people everywhere. For example this culture recognized the family as the primary unit of trade. This may seem Confucian in origin and therefore endorsed by the literati but it probably pre-dated Confucianism in origin and was deeply rooted in the agrarian society of pre-imperial China. The family and the central values associated with it did become a pillar of Confucian ethics, but as a cultural value, the primacy of the family in business was not dictated by Confucian concerns, nor was it forced on them by the literati and the mandarins. Confucian rhetoric was used mainly to reinforce what was a most practical and effective way to get business started and to expand and defend that business.

Another example of values not peculiar to the merchants were those of thrift, honesty, trust, loyalty, and industriousness. Like the family, all these virtues were endorsed in Confucianism. But they were not literati values as such, nor were they seen as qualities inspired by mandarins. Mandarins were certainly enjoined to value these qualities, but Confucius and his followers had given emphasis to these values as essential for order in an agrarian society, and therefore they applied to rulers and ruled alike. The merchants who recognized them as valuable for their class were not being imitative or derivative, but rational and practical. Merchants who respected these virtues were not elevated to become Confucians. Neither did the honouring of these virtues prove the importance of Confucianism in merchant culture. It would be more accurate to say that the merchants saw themselves as sharing a common culture with the literati, peasants and artisans and therefore accepted the orthodox wisdom that China should preserve its agrarian past.

But there were values which the other classes did not share. To name a few, I would list attitudes towards profit-seeking and risk-taking, towards business organizations like occupational guilds, native-place associations and trade coalitions and not least, towards the use of philanthropy. The differences here reflected values common to many varieties of merchants, but which in China marked them off most notably from the literati and the peasantry.

Profit-seeking and risk-taking, of course, were clearly seen as the values which merchants endorsed. The literati vigorously rejected the first because it challenged the public good and was therefore immoral. They also frowned on risk-taking because it was not only opportunistic but also endangered a family's fortune or reputation. As for peasants and artisans, their value-systems about honest hard work, thrift and caution could not have encompassed both these values and we would expect them to follow literati strictures about them without reservation. For the merchants, however, these values were central to, though not sufficient conditions for, the qualities of entrepreneurship which they valued. Given that there was literati disapproval, the merchants did tone down the profit-seeking motive and warned sensibly against excessive risks being taken. But they were fully aware that without high profits and the risks that had to be taken to produce such profits, the chances of encouraging entrepreneurship would be slim. And without entrepreneurship, the merchant class could not hope to rise above that of staid and respectable artisans.

Business organizations were peculiar to merchants operating in towns. The earliest and most common form they took were the guilds. These differed from the artisan's guild only in that there was no formal structure of training or apprenticeship to sustain professional skills. They were more like mutual-aid societies with welfare and other social functions. They were also agencies for representing merchant interests before officialdom. Knowing well how biased the mandarins were about merchant enterprises, the merchants were often in dire need of active help. Eventually there developed other specialized kinds of organizations, like the native-place associations and trade coalitions which would strengthen their hand against competitors and rivals as well. What is striking was that no philosophy of management and training emerged from these organizations. They seemed to have accepted that running business enterprises was no different from heading a family and these larger organizations were managed like extended families. In short, these organizations were not innovative but remained primarily organizations which provided a consultative machinery subscribed to for the defence of common interests. But, at another level, the welfare aspect was linked to something like a philosophy that stressed the importance of philanthropy.

Philanthropy was a multi-faceted phenomenon urged on all classes in China but most systematically developed among successful merchants. There were good reasons for their concern with this. As people from a class with low social status they saw their wealth as their only weapon for gaining respectability. How that wealth was used was an essential part of the strategy for upward social mobility. There were, of course, those who were more altruistic and their kind of compassion was certainly influenced by popular Buddhist teachings about the acquisition of merit for the next life. But it was part of a social strategy that made the rich merchants the most philanthropic group of people in China and made their brand of philanthropy unique to their class.

The above outline of key elements in the culture of Chinese merchants can perhaps show, at the same time, its strengths and weaknesses. Its strengths in the family system, in the simple agrarian values endorsed by literati orthodoxy are well known. Their guilds and their use of philanthropy were defensive strategies for their own advancement. But it was their appreciation of the profit motive and the taking of risks which gave them scope to encourage the qualities of entrepreneurship they came to be famous for in modern times.

Scholars like Liu Kwang-ching, Samuel Chu, Susan Mann and Hao Yen-p'ing have shown us how the Chinese merchants were transformed into a more respectable "merchant-gentry" during the late nineteenth and early twentieth century. Their studies confirmed that seeking a higher social status was a serious diversion of energy and capital for the traditional Chinese merchant. Their lack of confidence in cultural values which did not have literati approval had been inhibitive. Thus when they gained an honorary literati (*shen shi*) status, their performance was lifted and they felt better equipped to learn modern business methods and adapt alien institutions to mount a challenge to the foreign capitalists trading and investing in China. But the experiences of the China Steam Navigation Company, of various mining and railway enterprises, and of Chang Chien in light industry development suggest that mandarin supervision remained a major obstacle to the rise of an indigenous capitalist class. Entrepreneurship in the service of the State and of public trading organizations was initially encouraged but was invariably a contradiction in terms. But private entrepreneurship remained suspect and no Chinese government subscribed to the philosophy of free enterprise. Nor were there institutions that gave Chinese entrepreneurship the stimulation and momentum to create a modern sophisticated class. The autonomy that that class would have needed to carve business empires and build multinationals went against the deep-rooted tradition of mandarin or cadre control of all enterprises. The tradition remained strong in Nanjing and Beijing throughout the twentieth century.

The Chinese Merchant outside China

Let me now turn to the Chinese merchant outside China. For East Asia, the Chinese merchants clearly led the way and, after the twelfth century, they had become the leading merchants in Southeast Asia as well. By the fourteenth century, together with Central and West Asian traders active in Mongol Yuan China, they had reached a dominant position. Then, towards the end of the century, imperial policy changed. The Ming founder decided to ban all private foreign trade. This was applied to all borders, but the hardest hit were probably the coastal merchant networks of Fujian and Guangdong where most of these merchants came from. For a while, in the early fifteenth century, it appeared that aggressive trading overseas might take another form. Certainly, officially-approved traders participated in the enlarged tributary trade that accompanied the great naval expeditions under Admiral Cheng Ho to the Indian Ocean. Merchants both in Guangdong and Fujian benefited from the intensified activity along the Chinese coast. But the fleets were withdrawn after 1435 and the ban on private foreign trade remained in force. For the 200 years from the late fourteenth to the second half of the sixteenth century, private trade overseas was forbidden. This ban did not, of course, stop private trade, it merely made it more dangerous.

Eventually, the pressure for overseas trade became so strong — manifesting itself in extensive smuggling and increasingly destructive piratical raids along the whole length of the China coast between Hainan and the Shandong peninsula — that the Ming court decided to relax the ban. Chinese merchants were licensed to trade abroad, but controls remained and supervision by port officials was mandatory. The campaign to have the ban relaxed had been conducted by merchants — both Chinese and foreign (including Japanese and Portuguese) — in collusion with some literati families which had business interests. A split in the mandarin ranks allowed the case for foreign trade to be argued successfully. But it was only a partial victory. Thereafter, the permitted trade was closely monitored by mandarins and Chinese merchants were expected to know their place. There was only a modification of policy, not a change in the basic philosophy of the mandarin-dominated agrarian state.

Thus, Chinese sources about the Chinese merchants overseas, even the local gazetteers of Guangdong and Fujian where we would expect to find more references to them, remained limited and literati writings consistently underplayed the role of these merchants even after the ban was relaxed. Fortunately, there was external confirmation, largely in Western writings, that Chinese merchants were increasingly active, especially in Southeast Asia, where the Portuguese and the Spanish, followed quickly by the Dutch and the English, came to control most of the key trading ports. In all these ports, the Chinese merchants provided experience, skills and momentum. And Western officials and traders acknowledged that the Chinese were the most dynamic group in the region. From their reports, we obtain a picture of the Chinese merchants never found in Chinese sources. They emerge as ingenious and adventurous traders who had remarkable flair for profit-seeking and risk-taking under conditions that were often dangerous if not actually hostile. At the same time, they were aware that these trading environments were very different from those within China and that they could be turned to their advantage.

And to that end, the sources suggest that their entrepreneurial talents did succeed more often than not in making the more open trading conditions work for them. In short, they adapted well to the different conditions abroad. How did they manage to do that, given the great cultural differences that divided the Chinese from the others? What does that tell us about their own culture when it was transported abroad?

Merchant Culture at Home and Abroad

Western writings not only commented on Chinese courage, adaptability and entrepreneurship. They also confirmed those qualities of industriousness, thrift, honesty, trust and loyalty which bound most of them and gave their leaders strength and boldness. And, most of all, they noted the way the Chinese merchants organized themselves. There were guild-like associations and coalitions of various kinds. There were focal points built around temples for common use, notably temples to the Goddess of the Sea (*Tianhou*), the God of Wealth (*Guan Yu*, who was also the God of War), various Fujian and Guangdong deities and even local Southeast Asian deities and, not least the Buddha and several popular bodhisattvas. Around these temples and the secular organizations (including those better-known later as "secret societies", with their brotherhood ideology and sacred blood oaths) were built traditions of defence, protection, welfare, recreation and philanthropy. And where the more successful merchants had married and produced families, there were also tutoring arrangements to effect a degree of literacy. Underlying all these provisions, however, remained the contrast between Chinese official policies which limited foreign trade and the varying but much more open conditions for Chinese merchants in ports where it was considered normal to expand trade. At the same time, it must not be forgotten that Chinese merchants overseas received no official protection whatsoever. They really had to fend for themselves and that would have taxed their ingenuity and demanded great courage. Some of the traders from Fujian and Guangdong could be described as either desperate or exceedingly brave. However, the profits from overseas trade must have been considerable to have attracted so many people to leave their homes at a time when trading opportunities were expanding within China itself.

As far as culture was concerned, the Western sources and fragmentary materials in Chinese, Japanese and some Southeast Asian languages confirm, on the whole, that the picture outlined earlier of merchant culture in China was also true of the Chinese overseas before modern times. As one would expect, the Chinese merchants brought their culture with them and did their best to maintain those values which they believed would help them best. Only two of the key cultural traits, widely acknowledged in China, were rarely mentioned in the descriptions of merchants overseas. One concerned the important role of the family and the other concerned the lowly place of merchants and, consequently, the hold that mandarins had over merchants. The relative lack of comment on both these important features of merchant culture is understandable. The family did not feature strongly because the merchants and their relatives came as groups of single men. Few were successful enough to produce the kind of extended family system so pronounced in China, especially in provinces like Fujian and Guangdong. As for mandarin power over lowly merchants, this was probably obvious to those foreigners who had traded in China, but it would not have struck those who dealt with Chinese merchants in Southeast Asian ports or in Nagasaki as relevant. What was much more striking was the existence of "secret" organizations of guilds, alliances and brotherhoods with chosen leaders who wielded considerable "political" power and how effectively these organizations dealt with recalcitrant members and dangerous rivals as well as unfriendly or hostile foreign officials. But it was not obvious to non-Chinese observers that such organizations consisted of both relatives or clansmen and, when not originally related, "sworn" brothers, nor that, especially when abroad, they were ruled by leaders who acted as heads of families, with all the respect and power attributed to such heads. Nor was it significant that similar, less aggressive organizations also served to help merchants against mandarin interference and harassment within China, but these had to be upgraded by becoming more secret and more dynamic when in foreign lands. Suffice it to say that, having had considerable experience dealing with corrupt and officious mandarins in China, these merchant-led organizations were well-prepared to deal with greedy and extortionate foreign officials.

I shall not deal with all the major cultural traits identified with Chinese merchants here but shall concentrate instead upon three of them: the importance of the family as a primary unit of trade, the freedom from mandarin control and the risk-taking features of their entrepreneurship. Even then my aim is not an exhaustive study but a means of illustrating the different environment Chinese merchants had to adapt to outside China. And from the late nineteenth century onwards, my remarks would also apply to the relatively few merchants in North America, Australasia and elsewhere.

The family was vital to the overseas merchant, although not obviously so since only single men went to sea and few established families of their own abroad. Nevertheless, it is clear that, however adventurous or entrepreneurial each single man might have been, whether across the Pacific or across the South China Sea, he could not have started in business without some degree of family backing or without belonging to a family or an adopted family business network, such as the artificial brotherhoods operating as members under family discipline. This was fundamental even though it was less obvious abroad that their business organizations had strong family characteristics. From all accounts down to the twentieth century, all successful overseas Chinese merchants, whether originally from a merchant family or not, started by working for a relative who had a business. If they were close and direct kin, they were more worthy of trust and more likely to improve their position rapidly. If the relationship was less close, then hard work, honesty, thrift, and some early signs of initiative and talent would be essential if they were not to remain shop assistants and loyal retainers all their lives. The qualities of entrepreneurship became essential and were believed to be accompanied by luck and good fortune. When, as was often the case, spectacular successes followed for some of them, the collective efforts of family members in management, as well as production, transportation and distribution, would still be crucial. Without such support, no successful merchant would feel secure.

Equally interesting is the stereotype of short-lived family fortunes. Family businesses rarely lasted more than three generations. Again, foreign and Chinese accounts generally confirm this, but it has been difficult to explain the phenomenon. Were the causes cultural or structural? There have certainly been cultural or institutional methods of achieving continuity, but successful modern methods have mostly been developed in the West. One of the most important factors was the principle of separating ownership from management. Under a family system this would have been unthinkable. In China, the most interesting of the methods was the strategy of gentrifying the family, of turning a family member or two into literati not only through learning and examinations, but also through purchase of official titles and deliberate changing of lifestyle. In this way, it was sometimes possible to sustain business branches of the family through subtle links with literati cousins. Such a strategy was not available to the Chinese merchants overseas. Nor was it necessary for them to use it. Much more common was the use of marriage alliances in areas where families were bilateral in structure, that is, where descent and inheritance could follow both paternal or maternal lines. Where this was possible, as in Thailand and the Philippines, it was common for successful merchants, often themselves of part-Thai or Filipino descent, to have their children, whether sons or daughters, marry members of local aristocratic or patrician families and thus improve their chances of establishing business dynasties. Again, the family was important, but their readiness to adapt to inheritance systems that were not exclusively patrilineal as in China enabled some of them to escape the common fate of merchant families in China and help extend the life of their merchant empires in new and effective ways.

Of particular interest was the freedom from mandarin control when merchants traded overseas. There were, of course, great disadvantages when they had to trade among foreigners and under alien laws. Learning to do this was far from easy. Foreign officials were sometimes no more predictable than Chinese mandarins and no less venal, and foreign laws could be no less arbitrary than Chinese ones. In addition, there was always the danger of racial discrimination, political intrigue and instability and the machinations of Western powers in native affairs, often aimed directly against Chinese merchants. Thus it was inevitable that Chinese mercantile success depended on certain patterns of patronage. The major difference, however, was that the patronage was more open and flexible and often could be renegotiated under changing conditions in ways quite different from the dealings with mandarins in a centralized bureaucratic system. For example, when Chinese merchants dealt with native aristocrats in Thailand or almost anywhere else in the Malay archipelago not under Western control, local interest in and even dependence on foreign trade was so great that the Chinese were in strong bargaining positions. Also, it was sometimes possible for such Chinese to achieve social mobility through awards of local titles, through marriages or through acting as the rulers' merchant-representatives abroad. On the other hand, when such merchants dealt with Dutch or English officials, different tactics had to be adopted. Greater attention would have to be paid to rules and regulations and to significant cultural differences. But the merchants found that these officials were unlike Chinese mandarins in one very important respect. Westerners were dedicated to profit and appreciated Chinese trading ingenuity in ways impossible for the mandarins in China. Thus, although sub-ordinated to Western governance at key ports like Batavia and Singapore, Chinese merchants found that working to laws that encouraged and protected trade, and answering to officials who abided by such laws, gave them a freedom to develop their talents and expand their business empires in ways unknown in Chinese history.

There was one interesting consequence that deserves a mention. In China, merchants were morally and psychologically constrained to show extravagance only in approved ways. Against orthodox strictures about thrift and simple living, they could consume conspicuously only in the style of the literati officials. Buying land and building splendid mansions and gardens, stocking their homes with art objects, hosting banquets for officials on a grand scale, sponsoring scholarly endeavours and instigating extravagant community projects were all acceptable.

Even excesses in philanthropy were approved of. In these ways, merchants emulated their betters and this helped some of them to escape the stigma of low social status and eventually become members of the gentry themselves. But in lands far away from the mandarins, the same kind of extravagance in living style and philanthropy was less useful to the Chinese merchants. Although native and Western official classes were impressed, the Chinese style of philanthropy remained alien. Also, no sharing of power was possible in Western territories and, with native rulers, total assimilation and a denial of Chinese culture would have been necessary if the merchants aspired to high office. At the same time, conspicuous consumption and extravagance could dissipate family fortunes quickly and make them less likely to survive three generations. In short, patterns of behaviour useful in China were not necessarily helpful abroad.

What would have been more significant was the ability to produce succeeding generations of entrepreneurs to keep the family fortunes going. This brings us to the difficult question of what constitutes entrepreneurship. A dictionary would define an entrepreneur as one who manages, organizes and undertakes a commercial enterprise, including all the risks associated with it. At one level, Chinese merchants have been renowned for their boldness in risk-taking. This could be linked to an outlook that gave considerable weight to a very positive interpretation of destiny, one that assumed that good fortune was there for the bidding and would fall to those who were fated to get it. In this context, risk-taking was not blind gambling but part of a consistent and carefully calculated strategy that should yield handsome profits over a period of time. However, successes were rare and failures were not unexpected. Entrepreneurs are clearly not mere risk-takers. What was needed still were other qualities of industriousness, shrewdness, ruthlessness, something that might be called the will to profit. These qualities required considerable freedom to manoeuvre, room to think big and take risks at the right time and place.

Chinese merchants had this freedom when trading overseas because they were not held back by an agrarian bureaucratic State intent on keeping order in a society as little changed as possible. State Confucianism under mandarin control effectively hampered commercial enterprises by keeping merchants down. There was never any recognition that economic development was of value to China, that the State could promote such growth and that therefore entrepreneurship was a valuable quality. Outside China however, was a pluralistic world of many competing interests which rewarded those who learnt how to manoeuvre in it. Here the Chinese merchants had many of the right cultural ingredients to help them build business empires which even helped to develop and enrich their host countries. And, without orthodox Confucian mandarins to check and hold them back, they learnt to overcome discriminatory laws, to adapt to new methods of operation, to become more innovative themselves and to use the favourable parts of foreign cultures to help them modernize their minds as well as their institutions. It was altogether a remarkable transformation for those who were inhibited by an elite culture at home but whose own cultural values were given free rein abroad.

It is clear that, in comparison with the culture of merchants overseas, merchant culture in China was subdued and shapeless. The merchants at home did not identify it as a distinctive set of cultural values. Outside China, however, the various sources have described what may be justifiably called *Huashang wenhua* (Chinese merchant culture). Once we have this culture in focus, we can actually see it changing over the last two centuries, adapting and responding to modern trading patterns and methods, all the more rapidly the longer these merchants were open to new ideas and away from mandarin supervision and the dominance of mandarin culture.

We have ample evidence of this development in the twentieth century when the new merchant classes overseas became more confident and articulate. Since the end of World War II, they have become more self-conscious and professional about the values they espoused, the personal qualities that helped entrepreneurship and the methods needed to ensure business continuity and longevity. Their status is equal to that of any successful professional. They have combined what they have learnt from the West (just as the Japanese, Koreans and others have done) with what they recognized as their cultural heritage. Of the greatest importance to their recent successes has been their realization that they have done better without mandarin leadership. This is not to say that the overseas merchants did not see their culture as part of Chinese culture. On the contrary, they have recognized it as a dynamic part of Chinese culture that has survived the fall of the Chinese empire, the two World Wars and various Chinese civil wars as well as foreign discrimination and other harassments. The resilience of this culture has helped individual merchants to preserve their entrepreneurial qualities in competition against established enterprises. Some of them have risen above the status of a mere merchant and have become capitalists, financiers and industrialists in an increasingly diversified world economy. Chinese merchant culture has been significant as the most modernizing force among Chinese living overseas.

In China itself, however, the picture has been much more complicated. The tension between State ideology and merchant culture has never been resolved. Also, the deep-seated mandarin bias against any respectability for business values seems to have survived, albeit in a different form. From the traditional attitude that merchants were socially inferior and their profit-seeking ways immoral, there is now a strong political view that merchants are some kind of capitalists and therefore class enemies of the State. Thus, Chinese Marxism seems to have reinforced traditional Confucian attitudes. The merchants have returned to the bottom of the heap. Some of the prohibitions against commerce are familiar: party bureaucrats and families must not, like their mandarin predecessors, be involved in business enterprises in any way. That merchants were, in 1989, again forbidden to join the Communist Party, when almost everyone else can, suggests that once again they will not be allowed to play any significant role in the country's economic development. This does suggest that there is still a deep cultural divide that separates a suppressed merchant culture within China from the lively and vigorous *Huashang wenhua* outside.

This chapter does not attempt to explain the success of *Huashang wenhua* among the Overseas Chinese. I have tried, however, to show that in seeking to explain the phenomenon, we need to recognize that whether the culture of the Chinese merchants is appreciated or not can make a big difference to whether the merchants succeed as entrepreneurs or not. For merchants to be treated as the lowest class of people has, in terms of modernization and progress, done enough damage to China for centuries. We will wait to see whether Chinese leaders can appreciate that the cultural values that have made its people so prosperous outside China can play an important role in the future economic advancement within China itself.

CHAPTER 11

The Study of Chinese Identities in Southeast Asia

STUDIES OF THE CHINESE in Southeast Asia over the past decades have shown that the Chinese have changed and that they are capable of undergoing further change. There have been studies which point to people who are of Chinese descent but who no longer consider themselves Chinese. Others show descendants of Chinese who know little about what being Chinese means but who have rediscovered their Chineseness and have been trying to be re-sinicized. Yet other studies suggest that many Chinese have double identities. They identify with their country of adoption while remaining conscious of being Chinese. The studies suggest that there can be many Chinese identities which people admit to. These identities are difficult to define and, despite many efforts to refine them, are often dependent on nothing more than self-identification. This should not make us despair of finding usable definitions, but there is no doubt that the concept of identity is a slippery one which needs many qualifications. This chapter reviews the main ideas scholars have advanced about Chinese identities in Southeast Asia since the end of World War II, and will focus on the Chinese minorities in the new nation-states.

The Chinese have never had a concept of identity, only a concept of Chineseness[1], of being Chinese and of becoming un-Chinese. Although this implied that there could be differences in degree, that someone could be more Chinese and someone else less Chinese, this did not lead to a concept of identity. Thus the study of Chinese identities has been largely conducted by social scientists in recent decades.[2] From their studies, we can point to a number of identities which have received particular attention since the 1950s: national (local) identity, communal identity and cultural identity in the 1950s and 1960s and ethnic identity and class identity in the 1970s. For the period before 1950, before the concept of identity was much in use, I believe that there were at least two ways the Chinese saw their Chineseness which we could call their sense of Chinese identity: one might be called Chinese nationalist identity; the other, more traditional and past-oriented, I shall call historical identity.[3] It is obvious that ideas about identities have changed and from time to time new ideas were introduced because conditions in China and in the region had changed and the Chinese themselves were changing. This chapter examines the ways these concepts of identity have been used and suggests how some have been more useful than others. From our experience of studying these identities, we find that modern Southeast Asian Chinese, like most other peoples today, do not have a single identity but tend to assume multiple identities and that the whole range of identities they adopt must be taken into account if we wish to understand them. This question of multiple identities involves many variables and can be confusing.[4] I suggest it might be best approached through the idea of norms (that is, the ideal standards which they regard as binding to them as Chinese and others which they have to accept in their non-Chinese environments), and by trying to understand the changing ways which Chinese respond to norms and identify with them.

Before the Second World War, the question of Chineseness was thought to have been a simple one. All who thought of themselves as Chinese were Chinese. They were conscious of their family system, their place of origin in China (which usually determined their language group, or what we would call today their sub-ethnic group, as Hokkien, Cantonese, Hakka, Teochiu, Hailam, etc.) and their ties with other Chinese whether in China or in other parts of the region.[5] These factors had created a core of sentiment which could be strengthened and expanded by stories about the Chinese past and reasons for pride in a more or less abstract "Great Tradition" of Chinese civilization. This produced a kind of identity which could be appropriately called "historical" because it had emphasized the way traditional family values, clan origins and sub-ethnic loyalties, as well as symbols of a glorious Chinese past, all helped to sustain Chineseness.[6] And because this "historical" identity had been largely backward-looking and rarely assertive, Southeast Asian colonial officials and indigenous elites had found it acceptable for such Chinese to preserve their Chineseness in order to play their economic roles successfully. But, during the 1920s and 1930s, this historical identity was under attack by a new and aggressive nationalism from China which was built upon Sun Yat-sen's concept of *min-tsu* (translating the

Western concepts of "race" and "nation"). For this period, the bulk of writings about the Nanyang Huaqiao (Overseas Chinese) by Chinese, Japanese and Western scholars began to focus on the way local Chinese responded to the idea that their "racial" origins should lead them to identify with that nationalism in China. What then emerged was a Chinese nationalist identity that became real to the local Chinese because of the successful efforts of numerous teachers and journalists recruited from China to propagate the idea of such an identity. In particular, the establishment of hundreds of Chinese primary and secondary schools consolidated this identity for the next generation, and the expansionist activities of the Japanese in China leading to the Sino-Japanese War and ultimately to the invasion of Southeast Asia made that identity a stronger and more emotional one.[7]

Thus after the end of the war, there appeared to have been among the Southeast Asian Chinese a predominant Chinese nationalist identity which most of the new indigenous political leaders found alarming. The reactions varied from country to country depending on the numbers of Chinese in the population and each country's perception of future Chinese usefulness to the new nation-states that were being formed. In countries like the Philippines, Indonesia, Burma and Vietnam, where the numbers of Chinese were relatively small, that Chinese nationalist identity was believed to be ultimately containable and, in most cases, could eventually be replaced by the new local national identity that was being offered to the Chinese. In Malaya (then still including Singapore for all practical purposes), however, the picture was different. The Chinese nationalist identity which affected a large proportion of the Chinese population threatened to be an intractable problem requiring extremely careful handling. This was complicated by the fact that some of the younger Chinese nationalists had been influenced by the war to become members of the Communist Party of Malaya and had identified with a worldwide anti-colonial struggle for independence rather than with China as a nation.[8]

This last point reminds us that the Chinese sense of their own identity could be changed by changing events. The new indigenous elites seemed to have understood this and had good reason to expect the Chinese to change again when circumstances further changed. Thus, for several decades to 1950, Chinese historical identity seemed to have been partially superseded by Chinese nationalist identity. But, even when this nationalist identity was at its peak in the 1930s and 1940s, not all Chinese changed in favour of Chinese nationalism. Some had sought to identify with local indigenous nationalist movements, notably in Burma, Vietnam and the Philippines, and were prepared to accept a new identity based on anti-colonialism and modern principles of nation-building. These principles would have included the legal protection of minorities like the Chinese, but a few of the Chinese might have been prepared to be totally assimilationist even at this early stage. A few others had found a new kind of identity which in theory crossed racial and even national boundaries to focus on economic class. It had led some young Chinese to speak out for the ideal of class identity in the larger anti-imperialist struggle, that is, through identification with the oppressed peoples (both indigenous and immigrant), these Chinese could legitimize their minority rights after the colonialists were driven out. In this way, they could also, if they wanted to go further, be truly assimilationist. Neither of these gropings for new identities among the Southeast Asian Chinese, however, was the subject of scholarly study before the 1950s.[9] The point to note is that consciously changing their identity was an option which some younger Chinese were already exploring.

By the 1950s and 1960s, a number of strands in Chinese identities had been studied. The most obvious were the political strands. They included the dominant Chinese nationalist identity derived from *min-tsu* or "race-nation" which was being forced to give way to the new local national identity. For most of the newly independent states, to which Chinese migration had come to an end by 1950, the outcome was never in doubt and the process of change, however difficult and painful, was only a matter of time. The exception was Malaya (including Singapore) where the Chinese made up nearly half the total population. The strong local Chinese community was on the whole willing to abandon Chinese nationalist identity and replace it with the new Malayan national identity, but had at the same time developed a powerful sense of communal identity to assert the community's right to share power in the country. The community leaders still retained some sense of their earlier historical identity as Chinese and also sought to have the cultural features of that identity offically recognized as an integral part of a composite Malayan national identity. As can be expected, this created severe tensions in the country. The political struggles that followed have been the subject of several books, but because the political profile of Malaya (and Malaysia and Singapore) was so different from that elsewhere in Southeast Asia, the results of these studies cannot be usefully compared with those produced for other countries in Southeast Asia.[10] In particular, the forceful Chinese communal identity developed for political purposes in Malaya could not be found anywhere else because no other Chinese community was large enough to share power with the indigenous peoples to even a limited extent. For the other Southeast Asian Chinese, their political aspirations took different forms, in various kinds of community organizations and associations, and was not satisfactorily portrayed until the idea of ethnic (and sub-ethnic) identity was introduced in the scholarly writing of the 1970s.

National identity in each of new nation-states became an important part of every study of the nation-building process in Southeast Asia. But where the Chinese were concerned, their acceptance of that national identity did not tell us very much about the nature of that identity. It often began merely as a change of label and a putting on of a new legal personality and at most went on to become an affirmation of political loyalty. What many scholars wanted to know was whether there was, or could be, a fundamental change in values when a new national identity was adopted, and this was far more difficult to study. For example, many Chinese supported the nation-state and wanted to identify with the newly emerging ideals of nationhood. They saw no future in exclusive Chinese community organizations and were willing to adapt to new kinds of national needs. But how many of them were prepared to assimilate and lose their identity as Chinese? How many others would prefer to be politically integrated and be allowed to preserve some degree of Chinese cultural identity?

This takes us away from the political nexus of Chinese nationalist, local national and communal identities to the much subtler cultural realm (see Figure 5.1). By cultural here, I am referring to the inclusive way it is used in cultural anthropology, that is, everything related to traits which were learned and transmitted by and to members of society, including knowledge, beliefs, morals, customs, religions and law. These traits were similar in nature to those found in the traditional Chinese sense of identity. But the new cultural identity went further. Unlike what I have called historical identity, which was largely based on past cultural values and which depended on the persistence of these values among overseas Chinese communities, the new awareness of culture recognized the function and usefulness of modern non-Chinese cultures from which Chinese communities could learn new ways of ensuring their prosperity and success. Historical identity had co-existed, although not always comfortably, with native polities and colonial governments for centuries, but with the establishment of the modern nation-state, the question was no longer that of co-existence. The Chinese everywhere found that the choice now was between assimilation and integration and this called for a more flexible and more forward-looking attitude towards culture and a new sense of Chinese cultural identity.[11]

In the context of the assimilation or integration debates of the 1950s and 1960s, the great advantage of the idea of cultural identity lay in avoiding the emotive rhetoric behind "racial" identities, something most scholars eschewed after the unhappy uses of the word "race" before and during the Second World War. Instead, cultural identity as a concept implied that a nation-state could live with many cultures and that the new national culture would be enriched if the cultures of its various peoples were encouraged to survive and develop within the national framework. For the study of the Southeast Asian Chinese, the concept of cultural identity opened up the possibility of studying not only how they sustained their Chinese identity while adopting a wide range of non-Chinese values but also how some of them might seek total assimilation and accept a totally new non-Chinese identity. With this concept, scholars could explore the Chinese willingness to accept the local national identity and also examine the extent to which they would still identify themselves as Chinese in relation to other local nationals of Chinese descent, or in relation to Chinese outside the country. The adoption of some modern cultural values through Western schools in the region and higher education in Europe, Australia and North America was interesting. These values would include conversion to non-Chinese faiths (mainly Christianity), the mastering of non-Chinese language skills at the expenses of fluency and even knowledge of the Chinese language as well as the acceptance of behavioural patterns influenced by non-Chinese customs. Although these cultural elements were not Chinese, they were not necessarily incompatible with a Chinese identity and might even be accepted eventually as part of a new modern Chinese cultural identity.

The concept of cultural identity which was developed from the research of the 1950s continued to produce new insights and a better understanding of Southeast Asian Chinese cultural behaviour in the 1960s. It was especially valuable in the context of new and somewhat insecure nation-states when both Chinese and local elites needed to believe that a separate cultural identity did not conflict with the demands of political loyalty. Whether this was reassuring to the new national elites or not is uncertain. It was certainly comforting to many Southeast Asian Chinese and helped them defend their cultural identity against those who demanded nothing less than total assimilation to the national community.[12]

Nevertheless, there were limits to the usefulness of the concept of cultural identity. By emphasizing culture and avoiding the emotional overtones of racial origins and political competition, the study of cultural identity did not satisfy those who observed the relations between politics, race and minority groups in Southeast Asia in the late 1960s and early 1970s. Also, elsewhere in the world a new stage in race relations had arrived. Particularly relevant were the developments in the United States in the relations between the minority Blacks and Chicanos and the White majority. Broad cultural similarities were not enough to remove various forms of discrimination. Race and ethnicity had re-entered the political arena and scholars had to take them into account. Out of the wide-ranging debate came ethnic identity as a more accurate concept than cultural identity for dealing with contemporary race relations and minority problems. And this was found by some scholars to be so also for the study of the Chinese and other minorities in Southeast Asia.[13]

Ethnicity was no easier to define than culture because at its broadest it included race and culture, both difficult concepts. I shall not try to examine all the attempts to define it but will note only the key differences drawn between ethnic and cultural identity. The idea of cultural identity avoided explicit reference to biological heritage and focused on values, whether transmitted within the family, acquired through formal education or through immersion in the values of a society other than one's own. Ethnic identity was usually defined to include a cultural identity and thus avoid the worst connotations of race, but there was an undeniable connection between ethnicity and racial identification.[14] Put in another way, cultural identity emphasized a separateness between groups which could eventually be eliminated by cultural changes; ethnic identity, however, underlined differences which could only be reduced by long periods of physical intermingling through intermarriage between members of separate groups. Furthermore, ethnic identity had a strong political dimension through bringing out a link between identity and the organized actions of disadvantaged minorities. This stemmed from the fact that the word ethnic implied other, lesser, peripheral peoples excluded from positions of dominance. In this context, ethnic identity usually referred to the identity of minority groups seeking, or even fighting for, their legal and political rights.

To return to the Southeast Asian Chinese, most of them had by the 1970s been local nationals for a couple of decades and had become, to various degrees, politically domesticated. Events in China probably speeded up this process. The brutal policies of the Cultural Revolution towards families which had links overseas contributed to the alienation from both China and communism among most Southeast Asian Chinese and were the last straw even for the older China-oriented Chinese in the region. The process of domestication of local nationals of Chinese descent led local governments to view them with a different emphasis. Instead of viewing them as linked to some sort of external threat, most governments (with the exception of Malaysia) began to acknowledge that their Chinese minorities were probably less troublesome than some of their indigenous minorities, for example, the Karens in Burma, the Malays in southern Thailand and the Moros in the southern Philippines, who were all determined to undermine the authority of the new nation-states.[15] Southeast Asian Chinese welcomed this acknowledgement that they might be less of a threat than people had thought. Many had long hoped that their government and their critics both within and outside each country would stop focusing on issues like their stubborn communality, their dubious political loyalty and their cultural Chineseness and give more attention to an issue like their rights as one of the country's several ethnic minorities.

With this background in mind, it is easy to understand why scholarly writings turned more to questions of Chinese ethnic identity. This was particularly appropriate in countries where Chinese numbers were relatively small, but even in Malaysia where it had been usual to speak of the Chinese "communal" identity lying behind the political challenge to the Malay majority, the shift in emphasis to the legal protection of Chinese minority rights made ethic identity a more sympathetic and less threatening term than communal identity. Thus, in recent writings, there has been the tendency to use Chinese ethnic (or sub-ethnic for Hokkiens, Cantonese, Teochius, Hakkas, Hailams, etc.) identity to replace the nationalist, communal and cultural identities described earlier in this chapter. Figure 5.1 (p. 206) may be a useful summary of the discussion so far.

The discussion so far has said little about Chinese economic activities in the region. This is not because scholars did not write about such economic activities, but because they rarely linked such activities directly with questions of Chinese identity. I mentioned earlier

Figure 5.1

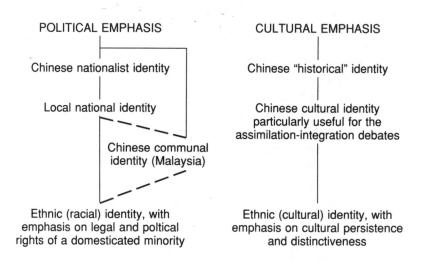

the gropings by some young Chinese for a class identity which crossed racial boundaries. These stirrings were overshadowed by the interest in nation-building and the issue of assimilation or integration of the Chinese, and it was not until the 1970s that more scholars spoke up against the neglect of economic and class interests in the study of Southeast Asian Chinese identities.[16] This was partly due to the strong counter-current in world politics in the 1960s which revived interest in Marxist-Leninist analysis, and criticized all scholarly studies which used superstructural models and ignored the economic base. But the more important reason for the renewed interest in economic activities may be found in the astonishing growth rates in some parts of East and Southeast Asia, especially in Korea, Taiwan, Hong Kong, Singapore and Malaysia. The question began to be asked as to whether the role of Chinese enterprise in the rapid economic development in Southeast Asia had any connection with, or more specifically, any effect on, Chinese identity. The Southeast Asian Chinese were responding more successfully than expected to the new opportunities offered by a rejuvenated capitalism led by Japan and the United States and by worldwide advances in technology and high finance. While their success has been attributed by some scholars to broadly ethnic and cultural factors, other scholars have felt that more fundamental questions about the class identity of the Chinese should have been asked. The eagerness of most Southeast Asian Chinese to look to

Western capitalist institutions and embrace their class counterparts across ethnic lines cannot be satisfactorily understood in ethnic and cultural terms.[17]

Nevertheless, various studies have shown that the concept of class identity has not been any simpler to grasp than that of ethnic or cultural identity. The crossing of ethnic and even national boundaries has been easier in theory than in practice. It could be done only in very narrow areas where business (in Malaysia, also trade union) interests could ensure mutual benefits for all the ethnic groups concerned. If business profits could be maintained for long periods, the class interests of the national economic elites of various ethnic backgrounds might override all other interests, but it was more likely to do so if there was already cultural integration or a degree of assimilation. We would expect that the stronger the degree of integration or assimilation, the more significantly it would contribute towards class identity within the country. If integration was weak or if national governments were seen to be discriminating against their citizens of Chinese descent, however, another kind of class interest would arise and economic elites of Chinese descent would be tempted to do business along ethnic lines with Chinese of other nationalities. This would tend to emphasize Chinese ethnic identity across the region and even with other parts of the world at the expense of a local identity with indigenous economic elites. The new stage of Chinese entrepreneurship is only just emerging and it is too early to determine in which direction it will develop. I would suggest that, while class identity among the economic elites within one country might help to weaken Chinese ethnic loyalties and encourage integration and even assimilation, political and social changes which steadily eroded away Chinese ethnic identity would have to be occurring at the same time if class identity were to have long-term consequences for the nation-states of the region.

There are obviously a variety of ways we can approach the subject of Chinese identities and I have shown how scholarly analyses tend to highlight one or another concept at different times according to changing circumstances. Let me now summarize the discussion so far and describe the picture of changing Chinese identities in Southeast Asia today as follows:

Historical identity as derived from past Chinese values still persists but is now encapsuled in the broader and much more useful concept of cultural identity.

Chinese nationalist identity is feeble and dying in most countries if not actually dead. The possibility of revival is there, but quite remote under present circumstances.[18]

Communal identity has been limited to Malaya/Malaysia, but the communalist road to political influence may be diminishing. Under heavy pressure, it might be replaced by the more neutral and less aggressive concept of ethnic identity.

National (local) identity is now common to the vast majority of Southeast Asian Chinese and is an important part of almost any mix of identities current among them, but at this stage, it it still regarded as little more than a legal and political identity for public and official use only.

Cultural identity has absorbed the traditional historical identity. It is still the most flexible concept of all, but it is less useful for those who believe that racial origins are still important as determinants in the idea of identity.

Ethnic identity corrects cultural identity on this point of racial origins. It is also more specific in conveying the idea of political purpose in the fight for legitimate minority rights and is a concept more likely to gain sympathy in the present climate of international opinion.

Class identity depends on crossing ethnic boundaries. It is emerging and may well be inevitable for most Chinese in the long run but, at this stage, it cannot but be conditional on Chinese ethnic identity being weakened by other political and social pressures to integrate or assimilate in the new state. Otherwise, the Chinese might identify with the class interests of other peoples, especially other Chinese, across national boundaries and this could be destabilizing for most nation-states.

By listing identities as I have done above, I may have given the impression that each of them is discrete and that "changing Chinese identities" means changing from one Chinese identity to another. This is clearly not the case. I have indicated from time to time how several of these identities overlap and why some concepts have been replaced by new ones in order to help scholarly analysis. Let me now say that all these concepts have helped our understanding of the Southeast Asian Chinese, some more so than others, but each of them is not enough to convey the complex reality of Chinese identities in the region. What is closer to reality is a picture of the Southeast Asian Chinese having multiple identities.

It must be clear by now that any idea of Chinese identity in Southeast Asia is an elusive one. Each of the concepts used so far may only fit some groups in some nation-states and only for some of the time. By using different concepts, scholarly writings have striven for greater accuracy and thus enriched our picture of the complex and often divided Chinese communities in the region. At the same time, they may also have given a picture of these communities that is far more fragmented and differentiated than they really have been or still are.[19] It is therefore necessary to find other ways to portray the complexity without fracturing the communities. To this end, some combinations of the different concepts may be put together and, in this way, allow us to approach the whole subject through the idea of multiple identities.

Such an approach assumes that it is perfectly normal for any individual or group to have more than one identity at one and the same time. I am not referring to the decades before the 1940s when the Southeast Asian Chinese seemed to have had dual identities by being Chinese nationals in China and foreign nationals abroad. That was merely a difference on paper which told us little about their own sense of identity. During the 1950s and 1960s, however, the picture changed radically. As citizens of the new nation-states, most Chinese slowly gave up their Chinese nationalist identity while acquiring a local national one. At the same time, they became more conscious of their cultural identity as Chinese and some of them also became more sensitive to their class (mainly middle-class) interests. Something akin to a class identity as an integrated part of their local national identity was emerging. But because racial factors would not go away, it had become necessary to bring forth the idea of ethnic identity to try and explain recent developments. Each of the four identities, whether national, cultural, class or ethnic, has sometimes been used as a new way of representing Chinese identity. Generally, however, there has been a recognition that most Chinese probably were a bit of each and none of these concepts could claim to convey what was really a mixture of multiple identities. Of course, not all Chinese would have had the same range of identities, nor could we expect each of these concepts to be given the same weight among those Chinese who have been aware of them. But we know enough about Southeast Asian Chinese today to believe that it would be usual for them to have had more than one identity at the same time.

How do we conceptualize the process of acquiring and maintaining multiple identities? To explore this question, I suggest that we approach it through the idea of norms. By norms, I mean the ideal standards which are binding upon members of a group and which serve to guide, control, or regulate their behaviour. Such norms are present in all the concepts of identity used so far and each of the identities described is based on the acceptance of specific sets of norms. For my purposes, I shall divide the major types of norms that determine Southeast Asian Chinese identity today into four groups.

PHYSICAL NORMS

For the Chinese, these are defined by endogamous marriages which give rise to vague notions of racial purity. In practice, these norms are not as absolute as they sound and are often subordinated to ideological principles about the male descent line, thus allowing for children of mixed marriages to be regarded as Chinese if they were born of Chinese fathers. If warranted by circumstances, children of Chinese mothers and non-Chinese fathers are also acceptable. After the first generation of mixed parentage, however, the norms would require a return to endogamous Chinese marriages. These physical norms have other ideological effects: they would breed narrow attitudes towards Chinese distinctiveness and exclusiveness, if not racial superiority as well. These attitudes which influence cultural and social values are often mistaken for cultural norms.[20] Of course, cultural norms can reinforce the ideological mystique about racial purity, but it is necessary to distinguish which set of norms is important here.

Physical norms directly contribute to a keen sense of Chinese ethnic identity and in some cases are the essential elements that define ethnic identity. When these norms are expressed in ideological terms, they could influence Chinese cultural identity to some extent and the political activities they stimulate in support of minority rights could in turn influence the development of national identity in each Southeast Asian country. But the normative identity determined largely by physical norms is that of ethnic identity.

POLITICAL NORMS

Modern political norms refer to ideas of political loyalty to the state, to the need for commitment to and participation in the tasks of nation-building and, often in the background, to the ideals of democratic rights. In practice, these norms are manifested in different ways

Figure 5.2

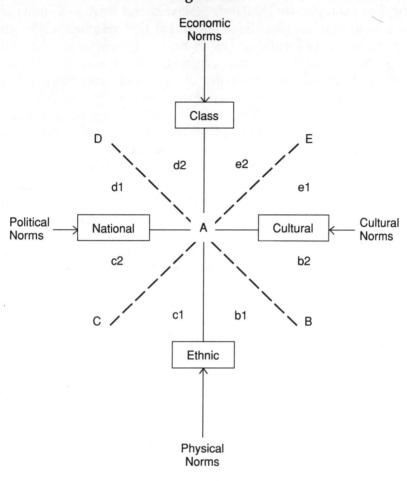

→   Direction of pressure.

      Normative identity if one set of norms is dominant. Also
      normative identity for combinations of multiple identities,
      for example, Ethnic for B & C, National for C & D, Class
      for D & E, and Cultural for E & B.

A   Equidistant and therefore free from normative pressures,
      the ultimate multiple identity.

Common multiple identities:
B + c1 + e1 = Ethnic and Cultural
C + d1 + b1 = National and Ethnic
D + c2 + e2 = Class and National
E + d2 + b2 = Cultural and Class

and the core principles are focused on different symbols and institutions. For example, in Thailand, Malaysia and Brunei, a monarchy and a state religion (Buddhism or Islam) that reinforce each other have primacy over secular norms. In Burma, Indonesia and Vietnam, the revolution and its symbols occupy the central position for determining political norms. While the Chinese and other "foreign" minorities are not totally excluded from these core principles, they recognize that political norms in these countries are largely defined by the elites of the dominant majority groups, usually indigenous, who control the governments of the new states. They also realize that, given the heterogeneous nature of Southeast Asian countries, such norms are rarely unchallenged. Therefore, they have learnt to expect that these norms are not consensual but really political decisions enforced through law or by the coercive powers of the state.

Political norms in new states are established to foster the new national identity. These norms are expected to help safeguard the nation-state against two immediate threats in the region. The first is the threat of strong local ethnic identities making demands that would weaken the new state from within. The second is that of outside economic and political interests which could either dominate the national economy through large-scale capital investments or propagate ideas of working-class solidarity across national borders in order to challenge the power of the new national elites.[21] The political norms need, therefore, the full support of all the institutions of the state. The normative identity defined directly by these norms is what I call national identity.

ECONOMIC NORMS
These refer to modern, rational standards of behaviour that influence the conduct of the national economy (overlapping here with political norms) and those standards regulating each group's pursuit of livelihood and profit. But when so broadly defined, their impact on identity is rather diffuse and not clear. We need to concentrate on those norms which either support the development of a national identity or those which reflect the cultural values of strong economic actors like the Chinese minorities in the region. But perhaps the most distinctive of those norms are those related to and which reflect class interests, interests which cross ethnic and national boundaries. Such norms can directly influence the sense of class identity, but without necessarily undermining an evolving natural identity or diminishing a residual Chinese cultural identity. In the long run, of course, a

strong commitment to class identity could weaken the identities of Southeast Asian Chinese as Chinese. But there are other variables involved. For example, economic successes may depend on the persistence of Chinese cultural values and the presence of Chinese ethnic identity and these may override class interests. Also, in most Southeast Asian countries, there are too few working-class Chinese to assert class interests at that level. Without that class, the middle-class economic norms of the Chinese in the region and elsewhere (including China, Taiwan, Hong Kong, North America and Australia) would tend to reinforce appeals to Chineseness. Only strong political pressures from within and powerful multinational organizations which could mobilize Chinese skills from without to serve their interests could keep such a resurgence of Chinese identity in check. No matter which direction the pressures of economic norms might go, I suggest that the normative identity they tend to shape is class identity.

CULTURAL NORMS
When broadly defined, these norms include everything in state and society (including political and economic norms) that influences the total value system of everybody. In that broad sense, it not helpful to our understanding of most Southeast Asian Chinese who have not been assimilated to such an extent that they deny their Chineseness and accept all the political and economic norms of the new nation-state. I prefer a narrower definition of culture which focuses on two kinds of norms. The first are Chinese cultural norms which the Chinese consider binding on them as Chinese (even when they are unable to attain them). They include the learning of the Chinese written language, the preservation of family ties especially through observing norms about birth, marriage and death, and the support given to clan, district, and other similar organizations which enhance Chinese social solidarity. The second are the modern cultural norms which the Chinese have found useful and necessary to accept. They include educational standards and career patterns outside the Chinese community, also non-Chinese language skills, even religious conversions and all the social customs which reflect the complexities of heterogeneous societies.

The two kinds of norms are obviously not given equal weight by the Chinese. In most Southeast Asian societies, the Chinese are relatively free to prefer one over the other. If they are inclined to assert their cultural identity as Chinese, they would give greater emphasis to the basic Chinese cultural norms (b2 in Figure 5.2). If they are confident that the minimal basic norms are enough to preserve their Chineseness, they would pay much more attention to modern utilitarian norms (e1 in Figure 5.2) which might help them attain the higher skills essential for professional betterment and upward social mobility. In any case, many Chinese would in fact regard these modern norms as more or less Chinese because they are acceptable to Chinese almost everywhere and can be seen to strengthen modern Chinese culture without threatening or interfering with basic Chinese norms. On this last point, they may in the long run have misjudged the situation, but it is too early to predict the outcome at this stage.

Both sets of cultural norms play a part in forming the sense of Chinese cultural identity. The difference in emphasis, however, means that the basic Chinese norms are more binding to those Chinese highly conscious of their ethnic identity, while the modern utilitarian norms would appeal more to those whose sense of ethnicity is not strong but who are anxious to attain social and economic success quickly. But the normative identity that is most clearly moulded by cultural norms is, of course, cultural identity.

Let me now return to the idea of multiple identities. I suggest that there are four common multiple identities, each based on a combination of the normative ethnic, national, class and cultural identities as defined above. There is, in theory, a fifth ideal multiple identity, the ultimate multiple identity because it is equidistant and therefore free from the normative identities, but I imagine that it is something impossible to achieve in practice. In Figure 5.2, I try to illustrate the relationship between the four sets of norms and the way they might influence the Chinese in their acquisition of multiple identities.

From the diagram, it would be apparent that I have used the idea of normative identity to give shape and form to various multiple identities. Thus, ethnic identity is the normative identity for a combination of identities which are influenced mainly by physical norms but also by political and cultural norms, and so on. But I would not wish to suggest that, in real life, the identities are all as neat, and have equal importance, as portrayed in the diagram. What is indicated are the positions that Chinese might find themselves in because of the norms they find binding to them as Chinese, the changes in direction they could make if they wanted to, and the new positions they could move to if they responded to other norms which bound them to identities that were less Chinese or more non-Chinese.

For example, if we assume that all Chinese grow up accepting physical norms as central to their ethnic identity, they could then be educated in an environment in which Chinese cultural norms are strong or be sent to national schools where nothing Chinese is available to them. They can retain their ethnic identity, but whether that identity is reinforced by Chinese culture and reflects hostility against the political norms (position B) or converted to national pride in their adopted country (position C) may depend on the options open to each Chinese community. For some Chinese, there are intermediate positions in which the normative ethnic identity determines everything, that is, it is so strong or its ethnic boundaries so prescribed by other ethnic groups that the Chinese involved would accept only Chinese cultural norms and make minimal commitments to political norms. For many others, however, their business and professional interests lead them to conform to economic norms across ethnic and cultural boundaries. Here again, they may have a choice, that is to say, whether they do so through emphasizing their Chinese cultural identity (route from position B to position E) or by stressing their political loyalty and seeking support from the state (route from position C to position D).

From observing the experiences of Southeast Asian Chinese during the past two decades, I would like to suggest how the above examples might fit some of the communities there. Let me begin with the totally untypical new nation of Singapore. It is the only country where all the multiple identities may co-exist to the same degree and where a large number of its citizens of Chinese descent (over 75 per cent of the population) may be equidistant from all normative pressures and approaching position A in the diagram.[22] Also untypical is Thailand, which is not a new nation-state, and where a century of largely assimilationist policies protected the country from the excesses of twentieth-century Chinese nationalism. For most Thai Chinese, their multiple identities would be guided by a strong normative national identity (that is, positions C and D).[23]

As for the larger nation-states, Malaysia stands out as the country where the Chinese are numerous enough to have real options whether to follow the cultural identity route (position B to E) or the national identity route (position C to D).[24] For quite different reasons, the Philippines provides similar options to its much smaller Chinese population. This is mainly because of its tough naturalization laws and its extraordinarily close relations with the Republic of China (Taiwan) until 1975. The situation has been changing since then and the national identity route may be increasingly favoured by the younger Chinese.[25] For Burma and Vietnam, the ethnic boundaries have always been less rigid and assimilationist policies have been relatively easy to implement. Clearly, for the majority of those citizens of Chinese descent, the national identity option had been acceptable for a long time. The only complications have arisen because of unpredictable strains which have surfaced from time to time in the relations between these countries and the People's Republic of China.[26] Finally, Indonesia provides the most complex, and even contradictory, picture. On the one hand, political norms weigh so strongly on people of Chinese descent that there are few options open to them. Access to Chinese cultural norms is kept to a minimum and the normative national identity is the primary standard for all. On the other hand, up to half the Chinese population are aliens and are unable to obtain Indonesian citizenship. For them, the cultural identity route to survival and success remains their only option.[27]

These comments are necessarily brief and are merely given to illustrate how the use of norms may be applied to the study of the multiple identities of Southeast Asian Chinese. Whether this approach will be useful in field research would need to be empirically tested. I do believe, however, that through the idea of norms and the concepts of normative identity, we can depict the pressures that determine multiple identities. In this way, I hope to have taken us a step closer to understanding the nature of Chinese identities in Southeast Asia.

NOTES

1 "Chineseness" is no easier to define than "Chinese identity" and tends to be defined tautologically. But both at least consist of concrete images that can be pointed to, whereas "identity" is abstract and the Chinese have found no word for it before the last decade or so. The technical term is now translated as *rentong* meaning "to identify that which is the same", but this is yet to be used in ordinary speech.

2 Modern social science research methods (including Marxist writings) originate from Western Europe and North America and may be described as "Western". In this essay, I have included Chinese, Japanese and Southeast Asian scholars who used these methods to study the Southeast Asian Chinese; most of them were either trained in the West or taught by those who had studied in the West within the past 30 years. The research they have produced has grown rapidly, with significant contributions coming first from economists and political scientists and then social/cultural anthropologists and sociologists. In this essay, it is obvious that I am greatly influenced by social/cultural anthropologists like Maurice

Freedman and G. William Skinner and their students. The most recent product of that tradition are the essays in L.A.P. Gosling and Linda Y.C. Lim (eds.), *The Chinese in Southeast Asia* (Singapore: Maruzen Asia, 1983), especially Vol. 2: *Identity, Culture and Politics*.

3 Perhaps "traditional Chinese" identity might be easier to recognize, but "historical" avoids the difficulties of being forced immediately to define what is "traditional" and what is "Chinese". "Historical" is neutral like "cultural" but emphasizes *past* cultural values and symbols.

4 As I shall show later, by multiple identities, I do not mean multiple ethnicities or multiple *ethnic* identities, like Sino-Thai and other mixed ethnic labels; nor am I speaking of categories or levels of *ethnic* identifications. Multiple identities are not situational identities, or alternative identities which one can switch around or switch on and off. What I mean by multiple identities is the simultaneous presence of many *kinds* of identities, e.g., ethnic, national (local), cultural and class identities.

5 I have used "ethnic groups" more broadly for Chinese, Malay, Indian and not for the separate speech groups like Hokkien, Cantonese, etc., as in C. Fred Blake, *Ethnic Groups and Social Change in a Chinese Market Town* (Honolulu: University of Hawaii Press, 1981). For the latter, I use "sub-ethnic", following Judith Strauch, *Chinese Village Politics in the Malaysian State* (Cambridge, Mass.: Harvard University Press, 1981), pp. 83–84.

6 This "historical" identity is, I believe, present in all who claim to be Chinese. In its most poignant form, where it was clung to when most Chinese characteristics had been lost, it was found among the *babas* and *peranakans* in Malaya and Java during the 19th and early 20th centuries.

7 The voluminous writings on nationalism among the overseas Chinese in the 1920–45 period are well known. Most of them are in Chinese and Japanese: see the useful list compiled by Hugh D.R. Baker in Victor Purcell, *The Chinese in Southeast Asia*, 2nd ed. (London: Oxford University Press, 1968), pp. 586–610. The most thorough study so far for any country in the region is Stephen M.Y. Leong, "Sources, Agencies and Manifestations of Overseas Chinese Nationalism in Malaya, 1937–1941" (Ph.D. thesis, UCLA, 1976, Xerox University Microfilms).

8 Where Chinese nationalism and communism are concerned, Malaya has for obvious reasons attracted the most attention and many political studies have been published, notably the work of Gene Z. Hanrahan, Lucian W. Pye and Anthony Short. A recent study that places the role of young Chinese in perspective is Cheah Boon Kheng, *Red Star Over Malaya: Resistance and Social Conflict During and After the Japanese Occupation, 1941–1946* (Singapore: Singapore University Press, 1983).

9 They are called "gropings" here because the young Chinese who identified with the early anti-colonial movements were rarely articulate enough to make clear whether they were really on the side of the new indigenous nationalism or on the side of the oppressed (largely indigenous) masses. Indonesian nationalism, too, attracted a few Chinese in the 1930s, but they were too few to be significant; Leo Suryadinata, *Peranakan Chinese Politics in Java*, rev. ed. (Singapore: Singapore

University Press, 1981), pp. 156–68.

10 See especially the pioneering works by Victor Purcell, K.J. Ratnam, Raj Vasil, where communalism is the key word and the communal identity of the Chinese was the basis for the demand to share power with the Malays.

11 I am indebted to the work of G. William Skinner here, especially to his *Chinese Society in Thailand: An Analytical History* (Ithaca, N.Y.: Cornell University Press, 1957), pp. 126–54; and his "Change and Persistence in Chinese Culture Overseas: A Comparison of Thailand and Java", *Journal of the South Seas Society* (Nanyang Hsueh Pao), 1960: pp. 86–100. I have used only assimilation and integration here, and not acculturation; I believe integration includes acculturation, but puts the emphasis on identifying with the new nation-states.

12 The pressure has been the greatest in Indonesia and the Chinese response is especially interesting. See the essays by Chinese nationalists, pluralists and assimilationists extracted in Leo Suryadinata (ed.), *Political Thinking of the Indonesian Chinese, 1900–1977* (Singapore: Singapore University Press, 1979), pp. 83–159.

13 A brief but trenchant comment on the renewed interest in race relations and politics may be found in the new Preface to R.A. Schermerhorn, *Comparative Ethnic Relations: A Framework for Theory and Research* (Chicago: University of Chicago Press, Phoenix edition, 1978), pp. xiii–xxii. For Southeast Asia, politics in Malaysia (for example, the work of Cynthia Enloe) had long been studied as communal politics, but ethnicity in the politics of other Southeast Asian countries became a focus of attention within the region only later, notably in the *Southeast Asian Journal of Social Science* (especially in Vol. 10, No.1 (1982): "Ethnicity in Southeast Asia"), *Southeast Asia Ethnicity and Development Newsletter* (Singapore, 1977–81), and various publications of the Institute of Southeast Asian Studies in Singapore.

14 Frederick Barth's use of ethnic boundaries and Judith Nagata's discussion of situational identity have been invaluable in clearing away some of the difficulties in differentiating ethnic from cultural identity. Ethnicity does not depend on race or biological heritage alone, but expressions of racial identification or "primordial sentiments" (C. Geertz) remain a vital part of ethnic identity. F. Barth (ed.), *Ethnic Groups and Boundaries* (Boston: Little Brown, 1969), pp. 9–38; J. Nagata, "What is a Malay? Situational Selection of Ethnic Identity in a Plural Society", *American Ethnologist*, 1/2(1974): pp. 331–50 and Clifford Geertz, "The Integrative Revolution: Primordial Sentiments and Civil Politics in New States", in C. Geertz (ed.), *Old Societies and New States: The Quest for Modernity in Asia and Africa* (N.Y.: Free Press, 1963), pp. 105–57. Although I am not specifically describing ethnic groups, I am greatly influenced by Charles F. Keyes, "Towards a New Formulation of the Concept of Ethnic Group", *Ethnicity*, 3(1976): pp. 202–13.

15 These minorities conform to the point made by Robert H. Taylor about "ethnic groups" being "those beyond the pale of religious, cultural or 'national' orthodoxy, and were not justified in sharing the benefits of membership in a select, chosen people". ("Perceptions of ethnicity in the politic of Burma", in *Southeast Asian Journal of Social Science*, 10/1 (1982): pp. 7–22, footnote 19). The Chinese are troublesome in other ways: they are urban and often particularly numerous at the political centre, the capital cities, and being highly competitive, they could threaten

the economic interests of the indigenous elites. But they are not agents of China: not enough weight has been given to the effect of China's change of policy in 1955 towards the Chinese outside China and how this policy change eased "the Chinese problem" for Southeast Asian new nations during the decade before the Cultural Revolution; Stephen Fitzgerald, *China and the Overseas Chinese: A Study of Peking's Changing Policy, 1949–1970* (Cambridge: Cambridge University Press, 1972), pp. 107ff. During the Cultural Revolution, of course, the majority of Southeast Asian Chinese were alienated by its excesses.

16 For post-colonial Southeast Asia, Hans-Dieter Evers cautiously explores the subject, "Group Conflict and Class Formation in Southeast Asia" in the collection of essays he edited, *Modernization in Southeast Asia* (Singapore: Oxford University Press, 1973), pp. 108–31. But fresh interest really began in studies about Malaysia in 1975–76 (B.N. Cham in *Journal of Contemporary Asia*, 5/4(1975): pp. 446–61, and Michael Stenson in *Bulletin of Concerned Asian Scholars*, April 1976). See also Micheal Stenson, *Class, Race and Colonialism in West Malaysia: The Indian Case* (St Lucia: University of Queensland Press, 1980), pp. 192–210, for the 1957–69 period; and Loh Kok Wah, *The Politics of Chinese Unity in Malaysia: Reform and Conflict in the Malaysian Chinese Association, 1971–1973* (Singapore: Maruzen Asia, 1982).

17 A valuable effort to link ethnicity with economic activity can be found in several original essays in Linda Y.C. Lim and L.A.P. Gosling (eds.), *The Chinese in Southeast Asia*, Vol. I (Singapore: Maruzen Asia, 1983); see specially the excellent introductory review by Linda Lim, pp. 1–29.

18 For a comparison of these "present circumstances", see my 1979 survey, "China and the Region in Relation to Chinese Minorities", in Wang Gungwu, *Community and Nation: Essays on Southeast Asia and the Chinese* (Sydney: George Allen & Unwin, 1981), pp. 274–85; and my 1984 survey, "External China as a New Policy Area", *Pacific Affairs*, Spring 1985, and Chapter 12 of this book. I suggest that relations between China and Southeast Asian Chinese could become more complex and subtle now that economic modernization along market-oriented lines is China's top priority, but there is no reason to believe that Chinese nationalism, not legitimate again in China, can be revived in Southeast Asia.

19 A recent example of sub-ethnic differentiation is the thorough description by Wolfgang Moese, Gottfried Reinknecht and Eva Schmitz-Seisser, *Chinese Regionalism in West Malaysia and Singapore* (Hamburg, 1979). In contrast, Judith Strauch, *Village Politics*, pp. 99, 153–59 and 169–71 and Loh Koh Wah, *Chinese Unity*, pp. 35–44 and 71–82, suggest that ethnicity in politics now overrides "regional" or sub-ethnic differences. For other social and economic reasons, this is also true in Singapore: Cheng Lim-Keak, *Social Change and the Chinese in Singapore: A Socioeconomic Geography with Special Reference to Bang Structure* (Singapore: Singapore University Press, 1985), pp. 166–200.

20 These attitudes are clearly derived from notions of racial purity and belong here to physical norms. They differ from attitudes drawn from notions of cultural maturity and sophistication which should be placed among cultural norms.

21 On the surface, this would mean the threat of capitalism to the survival of countries like Burma and Vietnam and that of communism to the survival of each of the

six ASEAN states. But, in terms of sovereignty and non-survival, the former could also be threatened by socialist or communist allies and enemies and the latter also by capitalist friends and the larger multinationals.

22 The question, "Why Should a Chinese Look for Chinese Identification in Singapore?" (Sharon A. Carstons, *Chinese Associations in Singapore Society*, ISEAS Occasional Paper No. 37, 1975, p. 17) can be answered at several levels. At one level, the answer is, Singapore is not a Chinese state, merely a city-state with a Chinese majority in the middle of a "Malay" world. At another level, Singapore Chinese are too close to Malaysian Chinese (and some Indonesian Chinese as well) not to share their concerns as a people whose Chinese identity is under attack. At yet another level, Singapore's policy of "multi-racialism" (similar to that of the colonial British?) will not allow the Chinese to forget their Chineseness (Geoffrey Benjamin, "The Cultural Logic of Singapore's Multiracialism", in Riaz Hassan (ed.), *Singapore: Society in Transition* (Kuala Lumpur: Oxford University Press, 1976), pp. 115–33. And there is a further point worth noting about government policy strengthening Chinese identity as "a bulwark against anomie" (John Clammer, "Chinese Ethnicity and Political Culture in Singapore", in Gosling and Lim, *Chinese in Southeast Asia*, Vol.II, pp. 266–84). All the same, I would suggest that, if Singapore is allowed to prosper and feel secure by its non-Chinese neighbours, the trend for its citizens of Chinese descent would be towards the balanced position where all four identities could be equally available to them. Those who move towards position A will remain ethnically Chinese, politically loyal and committed nationals, concerned for their class interests and share a mixture of basic and utilitarian culture values. A recent essay is suggestive: Chiew Seen Kong, "Ethnicity and National Integration: The Evolution of a Multi-Ethnic Society" in Peter S.J. Chen (ed.), *Singapore Development Policies and Trends* (Singapore: Oxford University Press, 1983), pp. 29–64.

23 I support the predictions in Skinner, *Chinese Society*, pp. 380–82, but do not believe they should be interpreted to mean that ultimately *all* Chinese will be totally assimilated (that is, will reach position D). My own understanding is that most Thais of Chinese descent will reach position D, but many will, for a long time to come, stay in position C while there will always be some in positions B and E; see Christina Blanc Szanton, "Thai and Sino-Thai in Small Town Thailand: Changing Patterns of Interethnic Relations", in Gosling and Lim, *Chinese in Southeast Asia*, Vol.II, pp. 99–125, for petty bourgeois Sino-Thai in what I have called position C.

24 That their options are real can be seen in the dozen or so papers describing Malaysian Chinese in the two volumes of Gosling and Lim, *Chinese in Southeast Asia*, notably those by Sharon Carstens, Tan Chee Beng, Moli Siow, Loh Koh Wah, Donald Nonini, Lim Mah Hui, Paul Chan and Judith Strauch. A recent study by Hua Wu Yin, *Class and Communalism in Malaysia: Politics in a Dependent Capitalist State* (London: Zed Books, 1983), is very critical of the Malaysian government's policies about local-national and communal (ethnic) identities, but it confirms that most Chinese still have real options as to which way they wish to go, from position B to E or from position C to D; see Chapters 7 and 8, pp. 150–94.

25 John T. Ornohundro, *Chinese Merchant Families in Iloilo: Commerce and Kin in a Central Philippine City* (Quezon city: Ateneo de Manila University Press, 1981) and

Charles J. McCarthy (ed.), *Philippine-Chinese Profile: Essays and Studies* (essays by McCarthy, Robert Tsai, Bernard C. Go and Robert O. Tilman), have been particularly helpful. Ch'en Lieh-fu, *Tung-nan-ya-chou ti hua-chi'iao, Hua-jen yu Hua-yi* (Taipei: Cheng Chung, 1979), pp. 241–50, 455–60, 508–11, and 535–64 also provides insights from the Chinese point of view.

26 There are no recent studies of ethnic Chinese in Burma and unified Vietnam. The only glimpses come from troubles with China: Burma during the Cultural Revolution (Ralph Pettman, *China in Burma's Foreign Policy* (Canberra: Australian National University Press, 1973)) and Vietnam since 1978 (Chang Pao-min, *Beijing, Hanoi, and the Overseas Chinese* (Berkeley: South Asian Studies Institute, 1982) and "The Sino-Vietnamese Dispute Over the Ethnic Chinese", *The China Quarterly,* 90 (June 1982): pp. 195–230).

27 Three recent studies bring out the complexity of the Indonesian picture: the essays by Charles A. Coppel and J.A.C. Mackie in J.A.C. Mackie (ed.), *The Chinese in Indonesia* (Melbourne: Nelson, 1976), pp. 19–76 and 77–138; Leo Suryadinata's *Pribumi Indonesians, the Chinese Minority and China* (Kuala Lumpur: Heinemann, 1978), pp. 138–64; and Charles A. Coppel, *Indonesian Chinese in Crisis* (Kuala Lumpur: Oxford University Press, 1983), especially Chapters 4 and 7.

CHAPTER 12

External China as a
New Policy Area[1]

THIS ESSAY SEEKS TO show that some recent developments in the People's Republic of China mark the emergence of a new policy area that may be called External China (*Waihua Zhengce*).[2] This policy area would focus mainly on people outside the PRC who are Chinese nationals of one kind or another as well as those people within China who are related to, and are identified with, ethnic Chinese outside China. This means that it is not simply about foreign policy or about matters outside China. Nor is it merely about the traditional Overseas Chinese or Huaqiao (Chinese sojourners) as commonly understood to include everybody who was of Chinese descent outside China. The new policy area includes people and problems inside China and therefore concerns aspects of domestic policy. For the moment, it seems to be a grey or ill-defined area that covers a large number of people inside and outside China, involves a mixture of foreign and domestic policies, and is the responsibility of a wide variety of central and local officials who have to work together on related problems. In addition, because it seems inclusive and ill-defined, it appears to be a growth area that has ramifications even more subtle and complex than the older policy area that concerned itself with all Overseas Chinese.[3]

The new policy area can best be understood through the groups of people that are included in it. Obviously, the vast majority of the Chinese living in China are not involved. Also, it is doubtful if External China concerns all those of Chinese descent who are presently living outside China, especially those who have adopted foreign nationality and have nothing to do with China. It is useful to start by distinguishing between two categories of people — those who are undoubtedly Chinese, and those who may be considered ethnic Chinese but are foreign nationals. Broadly speaking, the first category consists of three groups: the Huaqiao; the Tongbao of Taiwan,

Hong Kong and Macao; the Guiqiao (returned Huaqiao) and the Qiaojuan (Huaqiao dependents). As for the second category, one may distinguish those of Chinese descent in Southeast Asia from those who have settled elsewhere.

The Huaqiao

It seems appropriate to begin with Huaqiao. In some ways, the whole question of External China has evolved from the policy problems of dealing with Chinese outside China's borders. These problems really began during the second half of the nineteenth century. It began with Chinese born abroad acquiring foreign citizenship and emigrant coolie labour needing official protection from the Chinese government. It reached a climax with new policies offering to protect a category of people called Huaqiao by the turn of the century, and given formal legal recognition following upon the Nationality Law of 1909. Under the Republic of China, the issue of Huaqiao became increasingly important, especially with the Nanking government of the Guomindang from 1928 to 1949. The PRC inherited many of the same problems and policies, but since the late 1950s had initiated new policies stemming from an increasingly careful use of the term "Huaqiao", now defined to include only citizens of the PRC living abroad.[4] By this definition, Huaqiao may not now be used loosely to cover all Chinese overseas. During the Cultural Revolution period, the PRC went further and virtually abolished every office and organ that had to do with Huaqiao affairs whether inside or outside China. But since 1977, in a flurry of "restoration" of pre-Cultural Revolution institutions and their personnel, the Huaqiao issue has come to the fore again. For a while it appeared that Huaqiao affairs could return to their old prominence, especially under the leadership of the late Liao Chengzhi (1908–83).[5] But when the excitement died down, it became clear that there had been no fundamental change in Huaqiao policy. "Huaqiao" was still strictly defined, at least in official circles, to refer only to Chinese citizens living abroad.

But many significant changes had occurred during the two decades when the PRC was relatively isolated, which affected the use of the term Huaqiao. Many more people from Taiwan, Hong Kong and Macao had emigrated, especially to the Americas, Western Europe and Australasia. By the PRC's own definition, such people from Chinese territory are notionally citizens of China. Therefore, when they reside overseas but have not adopted foreign nationality, they may be called Huaqiao. This is made all the easier because the government of the Republic of China (Taiwan) certainly regards them all as Huaqiao. Indeed, it even counts the people of Hong Kong and Macao as Huaqiao, which in many contexts adds considerable confusion to our present use and understanding of the term.[6] If matters had been left to the countries in the Americas, Europe and Australasia, the ambiguities of who was or was not Huaqiao probably would not have mattered much. But the pressures from Southeast Asian governments leave no room for confusion. Countries like Indonesia in the 1950s had played a key role in China's adopting the strict definition of Huaqiao. Others have been equally firm that the term cannot be used to apply to their own citizens of Chinese descent. And diplomatic relations, especially those in the mid-1970s with Malaysia, Thailand and the Philippines, have served to confirm that narrower and more accurate usage.[7]

Equally significant is the sharp change in the post-World War II generation of Overseas Chinese — not least because of their perceptions of China's policies since 1957, especially during the years 1966–76 — who now seek to be citizens of foreign countries. Unlike their parents and grandparents, and now often with the encouragement of the same parents and grandparents, they seek to settle abroad and have no thoughts of returning to live, or to die, in China. The PRC government seemed to have anticipated that change and openly encouraged such Chinese to settle abroad and become loyal citizens of their adopted countries. Thus there is now no official misunderstanding about who should be called Huaqiao: Huaqiao are citizens of the PRC and may include those of the Republic of China (Taiwan) as well as Hong Kong and Macao passport-holders who are temporarily living abroad.[8]

Even by this narrow legal definition, Huaqiao may be found throughout the world. But the numbers are not what they used to be. No longer are we talking about a score of millions of Huaqiao, as many careless writings are still wont to do. The PRC itself seems to be working on the figure of about four million.[9] It is not clear how that figure was arrived at. It probably also includes every person abroad of Chinese descent who carries a Taiwanese or Hong Kong-British passport, as well as those who are stateless while awaiting naturalization in one form or another. A more careful estimate would put the figure closer to two-and-a-half million, most of them in Indonesia, North America and Japan. (It is difficult to know how to deal with the figures from Vietnam.)[10] The significance for the PRC of these Huaqiao, whether four million or two-and-a-half million, is not clear. Certainly most of those in Indonesia now hope to obtain Indonesian citizenship and most of those in North America who originated fairly recently from either Taiwan or Hong Kong/Macao are simply waiting for their chance to apply for foreign citizenship. Nevertheless, they are part of External China in the meantime.

The Tongbao of Taiwan, Hong Kong and Macao

The PRC would not officially consider these Chinese as Huaqiao. They are Tongbao — natural-born Chinese who, in theory, have the same rights as every PRC citizen. They can be said to belong to External China because they remain outside the PRC's jurisdiction. But a blunt statement of this kind would be quite meaningless. The complexities here are great and it is necessary to differentiate between the Tongbao of Taiwan and those of Hong Kong and Macao.

First, it does not appear, on the surface, appropriate to include the Tongbao of Taiwan here.[11] Taiwan is a distinctive and quite separate problem which the PRC can justifiably argue is largely a domestic issue. This was certainly true in 1949 and through the 1950s and 1960s. But since the PRC's admission into the United Nations, and even more so since China's new opening to the West after 1976 (perhaps best symbolized by the formal diplomatic relations established in 1979 between the PRC and the United States), the position has changed. The question of reunification is no longer the dominant, all-consuming issue it once had been. It is now closely linked with the future of Hong Kong and Macao; it raises matters concerning the status of the remaining Huaqiao abroad; there are problems related to Guiqiao who had originated from Taiwan and to Taiwan-dependents who are being treated like Qiaojuan, and there are Taiwan's modernization experiences and its example in dealing with ethnic Chinese who are foreign nationals.

The government in Taiwan, of course, still remains a special problem for China. The PRC cannot get rid of it as easily as it can the British administration in Hong Kong and, when it wants to, the Portuguese in Macao. And as long as that government in Taiwan claims to be the legitimate government of China, the people in Taiwan are not really *external* at all. Otherwise, the argument could be that, from the Republic of China's point of view, a thousand million Chinese on the mainland are parts of its External China, and that would not be helpful to intelligible analysis. Nevertheless, recent developments in PRC policy have now tied in the Taiwan question with a policy area which includes other Chinese not within PRC jurisdiction. The time has come to recognize that the Tongbao of Taiwan have become part of a larger question, that of External China.

As for the Tongbao of Hong Kong and Macao, their position in External China is not in doubt. For the Hong Kong Tongbao, living in a colony of the British empire, and thus second-class citizens in Britain and lesser members of the British Commonwealth, they are clearly different from the Chinese in the PRC or in Taiwan. The only question has been whether the PRC is right in calling them Tongbao or the government in Taiwan is right to include them as Huaqiao. The disagreement hinges on two definitions, whether or not Hong Kong is Chinese soil temporarily occupied by foreigners and whether the term "*qiao*" in Huaqiao refers to temporary residence anywhere (even within China), or whether it should now mean only residence outside Chinese soil. In early usage — that is, before 1858 — *qiao* had been used for migration within China. Only during the past century or so has it been changed to refer mainly to those outside China.[12] And since the mid-1950s, the PRC has defined it to refer to temporary residence abroad and, therefore, would not apply it to Hong Kong. But, although not Huaqiao, Hong Kong Tongbao have certainly been outside China's control and therefore clearly part of External China. By 1997, of course, Hong Kong will legally be part of PRC territory. However, the arrangements being envisaged for the fifty years after 1997 suggest that the people of Hong Kong will remain part of External China in one way or another.[13] If so, then together with the people of Taiwan and Macao, they would add about twenty-five million people to the new policy area: about nineteen million from Taiwan and some six million from Hong Kong and Macao.

It is possible to keep Taiwan clearly separated from Hong Kong and Macao, and regard the Taiwan Tongbao as a distinct group. But if emphasis is placed on the *external* nature of what they represent, then grouping all three kinds of Tongbao together is justified. In short, the key does not lie in all three being part of Chinese soil or all their people being undoubtedly Chinese, but in the kinds of common problems they pose for, and the nature of the contribution they can offer to, the PRC. Hong Kong, in particular, has much to offer directly in terms of China's modernization: capital, technical and managerial skills and, not least, its strong links with the industrialized world. In a different way, Taiwan too can offer much to the PRC. By being independent, capitalist and successful, it poses a challenge to the latter's socialist system. Yet, at the same time, Taiwan represents Chinese success and must be an inspiration to many in the PRC. Furthermore, the PRC could call on the services of many former Taiwanese citizens who have made their mark in the developed world. Altogether, the continued success of Taiwan might still be a major external contribution to China's modernization for years to come. And with the prospect of eventual reunification, there is always the expectation that Taiwan will be a sharp stimulus to the PRC until all its potential becomes part of the PRC's resources. To that extent, Taiwan would have an exceptional place in spurring the PRC to do well in the eyes of the world, not least in what it can achieve in Hong Kong both before and after 1997.[14]

The Guiqiao, Qiaojuan and Their Families[15]

The Guiqiao are former Overseas Chinese, most of whom had returned to China after 1949. The majority returned from Southeast Asia during the 1950s, but there have been sizable additions since then, notably some from Indonesia in the 1960s and many more from Vietnam since 1978. Some of them had returned to China voluntarily, but most of them had been pushed to do so for reasons beyond their control. Very few can be said to have been induced by the PRC to return, but they have all been welcomed with varying degrees of warmth and compassion. And most Guiqiao seem to have received preferential treatment in some ways. The group is a very mixed one, ranging from skilled professionals to indigent unskilled labourers. Most of them are now old; even the children they had brought back with them are now middle-aged.[16]

As for Qiaojuan, or dependents of Huaqiao, they are harder to define. As the term suggests, they were technically the close relatives of Huaqiao, but that was at a time when Huaqiao was loosely used to mean *all* Chinese overseas. Now that there are very few Huaqiao, Qiaojuan is a misnomer, for it now could refer to anyone who has relatives among the Chinese overseas, including those who are permanently settled abroad as foreign citizens. An added complication has been that the slight privileges allowed the Qiaojuan when their relatives abroad remitted funds home are hardly distinguishable from those permitted other Chinese whose relatives were Tongbao from Hong Kong and Macao. And, more recently, relatives of those who had followed the Guomindang government to Taiwan in 1949 have been encouraged to come forth and be treated in ways similar to the earlier Qiaojuan. Again, the name is a misnomer, since moving to Taiwan did not make such Chinese Huaqiao in any way. On the other hand, many such Chinese in Taiwan had sent their children to study in the United States and thus they themselves were now a kind of Huaqiao or even Qiaojuan, and in this way their relatives on the mainland may also be regarded as Qiaojuan.[17]

The question here is why Guiqiao and Qiaojuan should be included in External China. They all live in China today. Most of them are indistinguishable from other Chinese and few are likely to leave China. The reasons for their inclusion are both historical and practical. By historical, one could refer to event during the 1950s and early 1960s, but the most important single historical reason for their inclusion lies in what happened to most of them during the Cultural Revolution years, 1966–76. Most of them were affected by the backlash against the few privileges they had been given in earlier years, and many were accused — together with almost everyone who had been abroad before 1949 — of having "overseas connections" (*haiwai guanxi*). Their privileges, such as they were, were taken away from them and remittances from, or any other kind of contact with, their relatives abroad were discouraged. There were many personal tragedies, especially when their patriotic motives for returning were impugned and their every action since their return to China regarded with suspicion. Although Guiqiao and Qiaojuan were not singled out for unjust treatment, what befell them left terrible scars and also had an altogether negative impact on their friends and relatives overseas. As a consequence, the government since 1977 has sought to correct injustices and make restitution to some of the Guiqiao and Qiaojuan.[18] The most effective form that restitution could take was to let them re-establish their overseas connections.

This has also a practical aspect. As the government opens the country's doors to economic and technical influences from abroad and needs to demonstrate its new enlightened policy of order and progress, it is natural as well as humane not only to return all previous privileges to the Guiqiao and Qiaojuan, but also to tolerate the excitement and enthusiasm with which they have greeted the opportunity to deal with the outside world again. The government has recognized that there have been exceptionally deep resentments in South China where most Guiqiao and Qiaojuan are. It has, therefore, given encouragement to provinces like Fujian and Guangdong, and especially to their larger cities and their numerous Qiaoxiang (villages formerly with extensive Huaqiao connections), to restore all overseas links and contacts.[19] This has placed the Guiqiao and Qiaojuan very much in the External China policy area.

Of course, not everything about the Guiqiao and Qiaojuan has to do with External China. Many of their daily concerns are clearly domestic matters no different from those touching the lives of all other Chinese. But certain key features — for example, the investment of overseas Chinese capital in their home provinces, cities or towns, the financial contributions made by relatives overseas towards all levels of education, and even the simple remittances to assist the housing and living problems of Guiqiao and Qiaojuan — are directly matters concerning External China and need no elaboration. These have historical roots traceable to the end of the nineteenth century and have always been regarded as what was due to the people of the southern coasts of China.[20]

There are, as mentioned earlier, serious problems of definition. How serious this is becomes clear when we try to determine how many Guiqiao there are today and, even more difficult, how many may be officially recognized as Qiaojuan. There are no reliable figures. The authorities dealing with Guiqiao affairs estimate that there are about one million Guiqiao today, but they admit that many Guiqiao are only peripherally recognizable as former Huaqiao and that many others have simply given up their Guiqiao status, especially when they have been successfully assimilated and have no residual connections overseas. Other reasons given for the lack of reliable figures include the tendency of some authorities to empire-build and extend the meaning of Guiqiao while others are more exclusive.[21] As for Qiaojuan, few people would even venture a guess, although the figure of as many as twenty million was occasionally quoted.[22] The difficulty here was that not all Qiaojuan actively identified themselves as such. Sometimes it was only when enquiries were made from overseas or foreign funds were remitted that people would admit to be of that status. But, without doubt, the past six years or so have seen a spectacular revival of Guiqiao and Qiaojuan activity. The full domestic repercussions of this revival in China are still unclear and this is not the place to go into all aspects of this complex phenomenon. It has not been suggested that External China as a policy area includes all twenty-one million of Guiqiao and Qiaojuan, but merely that they belong to an area where domestic and foreign policies have consciously to mix, and that, if and when any of them should activate their connections abroad, each of these could influence local if not necessarily national development and welfare within China.[23]

The first category of people of External China, then, are those who are undoubtedly Chinese and who are not necessarily residing outside China. The second category are foreign nationals. Strictly speaking, they are foreigners and cannot be part of External China. The PRC government does not claim them for China in any way. In rejecting the old definition of Huaqiao during the 1950s, when the term had included everyone of Chinese ancestry living abroad, the PRC had officially disclaimed having any special connections with foreign Chinese. It remains committed to such a policy today.[24] Despite that, however, the activities of many such foreign Chinese impinge on PRC policies (both domestic and foreign) pertaining to the three groups described above, as well as on many other policies. In examining this second category, some comparisons should be made between the foreign Chinese in Southeast Asia and those in the rest of the world.

It is well known that the majority of all foreign Chinese have made their homes in Southeast Asia. It was, in fact, pressure from their new national governments in the 1950s that first made the PRC aware of the need to abandon the careless and inaccurate use of the term Huaqiao to apply to all Overseas Chinese. The major development of the past thirty years has been that, with the exception of Singapore, the ethnic Chinese of all Southeast Asian countries have become less obviously Chinese than they were. This is partly because there has been no new migration of Chinese into the region for over thirty years, and partly because of the determined efforts of all governments to integrate as many Chinese as they can into the national community. On the whole, the success of the latter was made easier by the fact that migration had come to an end. Today, most Southeast Asian Chinese no longer read and write the Chinese language, many can barely speak a dialect or two, some are barely recognizable as Chinese, and some may not even admit to being Chinese.[25]

The clear exception to this, of course, is Singapore. And the relatively large numbers of Chinese in Malaysia seem to have worked out an uneasy equilibrium in which gradual integration of the Chinese is balanced by official respect for the rights of those of Chinese descent to preserve their ethnicity. These rights are even better protected in Singapore where the Chinese are the ethnic majority and the government is run largely by citizens of Chinese descent. Furthermore, most ethnic Chinese there can speak, read and write Chinese, although not necessarily very well. In this respect, and in others where Singapore's leaders have demonstrated great foresight and financial and economic acumen, it has gained the PRC's attention. However, as with the other countries in Southeast Asia, the PRC recognized that the China connection is virtually a taboo subject which is politically sensitive, and one which could embarrass Singapore despite the strong sense of Chinese ethnicity there.[26] Given this situation in Southeast Asia, in what way could the region's ethnic Chinese be related to External China?

On the surface, the answer is simple. These Chinese could in no way be part of External China. The PRC government has not changed its policies about leaving foreign Chinese alone, especially those in Southeast Asia. But a number of recent developments seem to have blurred the picture, perhaps unintentionally. They stem from China's decision to open its doors gradually to the world. The excitement that this generated throughout the industrialized Western world (including Japan) is still unabated. And no less excited were many Huaqiao (especially those in the United States and Japan) and the Tongbao of Hong Kong and Macao. Even the Tongbao of Taiwan could not be unaffected by this turn of events, although there is little they could directly do. The entrepreneurial interest of some foreign Chinese, especially those of the United States, has attracted attention. As US relations with the PRC improved and various bans on trade and dealing with China were lifted, a number of Chinese Americans have openly invested in China, notably in the hotel and tourist industry. Others have proffered valuable advice in modernizing sectors of the economy, not least in science and technology research and in higher education. The background here is important. The close relations between the United States and Taiwan had set a pattern which permitted Chinese Americans to serve Taiwan in many capacities, in trade and industry, in education and training and even directly in government. Thus, when diplomatic relations were established with the PRC, there was no great difficulty for other Chinese Americans to look to the PRC in similar ways. And the PRC did not hesitate to welcome such foreign Chinese when they turned up, and even sought some of them out for their research institutes and universities.[27]

The ease with which these contracts were made and followed up was certainly assisted by overall US policy towards the PRC and, earlier on, towards the Republic of China in Taiwan. And foreign Chinese from other industrialized countries followed suit, if not directly to China, certainly via Hong Kong. And in so far as they are perceived as having been given privileges over other foreign entrepreneurs, their activities have become objects of close scrutiny abroad. For obvious reasons, many foreign Chinese in Southeast Asia would like to reap some of the benefits of more open trade and investment in China. While they cannot compete with those from the Americas who have family in and other connections with Beijing and Shanghai and the national enterprises, many would like to respond to the development needs of those parts of South China (Fujian and some regions of Guangdong) not catered for by other foreign nationals. What is important to note is that the desire to invest has little to do with sentiment and philanthropy, but comes from a keen eye for profit.[28] But there is a marked difference between national policies in the Americas and those in Southeast Asia. North American Chinese contributing to China's modernization do not comprise a threat to the countries of which they are nationals. This is not true of ethnic Chinese in the eyes of most Southeast Asian governments. Therefore, the level of involvement is much lower and more indirect. For most foreign Chinese in Southeast Asia, their contributions, if any, are probably not much more than occasional remittances to their relatives in South China. Nevertheless, there is involvement with Huaqiao, with Tongbao (especially in Hong Kong) and with Guiqiao and Qiaojuan, all three of which are groups of External China. These relationships are more subtle and private than those of the Chinese Americans, but at the level of Qiaoxiang (villages) with strong clan ties and a long history of having exported their men to trade and work in Southeast Asia, especially in Fujian and Guangdong, they were no less intense and significant.[29] If these relationships do not make all foreign Chinese part of External China, they certainly bring some of these Chinese close to External China and make them sensitive to policies taken on its behalf.

But there is another area which leaves the question even more ambiguous. This is the area of common Chinese ethnic consciousness as seen in Huaqiao history. Together with the excitement over modernization and open doors, the writing of Huaqiao history has aroused strong emotions in China.[30] This has always been so and the revival of public interest in the subject today has given it a new fervour. The authorities responsible are now aware of the dangers of reviving some of the chauvinist features of pre-1950s Huaqiao history and have warned specifically against certain traditional themes. For example, they have found it fit to underline that Huaqiao were migrants and not colonists, that the "tribute system" should not be glorified and that the image of Chinese suzerainty in Southeast Asia is totally misleading. In particular, there should be no chauvinist pride in traditional Chinese military exploits in the region. There is today no room for cultural superiority. On the contrary, Huaqiao history should emphasize the positive contributions: on the one hand, of patriotic Chinese supporting national revolution in China, and, on the other, of other Chinese who assisted the anti-colonial independence movements of various Southeast Asian nationalists and who contributed much to economic growth and the technical and educational progress of the region.[31]

The warnings have been necessary. There is a lot of Huaqiao history for the first half of this century which would make a case for a broader use of Huaqiao to include all Chinese residing abroad and thus support the notion of an External China that covers all foreign Chinese. If left in the hands of the sentimental chauvinists, that kind of history would expand the scope of External China even further. It might lead to a position where the ethnicity of the foreign Chinese was heightened until doubts were once again raised abroad about the sincerity and loyalty of such Chinese to their countries of settlement.[32] It would certainly make the question of how many ethnic Chinese there are outside China today one of increasing political significance.

It is not easy to say how many foreign Chinese there really are. The PRC seems to be working with a figure of about 16 million, that is at least 20 million Chinese overseas, of whom 20 per cent are still Chinese citizens.[33] When closely examined, it is clear that accurate figures of ethnic Chinese exist only for Singapore, Malaysia, North America, Japan, Korea and parts of Western Europe and Southern Africa. The estimates for Indonesia and Australia are acceptable, but there are no reliable figures for Latin America, the Soviet Union and Eastern Europe. As for Mainland Southeast Asia and the Philippines, official figures are so different from unofficial estimates that it is really difficult to decide who is ethnic Chinese and who is not.[34] If we consider that many people of Chinese descent do not wish to be identified as Chinese, or even as ethnic Chinese, the figure of 16 million may be far too high. A more realistic figure may range from between 12 million to well under 10 million.[35] But the situation is still fluid. Bearing in mind that figures for Overseas Chinese have varied greatly during the past three decades, they remain nothing more than rough estimates about a spectrum of Chinese ethnicity. At one end of it, ethnic Chinese are being fully assimilated and wish to be dropped out of consideration. At the other end, however, new foreign Chinese are appearing every day, including those who move from being Huaqiao to foreign Chinese. It is difficult at this stage to speculate whether this means that the global figure for ethnic Chinese by the end of the century will remain more or less the same, or whether many more may have to be added to present estimates. What is relevant here is that such ethnic Chinese (whether 16 million or less than 10 million) are not in fact part of External China. But there are both foreign and domestic policies concerning External China which touch the lives of many ethnic Chinese, especially those who have Huaqiao relatives in China, Taiwan, Hong Kong and Macao and also those who are sufficiently well qualified in one way or another either for China to be interested in them or for them to be interested in China, on their own behalf or on behalf of their adopted countries.[36] To the extent that these policies are being extended and are successful, many more ethnic Chinese may become closely involved in External China affairs.

It can be said that an old policy area covering the Overseas Chinese, broadly defined and once known as Huaqiao, was abandoned in the 1950s by the PRC (but not by the government in Taiwan). There was a genuine attempt to narrow the policy area to one which merely required that the PRC should offer protection to the real Huaqiao, its citizens abroad, in the normal internationally accepted way. But the domestic aspects of the old Huaqiao problem were so badly handled during the Cultural Revolution period that a new policy area had to be devised. This was initially characterized by the revival of the administrative structure for overseas Chinese affairs and by great expectations about restoring all overseas Chinese connections. But, as the "Four Modernizations" policy developed, it became clear that there was a new package of closely-related problems that should be taken together. This was not a substitute for the old overseas Chinese policy, although the narrower definition of Huaqiao had caused the PRC to consider what should be put in its place. What was critical was the importance of the Tongbao in Hong Kong and Macao for China's modernization. And no less important was the willingness to think positively about the economic achievements of Taiwan, and therefore about the Tongbao of Taiwan. Taken together with new Guiqiao and wider definition of Qiaojuan within China, the three groups required more focused thinking. Grouping them in External China as a new policy area is thus fully justified. But what is less certain is whether the PRC intends to include foreign Chinese in the package. From the point of view of deliberate official policy, that would be unlikely. But the policy will attract many foreign Chinese in an increasing number of ways, especially if it proves to be a successful method of encapsulating a complex problem and is flexible enough to permit their participation, however peripherally.

In this new policy area as outlined above, people within China have been included, although it is their *external* connections that are important. Also referred to are the closely related problems which bring in ethnic Chinese who are foreign nationals. And, not least, it has been pointed out how difficult it is to separate domestic from foreign policies where this new policy area is concerned. It seems understandable, therefore, why people both inside and outside China are somewhat confused, even perplexed, by the many ambiguities in some of these policies.

There are many officials who are trying to sort out these ambiguities and not leave this policy area blurred and undefined. They may not see it as External China but, whatever they call it, they recognize that it needs attention and definition. As long as it is unclear and somewhat inclusive, it can be misunderstood to mean that it is the old overseas Chinese policy in another guise and therefore is threatening to China's neighbours. That this is not the intention, and that it is inspired by China's own domestic humanitarian and modernization needs rather than by any desire to interfere in the affairs of other countries, seems to be clear. But misplaced enthusiasms among those who confuse External China and Overseas Chinese could lead to misconceptions and ultimately to new fears and suspicions in countries where ethnic Chinese are numerous. Only by carefully defining it can the new policy area be delimited and its ramifications kept within bounds. That would not only help to make the new policy area better understood, but also itself make the complex mixture of domestic and foreign policies work more effectively.

NOTES

1 Earlier versions of this chapter were presented as a lecture at the University of British Columbia, January 1984, and as a paper at the Asian Studies Association of Australia, Adelaide, May 1984.

2 "External China" was first used as the title of my article in B. Hook (ed.), *The Cambridge Encyclopedia of China* (Cambridge: Cambridge University Press, 1982), pp. 104–10. For that article, which was written in 1980, I included the Huaqiao, the Chinese of Hong Kong and Macau, and all ethnic Chinese outside China and Taiwan, but did not include the Chinese of Taiwan. Since then, I have made four visits to China and gradually realized that a new policy area has emerged. The term "External China" is not in use in China, and the Chinese translation, *Waihua zhengce*, came from discussions with Chinese scholars at Peking University, the Chinese Academy of Social Sciences and the Peking Foreign Languages Institute. An alternative term, "External Chinese" was considered, partly to replace the older term "Overseas Chinese," but that would shift the emphasis away from the policy area and place the stress on individuals or communities actually *outside* China. That would be misleading, so "External China" has been retained.

3 "Overseas Chinese" does not translate Huaqiao as it used to, but is now sometimes translated back into Chinese literally as *haiwai huaren*. It is slowly being replaced by "ethnic Chinese" in the sense of "anyone identifiably Chinese who is outside China."

4 For PRC policy up to 1970, see Stephen Fitzgerald, *China and the Overseas Chinese: A Study of Peking's Changing Policy, 1949–1970* (Cambridge: Cambridge University Press, 1972), esp. ch. 8, "An Experiment in Decolonisation." Also on the term Huaqiao, see the preface and p. 155.

5 Liao was born in Tokyo, his father Liao Zhongkai (1878–1925) was born in San Francisco. Appropriately, Liao's mother (1949–59) and then Liao himself (from 1959) headed the Overseas Chinese Affairs Commission. Since the end of the Cultural Revolution, this has been known as the Overseas Chinese Affairs Office, and it works directly under the State Council; see report on Liao's death by David Bonavia, *Far Eastern Economic Review*, 23 June 1983, pp. 15–16.

6 Ch'en Lieh-fu, *Tung-nan-ya-chou ti Hua-ch'iao, Hua-jen yü Hua-i* (Taipei, 1979), pp. 17–26, 88–91.

7 It is important to emphasize how much China has supported ASEAN since 1975, and how far it seems prepared to go to reassure ASEAN and try to win that group of countries to China's side. Its ideological decision to retain only minimal comradely links with the older communist parties in the region may have a reassuring side which is little appreciated: China would rather abandon close links with ethnic Chinese and allow them to assimilate to local loyalties in order to maintain its own ideological and party loyalties.

8 Popular usage is another matter. Many old people who are no longer Chinese citizens are still proud to call themselves Huaqiao, while many more recent migrants, whether from China, Taiwan, or Hong Kong/Macau, refuse to respond to the term Huaqiao.

9 Following Taipei practice, Ch'en Lieh-fu, pp. 17–18, uses the figure of twenty-two million, but this includes Hong Kong/Macau, and he admits that this would be "Huach'iao" in the broad sense. The PRC uses the figure of at least twenty million *haiwai huaren* (including Huaqiao and foreign nationals of Chinese descent), of

which about 20 per cent are Chinese nationals; Hong Sisi, "Huaqiao lishi yanjiu gongzuo di jige wenti," in *Qiaoshi* (published in Quanzhou by Jinjiang Office of Huaqiao Affairs), vol. I, January 1983, p. 2.

10 If the 1975 figures of the Overseas Chinese Affairs Commission in Taipei quoted by Ch'en Lieh-fu are correct, there were 1.55 million ethnic Chinese in United Vietnam; this may account for most of the difference of two million between the Taipei and the Beijing figures. On the other hand, if hundreds of thousands had left Vietnam since 1975, the explanations for the discrepancy may have to be found also in the half-million or so (1975 estimates) stateless or PRC/Taiwan/Hong Kong passport-holders left in Thailand, the Philippines, Malaysia and Singapore.

11 Not included in "External China" in *The Cambridge Encyclopedia of China* (see note 2).

12 Wang Gungwu, "A Note on the Origins of *Hua-ch'iao*," in *Community and Nation: Essays on Southeast Asia and the Chinese* (Singapore, 1981), pp. 122–3.

13 It is impossible to be precise here. Even if there were an agreement on nationality and most Hong Kong people were legally classified as PRC citizens, these citizens would have *external* privileges well beyond those available to ordinary Chinese.

14 There is a growing literature in and outside China on what the PRC might learn from the successes of Taiwan, South Korea, Hong Kong and Singapore. Where Taiwan is concerned, a recent compendium is most helpful: James C. Hsiung and others (eds.), *The Taiwan Experience, 1950–1980* (2nd edition) (New York: American Association for Chinese Studies, 1983), especially the foreword (pp. 1–7), introduction (pp. 9–18) and the section on economic development (pp. 119–217).

15 For a background on this subject, see chapter 4 "Domestic Overseas Chinese Policy: 1949–1966" in Fitzgerald, *China and the Overseas Chinese*, pp. 52–73.

16 Discussions with returned Huaqiao in Fujian, Guangdong and Beijing in September 1980, July–August 1983 and March 1984.

17 From discussions with local and central officials of the Returned Overseas Chinese Association in 1983 and 1984. They played down the remaining privileges for Guiqiao and Qiaojuan, but acknowledged that there were new extensions of the terms to cover those who had returned from Taiwan (usually via Hong Kong, Japan or the United States) or had family connections in Taiwan.

18 The literature on this subject is large, most notably as reported in Hong Kong magazines — e.g., *Cheng Ming, Ming Pao Monthly, The Seventies Monthly*. Conversations in China confirm the accuracy of the descriptions about Cultural Revolution experiences for Guiqiao and some Qiaojuan and about the efforts since then to make amends. For an example of a recent discussion on this topic, see *Huaren Monthly (Life Overseas)* (Hong Kong), nos. 5 & 6 (June & July 1984).

19 This has been particularly dramatic in Fujian province. Unlike most of Guangdong with its relatively easy access to Hong Kong and Macau, Fujian had been largely cut off from the outside world until 1980; conversations with officials and scholars in Fuzhou and Xiamen in 1980 and 1983. In 1980, there was great excitement at the

decision to locate a Special Economic Zone in Xiamen; in 1983, I was in Xiamen when the International Airport was opened and the joy with which this opening was greeted was very moving.

20 Provincial and municipal daily newspapers in Guangdong and Fujian report some of the larger contributions, especially philanthropic acts reminiscent of the traditional support for local education. Several Overseas Chinese Affairs newspapers have been revived and these publish news of Overseas Chinese relationships regularly. Others published locally give more intimate details: a typical one which I had not seen before, called *Wen-ling*, published in Jinjiang, Fujian, had published forty issues in the 1960s and was revived in 1982. Philanthropy is further encouraged by news of contributions to two universities for Overseas Chinese, Jinan at Guangzhou and Huaqiao at Quanzhou. No less important are commemorations of philanthropic deeds, the most famous of which was that of Chen Jiageng (Tan Kah Kee) to Amoy (Xiamen) University and to the Jimei Schools: for example, the 70th Anniversary volume, *Chen Jiageng xiansheng chuangban Jimei xuexiao qishi zhounian jinian kan* (Xiamen, 1983); also, *Jimei Xuexiao qishi nian* (Fuzhou: Renmin, 1983) and *Huiyi Chen Jiageng* (Beijing: Wenshi Ziliao, 1984).

21 Discussions with central officials of the Returned Overseas Chinese Association in 1984.

22 Discussions with local and central officials of the Returned Overseas Chinese Association in 1983 and 1984.

23 This is an important subject that deserves fuller study. Detailed official records are not available, but there are enough examples in local and provincial newspapers in China and in Hong Kong newspapers and magazines to suggest how much each linkage between Guiqiao or Qiaojuan and their relatives can contribute to local welfare and economic growth.

24 The most significant example of this is the Nationality Law of 1980; text in *Beijing Review* 40, 6 October 1980 (see Articles 3, 5, 8 and 9). Article 9 makes it clear that any Chinese who acquires foreign nationality of his or her own free will automatically loses his or her Chinese nationality.

25 Wang Gungwu, *The Chinese Minority in Southeast Asia* (Singapore: Chopmen, 1978), pp. 3–8.

26 As evidenced in the Chinese response to Mr. S. Rajaratnam's visit to China in March 1975 and Mr. Lee Kuan Yew's visit in May 1976 (*Peking Review*, 21 March 1975, pp. 5–6; 14 May 1976, pp. 3, 7–8; *Far Eastern Economic Review* 14 May 1976, pp. 22–24; 4 June 1976, p. 14).

27 There are no reliable studies on this sensitive subject. My main sources are Hong Kong newspapers and magazines, notably *The Seventies* (now *The Nineties*), *Cheng Ming*, *Horizon Bi-monthly* (now *Life Overseas*) and *Ming Pao Monthly*. From the point of view of China's needs, what foreign Chinese can directly contribute is limited. Japanese, US and European multinationals must play the much larger role. In the ASEAN countries, however, what is important is the extensive family and business connections which give the region economic coherence and indirectly benefit China's trade with the region; Roy Hofheinz, Jr. and Kent E. Calder,

The Eastasia Edge (New York: Basic Books, 1982), p. 200.

28 This is true for both the trade in traditional kinds of Chinese consumer goods as for the key rubber industry, John Wong, *The Political Economy of China's Changing Relations with Southeast Asia* (London: Macmillan, 1984), pp. 100–13. As for investment in China itself, the difficulty in ensuring an adequate return has been a deterrent even when governments like Singapore, the Philippines and Thailand do not forbid it (interviews with members of the Singapore Chamber of Commerce, 1982 and 1984). Another consideration is the diversification of risk (Hofheinz and Calder, *The Eastasia Edge*, p. 212).

29 This is particularly true at the Fujian and Guangdong end. See my report on a visit in July-August 1983, "South China Perspectives on Overseas Chinese", in *Australian Journal of Chinese Studies*, no. 13 (1985), and Chapter 13 of this book.

30 "Southeast Asian *hua-ch'iao* in Chinese History-writing", *Journal of Southeast Asian Studies*, vol. XII, no. 1 (March 1981), pp. 1–14, and Chapter 2 of this book.

31 Speech by Hong Sisi, vice-chairman, Federation of Returned Overseas Chinese, to the conference on Huaqiao history held in Beijing in December 1981, published in Qiaoshi (see note 9).

32 The most recent example of such doubts is the Malaysian government's response to the clandestine visits to China by Malaysian Chinese (K. Das report in *Far Eastern Economic Review*, 15 March 1984, pp. 48–9). An earlier report by Rodney Tasker in the same weekly underlines the deep-rooted problem (5 May 1983, pp. 21–6).

33 See note 9.

34 *The Cambridge Encyclopedia of China*, p. 106. This needs to be updated; also, it does not include figures for Western Europe, Southern Africa, the Soviet Union and Eastern Europe where the numbers are not significant.

35 Such a "realistic" figure allows for not only the well-known Filipino, Thai and Vietnamese phenomenon of their citizens of Chinese descent denying that they are Chinese, but also numbers of young people of Chinese parentage in Singapore, Malaysia and Indonesia who try to establish their full identity as Singaporeans, Malaysians and Indonesians. For the Filipino example, which is no longer exceptional, see Wong, *The Political Economy*, which says that ethnic Chinese "had been estimated broadly from as few as 100,000 to as many as 800,000" (p. 145).

36 Since early 1983, the Sino-British discussions over the future of Hong Kong have diverted attention from how foreign Chinese are responding to China's needs. Certainly the well-known Hong Kong publications from which relatively reliable information about Huaqiao and ethnic Chinese activities may be gleaned, have, on the whole, given far more space to the Hong Kong issue than to the wider question of External China. In addition to the magazines mentioned in note 27, I am referring to *Far Eastern Economic Review* and *Asiaweek*; also newspapers like *Da Gong Bao, Asian Wall Street Journal*, and *South China Morning Post*. The Sino-British joint declaration signed in December 1984 may now dispel some of the anxiety that has clouded the new policy area, and may encourage fresh thinking about how to proceed next.

CHAPTER 13

South China Perspectives on Overseas Chinese[1]

In July and August 1983, I travelled through four provinces of south China, stopping at the cities of Xiamen, Quanzhou and Fuzhou in Fujian and Guangzhou in Guangdong. From discussions with officials concerned with Huaqiao and related affairs and with scholars at four universities in each of the four cities (Xiamen, Huaqiao, Fujian Normal and Jinan Universities respectively) I found an enormous interest, or rather revival of interest, in the subject of Huaqiao, or in Overseas Chinese in general,[2] and was struck by the amount of work being done and by the difficulties both officials and scholars have to labour under. Several of those I spoke to gave me copies of their own writings on the subject, including copies of the journals their institutes or offices, or various scholarly associations, had published.[3]

The new interest in the question of Overseas Chinese includes various attempts to distinguish Huaqiao from Huayi (descendants of Chinese) and Huazu (ethnic Chinese), just to mention a couple of the alternative terms for what used to be known as Huaqiao. Drawing upon official statements and published essays and commentaries, as well as discussions with fellow academics and local specialists, the reasons for the renewed interest in Overseas Chinese can be summarized in the following five points.

Firstly, their value for the "Four Modernizations". Overseas Chinese may be encouraged to provide expertise at the scientific and technological levels or to invest capital in modern industrial enterprises. This is well known and needs no elaboration. Such Chinese may contribute to a faster rate of economic growth.

Secondly, what may be described as United Front work. This is primarily concerned with winning the sympathy of Overseas Chinese for issues like the final reunification with Taiwan, for the Chinese efforts to resolve the future of Hong Kong and for the overall achievements of the PRC.

Thirdly, the desire to correct erroneous policies of the so-called "Cultural Revolution" period towards Guiqiao (returned Overseas Chinese) and their relatives both inside and outside China. This is a much more contentious matter and, I believe, not one that is fully understood outside the two or three provinces of south China from where most Overseas Chinese came. These policies are seen today as among the most unjustifiable of the 1966–76 decade and a catastrophe for China's modernization. Given the desire to promote the "Four Modernizations" and United Front work, it is now thought essential to make good the injustices to all the victims of the disastrous campaign against returned Overseas Chinese and their families.

Fourthly, the more subtle question of dealing with ethnicity. This refers to the fact that the vast majority of the Chinese overseas have taken up foreign nationality during the past two decades. Figures are imprecise here, and there are many sets of unreliable estimates about the exact number of Overseas Chinese in the world. Chinese officials seem to be using the figure of 20 million, of whom some 20 per cent (that is, four million) are still Huaqiao, citizens of China who are eligible for Chinese passports.[4] The point, however, is that the vast majority, those of foreign nationality, still consider themselves to be ethnically Chinese or are considered so by others — not so much politically, as culturally and emotionally. China wants to respond warmly to such expressions of ethnicity, and to show that it recognizes an obligation to encourage such sentiments even while it firmly recognizes the rights and duties as foreign nationals of such Chinese.

Finally, the concern to write Overseas Chinese history. This is the most controversial among the Chinese themselves. There are several schools of thought here. One wishes to project this history as an epic story going back a thousand or even two thousand years, but limited to those Chinese who went *overseas* and therefore mainly those from the provinces of Guangdong and Fujian who left for various parts of first Southeast Asia and later the Americas, Australasia and elsewhere. Others take Huaqiao more broadly to refer to *all* Chinese who went beyond China's borders and temporarily resided abroad. Therefore, Huaqiao history should include those who went *overland* to Korea, Vietnam, the Soviet Union, Mongolia, Burma and Laos. But when taken historically, serious problems arise as to where China's borders were at different times, and this opens up a Pandora's box which creates other difficulties in definition. The idea that China's present borders (including Taiwan, Hong Kong and Macao) be used retrospectively through all time is anachronistic where the question of Overseas Chinese in concerned and not everyone is comfortable with it at the moment.[5]

There are those who would prefer to forget about Huaqiao history altogether. They want to concentrate on current problems which they think are complicated enough for China's modernization, its investment programme, and not least, for China's foreign policies and for the diplomats who have to implement them in the face of implacable hostility and deep-seated suspicions about the Overseas Chinese problem, especially in parts of Southeast Asia. This is probably a view common only to harassed bureaucrats and to those from provinces, especially in north and west China, which have never produced many such Chinese in the first place. They cannot comprehend why the Huaqiao should pose a special problem, why their families should have privileges and why their history should be separately treated. It is difficult to estimate the extent of the scepticism about the Huaqiao, or whether it is merely indifference and not real hostility towards them within China. But it is necessary to be reminded that not all Chinese in China care for the Huaqiao or even know who and what they are.[6]

Nevertheless, there is an official policy, there is renewed interest in provinces which produced many Overseas Chinese, and the subject has been given a higher profile than most people expected. There has been the revival of two Huaqiao universities in 1978, one actually named Huaqiao University in Quanzhou, and Jinan University in Guangzhou. Not surprisingly, both these universities are deeply concerned with Overseas Chinese history, as are others like Xiamen, Zhongshan, Yunnan Universities and elsewhere.

The subject of Overseas Chinese is clearly still bedevilled by many factors. Some are obviously political. Others are economic, technological, educational, even moral and sentimental. One common problem, however, underlies all these factors and that is the confusion over the use of the term Huaqiao and the understandable reluctance on the part of many Chinese concerned to face up to the need to define the term accurately. Popular usage has blurred the term so much that there is a case for accepting, as modern linguists are wont to do, the current wide variations in its meaning. But that is precisely where the problem lies. The Chinese government and most foreign governments, as well as most Chinese who have acquired foreign nationality, especially those in Southeast Asia, have not defined the term Huaqiao clearly to refer only to those who retain Chinese nationality. Outside China, Huaqiao is increasingly being used in that restricted sense. In short, the term is now recognized as having political significance. This fact, that the term has political significance, still needs stressing.

The term Huaqiao came into use very late in the nineteenth century and quickly became politically significant by being associated with nationalism and revolution.[7] Given the political implications of the term for over fifty years, it is necessary to be very careful how the term is used and to what periods of history it might accurately be applied. The Chinese, however, think that the fact that the term Huaqiao did not occur until the late nineteenth century should not mean that there were no Overseas Chinese before that time. The point about the *political* usage and meaning of the term was ignored or perhaps not understood. But now that there is so much activity about Huaqiao problems and Huaqiao history, this fudging of the term may not be so minor and merely academic. The confusion and sentimentality about the term is now so great that, if they persist, they will prevent the Chinese from ever becoming clear about its meaning.[8] This in turn will produce misunderstanding and suspicion, if not bewilderment, among those of Chinese descent abroad and among the people of those countries where these Chinese have become nationals.

The point about political significance needs restating. The argument hinges on the use of the word *qiao*, an ancient word whose main meaning is "to sojourn, or reside temporarily away from home". The first clear use of the word *qiao* to apply to Chinese residing abroad, i.e., in a foreign country, occurred in an official document in 1858. This was in the Sino-French Treaty of Tianjin and referred to the reciprocity implied in establishing diplomatic missions in each country.[9] Up to this time, a whole range of other terms, some most uncomplimentary, were employed to describe Chinese who resided overseas. The main reason for this was that, for most of the Ming and Qing dynasties, Chinese were prohibited from going overseas, and if they did go, were threatened with severe punishment on their return. The idea of sojourning, or temporarily residing *overseas*, was conveyed through other terms. The word *qiao* was never used; the other terms seem to have been adequate to cover the language needs of the time. What then was the significance of the introduction of the word *qiao* and later that evolution of the term Huaqiao as a noun?

The significance was largely political. The official use of *qiao* in

1858 applied only to officials on service abroad. But when rich merchants in Southeast Asia began to purchase titles by contributing to the imperial coffers, it became necessary to use more polite terms for them which acknowledged their official positions. The appointment of diplomatic officials to Europe, America and Japan followed, including the appointment of the wealthy businessman Hoo Ah Kay, better known as Whampoa, as a consul in Singapore in 1877. He already had official titles by purchase which would have made it quite appropriate for him to have been described as *qiaoju* in Singapore if it had occurred to anyone to do so.[10] But it was not until 1885 that an official document recognized all Chinese temporarily residing abroad as *qiaoju*. This was in another Sino-French treaty which described such Chinese as *qiaoju* in French Indo-China.[11] As for Huaqiao, it might have been in 1882–3 that Huang Zunxian first used the combination Huaqiao to describe the Chinese overseas. He was Consul-General in San Francisco at the time and was writing about commoners and not officials. This was supposed to have been in a communication to his superior, the Chinese Minister to the United States, Zheng Zaoru, but the authenticity of the text now preserved is uncertain. In any case, it was never published in his lifetime, and did not seem to have influenced any other writer. Zhuang Guotu of Xiamen University has pointed out the use of the term in two memorials by Zheng Guanying in 1883 and 1884 and a brief reference in the Veritable Records of Emperor Guangxu for 1884. Unfortunately, the memorials were not published until 1909 and the brief note even later. Thus, they are unlikely to have influenced contemporary writing. There is also the possibility that the texts were not the originals but were revised or edited before publication.[12]

Thus the first use of the term Huaqiao as a noun was the climax of a whole range of political awakenings that involved Chinese officials and intellectuals, but especially the southern Chinese of all classes. In this case, it did not matter when precisely the term was first used or who was the first to use it. It would not have been surprising if the word Huaqiao had crept into use from time to time between the early 1880s and the mid-1890s. That would have been a preparatory period while the political realization that something had to be done for southern Chinese who went overseas was being formed. It was a period when these Chinese from south China were asking for attention — and not merely the rich merchants — and a period when the bullying of a poor illiterate Chinese abroad was no less humiliating for a Chinese official than the discriminatory treatment of a better-off and better educated one.[13]

For the officials, therefore, the lifting of the overseas travel ban in 1893 was significant.[14] It freed them to think of how to harness the capital, the skills and the energies of the southern Chinese abroad to enrich and strengthen China. The fact that the ban was a dead letter in practice should not blind us to the psychological significance of its lifting to all kinds of Chinese, not least to the women of Fujian and Guangdong who now could move more easily to join their husbands and families abroad or travel out to marry those who were not pre-pared to marry locally. Once money could move back to China easily and women could move out, the bonds between south China and the Overseas Chinese were immeasurably strengthened, far more than technical questions of consular representation and legal points of nationality could have done. The more these bonds were strength-ened, the more demanding were the actual tasks of protection; and the more involved the imperial government became in Overseas Chinese welfare, the more unsatisfactory that government must have appeared to those who had had their expectations raised. The offi-cials found that they had to respond more positively to the clamour in south China for protection against discrimination. They now had a better grasp of the way Western governments protected *all* their nationals and, since *qiao* was already the official term for *approved* residence abroad in at least three treaties with the Powers by 1895, would have found no difficulty in applying it to *all* Chinese overseas once the official ban was lifted in 1893. In short, it was only natural by this time that *qiao* should be widely used to include all Chinese, but the political significance of doing so and adding *hua* to it to make a new general noun should not be underestimated simply because its time had come.[15]

Another important point was the potency of the term Huaqiao once it came into use. Once there was political recognition of approved residence abroad, the growing desire for official protection became stronger. But when the protection received turned out to have been feeble, other political emotions were aroused. A group of dissidents called for the government's overthrow and couched it in anti-Manchu, anti-Qing terms (with strong racist overtones), which warmly appealed to the southern Chinese who provided the bulk of the Chinese abroad. In this context, a crude but powerfully worded "revolutionary song", which seemed to have been specially addressed to the Huaqiao in Java, was published as an appendix to Zou Rong's very influential *Revolutionary Army* (*Geming jun*) in 1903.[16] It was a song that would not have greatly appealed to the rich and successful Chinese towkays of Southeast Asia but its political message was clear. It elevated the political role of these southern Chinese, it mocked the rich and successful who were likely to support both the Western colonial regimes and the Qing government, and it was the first direct call to the Chinese overseas to throw themselves into China politics. It was also the direct precursor to Sun Yat-sen's famous dictum made years later that "the Huaqiao were the mother of the revolution".[17] Whether deserved or not, they did not look back from that moment and maintained a high political profile abroad for the next five decades. Today, as China now defines them, they are merely ordinary aliens, in themselves without political significance. The period when it was politically significant to call all Chinese Huaqiao ended in the middle of the 1950s. That period may well be called the five decades of the Huaqiao.

It should be stressed that the Huaqiao decades should not be extended backwards in time. To use the term Huaqiao for earlier periods would be ahistorical. It would be contrary to Ming and Qing policies, to their thinking about Chinese who were resident overseas, and even to their ideas of government.[18] To be casual, even cavalier, in applying Huaqiao to every Chinese throughout history who ever went abroad for several years or more would make a mockery of the efforts so far to understand some key changes in modern Chinese history and put them in correct historical perspective.

In discussions with present-day Chinese officials and scholars, the distinction is often made between the Chinese who went to Southeast Asia and those who went elsewhere, for example, North America and Australasia. As is well known, almost all of them originated from south China. A few points of comparison can be made about the separate regions from the perspective of the people I spoke to in south China.

Relations between south China and Southeast Asia go back a long way. If the northern parts of modern Vietnam are included, they go back over 2,000 years. There have been Chinese settlers in the ports of Southeast Asia for at least a thousand years and people from that region and even further west have settled in China for even longer.[19] They were never that many at first but they could have been the basis of a healthy symbiotic relationship between south China and the region. That early relationship, however, was broken by Western expansion, from the Portuguese capture of Malacca in 1511 until the last decade or so.[20] And throughout these past 450 years, the main contacts to the mid-nineteenth century have been through trade, with some "piracy" and smuggling and a little politics, notably some Chinese political refugees from upheavals in China.[21] And it was not until the mid-nineteenth century that the large-scale labour movements brought the North American and Australasian regions into the picture.

For these latter regions, however, the ingredients were totally different. The connection was still first with south China, but it began with unskilled labourers, who were followed later in the United States by students. A few of the workers may have developed a low-level trade but trade was never the dominant feature of this connection. Even labour became insignificant once restrictive labour legislation discriminated directly against the Chinese.[22] By 1900, however, there were superficial similarities between Southeast Asia and the other regions as southern Chinese political leaders like Sun Yat-sen and his supporters and the supporters of Kang Youwei's Protect the Emperor Society competed everywhere they went for influence. The spread of nationalist feelings was also common, especially as the Chinese in Southeast Asia were in sympathy with their compatriots elsewhere who were being blatantly discriminated against. The increasing involvement of the Chinese abroad in China politics was another factor which made comparison possible.[23]

But the differences were far more significant. After the centuries of relative economic success in the Southeast Asian region, there had developed in this century the image of the "Nanyang Chinese" (Southern Ocean Chinese). It was an image projected by the southern Chinese themselves about sailing south to Southeast Asia, and it was characterized by vast numbers, by numerous success stories of the Chinese middlemen, entrepreneurs and even capitalists, and by the spectacular advances in Huaqiao education. For the Western colonial powers and the native political leaders, this image was projected as one of economic dominance. And for the people of south China, the Nanyang was both a land of wealth and opportunity as well as a romantic place filled with wild or charming and easy-going people.[24]

Until 1941, the Nanyang territories were obviously more attractive than anywhere else to any southern Chinese who thought of migrating. There was growing control of immigration by the colonial authorities and by Thailand, but they were never as restrictive as in North America and Australasia. The control of Chinese education for Huaqiao children was often dramatically described as an example of *paihua* (anti-Chinese) measures, but the acts of *paihua* were never as

248 • China and the Chinese Overseas

violent or legally systematic as those in the United States a few
decades earlier. With the exception of one group, the Nanyang was a
far superior place to go to. That group was the students who were not
limited to southern Chinese and who mostly went to the United
States. No one went to the Nanyang to study, though many went
there to teach, but the United States was second only to Japan as the
place to go to acquire new knowledge and/or a marketable foreign
degree.[25] This was indeed a vital difference and one which would be
increasingly significant in the future.

Of course, the most important single difference was not generally
recognized in south China at the time. The United States was an
independent, technologically advanced country, while, with the
exception of small and friendly Thailand, no part of the Nanyang was
independent, least of all powerful and advanced. The Nanyang was
profitable for the Overseas Chinese because the colonial and some of
the native ruling élites there found them useful for their purposes.
American ruling élites did not need the Chinese in any comparable
way. Thus, after the end of World War II, two sets of political events
totally transformed the relative positions of the Nanyang and the
North American region. Neither was expected by the Chinese
overseas.

The first was the rise of nationalism in each of the colonial territories of Southeast Asia. The Overseas Chinese from south China were,
on the whole, slow to understand the meaning of this development.
Most of them were too busy making money or struggling hard to eke
out a living. The others had their political antennae directed towards
their villages and towns in Fujian and Guangdong rather than
Southeast Asian affairs. Within years, the "Nanyang" was exposed as
a myth.[26] There was really no such arena for the benefit of Overseas
Chinese as had been fondly believed. It was a temporary phenomenon exaggerated by propaganda and wishful thinking. What
became rapidly clear was that each new nation had inherited a
different way of treating the Chinese problem because the Chinese
problem had never been the same for each territory. Each new nation
now enacted restrictive legislation, often directly against those in
their population of Chinese descent. The laws differed in intensity in
their attempts to circumscribe some kinds of Chinese activity, but
they seemed more legally systematic than ever before.[27]

The end of the "Nanyang Chinese" saw the end of the expansive
Chinese communities of Southeast Asia. Instead, most such communities became defensive and some have now virtually disintegrated

as communities and, in some places, much smaller social or kinship units are surviving as best they can. The transformation was not sudden but in comparison with the Chinese of the late 1940s, it may be said that the transformation is now complete.

The second set of political events impinge on the "Nanyang Chinese" as well, but has had more profound influence on the nature of the Chinese communities in North America. The victory of the Chinese Communist Party in China and the transfer of the Guomindang government to Taiwan produced unexpected changes in America's traditional policies towards China and Asia in general. Out of it came another kind of transformation for the Chinese, still mainly southern Chinese, in North America. The political and cultural connections were extended. There were political refugees, but more important, there were students, mostly from Taiwan, many of whom remained behind in the United States or returned to settle. Also, immigration policies were modified and the Hong Kong and Guangdong connection was strengthened. Within three decades, the Chinese population had risen to more than six times its original size. Now, in sharp contrast to the old "Nanyang", it is North America (and to a lesser extent, Australasia) that is the attraction for the new Overseas Chinese.[28]

In short, recent developments have led to sharp contrasts between conditions in Southeast Asia and North America where the question of Overseas Chinese is concerned. There are at least three major aspects to this question. The first may be described as the international aspect, the second as the national aspect and the third as the Chinese aspect.

First, North American and Australasian governments are relatively friendly towards China and do not feel threatened by the presence of their citizens of Chinese descent. For most governments in Southeast Asia, however, Vietnamese and Soviet propaganda about Overseas Chinese being China's fifth column in the region still rings a bell in some ears and everything China says or does about Chinese abroad, whether Chinese citizens or not, is a "sensitive" issue. This has consequences for the use of the word Huaqiao. The Chinese in ASEAN countries simply do not use it because it is wrong for most of them and it offends their respective governments. On the other hand, for North America, where there are many Chinese who have arrived more recently from Taiwan, Hong Kong and elsewhere, and where governments do not seem so sensitive about the word, Huaqiao can be more commonly and casually used without offending anyone.[29]

The national aspect is more subtle and involves, among other things, the question of political loyalty and that of ethnicity. The first is rather subjective and, one hopes, rarely needs to be fully tested. It is now expected that, in most cases, those of Chinese descent will be accepted and treated without blatant discrimination. History shows that integration into the adopted community is the norm and the Chinese are not an exception to that. But a deeper underlying issue is that of ethnicity, that sense of personal and cultural identity, deeper than that of nationality, which one may preserve even after one adopts a new nationality. While this is an ancient problem, the modern and international ramifications are much greater, much more sophisticated, than ever before. Ethnicity is linked with individual human rights, democratic rights and minority rights. It raises questions of power, the use of humane power, and that of national enrichment through variety in the cultural origins of a nation's peoples, especially in a world that is getting smaller and communicating faster every day. If ethnicity becomes fully accepted as a right — and North America and Australasia may be leading the way here — then two things might happen where the Chinese are concerned. Their ethnicity would be adequately conveyed through neutral terms like Huaren, Huayi or even Huazu, none of which carry legal and political significance in themselves. Enlightened modern governments which have tackled the question of ethnicity, and know that enforced and total assimilation of minority peoples is inhumane and quite unnecessary, should have no difficulty with such usage where ethnic Chineseness is concerned. And the Chinese who have settled abroad and adopted the nationality of their countries of settlement would, and should, be content with that.[30] And, not least, the word Huaqiao can be preserved to describe accurately those of Chinese nationality who are temporarily residing abroad, which is closest to its original literal meaning.

Finally, the Chinese aspect, that is, the aspect pertaining to China itself. The PRC has now sought to resolve the question through its 1980 Nationality Law,[31] but there is, of course, an extensive network of economic, social and cultural linkages that bind the Chinese outside China to their families in China. Will these linkages weaken further through time? Given the renewed interest and activity of the past five years in and outside China, it is obviously still too early to say. There are older Chinese abroad who are not happy to be told that they are not Huaqiao now. Some feel that they are in some sense being "disinherited" and a few point to the fact that the Taiwan government is prepared to call them Huaqiao. This may put some pressure on the government in China and its agencies abroad. But this may not remain a significant issue for very long.[32]

More serious is the wide-ranging application of the word *qiao* within China itself. One scholar in China has listed the scores of ways *qiao* has been used for people, for organizations, associations and work-units, for places, for economic purposes and even in very specific and technical terms arising from the importance the Chinese governments of this century have placed on the Huaqiao connection. They have developed from the vast apparatus that had been created to deal with Huaqiao affairs. There has been a virtual industry growing out of all the responsibilities the Chinese government had accepted at several levels for the Huaqiao and their families and other ties in China.[33]

The Chinese themselves have asked, how long will this last? Given the developments outside China where there have progressively been fewer people who could legitimately be called Huaqiao, and given that the earlier Guiqiao are getting older and their families are now mostly assimilated into Chinese life in almost every way, the answer seems obvious. But there is a large machinery in place and there are numerous people who are conscientiously working on its behalf. Given the nature of bureaucracy, and this is true of all countries, the wide range of its activities will probably continue for a long time. But if it is primarily concerned with activities *inside* China, and not too much spills over into work which has diplomatic implications, this can do no harm and even do some good. The work has many welfare and humanitarian features and it can help with some areas of construction and modernization in China. But it does need to be carefully supervised so that it does not confuse foreign governments or the Chinese of foreign nationality abroad.[34]

There is one hopeful development in China which is specially relevant here. It is related to the history of Chinese outside China which many scholars in China are very keen to write. As mentioned earlier, China's relations with Southeast Asia date back a long time and Chinese traders, sailors and refugees visited the region at least 800 years earlier than the American and Australian coasts and long before such Chinese could properly be called Huaqiao. There is an understandable urge to call all that a part of Huaqiao history and ignore the modern political significance of the term. If the historians do that, then Southeast Asia would be the centre of Huaqiao history.

But ironically, for China's modern history, the relatively few

Chinese who went to North America, Japan and Europe for modern science and technology, for educational advancement and for diplomatic duty on behalf of China, had a greater impact on China as a whole. Chinese scholars who were sent abroad to study and who subsequently worked abroad for three years or more are officially included in the definition of Huaqiao. There are many examples of those whose contributions to China's scientific growth are obvious. If they are considered returned Huaqiao, then intellectual and scientific quality takes on a significance that financial quantity from the Nanyang cannot match. For most of Southeast Asia, its historical role was mainly a question of mere wealth, that is, money for the development of provinces like Fujian and Guangdong, which was not a particularly impressive contribution in the eyes of high-minded mandarins in the central government.[35]

What amounts to the great irony that really deflates the importance of the history of the Huaqiao in Southeast Asia had emerged during the past five years. For example, because the Huaqiao is not a threatening concept to the ethnically conscious North Americans, the study of the history of the Chinese in North America is encouraged. Many books critical of past government policies have appeared and joint co-operative research involving American scholars and scholars in China has been possible. But since the Chinese in North America have mostly come from the Cantonese-speaking parts of Guangdong and since almost all other Chinese abroad, especially those from Chaozhou, Hainan and southern Fujian, went south to Southeast Asia, there is a growing gap in the quality of research possible. Considering the sensitivity of the governments of Southeast Asia towards their citizens of Chinese origin, it is almost impossible for scholars from China to do any meaningful research on the Chinese in Southeast Asia today. Thus, scholars in the Guangzhou counties have opportunities which those in other areas can only envy.

However, something constructive has developed in spite of this discrepancy in circumstances. There is an emerging awareness in China that the study of the Chinese in Southeast Asia cannot be separated from the study of Southeast Asian history itself, that their history may best be understood as an integral part of Southeast Asian history. This not only indicates that Chinese scholars have begun to respect the history of the Southeast Asian peoples and the region's efforts to become independent and modern, but it also lifts the level of their own historical scholarship to meet the more sophisticated demands of modern scholarship today. The fact is, a large part of the documentation of the Chinese in the region is in languages other than Chinese, not only the colonial languages of the time but also in native Southeast Asian languages. The history of these Chinese cannot be objectively and scientifically studied from the use of Chinese sources alone or supplemented from time to time by a few fragments of foreign language materials translated, often poorly, into Chinese. For the first time in history, some scholars in China have begun to admit that the historians of the Chinese overseas need to immerse themselves in the history of the countries to which such Chinese had gone.

It seems clear that some changes in perspective concerning ethnic Chinese abroad are occurring. It may be easy to write the Huaqiao history of those who went to North America or Australia because there are no great sensitivities about them. But, precisely because the historians do not need to be sensitive to other people's feelings, their history may well remain of the conventional, ethnocentric type. On the other hand, the need for sensitivity in Southeast Asia, as events in recent years have amply demonstrated, demands higher standards of understanding and greater efforts to be scientific and accurate about the Chinese who went south. It may still take a long time to produce results, but at least there is now a chance that the Chinese majority who went south from the middle of the nineteenth century will be the subject of history writing of a higher standard of historical comprehension than Chinese historians have ever produced in the past.

NOTES

1 Earlier versions of this paper were presented as lectures at the University of Hong Kong, and at the University of Toronto (Canadian Association for South-east Asian Studies) in 1983.

2 "Overseas Chinese" was the English term which translated the popular Chinese word Huaqiao. Both were commonly and loosely used to mean any Chinese residing overseas. But in recent years, various governments (including the People's Republic of China) have narrowed down the meaning of Huaqiao to refer to Chinese nationals who are living in a foreign country. For those of Chinese descent who are of foreign nationality, there are now other terms: more generally, *waiji huaren*, or, when identifying the country of nationality, *Mian-Hua* (Burmese Chinese), *Ma-Hua* (Malaysian Chinese) and so on. As for the English term "Overseas Chinese" (or others like "the Chinese overseas" or "the Chinese abroad"), this does not now necessarily translate Huaqiao but has been translated back into Chinese literally as *haiwai huaren*. This is a way of avoiding the political and legal connotations in the term Huaqiao, and the English term is used here in the ethnic

and neutral sense of "anyone identifiably Chinese who is outside China".

3 Most notably *Huaqiao shi lunwenji* (3 vols.) and *Huaqiao jiaoyu* published by Jinan University, Guangzhou, 1981–3; *Qiaoshi*, no. 1, 1982, published in Quanzhou in 1983; various university social science journals; and the writings of Professors Chen Bisheng and Lin Jinzhi.

4 Hong Sisi in his speech to the conference on Huaqiao history held in Beijing in December 1981 entitled *"Huaqiao lishi yanjiu gongzuo de jige wenti"* (Some problems of research into Huaqiao history), in *Qiaoshi*, no. 1, 1982 p.2 (but also published elsewhere).

5 Land borders are specially difficult. If all the minorities in China had always been part of the Chinese people, there could not have been Huaqiao living in the homelands of the Tibetans, the Mongols, the Turkic and Tungusic peoples or in Yunnan.

6 Anecdotes abound. One current joke describes young Chinese asking which country Huaqiao is, and another tells the story of a young Beijing Chinese who, when asked the way to the office of the Overseas Chinese Affairs, said, "Oh! You mean the Huaqiao Dashiguan [Huaqiao Embassy]".

7 Wang Gungwu, "A note on the origins of Hua-ch'iao", first published in *Masalah-masalah International Masakini*, no. 7, 1977, pp. 7–18 (Jakarta), and also in Wang Gungwu, *Community and Nation* (ASAA, S-E Asia Publication Series, Singapore and Sydney, 1981), pp. 118–127. Also additional notes on the subject in *"Hua-jen, hua-ch'iao yü Tung-nan Ya shih"* (Huaren, Huaqiao and S.E. Asian history), a lecture given at the Singapore Chamber of Commerce on 3 March 1976 which was published in *Nanyang Siang-pao* and then reprinted in Tsui Kuei-ch'iang and Ku Hung-t'ing (eds.), *Tung-nan Ya Hua-jen wen-t'i chih yen-chiu* (Studies on the Chinese in S.E. Asia) (Far East Book Co., Singapore, 1978), pp. 27–32. Also, Wang Gungwu, "Southeast Asian *hua ch'iao* in Chinese history-writing", *Journal of Southeast Asian Studies* (Special Issue edited by C.F. Yong), XII:1 (March 1983), pp. 1–14, and Chapter 2 of this book.

8 On new difficulties concerning Huaqiao, Guiqiao and other Chinese related to them, see Wang Gungwu, "External China as a New Policy Area", *Pacific Affairs*, Spring 1985, and Chapter 12 of this book.

9 Huang Yuebo *et al.* (eds.), *Zhongwai tiaoyue huibian* (Documents on Chinese-foreign Treaties) (Shangwu Yinshuguan, Shanghai, 1935), p. 76.

10 For the period background, see Yen Ching-hwang, "Ch'ing's Sale of Honours and the Chinese Leadership in Singapore and Malaya, 1877–1912" *Journal of Southeast Asian Studies*, vol. I, no.2 (Sept. 1970), pp. 20–32. Zhuang Guotu in his yet unpublished paper "'Huaqiao' yici mingcheng kao" (A study of the term Huaqiao) says that it was probably in 1878 that *qiaoyu* was first used to describe Chinese temporarily resident abroad. This was in a memorial by Chen Lanbin, Minister to the United States, Spain and Peru. He was recommending consular protection for Chinese who were relatively recent arrivals in the United States. Throughout the 1880s, the references to *qiaoju* seem to have been in the context of official protection.

11 *Zhongwai tiaoyue huibian*, p. 89. Leaving aside where Qing China really saw
An-nan (that is, modern Vietnam) as non-Chinese and therefore *foreign* soil, this
was the first legal use of *qiao* for Chinese residing on unequivocally foreign soil;
ibid., p. 151.

12 Huang Zunkai is the only source for his brother's correspondence from San
Francisco, in *Xianxiong Gongdu xiansheng shishi shulüe* (A brief account of the life of
my brother Gongdu) and quoted in Wu Tianren, *Huang Gongdu xiansheng zhuangao*
(A draft biography of Mr Huang Gongdu) (Chinese University of Hong Kong,
1972) p. 106. I am not sure that the text has not been touched up. I am grateful to
Mr Zhuang for the references to Zheng Guanying and the Veritable Records;
"'Huaqiao' yici mingcheng kao", pp. 7–8. Zheng's two memorials may be found in
Shengshi weiyan houbian (Warnings to a Prosperous Age: second collection) (first
published in 1909: photographically reprinted, Datong Shuju, Taibei, 1969), 10.1158
and 5.633. The earliest reference in the Veritable Records is for *yiwei*, 10th year of
Guangxu (1884), ch. 188, p. 8a. Mr Zhuang himself realizes that these texts were
published more than twenty years later, but thought they were probably reliable.
But the fact that Zheng Guanying invariably used Huaren or Huamin in his
writings published in several editions before 1909 makes this a little doubtful; see
the excellent collection, *Zheng Guanying ji* (Renmin Chubanshe, Shanghai, 1982),
vol. I.

13 The finest statement of this realization was Huang Zunxian's famous poem *Zhuke
pian* (On expelling guests) which he wrote about 1882; *Renjinglu shicao jianzhu*
(Annotated edition of Poems of Renjing Cottage) (revised edition, Gudian Wenxue
Chubanshe, Shanghai, 1957), pp. 126–130.

14 For the most recent study of this question, see Yen Ching-hwang, *Coolies and
Mandarins: China's Protection of Overseas Chinese during the Late Ch'ing Period
(1851–1911)*, (Singapore University Press, Singapore, 1985), chapter VII.

15 The opportunity I had to use the First National Archives in Beijing in March 1984
was too brief to enable me to determine when Huaqiao as a noun first appears in
official documents. Until I am able to do so, I stand by my views in "Origins of
Hua-ch'iao", p. 13 or p. 123–4.

16 I have translated parts of the poem in "Origins of Hua-ch'iao", pp. 17–18 or 126–7.

17 Zhang Yongfu (Teo Eng Hock), *Nanyang yu chuangli minguo* (Nanyang and the
foundation of the Republic) (Shanghai, 1933).

18 E.g., when Chinese were massacred in Manila in the 17th century, the Ming court
did nothing and when more Chinese were killed in Batavia in the 18th century, the
Qing court did not respond. There was no obligation to do anything for people
who were not on Chinese soil and were breaking the law in going abroad.

19 By "further west", I refer to the many Indians, Persians and Arabs, who followed
indigenous Southeast Asians to China and settled there during the first millenium.
By Chinese settlers, I include those who migrated to Vietnam *after* its independence in the 10th century.

20 Decolonization was mainly a phenomenon of the 1950s, but it may be argued that the last anti-colonial war did not end until the fall of Saigon and Pnom Penh in 1975.

21 Political (including tributary) relations stopped being really significant by the middle of the 15th century, more than half a century before the arrival of the Portuguese. Political refugees, however, were important in the 17th century, the 19th and parts of the 20th century.

22 The story is particularly well told in a recent study by Jack Chen, *The Chinese of America* (Harper & Row, San Francisco, 1981), Part 2.

23 This is a subject that has yet to be studied with a comparative approach. Several notable studies suggest that an approach which compares the political activities of the Chinese in different countries might be well worth doing. For example, Lea E. Williams, *Overseas Chinese Nationalism: the genesis of the Pan-Chinese Movement in Indonesia, 1900–1916* (The Free Press, Glencoe, 1960); Antonio S. Tan, *The Chinese in the Philippines, 1898–1935: a Study of their National Awakening* (n.p., Quezon City, 1972); C.F. Yong, *The New Gold Mountain: the Chinese in Australia, 1901–1921* (Raphael Arts P/L, Richmond, S. Aust., 1977); Yen Ching Hwang, *The Overseas Chinese and the 1911 Revolution, with special reference to Singapore and Malaya* (Oxford University Press, Kuala Lumpur, 1976); L. Eve Armentrout-Ma, "Chinese Politics in the Western Hemisphere, 1893–1911: Rivalry between Reformers and Revolutionaries in the Americas" (unpublished Ph.D thesis, Univ. of California, Davis, 1977); Edgar Wickberg (ed.), *From China to Canada: a History of the Chinese Communities in Canada* (Toronto, 1982), Parts 1 and 2.

24 Nanyang as applied to Southeast Asia is modern. It was wider in area in the late 19th century. Only after the first decade of this century did it stabilize in meaning, when Nanyang Huaqiao began to mean exclusively the millions of Overseas Chinese in Southeast Asia and was made to sound as if these Chinese formed one recognizable and uniform community of people likely to prosper in a land of plenty; Wang Gungwu, *A Short History of the Nanyang Chinese* (Eastern Universities Press, Singapore, 1959), pp. 33-4.

25 The story, largely of the role of US colleges and universities, has yet to be fully told. Some notable studies of Yale-in-China, Harvard-Yenching and the American interests in Qinghua, St. John's and Lingnam Universities have begun to appear. One study has attempted to be comprehensive: Y.C. Wang, *Chinese Intellectuals and the West, 1872–1949* (Univ. of North Carolina Press, Chapel Hill, 1966). But there is nothing in any Western language to match the studies of Chinese students in Japan produced by Saneto Keishu, especially his *Chugokujin teki Nihon Ryugaku shi* (Tokyo, 1969) (revised edition 1970).

26 "Nanyang" survived until recently in Nanyang University and is still used in the name of the research institute for Southeast Asian studies at Xiamen University. I questioned its use in 1958 (*Nanyang Chinese*, p. 42) and my book may have been the last work in a Western language to use the phrase "Nanyang Chinese" in its title.

27 Not all these laws were new. The Spanish and the Dutch had introduced restrictive laws almost from the beginning, in the late 16th and early 17th centuries. The

difference is that colonial laws hardly disguised the fact that they favoured the colonial élites, against Chinese aliens, while the new sets of laws are nationalistic in spirit and often seem to favour indigenous citizens against citizens of migrant origins, however long these migrants had lived in the country.

28 This is an area that is attracting serious study, e.g., the absorbing essays in Wu Yuan-li (ed.), *The Economic Condition of Chinese Americans* (Pacific Asian American Mental Health Research Center, Chicago, 1980, Monograph no. 3).

29 During my six months' visit to North America in 1983–84, I found the term Huaqiao commonly in use among the Cantonese-speaking Chinese, whether American citizens or relative newcomers from Hong Kong or China. On the other hand, those Chinese who had come from Mainland China since the 1940s or from Taiwan do not seem to like the term and use Huaqiao largely to refer to the descendants of early migrants and their modern Cantonese-speaking counterparts.

30 *Hua* ethnicity has become an increasingly subtle phenomenon as new generations are born and educated locally. It may not be long before terms like *huaren*, *huazu* and even *huayi* become quite inappropriate to describe them and their children.

31 Text in *Beijing Review*, no. 40, 6 October 1980.

32 This does not mean that there will be no more Huaqiao. On the contrary, as long as Chinese continue to emigrate from China, Taiwan and Hong Kong (or re-emigrate from one non-Chinese country to another), there will always be people who are legally Huaqiao or behave like Huaqiao. But whether Huaqiao will remain a significant issue for China and other governments is another question.

33 A list of standard compounds in China today using the character for *qiao* may be found in Chen Cunguang, "'Qiao' zi tanyuan ji youguan 'Huaqiao' gainian de yantao" (The origin of "qiao" and a discussion of the concept of "Huaqiao"), *Qiaoshi*, no. 1, 1982, pp. 25–9.

34 My talks with representatives of local *Guiqiao* bureaucracies in Fujian and Guangdong suggest that there is growing understanding of the problem, but there are emotional factors involved and it is easy to be carried away by bright ideas about how to modernize or build a profitable business with help from Chinese outside the country.

35 The late Mr Liao Chengzhi strongly favoured including everyone who had ever worked abroad for three years or more (including overseas students who, after graduation, stayed on to work for three or more years), as Guiqiao. The results of this extended meaning of Huaqiao have been patchy, but the presence of top scientists and engineers among Guiqiao will certainly help to make Guiqiao respectable if not influential as well. Recently, Guiqiao numbers seem to have risen, largely because of the returned *hoa* from Vietnam. That is a grim reminder that these numbers have often depended on sudden policy changes in Southeast Asian countries.

CHAPTER 14

Little Dragons on the Confucian Periphery

THE NEW CLICHÉ IS that South Korea, Taiwan, Hong Kong and Singapore should be grouped together because they have features in common. The obvious thing they have had in common for the past decade is that they have been economically successful. More specifically, they belong to that part of East Asia which has responded to measures dedicated to economic growth more rapidly than other regions of the developing world. They have led the way in their rates of development. This was apparent soon after the world discovered Japan's economic miracle of the 1970s. If Japan is *the* dragon of industrialized prosperity, then these four are the little dragons.

If Japan is the model, what have they got in common with Japan? If Japan reached the top by mastering what the West had to teach, what did the little dragons learn? Was what they learnt directly from the West as important, or more important, than what they learnt indirectly via Japan? Or was it something else, something each of them had in common with Japan, which enabled them to learn so fast from Japan — and helped them digest and adapt Western economic practices and institutions so successfully?

This is too complex a set of questions to deal with here. I shall limit myself to whether traditional Confucian values could be a determinant factor in helping these five countries use the capitalist model to facilitate modern economic development. The special focus on the heritage of Confucian values is because it has been seen to be the single most important factor that is common to Japanese, Koreans and Chinese, indeed, to all of East Asia and those parts of Southeast Asia where East Asians have been most active (especially the Overseas Chinese). This is an intriguing question that has been useful and challenging to recent scholarship but it is clear now that excessive claims have been made for Confucianism.

The possibility that this heritage of Confucian values might be the factor that made the difference for East Asia as compared with other regions will not go away. But there is a paradox in the theme for countries within the region which will not disappear either. This is the paradox that Confucian values were strongest in China and weakest in Japan, yet it was in Japan that industrialization took root and in Japan that capitalist development was achieved most rapidly. And where the little dragons are concerned, they are all on the periphery of China, with Singapore the furthest from the Confucian core. On the other hand, China itself (the PRC on the mainland) has chosen for most of the past forty years to reject the capitalist road to rapid economic growth. Significantly, North Korea and northern Vietnam close to the Chinese land borders have similarly preferred the socalist to the capitalist path. The paradox here also suggests that, while Confucian values might have assisted capitalist industrialization, having too much Confucianism or being too close to the Confucian core might be an obstacle to such a development.

During the past thousand years of history before the end of the Qing dynasty in 1912, official Confucianism occupied the core position in Chinese culture. This was the orthodoxy determined by culturally homogeneous élites with access to central power. Below these élites were peasants, artisans and merchants who formed a cultural periphery that supplied, fed and generally supported them. Outside the Chinese empire were neighbours who had more or less Confucianized élites: strongly Confucian in Korea, less so in Vietnam and barely Confucian in Japan. They were an external periphery to a great power with a strong ideological centre. And distinct from the cultural periphery within China and the external non-Han periphery, there was to develop in modern times also a detached periphery of areas with Chinese majorities which were outside China and outside central control. All three kinds are peripheries through their relationship to the idea of a Confucian core.

The Cultural Periphery

Let me begin with what I mean by cultural periphery. For this, it is important to distinguish varieties and levels of Confucian values. At least three are obvious and important. First, the values which Confucius, Mencius and their immediate disciples saw as at the core of Confucian values. This can be distilled from their writings and even by the countless attempts to explain and enrich them during the centuries of the empire. No matter how much Confucianism was adapted to suit a large empire, we must never forget that genuine Confucians in search of truth and wisdom existed down to the present times, but this endless quest is not central to the argument here.

Secondly, the values drawn from Confucian thought have legitimized the emperors and their political institutions for numerous dynastic houses. They were first fitted into a given imperial structure during the middle of the Western Han dynasty about 2,000 years ago. They were accepted and used by the bureaucracy; they in turn transformed that bureaucracy and gave it an enduring rhetoric as well as a set of standards to guide bureaucratic behaviour and even to check the excesses of imperial despotism from time to time. These Confucian values were also alternately rejected, modified and re-employed whenever necessary. Over time, they were so integrated into the mandarin system that it can be argued that imperial mandarin power and classical Confucian political values had become a seamless web. Certainly, by the Song dynasty (960–1276), it was almost impossible to tell which part of the imperial system was Confucian and which was not. Confucianism had made itself comfortable and strong within a power structure which could no longer deny its Confucian origins and foundations. An extraordinarily successful synthesis had occurred — and despite many compromises and distortions which damaged this public and State-sponsored Confucianism, it could not be said that true Confucian values were lost. They were still being upheld by those who sought to preserve the finer features of Confucian-Mencian ethics for themselves, their families and sometimes, their local communities as well.

The third variety of Confucian values are those practical and axiomatic parts of Confucianism which virtually all Chinese accepted over time as essential to their well-being. They are values about family and community relationships which were probably deeply rooted in Chinese society even prior to the times of Confucius and Mencius and whose essential elements were articulated by the two great teachers and their disciples. The key point is that they had always been broadly communal, tolerant of other values and ready to be inclusive of other belief-systems. Such values were not always recognized as Confucian; for example, respect for, and even a kind of worship of, ancestors as a central pillar of the family system, could sit with religious practices associated with Taoism and Buddhism. For most people before the Song dynasty, it was not even important to give these values the name of Confucianism. Only after Song Neo-

Confucians had reinterpreted and enriched Confucian values for their times did this variety of Confucianism find its voice among ordinary people. We still do not know enough about this process of localization and popularization of select bits of élite values. But because it was peripheral to State or official Confucianism and had developed a life of its own among those classes of Chinese for whom the mandarinate was remote, it is particularly important to our understanding of the role of Confucian values during the past few centuries.

Clearly, this third variety was peripheral to the first and second. It was peripheral to the first because it did not stress the universalist moral values of Confucian doctrine as espoused by those who had studied the classics closely and explicitly adhered to the central values in them. Among the non-literati classes, nothing was authoritative in philosophical terms. Confucian ethics had to be adapted to practical needs, to other religious institutions and to the requirements of the deities of different parts of China. It was accepted because it provided a backbone to what was often amorphous, poorly defined, even contradictory in local society. And it was upheld and reinforced by the mandarins and scholars sent to ensure its respectability. Its authority was the emperor, no less, but it was also bolstered by local teachers who imparted the rudiments of literacy through the basic classical texts. And these texts were interpreted inevitably in orthodox Confucian terms from at least the Ming dynasty (1368–1644).

But because relatively few Chinese got very far with the major classical texts, this variety of Confucian ethical values was also peripheral to State or mandarin Confucianism. Those who were introduced to these values recognized that the court insisted on being Confucian, and that they had to conform if they wanted to get on; but also that they were free to use other values to satisfy their material and spiritual needs as long as they did not openly oppose State orthodoxy. At the local levels, they would need to display conformity to satisfy the literati and the officials of the magistrate's court that they were not potential dissidents or rebels. The extent they needed to know their Confucian values depended on how much they had to deal with such literati and junior functionaries. Obviously, the peasantry and the artisans had the least to do with mandarins. Whether they had Confucian values or not was normally of little concern, especially when times were good. When times were bad, however, local mandarins expected that some adherence to key Confucian values like loyalty and filial piety would render peasants and artisans less likely to join secret societies and support outright rebellion.

The merchants were different, especially those with the capacity for long-distance trading between the larger cities, across provincial boundaries and to far corners of the empire and also those who traded abroad. Since the Song dynasty, they were no longer a restricted class condemned to a low status forever, although Confucian rhetoric still placed them officially below the artisan and the peasant. They had seen the relatively high status that had been accorded the wealthy *foreign* merchants at Changan, Loyang, Yangzhou and Guangzhou, and they had gradually replaced these foreign merchants during the Song. New classes of merchants had emerged, some with mandarin, landed gentry and military connections, others with capital, entrepreneurship and even family ties with the powerful, who could ensure that their trading activities received a measure of official protection. In turn, these merchants sought respectability through literacy and familarity with the Confucian classics — at least for their offspring and their descendants. With luck, the most successful could find themselves treated with respect by the literati because of the examination success of some members of the family or their extended clan. But for most of them, working to consolidate their business enterprises precluded them from being Confucian scholars or joining the mandarinate. And in so far as they needed to work closely with the producers of merchandise, whether artisans or peasantry, they had to retain the common touch. Thus, the merchants, however successful, remained an intermediate group on the periphery as long as they still needed to trade. They held some Confucian views, but were not burdened with too much Confucianism.

Being peripheral to Confucian scholars and mandarins was advantageous to the trading classes because it offered on the one hand some degree of freedom from strict behavioural codes and, at the same time, adequate points of contact with officialdom for traders to demonstrate their usefulness to the empire. In the context of the common saying that "Heaven is high and the emperor far away", the distance from the Confucian centre of the imperial court was much appreciated. Certainly, the idea of being distant from any mandarin-controlled administration allowed entrepreneurial activities which strict Confucians would discourage or disallow. From various studies of the Chinese merchant class, it is clear that merchants did better if they had access to mandarin protection but were operationally far enough away to be free and autonomous. Nevertheless, it is also clear that they were vulnerable at all times to official control; the application of Confucian values in an arbitrary political system encouraged nepotism, corruption, uncertainty and unprofitable mandarin interference. By the Ming and Qing dynasties, with tighter administrative controls and greater efforts at ideological indoctrination, central values were extended more effectively to the periphery. It became more difficult to escape the centripetal force of the core values of imperial Confucianism.

But many merchants traded abroad and were sometimes beyond the control of the imperial government. Thus, they worked in an intermediate position between being on the cultural periphery within China and being part of the detached periphery outside. Of special interest are those who specialized in foreign trade, especially from the sixteenth century onwards, when the combination of Ming and Qing policies and European expansion into Southeast Asia led to the rise of a new breed of Chinese merchant. The exploits of the overseas Chinese traders in Southeast Asia during the sixteenth to eighteenth centuries deserve closer study. This is not the place to examine them in detail. It is enough to point to some facts about the small Chinese communities that were learning to live under non-Confucian rulers and officials at various foreign ports.

Firstly, most of these merchants came from the three coastal provinces of southeast China, Guangdong, Fujian and Zhejiang, largely people from the cultural periphery. Although there is little direct evidence from these early centuries, we can expect these traders to have carried with them important elements of Confucian culture. They might have openly practised popular forms of Buddhism and Taoism, but those who came from merchant families were likely to have been literate and their literacy would have come from school texts as a kind of catechism based on the Confucian classics.

Secondly, these Chinese were rarely numerous enough to form stable communities; and where they were small, they either depended on their links with the larger communities like those in Manila, Batavia and Bangkok, or they were gradually assimilated into their respective local societies. But there is evidence that, in the larger communities, they valued their Chineseness and transmitted traditional values, including Confucian ones pertaining to the family, and especially to the web of kinship and locality connections on which their enterprises often depended.

Thirdly, they were largely traders and artisans who had to survive under non-Chinese rulers and non-Confucian cultural values. Most notably, they were merchants without mandarins, without mandarin protection and without mandarin extortion and interference. They had to adapt to other kinds of officials, and by and large, work with foreign élites and trading systems which did not despise commerce and the merchant class. At the same time, they came to understand Portuguese and Spanish officials who supported trade, Dutch and English traders who acted as officials, *and* local rulers and aristocrats who actively engaged in trade. It was a different kind of trading world from that in China and one that was highly competitive in quite different ways. Business life was probably no more predictable than under Chinese mandarins, but there was an openness in the trading between different foreign ports and a tolerance of merchants in a pluralist environment that they could not have found in China.

The cultural traditions of the Chinese merchants themselves would have included the experiences of the privileged foreign (Central Asian, Persian or Indian) merchants who had traded in China during the Han, Tang and Song dynasties and, more recently, of the Muslim traders under the Mongol-Yuan dynasty. Many of the foreign merchants had traded in Southeast Asia and the Chinese merchants must have been familiar with the conditions under which non-Chinese merchants made their fortunes. If so, they would have noted that, under the Ming Chinese rulers, foreign merchants were treated as tribute-bearing envoys and the foreign trading communities so well-known in China during previous dynasties had virtually vanished during the fifteenth century. Even Chinese were discouraged from doing any kind of overseas trade. They would have been aware of the irony that they could trade more freely and successfully with other foreign merchants *outside* China than on the China coast. Would they have wondered if the mandarins of a Confucian state and the imperial Confucian philosophy were more inimical to their trading opportunities than some "barbarian" trading systems?

No matter what comparative advantages there were outside China, the fact was that Chinese merchants abroad were relatively few in number, the overseas communities never reached a critical mass to dominate any port, and they never enjoyed from any Chinese government the political and military support which European, and some other Asian, merchants received. Indeed, until the nineteenth century, these Overseas Chinese were not only living on the periphery of the Confucian world; they were dependent on foreign goodwill, and even more so, on their own self-generated skills to make themselves indispensable to foreign rulers. But, it is possible nevertheless to argue that among the factors that made them succeed and become invaluable to others were traditional Chinese values best represented by Confucian ethics and social relationships.

During this early period, one part of the periphery illustrates what would eventually become an example of the detached periphery. This was the Chinese settlement of Taiwan from the sixteenth century. The role of Chinese merchants like Zheng Zhilong, those before him as well as his successors, in the opening of Taiwan is unique in Chinese history. Goaded partly by Dutch efforts to use Taiwan for both the China and Japan trade and partly by the political unrest in China, the merchant navies of Zheng Zhilong and his son Zheng Chenggong (Koxinga in European writings) laid the foundations of a maritime empire based on Taiwan. Although this "empire" failed and Taiwan came under Manchu Qing control after 1684, it remained a frontier area and was lightly administered as an overseas corner of Fujian province. There would have been among the early Chinese settlers the vestiges of Confucian civilization, but they formed a community without centrally-appointed mandarins for over a century and without its own Confucian literati until the middle of the eighteenth century. It could be argued that Taiwan started as a detached periphery that was later re-attached.

During the nineteenth and twentieth centuries, the rapid and fundamental changes that had reached the China coast began to penetrate to the centre of Confucian China. But although defeated militarily and diplomatically, China defended its core values with considerable success. Even after the May Fourth movement in 1919, when many Chinese intellectuals openly rejected Confucianism, most of the core values survived and revivals were organized from time to time until 1949. How successful these revivals were is doubtful. China had experienced some forty years of continual unrest, invasion and civil war. There was certainly nothing like a Confucian order managed by a central mandarinate. On the contrary, the coastal areas and peoples after 1840 were subjected to many new challenges, including partial and total detachment. They ranged from the cession of Hong Kong to the creation of extraterritorial treaty ports like Shanghai, Tianjin, Ningbo and Xiamen (Amoy). Eventually, Japanese ambitions led to the cutting off of Taiwan and then of Manchuria. And not least, Singapore had become a city with a Chinese majority who lived totally outside the control of the Chinese government.

Throughout the first half of the twentieth century, the detached periphery was extended and the centre weakened. This alarmed Chinese political leaders and the strong calls for openness and pluralism among those who lived in the detached areas were contradicted by equally strong cries for unity and stability under a strong centre that could defend the country against foreign imperialists and capitalists, and indeed against all undesirable foreign ideas and institutions. As we all know, the communists, better organized than the nationalists and more determined to exercise centralized power, were victorious. Under the banner of a different State ideology, they restored power to the centre with something like a new form of the mandarinate. They re-asserted control over the periphery in China, re-attaching the treaty ports and the provinces these ports had served as well as the rich and fast-developing region of Manchuria. What was left was the detached periphery of Hong Kong and Taiwan.

We have noted that this detached periphery of Chinese-majority territories has joined Japan and South Korea on the road to industrial capitalism. The periphery on the mainland (that is, the former treaty ports and their satellite cities in the interior and the three northeast provinces of former Manchuria), on the other hand, con-tinued to industrialize, but as the locomotives for industrial *socialism*, the centralizing and monolithic successor to the pre-industrial Confucian state. If the difference was merely one of political ideas and institutions drawn from a continuing Cold War, such a difference would have been easy to explain and accept. What is extraordinary now is that it is being argued that Japan and the four little dragons are spectacularly successful in achieving industrial capitalism because they share common features in a Confucian past. And, on the surface, this is appealing to many people in Northeast Asia because they can relate modern advancement to certain values that are non-Western and indigenous to the region. In this context, I return to the idea of the Confucian periphery. I have outlined the features of the cultural periphery, especially that of the merchants, and those of the detached periphery. It is now useful to compare these two with the external non-Han periphery whose élites, those of Korea, Vietnam and Japan, had shared the Confucian heritage with their Chinese counterparts for more than a thousand years.

Confucian Influence in Korea, Vietnam and Japan

First, some brief comments on their historical backgrounds. Korean rulers sent young scholars to study the Chinese classics during the Tang dynasty, but their State system did not begin to acquire Confucian orthodox characteristics until after the unification by the Koryo kingdom during the tenth dynasty. Even then, Buddhism remained much stronger in Korea than in China for several hundred years. It was not until the Yi dynasty's violent reaction against Mongol threats that Korea began to identify firmly with a revived Neo-Confucian identity centred on Ming China. From then onwards, the Korean élites became rigidly Confucian in almost every respect. Although it ruled a tributary kingdom outside China, the Yi dynasty rulers and mandarins of Korea prided themselves on being Confucian in ethical and political matters. The rest of the Korean people were very much placed in hierarchical relationships similar to those in China, with the merchant class lower socially than those in China.

Where the Vietnamese were concerned, they were always distant from the Chinese imperial centre although they too had sent young scholars to study the classics in Changan. Because they needed the Chinese less (they had no dangerous enemies comparable to the Mongols and the Manchus), they became more consciously nationalist from the tenth century onwards in defence of their independence. However, they too conceived of themselves as having their own central kingdom, albeit outside China, and their literati controlled the Vietnamese state like Chinese mandarins, on lines similar to those of Song and Ming China. After they regained their independence from Ming China in 1426, they gave even more power to their mandarinate to propagate their own version of Confucian orthodoxy. But, unlike the Koreans, the Vietnamese had a southern frontier that pushed southwards, so that they always had peripheral regions in the south that challenged the centre in the Hanoi delta areas. The more the Vietnamese became Southeast Asians, as they moved into the homelands of the Chams and the Khmers, the more non-Chinese alternatives (through Buddhist and Hindu values) were open to them. By the eighteenth century, the relation between their northern Confucianism and their southern frontier cultures had become finely balanced.

The Japanese were different from both Koreans and Vietnamese in even more significant ways. Firstly, Confucian values did not penetrate as deeply as Buddhist ones from the very beginning. The Japanese State was barely Confucian in rhetoric and early Japanese scholars sent to study in China were always more interested in Buddhism. Neither under the Fujiwara clan nor under the centuries of feudal division did there emerge a Confucian mandarinate. Certainly the question of Confucian influences before the Tokugawa shogunate period is a very doubtful one. This is not to say that, under the Tokugawa, the Confucian classics were not more widely studied, nor that strong Confucian values could not be found among the lords and their *samurai*, and even among the merchants whom the *samurai* professed to despise. But, without a powerful Confucian mandarinate, merchants were less bound to a rigid administrative structure. Non-Confucian ideas, whether indigenous or not, could thrive and provide alternative responses when wholly new stimuli eventually appeared in Western ships in the middle of the nineteenth century.

When we turn to modern economic developments and relate them to the theme of the Confucian centre and periphery, it is obvious that Japan's economic miracle has nothing directly to do with Confucianism in Japan or with having a close relationship with the Confucian centre in China. Of all the East Asian countries with a Confucian background, Japan has always been the most distantly peripheral to that centre. It is, therefore, significant that industrial capitalism took root first in Japan and not elsewhere in the region. It is no accident that, when Bakumatsu *samurai* and scholars used Confucian-sounding slogans to restore power to the Meiji emperor, there were no monolithic mandarin interests to stand in the way of wholesale acceptance of Western science and technology. There was also no uniform literati class who could be tempted to turn to another form of orthodoxy in order to reconstruct a post-Confucian mandarinate. Japan was pluralist enough to absorb wide-ranging ideas and lay the foundation of a capitalistic economy adapted to rapid industrialization. That tradition of pluralism owed little to Confucianism. It owed much to the Japanese ability to treat each set of imported ideas and institutions as merely another contribution to, and making another layer of, Japanese culture.

In contrast, none of the other countries and territories of East Asia had comparable experiences. It is intriguing then that four of them became little dragons along lines that seem to follow Japan, while three others did not. The four, South Korea, Taiwan, Hong Kong and Singapore, do not seem markedly different in their major traditional roots from the three which turned to communism, that is, China, North Korea and Vietnam. Yet their differences, rooted to a large extent in their respective encounters with contrasting colonial powers and imperialisms, are surely as important as their common Confucian backgrounds.

Of the former, three can be compared directly with mainland China, while South and North Korea might be contrasted separately. Vietnam is exceptional in that it was briefly divided between North and

South but the South, after a bitter war, became re-attached in a united Vietnam. It may be that Confucian values contributed little to that outcome. Vietnam was not only distant but also somewhat alienated from the Chinese imperial centre. It was, furthermore, "detached" in stages from that centre by the French when Vietnam came under colonial rule. Under the French, the Vietnamese were exposed to a model of capitalist economy. But their leaders rejected that model in their nationalist, anti-imperialist struggle and turned, together with the mainland Chinese, to a socialist ideology instead. And this in turn has so far not been helpful to their recovery and development. It is still too soon to predict future outcomes in Vietnam. There are also many variables peculiar to a Southeast Asian country which need to be separately studied, preferably in comparison with other Mainland Southeast Asian states like Laos, Cambodia and Burma.

Returning to the others, the two Koreas are of special interest. South Korean cultural values were hardly different from those of North Korea before 1945. Both were detached from Confucian China before that. Afterwards, the North Koreans were supported mainly by the Soviet Union (with help from the PRC) while the South Koreans were defended by the United States who later helped with their economic development. The Japanese also helped. The political determinants in both cases were obviously more essential between 1945 and 1952 than any cultural factors.

The Korean examples suggest that we should not concentrate on whether Confucian values predisposed a people towards capitalism or not. We should instead ask whether, if provided with different political ideologies and structures, various levels of Confucian values might be successfully adapted in different ways. In short, we should ask if a people with the same Confucian background might respond to different political circumstances by using different parts of the Confucian heritage. For example, North Koreans supporting an imperial Kim Il Sung and a centralized mandarin-type State may be acting in a way that is consistent with orthodox mandarin Confucianism. Similarly, it may be the mixed and more popular forms of Confucian values that are helping South Koreans make their form of industrial capitalism successful. That the former is assisted by Soviet and Chinese arms and the latter by American Arms and Japanese capital as well as more open and pluralist multinational organizations does not mean that Confucianism is irrelevant. When compared with regions with no Confucian background at all, there are still noteworthy differences. What we need to watch out for is any analysis of the four little dragons which over-emphasizes the degree to which cultural values are important pre-conditions for East Asian success.

One other similarity between North and South Koreans is also noteworthy. Both Koreas were under the same Japanese rule for thirty-five years. That should have had some impact in detaching Korea from the Confucian centre in China, but if it did, it was only a partial detachment. For example, it drove some patriotic Korean élites to become even more Confucian as an antidote to Japanese nationalism and Shintoism. At the same time, it encouraged many other Koreans to turn elsewhere, to Christianity or to communism, to preserve their national identity. Again we are faced with great ambiguity when seeking to link cultural values with rapid modern industrialization. On the one hand, some of these value systems may have inclined some Korean leaders towards socialist planning policies under a new kind of centralized mandarinate, as in North Korea. There are features in Confucianism which strengthen the tendency towards totalitarianism — its desire to make people conform to an idea of what a "proper person" ought to be, the belief in strong central control over all aspects of one's personal life, as well as the distrust of business and merchants. On the other hand, some Confucian personal values may have reinforced dissident Christianity in turning other Korean leaders to press for liberal democracy as a necessary part of advanced capitalism.

Thus, in the two Koreas, what was significant was the external political intervention by the two superpowers at the end of World War II. As a result, North Korea's development looked to the USSR and China and that of South Korea followed the US and Japan. This does not mean that cultural values do not have roles to play in the economic development of the two Koreas, but that their roles were only played on stages built by the superpowers. Weighed against the politics of ideology here, Confucian backgrounds seem distant and remote.

The Chinese in and outside China

Finally, we turn to the Chinese in and outside China. The peripheral areas that were restored to China and came under PRC control are now economically underdeveloped when compared with those which were detached and chose the capitalist way. But even for the detached periphery, there are differences. Singapore is likely not only to remain fully detached from China, but is also not fully Chinese. Its future as a little dragon lies in developing together with its ASEAN neighbours as part of the capitalist world. Taiwan, on the other hand, is much nearer to China geographically and culturally and actually insists that it is part of China. Indeed, it could have been re-attached to China together with the other peripheral areas on the mainland in 1949. There is little doubt that, Confucian values notwithstanding, had Taiwan been "liberated" together with Shanghai, Fujian, Guang-dong and Tianjin, it would not be greatly different from those places today. It is the fact of being detached for some forty years and the adoption of a different economic model that has enabled Taiwan to become one of the four little dragons.

As for Hong Kong, it lives under the shadow of re-attachment — even if the PRC keeps its promise that, for fifty years after 1997, there will be no change to its present structure. Will that make any differ-ence to Hong Kong's future? There are expectations that Hong Kong, together with the other dragons, could influence the coastal periph-ery areas of mainland China in the not-too-distant future. And if China really wanted that to happen, I have little doubt that such expectations would be fulfilled. But it would require China to take a big step away from the system in which a centralized bureaucracy controlled all economic activity. And that does appear at present to be unlikely. It is ironical, that in its present drive for ideological "pu-rity", China depends on a cadre bureaucratic system that reminds us of the traditional Confucian mandarinate. In some of the ways the party cadres are tackling the country's problems, including those related to its economic development, these cadres appear to have recreated the most Confucian of all the East Asian states.

Conclusion

What of the future? This is a big subject which I obviously cannot deal with here. There are indeed many factors that can influence the four examples of the detached periphery, but Confucian values will not be the most vital ones, certainly not a strong dose of such values. What is more important are the following: the degree of openness to the world, a willingness to value merit above ideological purity, and a system which is not capricious and arbitrary but one with laws which respect the individual and his property. If international trade and high-technology communications continue to expand dramatically, then there would be a good chance for this periphery to stay autonomous and free. Those Confucian values that help to support such an open system would continue to contribute to its future prosperity and progress. At the same time, other countries in the region which are exposed to industrial capitalism are expected to join the four little dragons before long. When that happens, we would need to question if the presence of Confucian values on China's periphery were so significant after all.

CHAPTER 15

Education in External China

... THE WORD "EDUCATION" IS used in this chapter in the sense of formal schooling. This is usually structured within a specific political framework, supported by economic surplus and social investments of some kind, and also subject to a greater or lesser degree of influence by a country's cultural traditions. For maritime Chinese (the Chinese communities overseas, in Hong Kong, Taiwan and some coastal communities of southeastern China, those in External China), the relationship of education to cultural tradition is particularly difficult to deal with, especially during this century. Most of them had to face more than one cultural tradition in their lives. Even in formal schooling, they were open to more than one culture, whether Western (sometimes colonial) or indigenous, as well as parts of their own Chinese culture. And even when they were considering what was Chinese, they could see that there were many layers to the various factors grouped together to form the basis of Chinese tradition. There was what has been described as the Great Tradition, often equated with Imperial Confucianism, supported by the literati and held in awe by most ordinary Chinese. There were also what have been loosely labelled Little Traditions, where commonly held Confucian values were mixed with different combinations of popular Buddhist, Taoist and other customs, beliefs and practices. For maritime Chinese, the Great Tradition was not always dominant or even relevant. Instead, local unorthodox variations of Little Traditions were encountered more frequently among Chinese who lived far from the Chinese capital and other major cultural centres. What each of these communities chose to pick from these traditions to harmonize with alien cultures in order to help them survive and succeed is a subject of great interest about which we still do not know enough. For my purposes here, I shall concentrate on their experience of culture in education.

Some historical background would be useful. Maritime Chinese communities can be broadly divided into three types. The small communities (including "Chinatowns") dispersed in countries of the West like Canada, the United States and Australia, are examples of the first. Largely merchant communities who lived among indigenous peoples in Thailand, Japan, Indonesia and Malaysia would be examples of the second. And the third type, the communities who are predominantly Chinese, are to be found in Hong Kong, Singapore and Taiwan.

The experiences of the three types where formal schooling was concerned varied greatly. For example, before the end of World War II, the education of the first type of maritime Chinese was predominantly one received in schools teaching in English or other Western languages such as French or Spanish. A few went to small private Chinese schools to learn the rudiments of the Chinese language, but their contact with Chinese culture of any kind outside their homes was negligible. Their education was Western and most of them were, to all intents and purposes, educated to be Canadians, Americans, Australians and so on. But in recent decades, there has been a surge in Chinese migration to the West (both directly from China, Hong Kong and Taiwan, and re-migration from one non-Chinese area to another), and Chinese communities abroad have become larger. As a result, aspects of Chinese culture are more visible, and there is easier access to the study of the Chinese language. Also, the consciousness about Chinese ethnicity has led many Chinese to explore Chinese cultural traditions in new and refreshing ways. Despite these changes, however, it would be true to say that schooling is still in the national language, whether English, Spanish, French or some other European language, and the cultural traditions encountered are largely Western. Unlike in the earlier period, however, Chinese acceptance of Western cultural values today is one of preference rather than compulsion. This has led to a most interesting juxtaposition of cultural attitudes. The children who have grown up among Europeans and North Americans are naturally Western in outlook and their Western values have been reinforced by their education in local national schools. At the same time, many of these same children have been encouraged by communal ethnic identity to try and rediscover Chinese traditions for themselves. At this level, where these young Chinese are comfortable and secure in their Western cultures and voluntarily confront Chinese tradition, there is curiosity, a little awe and some sentimentality, but no tension.

In contrast, the minority Chinese communities in Asia had, earlier this century, enjoyed formal Chinese education. Almost everywhere, they had been strong enough economically to run their own schools which taught in Chinese and most of these schools were modelled on those in China, often using textbooks prepared with the approval of the Chinese nationalist government. Where they were allowed to do so, the local-born Chinese were taught in their schools to see Chinese culture as the Chinese in China saw it. Of course, not all Chinese who went to such schools lived and thought like their counterparts in China. The local environment, especially indigenous cultural values as in Japan and Thailand, did influence their lives and their outlook to some extent. Over time, more and more young Chinese were sent to indigenous national schools. Today, especially in Thailand, Thai has become the language of communication even between people of Chinese descent. Chinese culture has become a sub-culture where it survives at all. There is still curiosity and sentimentality about China and its cultural artifacts, but again, like those in the West, they seem to be securely Thai and feel no need to be educated in Chinese traditions. Furthermore, intermarriage has become so common that most Sino-Thai families have assimilated their residual Chinese values into their Thai patterns of behaviour.

Where the Chinese lived under colonial rule (whether English, French, Dutch or American), however, the situation had been somewhat different. Many Chinese chose to send their children to colonial schools. There they received some diluted or even distorted Western cultural values which did not discourage them from asserting their Chinese identity. But for them, their understanding of Chinese values was indirect and often attenuated and highly selective, and they were often despised by those educated in Chinese schools for their lack of Chinese language skills. What was to make life more complicated in Western colonies was that the Chinese there were rarely interested in indigenous Javanese, Malay, Vietnamese or Filipino cultures. And this was to become a major disadvantage after World War II, when the Western powers withdrew and indigenous nationalisms created the newly independent governments of Southeast Asia. In order to survive, most of these Chinese communities had then to send their children to national schools teaching in indigenous national languages. Chinese schools have barely survived in such environments and the Chinese written language is now rarely taught in schools (except in Malaysia). In the national schools, Chinese schoolchildren have often to choose between becoming culturally indigenous or absorbing enough residual Western intellectual skills to enable them to study and get an education and perhaps emigrate to the West. Few would have the opportunity to learn Chinese cultural values, and even fewer would contemplate returning to China to do so.

In Hong Kong, Singapore and Taiwan, the situation early this century had been somewhat different. Education in Hong Kong and Singapore had resembled that in the British Malay states, but the size of the Chinese communities made Chinese culture much more prominent even in some of the English schools. Certainly, studying in an English school did not prevent young Chinese from retaining strong traditional values. As for Taiwan under the Japanese, despite the enforcement of Japanese colonial education, the Chinese there were never far from their own traditions. Indeed, it was the Japanese who were in a dilemma because they themselves had borrowed much from China, and had even adopted the Chinese writing system and professed admiration for many Chinese classical traditions. They therefore found it difficult to say that Chinese culture should be rejected.

Since World War II, the position has changed again. Taiwan returned to the Chinese fold. At the end of the civil war in China, the Nanking government moved to Taiwan and brought with it what appears to have been a keen sense of the Great Tradition and the surviving values of the Chinese literati. Within two decades, a national orthodoxy seemed to have returned to all formal schooling. But there has been a difference. The new orthodoxy is itself a mixture of modern and traditional cultures of the Treaty Ports of maritime China (for example, Shanghai, Ningpo, Fuchow, Amoy and Canton) and the Little Traditions of the maritime Chinese who have peopled Taiwan since the sixteenth century. Thus, the new orthodoxy is distinct from the culture of the Chinese heartland. It sees itself confidently as modern and the Great Tradition seems to have been integrated into a new and dynamic Chinese culture. This culture now sees no conflict between what is Chinese and what is modern. And the Taiwan Chinese need for close links with the United States and Japan for more than three decades has, if anything, reinforced the modern and self-critical traits that the younger generation had learnt from their schools. In addition, Taiwan provided Chinese education for thousands of students from other parts of External China and sent many of its well-educated graduates and entrepreneurs to the US. By so doing, this new form of Chinese culture has left its mark on other maritime Chinese communities, notably those of Hong Kong, Singapore and some cities in North America.

Hong Kong and Singapore have also changed since the 1950s, although in quite different ways. Singapore, with its own national government and its own civic identity, has created national schools in which English is the medium of instruction. However, some Chinese values have been preserved as the Chinese language is also taught to Singaporeans of Chinese descent. So far, the attitudes towards Chinese cultural traditions remain ambivalent and the modern content of what is being studied in schools is identifiably more Western than anything else. But, because Singapore is located in Southeast Asia with Indonesia and Malaysia as neighbours, Singaporean Chinese are not, despite what is taught in schools, simply caught between Chinese and Western cultural traditions. They are seeking to be Singaporean first while still struggling to build a new national culture out of an amalgam of Chinese, Southeast Asian and modern cosmopolitan elements. Until such a culture emerges, most of them are uncomfortable about the very idea of cultural tradition.

Hong Kong, on the other hand, being directly under the shadow of China but living on English law, international finance and Western technology, has to confront Chinese cultural traditions more directly. Also, most of its people have recently come from China or are children of those who did, and the traditions are still viewed as real and viable. Nevertheless, these traditions have already been transformed because the people have been educated in Hong Kong schools. There is a complex chemistry in the schools here. The mixture of what is Chinese and what is not, what belongs to the tradition and what does not, is unique. I would suggest that although education here is superficially similar to aspects of that available either in Taiwan or in Singapore, the emotional and intellectual tension in most Hong Kong people between pride in Chinese cultural tradition and the practical need for a cosmopolitan modernity is at its greatest and its most open. The experience derived from this tension deserves more attention. It is an experience which may have common features with that of all other maritime Chinese and especially with that of Taiwan or Singapore Chinese, but to try and define that commonality may lead to too abstract a formulation to be useful.

I have so far skirted the central problem of what constitutes Chinese cultural tradition. For the maritime Chinese communities, it has been, until recently, whatever the Chinese in China accepted as tradition. But since the idea of tradition itself has been challenged in

China for more than half a century, it is now less certain if anyone really knows what tradition means in China. Leaving aside the few who totally reject tradition in any form, there are broadly two approaches that dominate educational policy and are competing for attention. One emphasizes that there is an irreducible core of Chinese cultural heritage that must be studied and preserved at all cost. This is often emotionally presented as essential principles that define the quality of Chineseness in every educated Chinese. In a famous formulation, this was the *body* (*t'i*) of Chinese learning (as in *chung-hsueh wei t'i*). The other approach has been more pragmatic, teaching the younger generation to examine critically various strands from the past and helping them select what should be kept alive and further developed, something like *p'i-p'an ti chi-ch'eng* (inherit with a critical mind).

The first approach has been considered very respectable in educational circles. It is defensive but patriotic. The original meaning of Chang Chih-tung's famous phrase quoted above, which stressed the superiority of the Confucian heritage, has been attacked several times, not least during the ten years of the Cultural Revolution (1966–76). But it has never been totally rejected. It is interesting that the full quotation comparing the body of Chinese Learning with "Western Learning for practical applications" (*hsi-hsueh wei yung*), has resurfaced in vigorous historical debates in China today. It would appear that many Chinese still feel that there must be a body of essential principles for young Chinese to conform to if China is not to be corrupted by alien ideas and institutions. The trouble is, there is no agreement as to what these essential principles should be. What has concerned many is that by rejecting the old body of Chinese learning, they must find a new set replacing it, whether it be Marxism-Leninism in a sinicized form or Western liberalism.

The second approach starts from a different premise, to stop thinking about having an irreducible core of tradition (that is, to reject the idea of any kind of *t'i*), and begin instead with teaching the young to identify those parts of the heritage which might be worth preserving for the modern world. For most people, however, trying to be critical while using the language, rhetoric and methods of the Chinese heritage itself would not take them very far. The most fascinating example of this can be found in the Cultural Revolution attacks on all traditional ideas. For example, instead of arguing within a Marxist-Leninist framework, the radical leaders used less orthodox but largely Confucian ideas to attack the more orthodox ones. In other cases, the ideas of Taoist, Buddhist and other ancient Chinese philosophers were used to criticize everything Confucian. In other words, even this critical approach suffers from the tendency to argue within a closed system that embodies many of the very ideas that are to be criticized.

Preserving Chinese learning, or even modifying and improving it by making it more modern, represents structural and more abstract approaches to cultural tradition. There are other starting-points. One common example is to point to basic ethical principles in the tradition which are central to being Chinese and clearly must be taught to all Chinese. Indeed, it has long been thought that Chinese would not know how to behave without these principles. The young, therefore, are expected to learn through concrete examples and cultivate a deeper knowledge of vital social values and thus have a keener sense of how and when to take necessary action. This example of educating through tangible lessons in order to guide social behaviour comes from an ancient juxtaposition of knowledge and action which is still influential today.

The idea that knowledge and action (*chih* and *hsing*) are inter-related is an ancient one and a major pillar in Chinese moral philosophy. It has evolved through the centuries and one of the best and clearest statements about it came from the great Neo-Confucian philosopher, Chu Hsi. About 800 years ago, he said, "Knowledge and Action often need each other, it is like having eyes and no feet, which prevents you from going forwards and having feet and no eyes, which prevents you from seeing where you are going. In terms of priority, Knowledge comes first, but in terms of significance, Action is more important." Three hundred and fifty years later, Wang Yang-ming, who led an opposing school of Neo-Confucian thought, was inclined to regard *chih* and *hsing* as equally important and in separable. There have been other refinements since, but the issue was a lively philosophical and educational one till modern times. Both Sun Yat-sen and Mao Tse-tung were guided in their respective revolutions by the idea that *chih* and *hsing* were necessary and complementary. Sun was inclined to say that *chih* was more difficult than *hsing* whereas the young Mao Tse-tung, who was influenced by Chu Hsi, clearly believed that *hsing* was more important. Interest-ingly, when Mao expressed the relationship in modern terms as theory and practice, secular theory became equally important. As a Marxist, he had moved from moral knowledge to scientific theory and he was to argue that revolutionary action had to be guided by theory for it to succeed.

This is a good example of traditional formulations playing a part in moulding modern Chinese thought. Its influence on education in China is still being felt. The question remains as to whether it is necessary to identify an ethical principle as Chinese before it is worth learning, or by extending the same kind of logic, whether it has to conform to Marxist-Leninist principles before the young can learn it. Officially, Chinese education pays more attention to communist ideology than to Chinese tradition. However, the examples given above show that we can still identify a traditional attitude of mind in current debates in China about culture.

This is not to suggest that all Chinese in China subscribe to the abstract idea that Chinese learning must form the core of all knowledge, or to the view that concrete ethical examples provide the best guides to the Chinese heritage. But it would be useful to contrast traditional modes of thought still alive in China today with alternative ways of thinking that are more common among the maritime Chinese of External China. As outlined earlier, most maritime Chinese, living as minorities without power and without protection from China, had looked for practical and useful skills to cope with alien and often hostile environments. Learning for its own sake was of little value and they had moved away very early from the education of "gentlemen" (*chun-tsu*) for the few — that is, classical learning to be a literatus — to learning scientific, professional and business skills to cope with the rapid changes they saw around them. For those further away, living in the West or among other modernizing or nationalistic Asians, there was almost no appeal to cultural tradition and what has emerged is often a rather crude utilitarian approach to learning. This learning concerns only what is useful and can be quickly used. The few who fully accepted the Western cultural heritage would, in Chinese eyes, be somewhat beyond the pale. But I will not dwell on those whose education has been totally different from that available in China. Instead, let me concentrate on education nearer China, in Hong Kong, Taiwan and to some extent, also in Singapore. These are three of the "four little dragons" on the edge of China that have attracted so much attention in recent years.[2] Their example raises one important question about the relationship between wealth and culture and throws light on one particularly interesting aspect of culture, the culture of trade, which can help illuminate the theme of education and cultural tradition.

Historians have long debated on the relationship between wealth and culture, on what might seem to have been an essentially chicken and egg question. There has been disagreement whether cultural factors determined how much wealth a society could produce or whether it was the wealth produced which determined the level of civilization attained. For our purposes, it is enough to point out that the standards of living of the people of China are very low compared with those of the three "dragons" and all Chinese people everywhere are perturbed by this fact. Hence the emotional reactions to a range of views on this topic; for example, a wealthy imperial China had produced the great cultural traditions, therefore China needs prosperity if its culture is to flourish again. Or, key ancient ideas had brought about the wealthy Chinese empire; if they could be adapted for modern use, could they not help China become wealthy again? Or, more confusingly, statements that China under Mao Tse-tung had rejected Chinese values in favour of Marxist-Leninist ones, hence the decline in prosperity, are heard almost as often as others saying that China remained poor because its socialist leaders never really freed themselves from traditional modes of thought that have outlived their usefulness.

This is not the place to examine such a complex question on which historians and modern analysts disagree. The fact is, the Chinese in China are poor and the Chinese outside are much richer. And it appears that Chinese cultural tradition did not stand in the way of wealth production in Taiwan, and in Japan, it is widely agreed that Japanese traditions have actually helped to speed up Japan's economic development. Also, in Japan and the "four little dragons", wealth seems to be supporting not only the creation of new cultural traditions but also the revival of viable ancient traditions. And, although it is debatable if there is consensus anywhere that the new cultures are all that desirable, or that what have been preserved from the old are the best and the essential parts of their respective heritages, the fact is that wealth can provide the means for such questions to be studied. Education has benefited from additional resources being made available. It has become more open and pluralistic and this can only help lead to fresh understanding of cultural traditions and to new developments in a people's culture itself.

Much of the wealth in Hong Kong, Taiwan and Singapore has been created by successful trade and industry policies, and these include education and training policies aimed directly at encouraging trade and industry. It is therefore particularly useful to examine the example of attitudes towards trade and industry as an aspect of Chinese cultural tradition. There is no question that education today in the three territories has business and technological interests very much in mind. What is often forgotten, however, is that while the modern skills acquired are new, attitudes towards acquiring these skills are deeply rooted in the Chinese cultural tradition. These attitudes have both positive and negative features and illustrate some of the ambiguities in the Chinese heritage itself, especially in what I have called "the culture of trade".

By "culture of trade", I mean that culture derived from the values of traders, that is, what traders would or would not do for profit and how far they would be prepared to go to expand their markets. This would also have to take into account the cultural framework in which the traders had to operate and the prevailing social attitudes towards wealth, especially towards those who had made their fortunes from trading activities. For example, in the Great Tradition in China, merchants were given a very lowly position; in fact, they had traditionally been placed at the bottom of the social scale. Imperial mandarins did not recognize that merchants created wealth for the society, but merely thought they did so largely for themselves. In a large agrarian state, this was understandable. It did mean, however, that trading skills were rarely employed to enrich China, only to assist the imperial coffers from time to time. When merchants were performing valuable service, they were closely supervised by mandarins and made to feel that they traded only on sufferance. The small class of successful merchants always saw themselves as personally dependent on mandarin protection. The culture of trade was, therefore, apologetic, defensive and always imitative of that of the literati.

This key feature of the Chinese cultural tradition has been largely rejected in External China. Even in Taiwan, where traditions remain strong, this part of the tradition has been largely suppressed in the education of the young. And in Hong Kong and Singapore, the contrary practice of favouring investors and entrepreneurs has been given a new respectability unknown in traditional China. How this culture of trade gained acceptance provides a good measure of how a society can modify a cultural tradition to suit its needs.

In China, however, the picture is much more complex. Changes in the status of merchants had only just begun to take place at the beginning of this century when two successive revolutions checked that development. The first was led mainly by nationalist literati and soldiers while the second was dominated by communist intellectuals and the peasantry. The latter inherited a particularly strong bias against the culture of trade and, by identifying it as similar to the exploitative values of capitalism and imperialism, suppressed all signs of that culture for nearly three decades. Thus, while the culture of trade was seen positively and actually encouraged in education in External China, the same features in China were condemned. Even now, the new open policy in China is hesitant about the role of merchants. On the surface, entrepreneurship is officially promoted as a means to increase production and national wealth. Extreme voices even speak of "the whole people engaging in trade" in response to market forces, but the very tone of that extreme "slogan" reminds us of traditional attitudes. The tone suggests that many people are uncomfortable and ambivalent about it in traditional ways and fear that people with power and influence would, as in the past, take advantage of their positions to exploit the trading classes. The place of merchants is still being fiercely debated. In reality, they are still to be tightly supervised by cadre-officials and their traditionally suspect and inferior place is being upheld. It may be quite a while before education that respects the culture of trade will find its place in China.

We have here an example where an important part of a cultural tradition has remained essentially unchanged in China and the damaging results of failing to deal with that tradition rationally and in practical ways have had serious consequences for the country's wealth-creating capacities. This experience has been accompanied by convoluted rationalizations partly because it is not clear whether China seriously believes some parts of its cultural traditions should be preserved, or whether it really wants to abandon all traditions that do not conform to socialist principles, or whether it now thinks that such cultural concerns are simply not very relevant. We certainly cannot tell from this example of how merchants have been regarded what China will ultimately do with all other parts of its cultural traditions. What has been highlighted here is the contrast with what maritime Chinese communities have done with traditional attitudes towards the merchant classes, and especially with the way the changes in attitudes were introduced into formal schooling. These communities have demonstrated that, by adapting to changing values out of necessity, and having educational methods and goals changed in response to new circumstances, they have been able to produce great benefits. This need not apply to each and every part of cultural tradition, but rational and hard-headed decisions have to be made about many of them with regard to "pedagogy, curriculum and policy".[3] It would seem that only by doing that could the role of education in harmonizing cultural heritage with the utilitarian demands of the contemporary world be truly valuable. Education in External China today is the result of many decisions made over several decades. There are no easy lessons for the Chinese in China to learn, because conditions in China are very different. But it would be surprising if the extensive contacts it has with External China, and especially the intensive contacts with Hong Kong, did not provide some useful lessons for education in China.

NOTES

1 This chapter was originally presented as part of a lecture at a conference on "Cultural Tradition and Contemporary Education" at the Chinese University of Hong Kong on the occasion of its 25th anniversary, 13 October 1988. It has been slightly amended for the present publication.

2 See Chapter 14.

3 "Pedagogy, curriculum and policy" were subjects included in the subtitle of the conference theme.

CHAPTER 16

The Chinese: What Kind of Minority?[1]

SOME TIME AGO, I spoke of the end of the Nanyang Chinese as a "multinational" community in Southeast Asia. I said this at a time when strong demonstrations of communal strength had brought about the foundation of Nanyang University in Singapore, theoretically to serve all the Chinese in the region. The new university suggested that we were about to witness the growth of an intellectual and cultural centre for what might be described as a multinational minority people. But there were other signs that this was a phenomenon akin to a Parkinsonian law, the building of grand buildings after the period of glory was over. First, there was the proven strength of indigenous nationalism all over Southeast Asia and even to some extent in the Federation of Malaya. Then there was the shift in policy towards Overseas Chinese by the People's Republic of China which Chou En-lai announced at Bandung and began to institutionalize soon afterwards. And not least was the rise of local-born leaders of Chinese descent who had become better organized to resist the continuation of "multinationalism" and were being encouraged by the new national governments to be more articulate and more independent of the old-style Nanyang "chauvinism".

The fear that the Chinese would continue to be "multinational", however, remained. Much was made of the fact that China was communist and communism offered a new basis for establishing internationalism which the Chinese could easily translate into a multinational communalism where they were concerned. Those Chinese who looked to China and admired the achievements of Maoist communism would not give up their efforts to keep the "Nanyang Chinese" idea alive. The radicalism of Nanyang University students in the late 1950s and 1960s confirmed these fears, so much so that few people noticed how few of the university's students had come from outside Singapore and Malaysia and how much the university had become a Malayan-Chinese university, and later, a Singapore university.

The fear of a Chinese communist multinationalism did not subside during the Vietnam War. If anything, it was strengthened by the growing proximity of that war to areas of large "Chinese" population like Bangkok, Penang, Kuala Lumpur and Singapore. But it was noted that the Cultural Revolution in China had some strong negative effects on most of those of Chinese descent in the region. It was the first time the majority of "Chinese" were alienated from what was happening in China, especially as some of the violence and aggression had been directed against returned Overseas Chinese and the families of Chinese still outside China. This, together with the grinding poverty of the people as revealed during the years of crop failures in 1959–61, confirmed that China was not for most of them. Also, the continued failure of China to protect the lives (and property) of Chinese citizens in Indonesia since 1959 culminating in the killings occasioned by the Gestapu coup in 1965 further convinced the still doubtful that they should make their peace with their national governments and forget what few remaining ties there still were with China.

At least so it seemed until the Nixon visit announcement and the UN admission in 1971 and the successful Chinese "diplomatic offensive" since 1969. China was at last legitimate to the vast majority of the world. Once again, questions were asked as to whether this might affect the loyalties of the Chinese. Again the spectre of the multinational Chinese came to mind. But before this new spate of speculation got off the ground, the war in Indo-China reached its inevitable conclusion and, within months, it became quite clear that communist victories did not lead to Chinese dominance or to any renewal of the multinational nature of Chinese minorities in Vietnam, Laos and Cambodia. On the contrary, those "Chinese" who remained behind and survived the transition have become more submerged in the indigenous populations than ever before.

All the same, some old anxieties about the future role of the "Overseas Chinese" have reappeared. All the fears of the 1950s concerning these Chinese were quickly revived and a large variety of questions were asked. Most of them centred on two related problems with wide ramifications: firstly, would the Chinese in Southeast Asia be the targets of subversion? Secondly, would they be encouraged to resist assimilation and reassert their Chineseness?

On both these questions, opinions were divided. There were many

who felt strongly that the diplomatic re-emergence of China necessarily meant trouble for Southeast Asian countries with Chinese
minorities, although some concentrated more on the consequences of
American military withdrawal than on what the Chinese planned to
do. Others were confident that the time for such fears was over. Most
of the Chinese had settled down and made their peace with the new
nationalist governments that had emerged since 1945. Most of them
were economically well off and too committed to the more or less
laissez faire economies of the region to want to destroy them. Where
there was danger, it would come from the growing discontent among
the indigenous poor and the political awakening of the indigenous
young. Thus one view concentrated on the intentions of China and
the other on the effectiveness of Southeast Asian governments. There
was also a third which looked more closely at the reactions of the
local Chinese. Although no great threat was necessarily to be
expected from them, there would be specific changes, for example,
as far as citizenship among those who had been nationals of the
Republic of China in Taiwan was concerned, or the new perspectives
on issues of loyalty and assimilation. These changes would depend
on the current policies of Southeast Asian governments, the numbers
of Chinese and the degree of assimilation already achieved in each
country and not least on the attitudes of individual Chinese about
their countries of adoption.

By May 1974, China's own policies towards Southeast Asia became
clearer. They emphasized the acceptance of the existing international
system and the desire for a new start with governments so far hostile
to China. Over forty countries which had previously recognized
Taiwan or refrained from recognizing either of the Chinas had established full diplomatic relations. Changes within China, too, confirmed
a desire for stability and development. Lin Piao had fallen in September 1971, the Chinese Communist Party had been restructured in the
provinces and a new Central Committee was elected at its Tenth
Party Congress in August 1973. Although a fierce political campaign
against Lin Piao and against Confucius continued in 1974, the trends
were towards firm control within and a steady policy without, and
this has continued even after Chou En-lai's death. In particular,
foreign policy statements concerning the United States, Japan and the
Third World, even when laced with violent anti-Soviet sentiments,
could be described as reassuring to Southeast Asian governments.
Also, in the treatment of visitors to China, the distinction made
between foreigners of Chinese descent and "Overseas Chinese" with

Chinese passports had been widely noted. Taken together with other assurances the Chinese government was given at the protracted negotiations with Malaysia's representatives through 1972 and 1973, the key developments did assuage old fears. When Tun Razak agreed to visit Peking in May 1974, his decision suggested that he saw more advantages than risks in taking Chinese assurances at their face value. A year later, both President Marcos of the Philippines and Premier Kukrit of Thailand were to accept the need for change for similar reasons. It was expected that the Singapore government would follow the same path, especially when Indonesia indicated its willingness to restore relations with China.

Now that China has largely achieved its aim of conciliation with the ASEAN countries, it remains to be seen if China might act differently towards people of Chinese origin who had settled in the region and begin to urge them to act on China's behalf in any way and whether the local citizens of Chinese descent themselves might re-discover their Chineseness and slow down if not stop the process of assimilation altogether. Since Malaysia's recognition of China, a number of developments have been relevant to the problem of "Overseas Chinese", especially to the need to clarify further what the term "Overseas Chinese" really means now.

The three most important developments were (a) the political changes in the pivotal state of Thailand, (b) the transformation of Indo-China and its impact on United States policies for ASEAN countries and ASEAN policies towards China and the Soviet Union and (c) the consequences of worldwide inflation and recession on the economic conditions of the non-communist states in the region. Related to these three were a number of other events also important for those of Chinese origin. These included the strength of insurgency forces in Thailand and Thai efforts to prevent its eastern neighbours, Laos and Cambodia, from supporting these insurgents, the residual United States support for Thailand as the new line of defence against the spread of communism and the Thai-Malaysia border campaigns against a combination of Malaysian Chinese, Thai and Thai-Malay insurgent forces. Also notable is the rise of *bumiputra* (prince of the earth) discontent in Malaysia and Singapore's concern with non-communist subversion: both had long-term implications for those of Chinese origin, especially if the more crucial developments in Thailand were not resolved and its security problems endangered the whole length of the Malay peninsula.

With each development, it became more imperative to question the use of the term "Overseas Chinese". It had been used in its broadest sense to cover all people of Chinese descent resident abroad and it roughly translated the Chinese term "Huaqiao" (Chinese sojourners). For Southeast Asia, the more specialized "Nanyang Huaqiao" or Nanyang Chinese was widely used until the 1960s. This is a term which has implied a single community with a considerable solidarity. It still survives largely because the government in Taiwan has retained it in its official publications. The People's Republic became more wary of the term after the Bandung conference in 1955 but was not always consistent. It has distinguished between "Foreign Chinese" and "Overseas Chinese", that is, the large majority of those who are foreign nationals but of Chinese descent and the small minority of Chinese nationals who more or less permanently reside abroad. The fact that the two governments used "Huaqiao" with different meanings has not helped clarify the term for Southeast Asian governments. Specially confusing has been the way the government in Taipei had encouraged the view that all those of Chinese descent are Chinese first and foreign citizens second. This has often made China's position very difficult. On the one hand, foreign governments doubted its sincerity when it declared that all Chinese abroad should become loyal citizens of their respective adopted countries. On the other, some foreign nationals of Chinese descent retained hope that, at the crunch, China would offer them refuge and help, if not full protection. The classic example of how awkward the problem could be for the two Chinese governments, for Southeast Asian governments and for various types of Chinese abroad alike was that of Indonesia. For the past twenty years, there had been (a) Indonesians of Chinese descent; (b) Chinese who were citizens of the People's Republic; (c) Chinese who were citizens of the Republic of China (Taiwan) whom the Indonesians treated as "stateless"; (d) Stateless Chinese waiting for Indonesian citizenship willing to be protected by the People's Republic and by the Republic in Taiwan while waiting; and (e) Stateless Chinese awaiting citizenship who wanted to have nothing to do with either government.

Within Southeast Asia, the term "Overseas Chinese" or "Huaqiao" is now less widely used. In government publications and in the media, including those in Chinese, the trend is to avoid any reference to Chinese except, when necessary, as *Ma-Hua, Yin-Hua, Tai-Hua* and *Fei-Hua* (Malaysian, Indonesian, Thai and Filipino Chinese). Those of Chinese descent sometimes refer to themselves as Huaren (Chinese person) or Huayi (descendant of Chinese), self-consciously dropping the "qiao" in "Huaqiao" which had emphasized that they were merely sojourners always intending to return to China. It is still not certain whether this simply marks a formal and artificial avoidance of "Huaqiao" for most of those of Chinese descent. Nor is it certain that the various governments take the formal change in terminology as a real indication that their subjects had really changed their attitudes towards their new homes. But it is an important step to drop the term "Huaqiao" for all but those who are citizens of China or Taiwan if we are to reduce the confusion and encourage more accurate understanding of a complex situation.

To return to the case of Indonesia, it is obviously unscientific, and verging on racism, to refer to all five categories as Chinese or Overseas Chinese. Categories (a) and (e) should normally be called Indonesians except when circumstances make it necessary to call them Indonesian Chinese. Category (d) should also be called Indonesian Chinese, although there might be times when (Overseas) Chinese would be more appropriate. Categories (b) and (c) are clearly (Overseas) Chinese. A slightly less complex situation existed in Cambodia (until April 1975) and Laos (until July 1975) where relations with China had undergone various changes. Categories similar to the five found in Indonesia had existed since about 1955, but the picture had become much simplified by 1971 when Prince Sihanouk was overthrown and Lon Nol seized power. And since the middle of 1975, only two categories remained: Cambodians and Laotians (of Chinese descent) and (Overseas) Chinese. Such a development had already occurred in Burma where relations with China since 1950 have been relatively steady. There are Burmese (including Sino-Burman, Sino-Shan, etc. if local identifications were pursued further) and there are (Overseas) Chinese. A rather curious but aberrant development occurred in Vietnam. In North Vietnam, the question of being of Chinese descent had long been meaningless and Chinese was used only for those who came from China or carried Chinese passports. In South Vietnam where the numbers of Chinese had been much larger since the nineteenth century and where the government in Taiwan was recognized as China until April 1975, most Chinese were forced to take Vietnamese nationality by the government of Ngo Dinh Diem (1955–63). While this did not reconcile such Chinese to Vietnamese aspirations, it did make the position simpler for the new government when it took over power in May 1975. It would be interesting to see if the Vietnamese of Chinese descent who had not escaped from the country have been given a choice of becoming (Overseas) Chinese again or have been treated as Vietnamese in every respect.

Obviously the question of which government was recognized had been an important factor in determining who was or was not Chinese. Where a Southeast Asian government had consistently dealt only with China, the definition of Chinese had steadily narrowed and only those who are citizens of the People's Republic are Overseas Chinese or Huaqiao. This had not been so clear when diplomatic relations were with the Republic in Taiwan, or when neither China nor Taiwan was officially recognized. In such cases, as with Thailand and the Philippines before 1975 and with Malaysia and Singapore, a new stage in definition was due. On 31 May 1974 Malaysia established diplomatic relations with the People's Republic, recognized it as the sole legal government of China and decided to close down its consulate in Taipei. On 9 June 1975 the Philippines followed suit and announced that it would remove all its official representatives from Taiwan and ask Taiwan to withdraw its representatives within one month. On 1 July 1975 Thailand also agreed to do the same. For all three countries, the implications for its citizens of Chinese origin, for both its Chinese and for those who might have been stateless, were great.

The official and legal position is relatively simple. Despite the variations in the three joint communiques signed, they all agreed that those of Chinese descent who adopted the nationality of any of the three countries automatically forfeited Chinese nationality. Dual nationality was therefore untenable. It was also understood that China did not recognize "stateless" Chinese and by this, China hoped to encourage the three governments to facilitate the acquisition of local citizenship by those of Chinese origin. No exact figures of those involved have been published officially, but it has been generally assumed that, for Malaysia, some 120,000 non-citizens were involved and, for Thailand and the Philippines, about 300,000 and 100,000 respectively of "Taiwan citizens" were asked to choose between local and Chinese citizenship. The Chinese government repeatedly emphasized that those who chose to be Chinese should abide by the laws of the land, respect local customs and live in friendship with the people of the three countries. For such Chinese, China pledged to protect their rights and interests in accordance with international practice.

From the point of view of the three Southeast Asian governments, the question was also a political one. The "Taiwan Chinese" in Thailand and the Philippines had never worked against the local governments before. Would they acquiesce easily with their changed status? As for Malaysia, with its history of suspicion concerning the loyalties of those of Chinese origin, how sure could it be of the loyalty of another 100,000 more if most of those who had not previously qualified were now given the local citizenship they wanted? Malaysia had the additional problem of associating the Malayan Communist Party with the Chinese and those of Chinese descent. In this way, communist opposition was always linked with external intervention. If there should be virtually no more Chinese but only Malaysians of Chinese descent who might or might not support the MCP, would this now be a largely internal matter which could not so easily be blamed on others? The problems for each of the three Southeast Asian countries were obviously different, but the governments were assured loudly and clearly by the Chinese government that the "Huaqiao" of the past were almost extinct, that "foreign Chinese" were not China's concern and not the target of subversion by China and that such Chinese were not encouraged to resist local assimilation and assert what was left of their Chineseness. It seems, therefore, that China has not been ambiguous about these problems. The ambiguity stems more from the attitudes and the experiences of those descendants of Chinese who have made their homes in the region.

The Chinese Communities in Malaysia, Thailand and the Philippines

The rest of this essay will concentrate on the *Ma-Hua, Tai-Hua* and *Fei-Hua*, that is, the Huaren or Huayi of Malaysia, Thailand and the Philippines. The first and most obvious point to note is that "Chinese" has been defined differently for each country. The Filipino definition has been the most clear-cut: only those who are aliens are counted as Chinese, and both local and foreign demographers respect this form of counting. For Thailand, the definition has been less consistent. Officially, the Thai definition is the same as that of the Philippines, but demographers and political commentators consistently blur the picture by making rough estimates of all Thai nationals who are part-Chinese and of Chinese descent together with alien Chinese and using figures of Chinese ranging from two-and-a-half to four million. As for Malaysia, the official definition is itself confusing. Apart from a few part-Chinese who are unequivocally Malay and have been acknowledged as such, everyone of Chinese descent, whether he is a Malaysian citizen or not, has been counted as Chinese. There are understandable historical reasons for this method of counting, but its retention in the official census and other publications makes it difficult to get rid of the residual sense of all such Chinese being in some way "Huaqiao" whether they are citizens or not. It emphasizes that they are culturally unassimilated and that this is more important than their protestations of loyalty to Malaysia. This encourages a feeling of separateness that keeps alive the idea of being discriminated against and makes some Malaysian Chinese adopt a negative attitude towards the country. This in turn sustains doubts about their political loyalty.

Another critical point to note is the attitude towards China of all those who may be counted as Chinese in one way or another, whether they are aliens or local citizens of part-Chinese or Chinese descent. It has become clear that very few such Chinese are interested in returning to China to live. This is only partly because of the fact that returning to China had almost always been an irreversible act. More important is the fact that China does not welcome them back. It may still want them to remit funds to assist relatives in China, but it recognizes that Chinese who have lived abroad all or most of their lives are unlikely to settle easily in China. Equally important is the realization among most of those who have settled in countries which are more or less capitalist that they could not do well in a planned socialist society. They may or may not believe that the political and economic system in China is the best possible for the people in China, but they know that they would not be able to adjust unless they rejected their present way of life altogether and became committed to the new Chinese ideals. Furthermore, those few who are ideologically committed to the Marxism-Leninism of China might well feel that their contribution to the historical process could be better made by fighting social injustice and economic exploitation in their adopted countries where the need for revolution was greater. They might be inspired by Marxist ideals, but they would be far more effective if they identified with local grievances and supported indigenous movements and played down their own Chinese origins. The choice might be more difficult if the indigenous revolution itself succeeded, as in the Indo-China states. Those who did not leave Saigon-Cholan and Pnom Penh in April 1975 could choose whether to live in a Vietnamese/Cambodian socialist society or to return as a Chinese to live in a Chinese form of it.

All this is not to say that there is no residual nostalgia for "the old

294 • *China and the Chinese Overseas*

country" nor any sympathy at all for the goals of the Chinese revolution. The important thing is to set this beside a general suspicion of, if not hostility towards, the spread of communism into their adopted country. This was the case not only among traditionalists, capitalists and pro-Taiwan loyalists but also among the petty bourgeois traders and artisans who form the majority of Huaren or Huayi in every country in the region except in Malaysia and Singapore. Such a situation could not remain constant but was susceptible to radical change if government policies failed to give them a firm stake in their adopted countries and win their loyalties. But there is little doubt that fewer and fewer of them would be tempted to identify with China unless they are pushed or forced to do so. Nor would they be happy to contemplate their fate if local communists should seize power and declare them to be among the exploiters of the indigenous peoples.

More specifically, what have been the attitudes of *Ma-Hua*, *Tai-Hua* and *Fei-Hua* towards Malaysia, Thailand and the Philippines respectively since the establishment of diplomatic relations with China? Although all three countries are members of ASEAN, their security problems are quite different and these problems directly influenced their views about China, communism, and their present and future citizens of Chinese descent. And the attitudes of these Huayi would also depend on the nature of these security problems and their respective governments' policies towards them as trustworthy citizens. As mentioned earlier, the most critical developments since the Vietnamese and Cambodian victories in April 1975 had concerned the politics of Thailand and the insurgent forces in Thailand and Malaysia. Of more general concern for all ASEAN countries is the question of United States policy in Asia and the duration and impact of economic uncertainty in Japan and the United States on the region.

THE PHILIPPINES

Let me begin with the Philippines where the problem is simplest and where the numbers of Chinese are comparable to those in Indonesia, Burma, Cambodia, Laos, Vietnam, the "outer ring" of the region. Here part-Chinese (mestizos) are almost wholly assimilated and barely distinguishable from Filipinos. Some of them may be specially enthusiastic about close trading relations with China, but there is no problem of subversion from this group at all. As for the 100,000 alien Chinese, there had been a degree of alienation because most of them who had been born in the country felt that they were discriminated against and had been prevented from becoming naturalized Filipino

citizens by the simple operation of law. But in anticipation of diplomatic relations with the People's Republic of China, ex-President
Marcos' Letter of Instruction No. 270 had relaxed the conditions for
citizenship and encouraged those who still wished to become Filipinos to fill in the new application forms provided. The first closing
date for such new applications, 31 May 1975, gave very little time for
the aliens to respond. This was extended to 30 June, by which date
about 19,500 applications had been submitted covering about 60,000
individuals (including children who were still minors). This meant
that about 60% of the alien Chinese sought naturalization immediately and submitted themselves to scrutiny by the National Bureau
of Investigation and the National Intelligence and Security Authority.
At that stage, there remained about 40,000 who for various reasons
did not apply. Some were unable to find the 6–10,000 pesos needed to
submit their applications, some might have preferred to become
citizens of China and others might have wished to retain their
Taiwan passports even if it meant that they would be "stateless"
while they lived in the Philippines.

There is no reason to doubt that those seeking naturalization would
eventually identify with the larger Filipino community, especially if
they are Christians, speak the National Language or local dialects
and had begun to be active in local political and cultural affairs. Their
assimilation was to be assisted by organizations like the *Pagkakaisa Sa
Pag-unlad*, which had been preparing the ground for just such a
situation for several years. As for the remaining 40,000 (including
children), it was not clear how many would eventually become
Chinese citizens or be treated as such by the Chinese and Filipino
governments. Initially, it did not appear that there would be more
than 20,000 adult Chinese citizens in the country for the following
decades, a figure both governments could live with without serious
difficulty. The detailed arrangements for each individual and his
family would naturally take time to sort out and considerable dis-
locations were expected to begin with. Nevertheless, it was felt that
there should be no threat to good relations between China and the
Philippines from this source, and it was expected that, after a period
of uncertainty, this aspect of the Chinese problem in the Philippines
would essentially be settled. Only one area of concern remained.
If Taiwan does become part of the People's Republic and the
Philippines-China boundary is drawn along the Luzon Strait (Bashi
Channel), is a dispute likely? One could speculate for years about
this, but there is nothing to suggest that these questions would

involve the Chinese citizens or the Filipino citizens of Chinese descent.

THAILAND

A more complex problem faced the government of Thailand and the Chinese in Thailand. There were three major reasons for this. Firstly, the legal and the social definitions of Chinese have not coincided as clearly as in the Philippines. Secondly, Thailand had been deeply involved in the wars in Indo-China in which China had invariably supported the opposite side. Thirdly, the problem of insurgency was serious and the insurgents had been receiving encouragement and help from the Chinese Communist Party if not from the government itself.

The question of how Chinese are counted in Thailand has already been mentioned. The position of the 310,000 alien Chinese was similar to that in the Philippines. The Thai government would speed up the granting of Thai nationality to those who wanted it, but it expected the majority to seek Chinese nationality or try to retain their Taiwan passports under special arrangements. Unlike in the Philippines, the proportion of those seeking Thai nationality was likely to be fewer because Thai nationality had always been easier to obtain and most of those who wanted it would have got it before 1975. Should large numbers, say some 200,000, become Chinese nationals, the government might have been a little anxious. But the real anxiety would have come from another source. A large number of those who had acquired Thai nationality since the 1930s might still not have been fully assimilated into Thai society. This has not previously troubled the Thai government because it had never placed great store on the artificial "conversion principle" of naturalization, but depended on the more natural but time-consuming "continuum method of cultural assimilation", a method whereby the Sino-Thai assimilated in the nineteenth century drew other Thai Chinese gradually across the bridge they provided into Thai society. Given time and patience, the policy has been remarkably successful. Today the large majority of Thai Chinese are Sino-Thai and their fierce loyalty to the social structure in which they have a large stake is not doubted. Their numbers, their cohesion and their determination to persist with the assimilationist policy may overcome any fear that this process might be arrested. But the continuum picture never looked complete and there have always been questions about whether the method could not work both ways and whether there might not be pressure to have the process reversed. The persistent doubts about this have led to the loose way all writers refer to "Chinese" in Thailand and count all those who are of Chinese ancestry, adding to the alarming figures often used of two-and-a-half to four million "Chinese". This kind of counting reflects an underlying suspicion that many Thai Chinese might be willing to revive their Chinese connections, if not actually identify themselves as Chinese, if the circumstances were different and it was expedient or profitable to do so.

Another facet of the question is the composition of this large more or less "Chinese" population. If indeed Thais of Chinese or part-Chinese origin number some 8% of the total population and are largely living in urban centres, it would mean that a large proportion of them are petty bourgeoisie and proletariat as they certainly are in Bangkok. Such urban centres produced the restless reformist intelligentsia that had shaken the political structure since October 1973, and these certainly included many of Chinese or part-Chinese origin. There is still no doubt that these Thai Chinese would act primarily as Thais rather than as "Chinese". But in the context of the communist-dominated states east and north of the country and renewed close trading relations with China, any Thai Chinese political activity against the status quo could create the doubt as to how many of these Thai Chinese could stand to have their loyalty tested. But it would be tragic if this should lead to Thai leaders forgetting that, although many Thai Chinese have maintained kinship links with town and villages in South China, most of them have done well in the traditionalist, conservative and capitalist system of Thailand and very few have ever identified with the government and dominant ideology of China, whether militarist, nationalist or communist.

MALAYSIA

As for Malaysia, the Chinese problem is much more obvious and the late Tun Razak took the greatest risk of his career to go to Peking, normalize relations between Malaysia and China and showed that he was not anti-Chinese. The chief reason for the bold step was his concern to move Southeast Asia towards a "zone of peace, freedom and neutrality". Considerations of trade with China, channelled through government agencies wherever possible, were also important. At the same time, an acknowledgement by China of his government's legitimacy, China's official assurance of non-interference in Malaysia's internal affairs, its firm confirmation that Malaysians of Chinese origin can expect nothing from China while those who chose to be

Chinese had to abide by the laws of Malaysia did improve Tun Razak's position as a wise and clear-sighted national leader. The risk had been worth taking because it finally took the ambiguity out of the nationality problem for the Malaysian Chinese. If many of them are still not satisfied with the government, they would have to seek a Malaysian solution. Their attitude towards their adopted country is likely to be better focused and they are more likely to seek common cause with those equally dissatisfied of whatever ethnic origins and seek to right injustices as Malaysians. Thus, although the developments since independence have shown that Malaysian Chinese must learn to accept a subordinate political position, that their communal economic power is limited in an economy tied to a larger global system, and that full cultural assimilation with the *bumiputra* is almost impossible, the same period has confirmed that such citizens of Chinese origin are capable of making a political commitment to Malaysia and of adapting to the change from an Anglo-Malayan framework of the 1950s to the established Southeast Asian state it is today.

There was, of course, a resumption of violence by the Communist Party of Malaya after May 1974, and the Party continued to be dominated by Malaysians of Chinese origin, although many of the original leaders had never been citizens of independent Malaya or Malaysia and are now either aliens or "stateless". (Chin Peng claimed to have been a Malaysian citizen when he appeared on the Thai-Malaysian border to proclaim the end of the MCP insurgency in December 1989.) Also, there were sporadic outbreaks of urban violence by groups unknown, notably around Merdeka Day 1975, most likely by Malaysians of Chinese origin. These represented at least two sources of possible danger to the political stability of the country. But neither of them was the straightforward matter of good versus evil or Chinese versus Malay which some observers and analysts had continued to advocate. The MCP violence stemmed from a view of history that saw revolution as inevitable, that saw the country, and the region as a whole, as ready for radical change. It had been encouraged by the diplomatic successes of China and the communist victories in Indo-China, but it was no longer specifically Chinese in origin. In fact, the MCP's capacity to make political gains depended more on its fraternal relations with Thai and Malay rebels on both sides of the Thai-Malaysia border than on overt Malaysian Chinese support. As for the urban violence, if it arose, as it appeared to, from the increasing discontent of some Malaysians of Chinese origin, it would have been primarily the product of an ongoing complex historical process. This was the process of transforming a post-colonial plural society into a nation-state founded on *bumiputra* sovereignty. However just might be the efforts at economic redistribution and however necessary the "melting-pot" philosophy is to the cause of nation-building, it must be recognized that the process will be painful and divisive. And should the process be poorly managed, it could be far more disruptive to the country than a Marxist-Leninist-Maoist world view so alien to most Malaysians.

In short, the government of Malaysia had good reason to be anxious about a sizeable urban proletariat of Chinese origin, but the operative word need not be "Chinese" but "proletariat". There had never been any serious threat to political stability from the middle-class professionals and the successful traders, whatever their origins; the main threat which had failed in the 1950s had been abstractly ideological and revolutionary, but it had since been reshaped in terms of reduced opportunities, aborted expectations and actual downward social mobility. Here the nature of the newly settled communities of migrant background needs to be taken into account. Immigrants are notoriously restless. They long for upward mobility, at least for the promise of future upward mobility. In the new nation-state where those of Chinese origin form some 35% of the population, upward mobility for all is obviously impossible. Thus the majority over a time would have to accept a levelling and stabilizing of certain classes which all settled peoples are forced to recognize as the norm. For most, therefore, their proletariat class will grow and persist, and as they seek and find protection in the defensiveness of their class, they will be more and more Malaysian in their use of legitimate local institutions to enhance their standard of living and reduce their social grievances. A secure firmly established proletariat is rarely revolutionary, and if it does gain class solidarity, rarely racist. The time seems to have come for much less emphasis on ethnic origins and much less fear of the proletariat. This is not to say that there is no revolutionary potential in the countryside. In Southeast Asia, it is still agrarian unrest that threatens the residual traditional political structures. But this is not a Malaysian Chinese threat, it is not a force that can benefit either the Malaysian Chinese bourgeois or proletariat. The recent developments suggest that Malaysian Chinese have little to gain from political instability and it is not too late for their leaders to hammer this home to their supporters, to other Malaysians and to the government alike.

Conclusion

It would be difficult to summarize the minority Chinese problem for Southeast Asia as a whole. The following should serve merely as a framework for a better understanding of the more general aspects of the problem:

From the point of view of the Southeast Asian governments:
1. The suspicion remains that some of their own citizens of Chinese descent may still be Chinese first and loyal citizens second. On the assumption that the Chinese are inclined to act on behalf of China, the distrust of revolutionary China encourages the distrust of all Chinese, even their own citizens.
2. The political and cultural assimilation of Chinese is regarded as being only skin-deep, hence assimilation is no guarantee against subversion. Only racial mixture over a long period of time can eliminate "the Chinese problem".
3. The economic power of Overseas Chinese and their own citizens of Chinese descent is a long-term threat. It has so far been contained by the Western-dominated "neo-colonial" or multinational trading system. If Western power withdraws, more draconian measures will be needed to keep this "Chinese" power down.

From the point of view of China:
4. Southeast Asia, like the rest of the Third World, is ready for independence, liberation and revolution. China can help by using the right tactics. The key strategy lies in the success of China and the socialist camp. Those of Chinese origin in the region are largely unrevolutionary and must not be allowed to stand in the way of that success.
5. Not only will the revolution be ultimately victorious, Chinese influence in the neighbourhood must inevitably grow. Time is on its side. China can afford to ignore the minority Chinese; they are now dispensable. In any case, when Chinese influence is overwhelming, those who still wish to do so may identify with China again.

From the point of view of the Chinese settled in Southeast Asia:
6. The majority owe no loyalty to China, but the habit of sojourning is being kept alive by discrimination, by insecurity,

by cultural arrogance, by irrational hopes about China's ultimate protection and by false ideas about greener pastures elsewhere.

7. Where those who are identifiably Chinese are numerous enough, there is the defence and withdrawal into ghettos. This phenomenon is already noticeable in the major cities, especially in those of the "outer ring" of countries like Indonesia, Burma, the Philippines and the Indo-China states.

8. Only in the core countries of Thailand, Malaysia and Singapore can the citizens of Chinese descent still play a positive, meaningful and worthwhile role. This could in theory be in the name of the world revolution, but is more likely to be on behalf of their respective nation-states if their stake in them can be better defined.

Thus the "Chinese" have still to find their identity as a particular kind of minority. Their difficulties have been almost insurmountable largely because they have been seen as so many different kinds of minorities. For the moment, it might be useful to make a preliminary attempt to determine the kinds of minorities that the "Chinese" are not and to consider the kinds that they might still be. They are certainly *not* the following types of minorities:

1. They are not indigenous minority peoples with full birthrights;
2. They are not a minority with a largely exclusive territory and are therefore not rural peoples;
3. They are not border minorities who may feel at home in two neighbouring countries;
4. They are not a minority whose *only* home is where they are at present.

The "Chinese" have, however, the following characteristics in common with other minorities:

1. They consist of many rival groups, are normally fragmented and unite rarely and only temporarily when badly discriminated against;
2. They prefer to keep their own culture but, given the right incentives, would be prepared to give it up gradually;
3. They can assimilate and "de-assimilate" within certain limits;

4. They may themselves become migrants again and become new kinds of minorities somewhere else;
5. They can be "multinational" minorities abroad (like Indians, various Europeans, various Arabs, some Vietnamese, Japanese, to mention a few).

But where the "Chinese" are totally different is as follows:

1. Their "mother country" is near Southeast Asia, very large and populous, potentially powerful and *traditionally* contemptuous of the peoples and cultures of the region;
2. Their "mother country" has a communist government and is perceived as part of an international conspiracy to dominate the world through the direction and encouragement of revolutions.

In short, the *special* kind of minority the "Overseas Chinese" constitute has been largely determined externally. It is a minority haunted by its proximity to its place of origin, by a turbulent past and by a resurgent revolutionary China claiming to represent a universal force that is attracting the world's attention. As a minority, it has acquired a tragic quality because China is so much greater in everyone's eyes than it will ever be.

NOTE

1 An earlier version of this essay was published in 1976. The essay has been slightly revised and updated for the present publication.

Chronological Table of China's Dynasties

Several of these dynasties started earlier in other parts of China, but did not exercise full control over the country until the dates stated.

Xia	2140–1711 BC
Shang	1711–1066 BC
Western Zhou	1066–771 BC
Eastern Zhou	770–256 BC
Warring States	475–221 BC
Qin	221–206 BC
Western Han	206 BC–AD 25
Eastern Han	25–220
Three Kingdoms	220–280
Western Jin	265–317
Eastern Jin	317–420
Southern and Northern Dynasties	420–589
Sui	589–618
Tang	618–907
Five Dynasties	907–960
Northern Song	960–1127
Jin (Golden Tartars)	1115–1234
Southern Song	1127–1279
Yuan	1279–1368
Ming	1368–1644
Qing	1644–1911

Source: *Xiandai Hanyu Cidian* (Dictionary of Modern Chinese).
Beijing: Shangwu Yin Shu Gan (Commercial Press), 1980.

Index

China, 7–29, 34–37, 41, 47, 51–55, 59, 62, 67, 68, 79, 81, 84, 86, 107, 117, 140, 142, 143, 147, 148, 153, 157, 158, 167, 168, 172–178, 182, 185–187, 194, 195, 199, 200, 205, 213, 259, 263–271, 275–287, 290–297, 300, 302; External, 222–239, 273–284; Nationality Law (September 1980), 35; -Mexico trade, 92; Steam Navigation Company, 188

Chinese, 181; as middlemen, 137; classical studies, 154, 266; Chinese Communist Party, 7, 135, 178, 287, 296; Consul, 172; culture, 6; customs, 169; economy, 126; governments, 8; heritage, 282; identity, 198–221; labour, 168; literature, 149; mestizo community, 91; national politics, 132; Nationality Law of 1909, 25; quarter, Nagasaki, 96; society and culture overseas, 18; superiority, 138; tradition, 152, 280

Ching-tung, 65
Chip Bee School, 157
Chongfu (Fuzhou) Temple, 96
Chou En-lai, 32, 285, 287
Chouhai tubian, 114
Christianity, 183, 270, 295
Chu Hsi, 279
Chu Hsiu-hsia, 31
Chu Ying, 122
Chu Yu-lang, 70
Chu'uan-chou, 41
Chung-hua min-tsu t'o-chih Nan-yang shih, 30
Chung-kuo chih-min pa ta-wei-jen chuan, 27
Chung-kuo chih-min shih, 30
Chung-shan universities, 32, 33
Citizenship, 287, 292
Civil War in China, 8
Clans, 4, 137, 199, 213, 232, 262
Class identity, 198, 201, 206, 207, 208, 213; struggle, 32
Classical studies, 152; texts, 261
Clementi Smith, Sir Cecil, 174;
Colonial administration, 136; governments, 135, 137, 142; languages, 143; powers, 268; rule, 131, 275; schools, 275; withdrawal, 139, 145
Colonialism, 134, 145, 201, 233
Colonization, 26, 27, 28, 29, 177
Columbus, Christopher, 153
Commerce, 182
Commercial success, 133
Communal identity, 198, 202, 205, 208
Communalism, 205, 285
Communications, 120, 122, 138, 271, 275
Communism, 32, 130, 139, 157, 178, 196, 205, 270, 280, 282, 285, 288, 294
Communist Party of Malaya, 200, 298
Communists, 30, 135, 266
Communities, 22–26, 28, 36, 83, 121, 130, 132, 134, 144, 202, 209, 215, 248, 260, 263, 273, 275, 276, 283, 292–302; leadership, 133;

politics, 132; solidarity, 139
Concept of Chineseness, 198
Confucian attitudes, 69, 70, 109, 121, 122, 124, 126, 196, 258–272; classics, 263, 268; officialdom, 119; orthodoxy, 81; values, 182, 185, 258–261, 263, 269–273
Confucianism, 123, 125, 147–165, 185, 186, 195, 258–273
Confucius, 119, 150, 184, 259, 260, 287
Conversion to non-Chinese faiths, 203
Coolie pattern, 4, 6
Coolies, 8, 15, 20, 21, 33, 175, 223
Cotton, 85
Cultivation, 120–124
Cultivators, 166, 167
Cultural assimilation, 296, 298, 300; change, 131; heritage, 196, 278, 280, 283; identity, 198, 202–210, 213–216, 250; origins, 250; periphery, 259–272; revival, 17; Revolution, 205, 223, 228, 234, 241, 278, 286; status, 188; superiority, 233; tradition, 273, 277, 279–283; values, 178, 182, 195, 197, 203, 212, 213, 269, 276
Culture, 19, 20, 130, 142, 145, 181–197, 202–204, 213, 215, 259, 273–276, 280, 301; of trade, 282, 283
Dade Nanhai lu, 107
Dai states, 110
Dali, 105, 106, 110
Daoyi zhilue, 107, 108, 114
Dashi, 103
Daxia University, Shanghai, 156
Deli (Medan), 170
Demiéville, Paul, 158
Democracy, 270
Descendants, 19, 20
Descent or re-migrant pattern, 4, 8, 21
Deshima, 96
Destruction of Cham kingdom, 1471, 66
Development, 258, 259, 287
Discrimination, 24, 196, 207, 245, 250, 294, 300
Dongxi Yang kao, 90
Drugs, 118
Du-ton, 47
Dual identities, 209
Dual loyalties, 173
Due-ton, 47, 48
Dutch, The, 7, 29, 45, 63, 87, 88, 94, 97, 98, 170, 171, 189, 193, 264, 265; administration, 167; East India Company, 95, 98
Dyes, 124
East Africa, 45, 59, 104, 113; Asia, 206, 258; Asian merchants, 181; Java, 60; Timor, 14
Eastern Europe, 233; Oceans, 41, 51, 116; Tibet, 106, 109, 111
Economic development, 122, 145, 182, 271, 281; growth, 169, 258; modernization, 144; power, 140, 300; redistribution, 299;

Labourers, 17, 175, 227, 247
Land, 183
Language, 111, 142, 145, 158, 172, 203, 213, 230, 243, 253, 275, 277, 295
Laos, 41, 42, 46, 57, 58, 61, 66–68, 107, 113, 241, 269, 286, 288, 290, 294
Lat Pau, 25
Latin America, 233
Law and order, 138, 277
Lê dynasty, 58
Lê Loi, 56, 67
Lê Quily, 48
Li Ch'ang-fu, 30, 31
Li Dan, 94, 96
Li Jui-hua, 31
Liang Ch'i-ch'ao, 27–29
Liao Chengzhi, 223
Lim Boon Keng, 147, 149–165
Limahong, 90
Lin Chin-chih, 33, 35
Lin Feng, 90
Lin Hsien, 50
Lin Piao, 287
Lin Shuqi, 156
Lin Wenqing, 156
Lin Yutang, 147, 148, 151, 155
Lin-an, 126
Lingwai daida, 103
Literacy, 19, 134, 176, 190, 261, 263
Literati, The, 183–189, 193
Little Traditions, 273, 276
Liu Chi-hsuan, 30
Liu Kwang-ching, 188
Liu Sung, 123
Liu Sung-heng, 28
Liu-ch'iu, 51, 116
Lizong, 104
Lo Hsiang-lin, 62
Lo-ho, 46
Local authorities, 14; Chinese leaders, 169; citizenship, 176; communities, 4, 13; families, 5; identities, 20; Malay rulers, 170; nationalism, 19, 209
Lohu, 114
Lon Nol, 290
Lopburi, 114
Loyalty, 32, 135, 136, 140, 142, 170, 171, 172, 174, 176, 177, 186, 190, 202, 203, 205, 207, 210, 215, 233, 250, 292– 297, 300
Loyang, 82, 118, 262
Lu Xun, 147, 149–165
Lu-ch'uan, 53, 57, 58, 64, 65
Luang Prabang, 67
Lukchins, 19
Lung-chou, 48, 49
Luzon, 45, 89, 90, 93, 97, 113
Luzon Strait, 295
Ma-Hua, 34, 35, 142, 289, 292, 294
Ma-lai-ya hua-ch'iao, 31

Mac regime, 66, 69
Macao, 88, 94, 223–227, 231, 234, 242
Maize, 98
Majapahit empire, 51, 108
Malacca, 58, 60–63, 68, 86, 87, 93, 167, 170, 246
Malacca Straits, The, 113
Malay archipelago, 29, 88, 166, 168, 193; nationalism, 139; peninsula, 6, 50, 58, 69, 70, 81, 84, 103, 288
Malaya, 11, 139, 200–202, 208, 285, 298
Malayan Communist Party, 292, 298
Malays in southern Thailand, 205
Malaysia, 9, 14, 34, 35, 178, 201, 205–208, 212, 224, 230, 233, 274, 275, 277, 285, 288, 291–299, 301
Manchu dynasty, 29, 171, 265
Manchuria, 43, 265, 266
Manchus, The, 148, 267
Mandarin system, 260
Mandarins, 79, 80, 98, 172, 184–196, 252, 261, 263, 264, 268, 269, 282
Manila, 22, 80, 87–92, 263; fort, 91
Mao Tse-tung, 279, 281
Maoist leanings, 141
Marcos, President, 288, 295
Maritime Trade Commission, Quanzhou, 81
Marxism, 32, 196
Marxism-Leninism, 278, 280, 281, 293
Massacre of Chinese, Batavia, 88; of Chinese, Manila, 88, 90, 91
Mauritius, 14
Maw Shan chiefs, 64
Maw Shans, 57, 58, 61
May Fourth Movement, 149, 157, 265
May Thirtieth Affair (1925), 152
Meiji emperor, 268
Mencius, 259, 260
Merchant communities, 274; culture, 181–197; values, 183; gentry, 188
Merchants, 4, 5, 18, 42, 60, 61, 79–101, 79, 80, 109, 110, 134, 167, 168, 172, 175, 181–197, 244, 259, 262, 263, 268, 270, 282; status of, 183
Merdeka Day 1975, 298
Mestizos, 294
Middle East, The, 104, 181
Migrant communities, 3, 4, 232, 302
Migration, 3, 135, 168, 201, 230, 274; history of, 12–21; patterns of, 1–21; policy, 7
Min Guangren, 7
Min Pao, 28
Min Yueren, 7
Min Zhong, 156
Min-tsu, 199, 201
Miners, 5
Ming calendar, 44, 112; dynasty, 23, 29, 35, 43, 44, 57, 62, 82, 110–116, 119, 125, 243, 246, 261, 263, 267; fall of, 95; foreign